Business Process Management Cases Vol. 2

Jan vom Brocke • Jan Mendling •
Michael Rosemann
Editors

Business Process Management Cases Vol. 2

Digital Transformation - Strategy, Processes and Execution

Springer

Editors
Jan vom Brocke
Department of Information Systems
University of Liechtenstein
Vaduz, Liechtenstein

Jan Mendling
Institute for Information Business
WU Vienna
Vienna, Austria

Michael Rosemann
Centre for Future Enterprise
Queensland University of Technology
(QUT)
Brisbane, Queensland, Australia

ISBN 978-3-662-63049-5 ISBN 978-3-662-63047-1 (eBook)
https://doi.org/10.1007/978-3-662-63047-1

This Springer imprint is published by the registered company Springer-Verlag GmbH, DE part of Springer Nature.
The registered company address is: Heidelberger Platz 3, 14197 Berlin, Germany

Foreword

Beyond the obvious advantages of business process management, we here at Hilti are most interested in three types of processes: global processes, transformational processes, and resilient processes.

Hilti has expanded the scope of many of our BPM projects from the individual process to a portfolio of processes. In particular, BPM has proven to be successful in fostering the standardization of Hilti's *global processes*. This has not only reduced operational costs dramatically, but also ensures consistency in the provision of our services, and it has enabled Hilti to develop new business models, such as introducing fleet management as a combination of our hardware and service offerings, which today marks an important share of our business. As a result, role definitions, data standards, resources requirements, and performance measures have become comparable.

While we have matured our ability to master our high-volume transactional processes over the last decade, we are now entering the stage of improving the management of our *transformational business processes*. This includes processes such as corporate innovation or digital transformation. This type of process might not be the main focus of traditional BPM, but I very much envisage that we will see more applications of BPM in the domain of transformational processes.

Finally, we are increasingly extending the scope of our process design and analysis activities. No longer is the streamlining and automation of a process our only area of interest. Rather, recent environmental changes have motivated us to explore the notion of *resilient processes*, i.e., processes that are robust, responsive, and agile. While we explore the edges of contemporary BPM, we appreciate that books like this one help us to stay in touch with current methods and techniques so we can continue to grow our BPM maturity and tackle even more challenging process requirements.

This book demonstrates both opportunities and challenges of adopting BPM in practice. It is a rich collection of real-world cases from well-known organizations around the world. The cases clearly show how organizations, very much like Hilti, nowadays go beyond the mere modeling of processes, and build process management capabilities in areas such as governance, strategic alignment, people, culture, methods, and information technology. The BPM Billboard, presented in the introductory chapter by Jan vom Brocke, Jan Mendling, and Michael Rosemann, is a very useful tool to comprehensively plan and scope process management initiatives. At Hilti, we are currently redesigning our BPM methodology and, following the principles of the BPM Billboard, we have been able to identify different requirements for BPM depending on the type of business we are looking at.

I would like to congratulate all authors on their ambitious projects and their insightful cases which make up this book. This volume adds another compelling 22 cases to the already existing 31 cases from volume 1. Together these two books make the BPM Cases series a highly valuable source both for practitioners and for students to master the challenges and emerging opportunities of our fast-changing world.

Hilti CIO
Schaan, Liechtenstein
March 2021

Martin Petry

Preface

We are excited and overwhelmed by the uptake of the BPM Cases, which today is used around the world by both practitioners and educators to showcase and study business process management.

Our BPM Cases Collection is dedicated to providing a contemporary and comprehensive, industry-agnostic insight into the realities of BPM. In particular, we focus on the lessons that only authentic, case-based insights can provide. As a result, the experiences documented cover both the positive impact of deploying BPM and the lessons learnt from failed attempts. Together, both BPM Cases books form the most extensive account of real-world BPM cases, and it is continuously growing. Each case takes a holistic approach on BPM and by doing each chapter recognizes that BPM in practice is a multidimensional endeavor covering strategy to operations, systems and infrastructure, governance and culture, models and running processes. The fact that each case combines these dimensions in a unique way is the main contribution of this book, a contribution that in an academic and educational world, in which we tend to center on isolated BPM features, is often missing.

In this volume, we also introduce a new device to plan and scope BPM initiatives: the BPM Billboard (http://www.bpm-billboard.com). The Billboard helps BPM professionals to link BPM projects to the corporate strategy and to build the organizational capabilities to reach such a strategic directive.

We keep the very successful unified structure of each case, which makes it easy to access the single cases:

- Introduction—What is the story of the case? The authors give a brief narrative of the entire story to grasp your interest in the case. This part includes a summary of the key figures of the case company.
- Situation faced—What was the initial problem situation? What situation led to the actions taken? The authors specify the context of the case as to needs, constraints, incidents, objectives, and beyond.
- Action taken—What has been done? What measures have been taken, e.g., regarding the process redesign or process innovation? Which methods and approaches have been used? The authors share a factual passage of the course of events.

- Results achieved—What effects could be observed resulting from the action taken? This could be changes in performance measures as well as qualitative statements from employees, customers, or other stakeholders. Here, the authors also discuss how far expected results materialized and how far expectations were met, or not.
- Lessons learned—Reflecting on the overall case, what can others learn from it? The authors derive around five lessons learned, which are grounded in the case and which have the potential to impact the planning and acting of BPM professionals beyond this case.

The cases of this book are grouped into three major blocks:

- Process technology and automation: including cases on blockchain technology, sensor networks, industry 4.0, and process-aware information systems.
- Process analysis and monitoring: including cases on process mining, deep learning applications, and process prediction.
- Governance and strategic alignment: including cases on governance structures, the management of business transformation initiatives, the adoption of global process standards, strategic alignment, and business process architecture.

The material presented in this book is complemented by online material for teaching, training, and advisory. The website http://www.bpm-cases.com makes slides and additional content available which can be helpful for using the cases both in teaching BPM and in preparing for BPM projects in practice.

We would like to thank the following people and institutions for their continuous support with the compilation of this book.

- First, we thank our research teams both in Liechtenstein and in Vienna. There have always been strong ties between Liechtenstein and Vienna not only in BPM but in history, and we emphasize this connection with our book cover that refers to the pattern of the parquet floor of one room in the Palais Liechtenstein in Vienna.
- Second, we thank the organizers of the BPM Conference in Innsbruck 2015 and Vienna 2019 who gave us the chance to bring together many of the case authors of this book by inviting us to organize the industry program of the conference. In Innsbruck, half way between Liechtenstein and Vienna, the idea of this book emerged.
- Third, we thank our colleagues and friends who served on the editorial board of this book and who have dedicated much time and effort in multiple rounds of reviews to further develop the cases presented in this book.
- Fourth, we thank our BPM research colleagues from around the world for their continuous inspiration and support.
- Special thanks go to our colleagues from the University of Münster who initiated and coordinated the ERCIS (European Research Center for Information Systems) network. Thanks to this network, we have the opportunity to collaborate with

many of our BPM colleagues and friends, in the EU Horizon 2020 project RISE_BPM, provided by the European Commission under the Marie Sklodowska-Curie grant agreement No. 645751 and the Liechtenstein Government. We are grateful for the financial support through this project, which was essential in making the idea of the BPM Cases Book come to life.
- Last but not least, we are grateful for the support of AIBA, the Liechtenstein Agency for International Educational Affairs, for fostering the collaboration with international colleagues to further develop educational programs in the area of BPM, specifically the two ERASMUS+ projects, "Reference Module Design for Explorative Business Process Management" (grant agreement No. 2018-1-LI01-KA203-000114) and "BPM and Organizational Theory: An Integrated Reference Curriculum Design" (grant agreement No. 2019-1-LI01-KA203-000169), which have strongly contributed in shaping this case collection.

We hope you will enjoy reading this book and that it may help to further convert the potential of BPM into reality. We hope you will benefit in multiple ways from these cases and we very much look forward to your feedback.

Vaduz, Liechtenstein — Jan vom Brocke
Vienna, Austria — Jan Mendling
Brisbane, Australia — Michael Rosemann
March 2021

Contents

List of Contributors

Wil M. P. van der Aalst RWTH Aachen University, Aachen, Germany
Eindhoven University of Technology, Eindhoven, The Netherlands

Ahmad Alibabaei Shahid Beheshti University of Medical Sciences, Tehran, Iran

Elheme Azemi Raiffeisen Bank J.S.C., Prishtina, Kosovo

Saimir Bala Vienna University of Economics and Business (WU), Wien, Austria

Wasana Bandara Information Systems School, Queensland University of Technology, Brisbane, QLD, Australia

Gunter Beitinger Siemens AG, Amberg, Germany

R. F. M. Bergmans Data Intelligence Department, APG Algemene Pensioen Groep N.V, Heerlen, The Netherlands

Antonio García Bernal Airbus Defence and Space, Seville, Spain

Agnieszka Bitkowska Warsaw University of Technology, Warszawa, Poland

Kurt Blümlein Bizagi Deutschland GmbH, Munich, Germany

Seyed Amir Bolboli Bilfinger SE, Mannheim, Germany

T. A. E. J. Boymans Maastricht University Medical Center+, Maastricht, The Netherlands

Jan vom Brocke University of Liechtenstein, Vaduz, Liechtenstein

Jenny Bruhin Hirslanden AG, Zurich, Switzerland

Iris Bruns ConSense GmbH, Aachen, Germany

J. C. A. M. Buijs Data Intelligence Department, APG Algemene Pensioen Groep N.V, Heerlen, The Netherlands

Cristina Cabanillas University of Seville, Sevilla, Spain

K. F. Canjels Maastricht University Medical Center+, Maastricht, The Netherlands
Eindhoven University of Technology, Eindhoven, The Netherlands

Klaus Cee Marabu GmbH & Co. KG, Tamm, Germany

Angelo Corallo Department of Innovation Engineering, University of Salento, Lecce, Italy

Marcus Dees Uitvoeringsinstituut Werknemersverzekeringen (UWV), Amsterdam, The Netherlands

Jean Duell SeMa Application Owner and Operational Management, Deutsche Bahn AG, Berlin, Germany

Matthias Ehrendorfer CDP GmbH, Vienna, Austria

Andreas Ermer Maxsyma GmbH & Co. KG, Floß, Germany

Antonio Manuel Gutiérrez Fernández ISIS Papyrus Europe AG, Brunn am Gebirge, Austria

Johannes Franke duisport (Duisburger Hafen AG), Duisburg, Germany

Renata Gabryelczyk University of Warsaw, Warszawa, Poland

Jens Geiger N-DECT, Pretzfeld, Germany

María Teresa Gómez-López Universidad de Sevilla, Seville, Spain

Artur Grygorowicz Ministry of Finance in Poland, Warszawa, Poland

Garrett Harper AgriDigital, Sydney, NSW, Australia

Ludger Hasenauer Bilfinger SE, Mannheim, Germany

R. El Hasnaoui Data Intelligence Department, APG Algemene Pensioen Groep N. V, Heerlen, The Netherlands

Tecwyn Hill Signavio GmbH, Berlin, Germany

M. S. V. Imkamp Maastricht University Medical Center+, Maastricht, The Netherlands

Stefan Jablonski University of Bayreuth, Bayreuth, Germany

Thomas Jansen duisport (Duisburger Hafen AG), Duisburg, Germany

Lena Franziska Kaiser University of Liechtenstein, Vaduz, Liechtenstein

Klaus Kogler CES Clean Energy Solutions, Wien, Austria

Thomas Kuhn Hirslanden AG, Zurich, Switzerland

Mariangela Lazoi Department of Innovation Engineering, University of Salento, Lecce, Italy

Massimiliano de Leoni University of Padova, Padova, Italy

Cesare Liaci Società Cooperativa Coolclub, Lecce, Italy

Fabian Ludacka TIM Solutions GmbH, Munich, Germany

Juergen Mangler Faculty of Computer Science, University of Vienna, Vienna, Austria

Jan Marek Generali CEE Holding, Praha, Czechia

Manuela Marra Department of Innovation Engineering, University of Salento, Lecce, Italy

Paul Mathiesen Information Systems School, Queensland University of Technology, Brisbane, QLD, Australia

Jan Mendling WU Vienna, Vienna, Austria

John C. Merideth Enterprise Systems, Commonwealth Bank, Sydney, Australia

Andreas Metzger paluno (The Ruhr Institute for Software Technology), University of Duisburg-Essen, Duisburg, Germany

Bridie Ohlsson Geora, Sydney, NSW, Australia

Dan O'Neill Enterprise Systems, Commonwealth Bank, Sydney, Australia

Florian Pauker EVVA Sicherheitstechnologie GmbH, Vienna, Austria

Sebastian Petter University of Bayreuth, Bayreuth, Germany

Luise Pufahl Software and Business Engineering, Technische Universität Berlin, Berlin, Germany

Louis Püschel Project Group BISE of the Fraunhofer FIT, University of Bayreuth, Research Center FIM, Bayreuth, Germany

Lorenzo Quarta Bit.Arts SRL, Lecce, Italy

Belén Ramos-Gutiérrez Universidad de Sevilla, Seville, Spain

Hajo A. Reijers Utrecht University, Utrecht, The Netherlands

Freddie Van Rijswijk ISIS Papyrus Europe AG, Brunn am Gebirge, Austria

Aurora Rimini Department of Innovation Engineering, University of Salento, Lecce, Italy

Stefanie Rinderle-Ma Faculty of Computer Science, University of Vienna, Vienna, Austria

Maximilian Röglinger Project Group BISE of the Fraunhofer FIT, University of Bayreuth, Research Center FIM, Bayreuth, Germany

Michael Rosemann Queensland University of Technology, Brisbane, QLD, Australia

Christoph Ruhsam ISIS Papyrus Europe AG, Brunn am Gebirge, Austria

Andreas Schachermeier ConSense Management Systems GmbH, Aachen, Germany

Konrad Schießl Siemens AG, Amberg, Germany

Stefan Schönig University of Regensburg, Regensburg, Germany

Anna Shadrina AIT Austrian Institute of Technology, Seibersdorf, Austria

Rehan Syed Information Systems School, Queensland University of Technology, Brisbane, QLD, Australia

Angsana A. Techatassanasoontorn Faculty of Business, Economics and Law, Auckland University of Technology, Auckland, New Zealand

Denise Toman Business Process Improvement Office, Queensland University of Technology, Brisbane, QLD, Australia

Álvaro Valencia-Parra Universidad de Sevilla, Seville, Spain

R. J. B. Vanwersch Maastricht University Medical Center+, Maastricht, The Netherlands
Eindhoven University of Technology, Eindhoven, The Netherlands

Ángel Jesús Varela-Vaca Universidad de Sevilla, Seville, Spain

Imesha Denagama Vitharanage Information Systems School, Queensland University of Technology, Brisbane, QLD, Australia

Philipp Waibel Institute for Information Business, WU Wien, Vienna, Austria

Ingo Weber Software and Business Engineering, Technische Universität Berlin, Berlin, Germany

Charlotte Wehking University of Liechtenstein, Vaduz, Liechtenstein

Andreas Weigert Siemens AG, Amberg, Germany

Emma Weston AgriDigital, Sydney, NSW, Australia

Gerhard Zucker AIT Austrian Institute of Technology, Seibersdorf, Austria

Part I

Introduction

Planning and Scoping Business Process Management with the BPM Billboard

Jan vom Brocke, Jan Mendling, and Michael Rosemann

1 Introduction

Business Process Management (BPM) has proven successful in fostering efficiency and productivity in many application areas (Hammer, 2015) and it has also demonstrated great potential to drive innovation in the digital world (Schmiedel & vom Brocke, 2015). However, planning and scoping Business Process Management (BPM) initiatives is a complex task and has been experienced as challenging by many organizations (vom Brocke et al., 2014). A plethora of aspects need to be considered, comprising both deep technical knowledge as well as strategic organizational considerations, just to name a few (Dumas, La Rosa, Mendling, & Reijers, 2018; vom Brocke & Mendling, 2018; vom Brocke & Rosemann, 2015). Instead of focusing on single processes and their management, companies must ensure that

This is the author version of the manuscript currently in press with Springer Nature publishers. Please cite as: vom Brocke, J., Mendling, J., Rosemann, M. (2021), Planning and Scoping Business Process Management with the BPM Billboard, in: J. v. Brocke, J. Mendling, M. Rosemann (Eds.), Business Process Management. Cases, Volume 2, Springer, 2021.

J. vom Brocke (✉)
University of Liechtenstein, Vaduz, Liechtenstein
e-mail: jan.vom.brocke@uni.li

J. Mendling
WU Vienna, Vienna, Austria
e-mail: jan.mendling@wu.ac.at

M. Rosemann
Queensland University of Technology, Brisbane, QLD, Australia
e-mail: m.rosemann@qut.edu.au

J. vom Brocke et al. (eds.), *Business Process Management Cases Vol. 2*,
https://doi.org/10.1007/978-3-662-63047-1_1

their BPM initiatives are contributing to their organizations' strategic plans and are designed according to their capabilities. The capabilities required in this context include business competencies, technology expertise, and social skills. To develop such capabilities, organizations must understand their own strategic ambitions and roadmaps, as well as their performance goals, whether improved productivity, compliance, agility, new revenue generation, or something else (vom Brocke et al., 2014). Moreover, the idiosyncratic nature of the organization's processes must be understood, be they crucial, transactional processes (e.g., the billing process in a telco company), data-intensive processes with complex business rules and algorithms (e.g., online advertising in a marketing company), creativity-intensive processes that depend heavily on staff (e.g., postproduction processes in a media company), or low frequency, highly important processes (e.g., annual budgeting in the public sector). All these factors, plus further contextual elements such as culture, economic climate, and regulatory setting, influence how BPM initiatives should be planned and scoped if they are to be successful (vom Brocke, Zelt, & Schmiedel, 2016). Once an organization has mastered the ability to understand and plan all these aspects of its BPM initiatives, it can manage its process portfolio by defining and setting up projects and sketching out how they relate to one another.

Many companies have mastered the management of well-defined process lifecycle models and related methodologies, such as Lean Management, Six Sigma, and Robotic Process Automation. However, the broader strategic management of processes as a corporate asset and its integration into the organizational setting is far less mature in the professional BPM practice and its related academic body of knowledge is still under-developed.

As a result, organizations' broader appreciation of BPM as an essential enterprise-wide capability remains often limited, and BPM is too often seen as a supportive "back-office" activity only.

We developed the BPM Billboard in order to improve the alignment between BPM initiatives and organizational goals, context factors, and capabilities. The BPM Billboard is a framework that supports organizations in planning, scoping, and integrating their BPM projects and programs. It is designed in such a way that all considerations that are relevant to a BPM initiative can be visualized on one page, an approach that has proven popular and valid in the use of strategic tools like BCG matrix (Hambrick, MacMillan, & Day, 1982), Strategy Maps (Kaplan & Norton, 2004) and Balanced Scorecards (Kaplan & Norton, 1996). This "BPM on one page" approach facilitates intuitive and shared planning by various stakeholders, along with transparent and effective communication of actions taken. This chapter introduces the BPM Billboard and outlines how the cases in this book relate to the layers of the BPM Billboard.

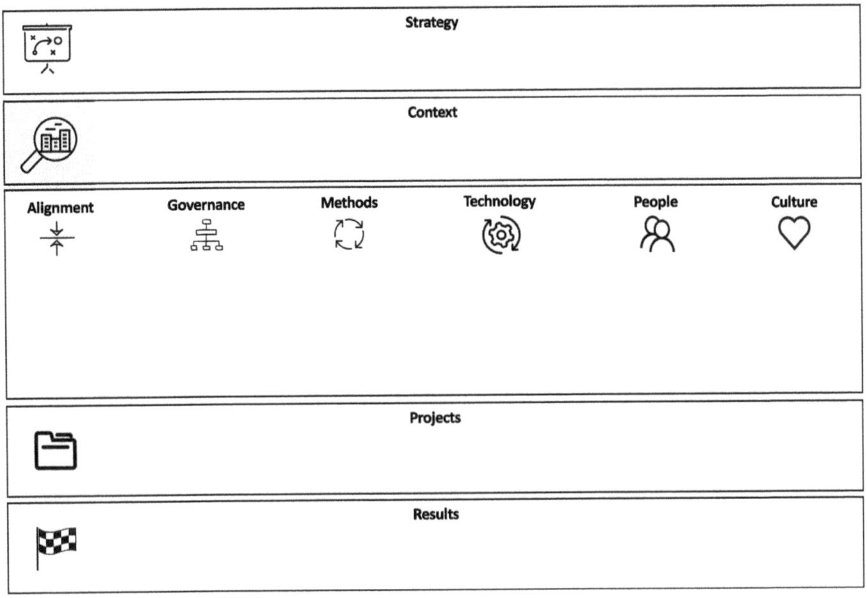

Fig. 1 BPM Billboard

2 The Structure of the BPM Billboard

The BPM Billboard is a one-page visualization of all the key components to be considered when planning and scoping a BPM project or program (Fig. 1). It builds on previous research and in-depth empirical insights gained from global BPM initiatives, including the Ten Principles of Good BPM (vom Brocke et al., 2014), the Six Core Elements of BPM (Rosemann & vom Brocke, 2015), and the BPM Context Framework (vom Brocke et al., 2016; Zelt, Recker, Schmiedel, & vom Brocke, 2019). The billboard is further inspired by the idea of a one-page representation, as it has been suggested and applied in the design of visual inquiry tools (Avdiji, Elikan, Missonier, & Pigneur, 2019), such as the business model canvas (BMC), which has been designed to plan and communicate business models (Osterwalder & Pigneur, 2010).

In the following, we introduce its components and describe how to use the framework to plan and scope BPM initiatives.

The BPM Billboard is a holistic tool that is structured along five interrelated layers. Comparable to other holistic approaches like BCG matrix (Hambrick et al., 1982), Strategy Maps (Kaplan & Norton, 2004), and Balanced Scorecards (Kaplan & Norton, 1996), the BPM Billboard helps to build a consistent, intuitive narrative based on the relationships between five components: strategy (BPM's strategic alignment with the organization), context (BPM's relation to the organization's context), capability (identifying and developing the organization's BPM-related capabilities), projects (actual BPM-related projects that provide a strategic impact), and results (achieved by the different projects and programs).

2.1 Strategy

Before taking any action, those involved in a BPM initiative must relate the initiative to a strategic objective: Where does the organization want to go? What is the board currently most concerned about? What is the strategic agenda? What are sources of competitive advantage, and challenges that lie ahead? What does the CEO think about first in the morning, and what would the board be excited about if it was taken care of?

BPM should relate to and help to address these kinds of issues. For example, Porter's generic strategies can serve as a guide for the identification of an organization's strategic position (Porter, 1980). BPM can then contribute to increasing productivity and innovation capabilities (Mendling, Pentland, & Recker, 2020), and it can foster the organization's adaptability to respond to change more quickly and more successfully. Such matters are well known in organizations, but their consideration is typically not part of BPM methodologies, most of which are exclusively concerned with individual processes.

BPM initiatives are an important means for addressing these matters. Indeed, BPM is a means to an end, not the end itself. In our applied BPM research, we observed that many BPM initiatives are centered on the means, that is, for example, how a process architecture is structured, how processes are modeled, or the role description of a process owner. However, successful BPM centers on the ends. What is the net impact of an improved understanding of or performance of a business process? It is not necessary to know all of a car's operational details to be able to drive it; we need to know only a few relevant parameters, such as steering, accelerating, and braking, to drive it. BPM should do the same; it should hide the details most people do not need to know but needs to deliver results that matter.

2.2 Context

There is no such thing as a "one best way" without considering context (Burnes, 1996). To plan and scope a BPM initiative, we must consider the organizational context. Porter's five forces, for instance, show that the buyer and supplier power as well as threats of new entries and substitutes determine competitive rivalry (Porter, 2008). What are constraints and opportunities? Company-specific factors like size, domain, and regulations are key elements of context (Zelt, Schmiedel, & vom Brocke, 2018), but it is not only these kinds of factors that characterize the organization as a whole, as each organization has its own requirements related to the nature of the processes that make up the organization. Some processes might be repetitive and well structured, while others are less frequent, highly variable, data-intensive or require certain kinds of knowledge and skill. When a company scopes a BPM initiative, it must analyze the spectrum of requirements, which tend to be homogeneous when a certain process area is focused and heterogeneous when multiple processes across the organization are addressed. Some processes benefit from semiformal process models and workflows, while others may benefit from process videos, stories, and social network forums. Many companies have struggled to introduce unified BPM approaches, but there is no one-size-fits-all solution to BPM. Since processes can differ widely, they must be managed individually. Realizing that a unified approach will not work is probably one of the key success factors for introducing BPM in a way that creates value for the organization and is appreciated by the executives, staff, and customers who benefit from high-impact, tailored BPM initiatives.

2.3 Capabilities

Once the strategic environment and the context are captured, the capabilities required to deliver BPM should be addressed. A wide spectrum of capabilities, not only process modeling and process-aware information systems, is needed. In our BPM engagements, we look at organizational capabilities, described as the six core elements of BPM: strategic alignment, governance, methods, IT, people, and culture (Kerpedzhiev, König, Röglinger, & Rosemann, 2020; Rosemann & vom Brocke, 2015).

1. *Strategic alignment* relates to the capabilities that ensure that BPM is aligned with the organization's strategic objectives (e.g., via a hierarchy of process-performance metrics).
2. *Governance* refers to appropriate control of BPM (e.g., by defining roles and responsibilities to ensure all decision-making processes related to a BPM initiative are well defined).
3. *Methods*, which describes how BPM is conducted, consolidates the set of tools and techniques that are specific to the organization's requirements (e.g., process-modeling standards, facilitation techniques), as well as a diverse set of new methods (e.g., design thinking, NESTT) (Grisold, Gross, Röglinger, Stelzl, & vom Brocke, 2019; Rosemann, 2018).
4. *Information technology* covers all direct solutions (e.g., Robotic Process Automation) and indirect solutions (e.g., sensor and distributed ledger technology, analytics, artificial intelligence) that support BPM initiatives (Grisold, Wurm, Mendling, & vom Brocke, 2020).
5. *People* and (6) *culture* account for the human and social aspects of BPM. "People" refers primarily to the BPM skillset, while "culture" relates to organizational values, attitudes, and a process mindset.

A brief assessment of each of these capabilities should be carried out to determine the extent to which the organization's current capabilities suffice or need further development to deliver the project in the given context.

The spectrum of these six core capability areas shows that a multiplicity of measures is relevant to BPM and how to best align these with other areas in the organization. Our research shows that all areas should be considered, although some of the capability areas might be prioritized depending on the strategy and context so they are developed within different timeframes. BPM should not be considered a one-off project but a journey (Trkman, 2010; vom Brocke et al., 2014; vom Brocke, Petry, & Gonser, 2012) that continually develops these capabilities to serve the organization's strategy.

2.4 Projects and Programs

BPM comes to life in process-centric projects and programs. In this regard, by using the BPM Billboard, companies can align their initiatives with the four other layers of the BPM Billboard. By continuously reviewing strategy, context, capability areas, and results, organizations can ensure that new projects that enter the project portfolio make a distinct contribution to strategy.

2.5 Results

BPM initiatives should be directed toward and evaluated based on tangible results. What is it that a project or program should deliver, what is the specific expected result that further develops the organizational capabilities and helps to achieve the strategic objectives in the given context situation? Beyond planning for results when scoping the BPM initiative, concurrent evaluation should be conducted when running the BPM initiative. Which improvements can be substantiated based on key performance indicators and what learning experiences inform the adjustment and further progression of the BPM initiative?

Working with the BPM Billboard, we keep track of the capabilities, how they contribute to BPM projects, and what stage they occupy. Stages in this context are best captured in a simplified Kanban style:

1. Backlog: Projects that have not yet been started are assigned to the backlog. When capacity to work on projects becomes available, a project from the backlog can be started.
2. Ongoing: Projects that are in progress are assigned to the set of ongoing projects. Projects are meant to be completed, but they are also continually reviewed. In this way, projects that cannot achieve their original objectives can be terminated. The phases of the BPM lifecycle can also be used to represent the projects' status.
3. Completed: Projects that have been completed are assigned to this category. To keep track of what results have been achieved and to create templates for future projects, these projects should not be deleted from the BPM Billboard.

When the BPM Billboard is used, BPM contributes to an organization in a way that is clearly aligned with its strategies and objectives. It is not a "stranger" in the organization but a natural means by which to develop projects and programs that help to deliver the strategy. Hence, BPM provides a lens for identifying the projects that are most relevant to strategic goals by building on the body of knowledge and toolkit to assess and develop BPM capabilities in organizations' specific contexts. This lens makes BPM approaches both efficient and well recognized in organizations. Maintaining BPM projects in the BPM Billboard allows interrelationships (e.g., flow-through effects between projects), synergies (e.g., knowledge spill-over between projects), and hierarchies (e.g., consolidating projects to programs) to be identified.

3 Illustrating the BPM Billboard

Here we present an example of how to apply the BPM Billboard. For illustration purposes, we re-construct the SAP case, "How to Move from Paper to Impact in Business Process Management: The Journey of SAP" (Reisert et al. 2018). We use the BPM Billboard to present the essential elements of the case in the form of "BPM on one page" (Fig. 2).

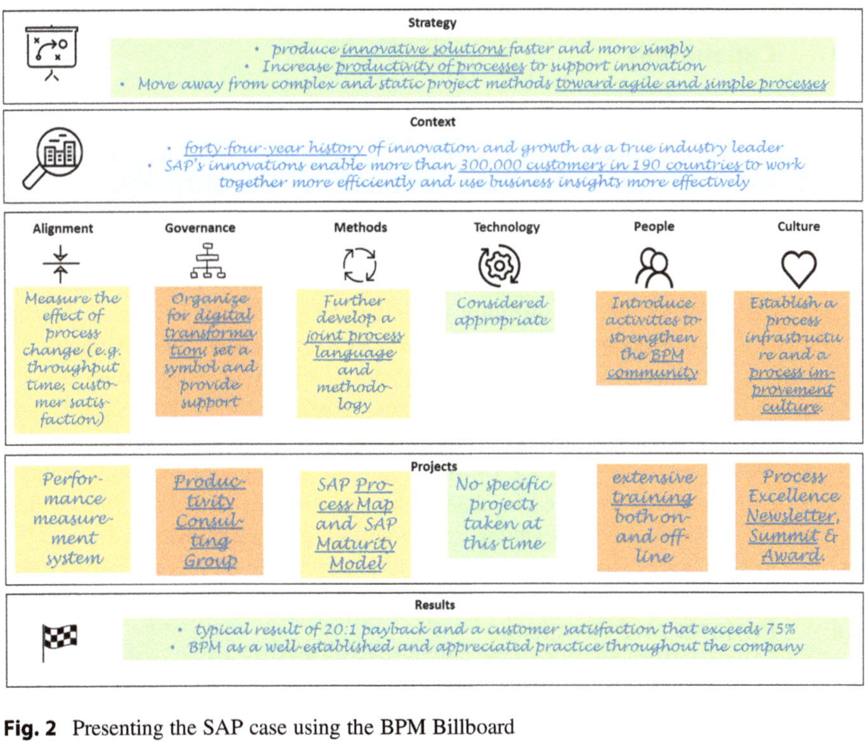

Fig. 2 Presenting the SAP case using the BPM Billboard

3.1 Strategy

The SAP case is oriented to the clear strategic objective of "producing innovative solutions faster and more simply," which gave focus to the BPM program as was being designed. Countless actions could have been taken, and many objectives may have appeared desirable, but defining a clear focus for the BPM initiative helped SAP deliver tangible, valuable results.

3.2 Context

Planning and scoping the BPM initiative required paying close attention to SAP's unique context. As the case description states with reference to 2017, "SAP has a forty-four-year history of innovation and growth as a true industry leader, has an annual revenue (IFRS) of €20.793 billion, and employs more than 77,000 employees in more than 130 countries. SAP's innovations enable more than 300,000 customers in 190 countries to work together more efficiently and use business insights more effectively." In such a large-scale, demanding context, BPM executives had to set an example in using an effective and innovative BPM approach, although the approach faced a number of challenges, such as those related to the company's size and the global distribution of the units and people involved.

3.3 Capabilities

SAP initiated a comprehensive approach to develop organizational capabilities in all core areas, including methods, IT, strategic alignment, governance, people, and culture. SAP addressed the governance structure from the outset of the initiative and communicated its vision to move "away from complex and static project methods toward agile and simple processes." A process map and a process maturity model communicated process thinking and, together with innovative process technologies, enabled the organization to change its processes. SAP also defined metrics by which to measure process performance and process improvement. To make BPM meaningful in the large organization, emphasis was placed on the employees' role, and a wide range of activities, including the SAP Process Excellence Newsletter, the SAP Process Summit, and the SAP Process Excellence Award, was introduced to build a strong BPM community throughout the organization. Extensive training was provided in classrooms and through virtual training, which helped to build skills and joint values for the initiative systematically.

3.4 Projects and Programs

Each of these measures was implemented in projects like developing the SAP Process Map and analyzing and communicating SAP's key processes, roles, and responsibilities. Thus, the BPM initiative was run as a portfolio of projects, each leading to the further development of BPM capabilities to meet the strategic objective to "produce innovative solutions faster and more simply."

To support the project and program management, the Productivity Consulting Group (PCG) offered a portfolio of well-structured, innovative services that can support BPM experts in their efforts to improve processes, including project management support. SAP developed a service catalog that clustered the PCG's services along the primary dimensions of improvement and levels of intensity.

3.5 Results

In each of the projects at SAP, a strong emphasis was put on specific results to be achieved. For instance, regarding the development of a process improvement culture, specific artifacts have been defined to deliver such culture, namely the process excellence newsletter, summit, and award. Further, continuous measurement has been conducted in order to evaluate to what extent the strategic objectives have been met by the initiative. Success for SAP's BPM activities has been defined "as creating measurable and sustainable positive impact by which it contributes significantly to the corporate strategy." (Reisert et al. 2018, p. 32).

It has been reported that by 2017, when the case study was written, based "on a sample of 100 projects per year, SAP currently achieves a typical result of 20:1 payback and a customer satisfaction that exceeds 75%. In addition, many processes' processing time has been reduced significantly, including a process in marketing services team that eliminated eleven process steps and reduced processing time by up to 74%."

Beyond quantitative measures, also wider organizational effects have been observed. For example, the Process Managers' opinion has changed from "viewing process modelling as an administrative burden to seeing it as a critical activity in fully understanding the complexity and dependencies of processes as a first and necessary step in process improvement initiatives." (Reisert et al. 2018, p. 32). One manager reports process modeling "actually made an impact on the daily project work of the GCMS Team, as it changed the way we visualize processes. It accelerated and improved our collaboration..." (Reisert et al. 2018, p. 32). Also, the SAP process map is used for company-wide idea management and it has been a meaningful reference structure for discussions. Through the well-positioned and scoped projects, processes have become a valuable management focus throughout the organization.

The SAP case reports on a successful, large-scale BPM initiative that not many organizations have been able to accomplish. The case illustrates the key principles of the BPM Billboard. By linking the BPM initiative to a clear set of strategic objectives and by considering SAP's situational context, the company defined a portfolio of projects that systematically developed the organization's capabilities in support of its strategic objectives. SAP reported having significantly simplified its internal processes and raised overall productivity.

4 Using the BPM Billboard

The SAP case illustrates the key elements of the BPM Billboard and how they relate to one another. Typically, the BPM Billboard supports a BPM initiative's entire life cycle, as exemplified in four scenarios.

Planning a BPM Initiative The BPM Billboard, a powerful tool for planning and scoping BPM initiatives, is often applied during a half-day workshop in which ideas for impactful BPM projects are generated.

- We start by noting down some key strategic objectives that are meaningful and strategically important to the organization, followed by ideas for how a BPM initiative could help deliver these objectives.
- Then we characterize the context by identifying constraints to be considered, as well as potentially hindering and supporting factors for the BPM initiative.
- In the next step, a round of discussions gives each of the capability areas a rough assessment of the extent to which they need to take action to develop, such that they can contribute to achieving the strategic objectives.
- Then the capability areas are prioritized, as some capability areas may be more important than others. To ensure focus is sustained, for instance, the three most pressing capability areas are identified to work on.
- For each capability area, project ideas are generated, along with how the capability area might be further developed, resulting in a list of strategic BPM project ideas to be further described and evaluated as to budget, timing, interdependence, and so forth.
- Projects of particular interest can then the further sketched out and described in two- or three-page project proposals.
- Projects include specific results to be achieved and continuous assessment is set in place to evaluate strategy delivery through the respective projects.

Managing a BPM Initiative The BPM Billboard serves as a structuring device for managing BPM initiatives. Process managers can use the BPM Billboard to revisit and coordinate the set of projects that are running and planned.

- Revisit the strategy continually in regard to new objectives and priorities coming up, and double-check the initiative's overall direction.
- Revisit the context of the BPM initiative regarding new constraints that might have come up, such as changes in the economic or socio-technical environment.
- Check on the progress of running projects as well as the results achieved to ensure the required capability areas are being developed, and decide on the projects that help with that development.
- Consider re-dimensioning projects and stopping projects or launching new projects in light of the updated situation, as sketched out in the BPM Billboard.

Assessing a BPM Initiative The BPM Billboard helps in assessing BPM initiatives. Many companies want to know where they stand in BPM and what the most valuable next steps would be. Using the BPM Billboard, we evaluate the current state and develop recommendations for future action.

- Capture the set of current BPM activities and structure them according to the six key capability areas.
- Then refer to strategy and identify the organization's key strategic objectives.
- Check the context of the BPM approach by identifying key constraints.
- Assess the organization's BPM practice against the background of the strategic and contextual requirements.
- Decide which activities to stop, which to adjust, and which to add based on the assessment of results (to be) achieved.

Communicating a BPM Initiative The BPM Billboard is a useful tool for communicating what a BPM initiative does and how it contributes to strategy. Given BPM initiatives' complexity, the BPM Billboard's one-page summary of the initiative's essential elements is an advantage.

- Clearly state a strategic objective that is also meaningful for people who are not involved in BPM activities.
- Explain how the BPM initiative can help and has helped to achieve the organization's overall strategy in the given context.
- Clearly communicate how each project delivers measurable results and which strategic objectives it aligns with.

5 Outlook

The cases in this book reflect the intention of the BPM Billboard, as they all deliver strategic value through BPM projects. Each case focuses on a different set of capability areas, strategic priorities, contexts, and results.

The cases cover BPM applications in various industries, including agriculture; manufacturing of paper and paper products; manufacturing of fabricated metal products except machinery and equipment: manufacturing of computer, electronic, and optical products; manufacturing of machinery and equipment; repair and installation of machinery and equipment; building construction; transport; computer programming, and consultancy; financial services; insurance; professional, scientific, and technical services; public administration; education; healthcare; and creative arts and entertainment. The cases are grouped into three categories: process technology and automation, process analysis and monitoring, and governance and strategic alignment.

1. Cases in the categories of process technology and automation discuss contemporary BPM technologies and the challenges and benefits of rolling them out.
   (a) Marek et al. describe how process automation supported the digitalization journey at a major insurance company.
   (b) Schönig et al. report how sensor-enabled wearables supported processes in the production industry.
   (c) Pufahl et al. present the case of a blockchain implementation and how it enabled financing along agricultural supply chains.
   (d) Ludacka et al. show how the global accounting function of a major European railway operator benefited from process automation.
   (e) Gutiérrez Fernández et al. share an application of energy efficiency performance tracking at a clean-energy provider.
   (f) Pauker et al. describe how an industry 4.0 application helped a major energy provider.
   (g) Geiger et al. discuss how the development of a process-aware information system enabled the agile management of business processes.
2. Cases in the process analysis and monitoring category describe the challenges and benefits of applications of process analytics and prediction.
   (a) Buijs et al. report on the application of process mining at an insurance company for analyzing customer journeys.
   (b) Valencia-Parra et al. present findings from adopting process mining at Airbus.
   (c) Canjels et al. report their analysis of the arthrosis care process at a major Dutch university hospital.
   (d) Metzger et al. document how a major inland port adopted deep learning to improve terminal processes.
   (e) Dees et al. discuss lessons learned from applying process predictions at a major Dutch institution.
   (f) Denagama Vitharanage et al. present insights into the benefits of process improvement at an Australian university.
3. Cases in the governance and strategic alignment category discuss the challenges and benefits of BPM adoption, digital transformation, and holistic approaches to managing business processes.
   (a) Bandara et al. describe insights from defining BPM governance at a major Australian bank.
   (b) Alibabaei presents how BPM governance can be realized beyond the BPM office.
   (c) Kuhn et al. describe the process-based ERP transformation of a major hospital group.
   (d) Bolboli et al. discuss lessons learned from adopting BPM at a major industrial services provider.
   (e) Cee et al. report on the adoption of global process standards at a production company.
   (f) Corallo et al. present a process reference framework for the creative and cultural industries.

(g) Azemi et al. discuss the adoption and strategic alignment of BPM at a European bank.
(h) Gabryelczyk et al. describe the development of a business process architecture for a ministry of a European state.
(i) Schießl et al. report on the integration of BPM with other approaches at a major manufacturing company.

In sum, these cases provide a compelling overview of the diversity, potential, and impact of BPM initiatives. Despite their obvious differences, they have one commonality, i.e., they can be categorized along the five layers of the BPM Billboard, and it is only via this integration of BPM initiatives across these layers that the success documented in these cases has been catalyzed.

References

Avdiji, H., Elikan, D., Missonier, S., & Pigneur, Y. (2019). A design theory for visual inquiry tools. *Journal of the Association for Information Systems, 21*, 3.

Burnes, B. (1996). No such thing as… a "one best way" to manage organizational change. *Management Decision, 34*(10), 11–18.

Dumas, M., La Rosa, M., Mendling, J., & Reijers, H. (2018). *Fundamentals of business process management* (2nd ed.). Berlin: Springer.

Grisold, T., Gross, S., Röglinger, M., Stelzl, K., & vom Brocke, J. (2019). Exploring explorative BPM – Setting the ground for future research. In T. Hildebrandt, B. F. van Dongen, M. Röglinger, & J. Mendling (Eds.), *Business process management. BPM 2019* (Vol. 11675). Cham: Springer.

Grisold, T., Wurm, B., Mendling, J., & vom Brocke, J. (2020). *Using process mining to support theorizing about change in organizations.* Paper presented at the proceedings of the 53rd Hawaii international conference on system sciences, Maui, Hawaii.

Hambrick, D. C., MacMillan, I. C., & Day, D. L. (1982). Strategic attributes and performance in the BCG matrix—A PIMS-based analysis of industrial product businesses. *Academy of Management Journal, 25*(3), 510–531.

Hammer, M. (2015). What is business process management? In J. vom Brocke & M. Rosemann (Eds.), *Handbook on business process management 1* (pp. 3–16). New York: Springer.

Kaplan, R. S., & Norton, D. P. (1996). *Focusing your organization on strategy—With the balanced scorecard* (2nd ed.). Harvard Business Review (On Point Collection).

Kaplan, R. S., & Norton, D. P. (2004). *Strategy maps, converting intangible assets into tangible outcomes.* Boston: Harvard Business School Publishing.

Kerpedzhiev, G., König, U., Röglinger, M., & Rosemann, M. (2020). *An exploration into future business process management capabilities in view of digitalization: Results from a Delphi study.* Business & Information Systems Engineering.

Mendling, J., Pentland, A. B. T., & Recker, J. (2020). Building a complementary agenda for business process management and digital innovation. *European Journal of Information Systems., 29*(3), 208–219.

Osterwalder, A., & Pigneur, Y. (2010). *Business model generation: A handbook for visionaries, game changers, and challengers.* Lausanne.

Porter, M. E. (1980). *Competitive strategy: Techniques for analyzing industries and competitors: With a new introduction/Michael E. Porter.* New York: Free Press.

Porter, M. E. (2008). The five competitive forces that shape strategy. Competitive strategy. *Harvard Business Review, 86*(1), 78–93. 137.

Reisert C., Zelt S., Wacker J. (2018) How to Move from Paper to Impact in Business Process Management: The Journey of SAP. In: vom Brocke J., Mendling J. (eds) Business Process Management Cases. Management for Professionals. Springer, Cham. https://doi.org/10.1007/978-3-319-58307-5_2

Rosemann, M. (2018). The NESTT – Rapid process redesign at Queensland University of Technology. In J. vom Brocke & J. Mendling (Eds.), *Business process management cases. Digital innovation and business transformation in practice.* Berlin: Springer.

Rosemann, M., & vom Brocke, J. (2015). The six core elements of business process management. In J. vom Brocke & M. Rosemann (Eds.) *Handbook on business process management 1* (pp. 105–122). Berlin: Springer.

Schmiedel, T., & vom Brocke, J. (2015). Business process management: Potentials and challenges of driving innovation. In J. vom Brocke & J. Schmiedel (Eds.), *Business process management. Driving innovation in a digital World.* New York: Springer.

Trkman, P. (2010). The critical success factors of business process management. *International Journal of Information Management, 30*(2), 125–134.

vom Brocke, J., & Mendling, J. (2018). *Business process management cases. Digital innovation and business transformation in practice*. Berlin: Springer.

vom Brocke, J., Petry, M., & Gonser, T. (2012). Business process management. In *A handbook of business transformation management methodology* (pp. 137–172). London: Routledge.

vom Brocke, J., & Rosemann, M. (2015). Business process management. In *Encyclopedia of management* (pp. 1–9). New York: Wiley.

vom Brocke, J., Schmiedel, T., Recker, J., Trkman, P., Mertens, W., & Viaene, S. (2014). Ten principles of good business process management. *Business Process Management Journal, 20* (4), 530–548.

vom Brocke, J., Zelt, S., & Schmiedel, T. (2016). On the role of context in business process management. *International Journal of Information Management, 36*(3), 486–495.

Zelt, S., Recker, J., Schmiedel, T., & vom Brocke, J. (2019). A theory of contingent business process management. *Business Process Management Journal, 25*(6), 1291–1316.

Zelt, S., Schmiedel, T., & vom Brocke, J. (2018). Understanding the nature of processes: An information-processing perspective. *Business Process Management Journal, 24*(1), 67–88.

Part II

Cases on Process Technology and Automation

Process Automation at Generali CEE Holding: A Journey to Digitalization

Jan Marek, Kurt Blümlein, and Charlotte Wehking

1 Introduction

The international insurance organization Generali provides life and other types of insurance for a range of clients, including individuals, small- and medium-sized companies, and corporations. As part of a service industry, the organization helps to protect its customers against various risks. With more than 14,000 employees, 24% market share, and 8 million insurance contracts, Generali CEE Holding is a market leader in the Czech Republic. Generali CEE Holding offers motor, home, accident, and health insurance, as well as commercial and industrial risk solutions in their property and casualty insurance segments.

Generali CEE Holding faced several digital-innovation-related challenges from the insurance market, governmental requirements, and with regard to employees' daily work routines related to process and workflow management that resulted in inefficiency and productivity losses. It is a great case showing how to develop a BPM approach that is closely linked to specific challenges the organization was facing (vom Brocke, Mendling, & Rosemann, 2021). To remain successful in the insurance market, the company must address internal and external challenges simultaneously. From an internal perspective, Generali CEE Holding faced challenges related to data redundancy and inconsistencies that resulted in decreased efficiency.

J. Marek
Generali CEE Holding, Praha, Czechia
e-mail: jan.marek@generali.com

K. Blümlein
Bizagi Deutschland GmbH, Munich, Germany
e-mail: kurt.blumlein@bizagi.com

C. Wehking (✉)
University of Liechtenstein, Vaduz, Liechtenstein
e-mail: charlotte.wehking@uni.li

J. vom Brocke et al. (eds.), *Business Process Management Cases Vol. 2*,
https://doi.org/10.1007/978-3-662-63047-1_2

For example, its internal processes were paper-based, which duplicated data and resulted in time- and resource-consuming tasks for employees. From an external perspective, new regulatory legislation came into force that obliged Generali CEE Holding to change its internal processes. Generali CEE Holding looked at the challenges as opportunities, so it initiated an organization-wide transformation project and implemented several digital technologies. The goal of this project was to exploit digitalization (vom Brocke, Zelt, & Schmiedel, 2016) to increase productivity and efficiency in the area of corporate risks underwriting by ditching labor-intensive, paper-based processes in favor of robotic process automation technology. Process automation can be used for both simple, single-process activities or entire complex processes (Dumas, La Rosa, Mendling, & Reijers, 2018).

Business process management (BPM) has been recognized as a success driver in dealing with such transformation projects, especially in a digital world (Schmiedel & vom Brocke, 2015). Because such transformation projects are large and complex, BPM's holistic view helps an organization to break complexity into small, compatible parts (Rosemann & vom Brocke, 2015). BPM's holistic view consists of BPM's six core elements, a framework of critical success factors from Rosemann and vom Brocke (2015) that helps organizations to achieve transformation. The six core elements are strategic alignment, governance, methods, information technology, people, and culture.

In 2010, Generali CEE Holding teamed up with Bizagi, an international software organization for digital process automation solutions, to manage this transformation using Rosemann and vom Brocke's (2015) six core elements. In this case, the transformation focused on digitizing processes and process and workflow automation, including robotic process automation software. The automated processes and workflows delivered immediate benefits for Generali CEE Holding. This chapter describes the situation and the challenges Generali CEE Holding faced in the beginning, actions that were taken to overcome these challenges, the results achieved, and the lessons learned from the digital transformation journey.

2 Situation Faced

Before Generali CEE Holding decided to follow a path toward digital transformation of its processes, it faced several challenges. From an external perspective, a changing regulatory backdrop and new legislation from the Czech and European governments forced Generali CEE Holding to change its processes. For example, the company had to meet the requirements of data protection legislation and changes to the International Financial Reporting Standards and Insurance Distribution Directive. Generali CEE Holding also faced new challenges as digitalization found its way into the insurance industry. The power of digital technologies radically changed the insurance landscape. For instance, new digital ecosystems and platforms allow insureds to provide their information quickly and directly but also increase customers' demands and rights, along with optimizing the customer experience and enhancing customer loyalty. Therefore, Generali CEE Holding needed to act quickly to remain competitive.

From an internal perspective, Generali CEE Holding struggled with inconsistencies in its processes and workflows. Its processes used paper-based documentation almost exclusively, resulting in wasted time and resources. Searching for the right document, filing documents, passing them back and forth to update process information, creating duplicate entries, and dealing with lost documentation resulted in inefficiency and unstructured processes. Valuable information that might be necessary to ensure customer satisfaction was easily lost. Because some processes were already documented digitally, employees also had to switch between paper-based and digital-based processes and systems (e.g., an internal data management system, policy system, and client overview) to find the information they needed. In addition, a high number of customer contacts, including complaints or data protection regulation information, had to be handled quickly, but employees struggled with finding the right information from the right database (e.g., digital vs. paper-based). To overcome these internal and external challenges, Generali CEE Holding initiated a large-scale digital transformation project that used the six core elements of BPM as success drivers (Rosemann & vom Brocke, 2015).

3 Action Taken

As part of the transformation strategy, Generali CEE Holding sought to deliver structured processes for the underwriting process lifecycle to enhance productivity and efficiency. The project focused on the policy cancellation and policy binding processes using an agile project management approach (i.e., Scrum). The core elements of *strategic alignment* and *methods* were addressed right at the beginning of the journey. Key stakeholders, such as top management, supported the transformation project from the start, understanding that a close connection between the organization's priorities and the new business processes would help to drive success in the effort to improve the overall business performance (Rosemann & vom Brocke, 2015). The entire transformation journey was triggered and executed using the agile methods that originated in the field of software development and found their way into project management (e.g., Dingsøyr, Nerur, Balijepally, & Moe, 2012). Now the approach enjoys considerable popularity among practitioners because of its fast-developing nature and user-centeredness. In the agile method, a self-organizing team works at a fast pace that still balances creativity with productivity while responding flexibly to changes from both the business and the technical sides (Highsmith & Cockburn, 2001). In addition, employees and customers were actively involved in the development process to provide timely feedback. New technology by itself does not create value right away, as it needs people and processes to incorporate the technology, thus making innovation possible and creating value for the organization (Schmiedel & vom Brocke, 2015).

Generali CEE Holding followed a multistep approach to change from paper-based, labor-intensive processes to robotic, automation-driven processes. The journey took four main steps: First, Generali CEE Holding's IT and business departments came together to form a project team, as the core element of *governance* asks for transparent roles and responsibilities on several levels. As the core team that led the change process, this team was responsible for the decision-making process and for guiding and documenting all actions related to the transformation (Rosemann & vom Brocke, 2015). Other than the software solution provided by Bizagi, the project was handled in-house because of initially unclear user requirements and the demand for fast delivery. (The entire project had a timeframe of 8 months.) A team of three BPM developers and two business analysts worked together in workshops and interviewed employees to ensure they had the information they needed about the requirements of the new BPM platform. Considering the principles of BPM, such as the principle of joint understanding and the principle of involvement, allowed the team to master the challenges they encountered (vom Brocke et al., 2014). Over a period of 5 months, the project team presented users with new versions of the system weekly, and based on the users' feedback, developed the prototype and added new functions. Each week, a new feature of the platform was introduced, which helped to keep the users interested. Consequently, all of the stakeholders were well integrated into the project, and a common understanding of the problem and solution emerged. At first, the target group—employees of the business and IT departments—disliked the idea of the new platform, and the project team faced resistance to the change. At that time, the employees expressed their preference for the stability and continuity of their existing work methods and feared the new changes—and even that they might be fired. The core elements of *people* and *culture* were addressed in this step. Later, when the system was implemented, the employees had to apply the new processes and systems to improve business performance, so they need a certain level of expertise and process management knowledge (Rosemann & vom Brocke, 2015) along with acceptance of the change, or the newly implemented system would not be used. The response to a particular process change often relates to the organization's overall receptiveness to change and new circumstances (Rosemann & vom Brocke, 2015). Employees are more responsive to change when they are part of the change process itself and can provide feedback. Both success factors (i.e., people, culture) were addressed in this transformational journey through proper communication and extensive training and workshops. Often, as in this case, communication is essential to the success of organizational change (Simoes & Esposito, 2014), but success also depends on top management's support of the communication, training, and workshops (Aladwani, 2001). Generali CEE Holding continually communicated to employees that they would be able to work on tasks that have a significant impact on customer satisfaction. As soon as the users understood that the new platform would simplify their work, help them to be more efficient, and remain of great value to the organization, the users' resistance to the change disappeared. In the end, all employees kept their jobs.

The second step in Generali CEE Holding's multistep approach to change to robotic, automation-driven processes was the introduction of a robust BPM platform prototype to facilitate the management of processes and workflows. The new platform consisted of four systems: web service integration, a document

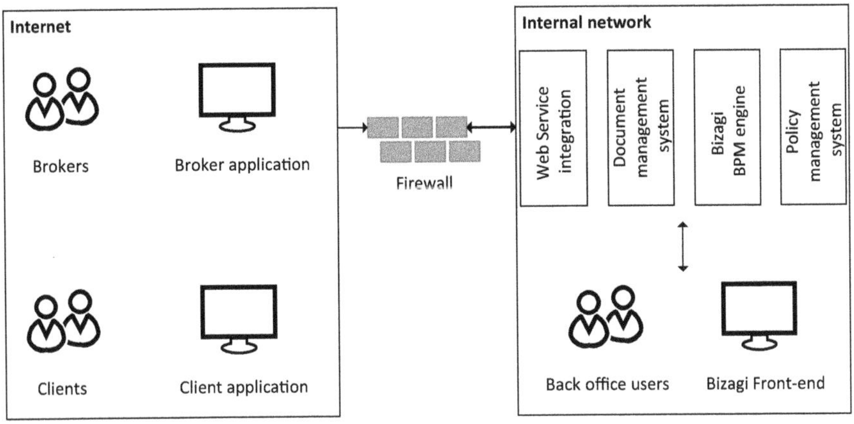

Fig. 1 Overview of the new BPM platform

management system, the BPM engine, and a policy management system. Figure 1 provides an overview of the new BPM platform. The core element *information technology* refers to software or hardware that enables and supports process activities (Rosemann & vom Brocke, 2015). The new BPM platform was the heart of the transformation. Generali CEE Holding implemented a workflow system and a (robotic) process automation software, as various industries have already recognized the enormous potential of business process automation to improve product quality and efficiency.

This new solution allowed Generali CEE Holding's customers and employees to interact smoothly (Fig. 1). The web service integration in the form of an Oracle Enterprise Service Bus allowed the company to communicate with its clients and brokers via the internet, and several of the application's programming interfaces allowed collected information about customers to be distributed to the BPM engine and document management system. It was then possible to handle customer cases like quotations, complaints, and data protection regulation requests automatically and to send them directly to the corresponding back-office departments. The new application facilitated the replacement of paper-based documentation with digital process documentation, and the use of a single platform allowed easy and fast distribution of process information across departments with defined business rules. All business data could be retrieved directly from the workflow system itself and the corresponding integrated database. Employees no longer had to switch between systems or between paper-based documents to get the information they needed. Valuable information was no longer lost, and time and resources were saved. The graphical representation and real-time monitoring of process elements delivered a high degree of control and visibility of service level agreements, the service portfolio, and complaints. The loosely coupled connectors between the process layer and respective integration points enabled the company to create working processes quickly and to rewrap them quickly to distribute or reuse, even across other member countries.

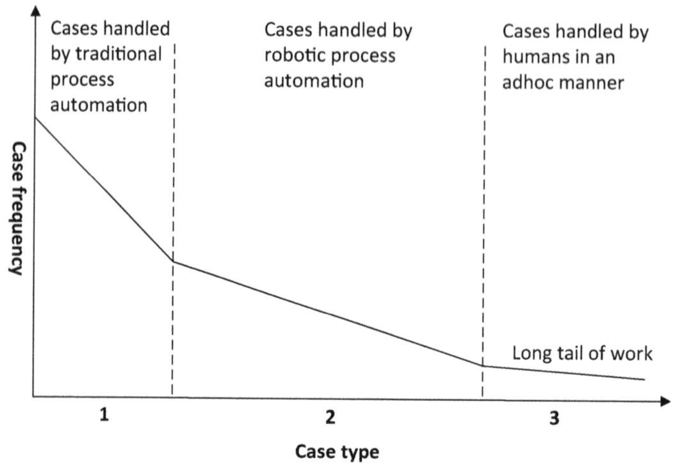

Fig. 2 "Positioning RPA," adapted from van der Aalst et al. (2018)

The third step of the journey focused on the optimization and simplification of the company's processes. All the user forms were kept manageable to avoid the need for complex adjustments later. For instance, changes in the production parameters or in product behavior could be adjusted easily. Generali CEE Holding also minimized process activities and collected additional business rules to facilitate decision-making.

In the fourth step, in addition to process optimization and new software, the project introduced advanced technology in the form of robotic process automation (RPA). RPA is defined as a "software-based solution to automate rule-based business processes that involve routine tasks, structured data, and deterministic outcomes" (Aguirre & Rodriguez, 2017, p. 65). Generali CEE Holding used such an RPA software for its digitalization strategy. (We report on our results, including concrete numbers and examples, in Sect. 4.) RPA software sits on top of other IT systems, in this case operating with the existing BPM systems (Willcocks and Lacity, 2016). The software collects structured data from several systems and performs predefined calculations and decisions. It does not store any data (Osmundsen, Iden, & Bygstad, 2019), as Generali CEE Holding's internal IT infrastructure takes care of data storage. With this additional technology, the core element of information technology is once again a success driver (Rosemann & vom Brocke, 2015). Figure 2 shows an overview of positioning RPA (van der Aalst, Bichler, & Heinzl, 2018). The "long tail of work" is split into three case types: The first type includes cases that occur with a high level of frequency and that have a common structure that can easily be automated, the second type refers to cases that occur with a medium level of frequency but not enough to justify process automation, and the third type are cases that occur infrequently and should be handled ad hoc. Especially, in the second type of case, RPA software can provide benefits for an organization, as robotic agents imitate human workers. According to Fung (2014), this type of case is particularly suitable for RPA, as it is typified by five characteristics: low cognitive requirements, so tasks do not require subjective knowledge or creativity; high volume, so tasks are performed frequently basis; access to multiple systems, so tasks require access to various applications; limited exception handling, so tasks have a high degree of standardization; and human error, so tasks are likely to fail because of mistakes. Based on these characteristics, Generali CEE Holding started to use RPA for all policy cancellation processes and so relieved their employees of monotonous tasks. All other processes connected to policy binding were still done manually and ad hoc. Testing on the current pilot phase shows promise for extending RPA into other process areas at Generali CEE Holding.

4 Results Achieved

The transformation project was strategically relevant to the organization and resulted in great success, as the introduction of the workflow system and the RPA software delivered immediate benefits. The two main results are concerned with process documentation and process automation.

Process Documentation Changing the documentation style from paper-based processes to digital-based processes allowed Generali CEE Holding to improve the *efficiency* of process documentation, to eliminate duplicate data entries, and to improve accuracy and the use of resources. As a result, process *control* increased and *responsibilities* were clearer. For example, the time to prepare quotes and offers for customers declined by 40%. Furthermore, employees can write complex customer offers in half of the time it took prior to the digital transformation project. All important information is now documented and structured, and everyone knows where to find which pieces of information, saving time that employees can now spend with customers to get detailed feedback or to record user requirements. The brokers can also generate a snapshot of the current business portfolio in real time, facilitating smooth consultations with customers.

Process Automation After the transformation project was introduced, Generali CEE Holding automated through RPA and fully operationalized 38 processes within 2 months.

The use of RPA software resulted in *cost reductions* based on increased productivity and reduced processing time. In particular, the company's new solution increased cost savings as much as 50%. In addition, the use of RPA software increased productivity, with 24/7 potential, while also guaranteeing the quality of work, as the chance of human error was zero. Process decisions are now made based on clear and predefined logical rules instead of subjective knowledge or workers' experiences, improving quality and reducing errors, as the robots run with less than 1% error by default. It is possible to get rid of the errors, but doing so would require complex changes in the policy systems themselves. Implementing these changes would require many resources that would no longer present a good business case.

Besides the benefits of cost reduction, even *employee satisfaction* increased, as monotonous activities (e.g., copy–paste activities) were eliminated from their daily tasks, allowing them to focus on more value-adding tasks that required creativity and decision-making skills.

Furthermore, the new platform ensured greater *visibility and auditability* of transactions, which improved control of the overall underwriting process lifecycle. Generali CEE Holding can now follow new regulatory requirements quickly, and compliance has improved. For instance, the process audit is fully automated now, enabling an agile response when new regulations come into force or existing regulations and legislation change. Further, if new legislation or regulations come into force, Generali CEE Holding can implement them in just a few days. The company can now respond to customers and regulators more flexibly and faster. Based on faster handling of customer queries, not only are the employees of the contact center that manages complaints satisfied, but the customers themselves also benefit, as waiting time is reduced.

In addition, the introduction of RPA software-enabled Generali CEE Holding to enhance *business agility* and make use of *scalability* effects. Besides responding to changing regulations, seasonal demand could be addressed by deploying virtual resources (i.e., robots) at a fraction of the cost for a short period. As RPA had minimal impact on the company's existing IT landscape, using such software did not necessarily require the company to make major changes in IT, so it could remain agile.

Generali CEE Holding reached these fast results because of the work of a mixed transformation team and the special architecture of the BPM solution. The social side (e.g., people's attitudes and skills, authority structures) and the technical side (e.g., processes, tasks, technology) interacted successfully (Bostrom & Heinen, 1977).

5 Lessons Learned

The digital transformation journey from paper-based, labor-intensive processes to their automated replacements offered several lessons.

Integrate Data and Processes An integrated data model provides a sound foundation for process success, as information and data can be shared across departments and stakeholders at any time but with fewer resources. The model also enhanced the capacity for decision-making and forecasting, as it is based on accurate data. Considerable effort is required to *consolidate data* and *processes*, but it paid off for the organization in this case. For example, it reduced data complexity, eased collaboration with internal and external stakeholders, and increased the speed and ease with which changes to the entire production environment could be made and deployed while taking care to maintain the processes and data quality.

Start Small Generali CEE Holding started to define and automate its processes and workflows with a few work processes in *one area*. Learning from a small sample facilitates later simplification and adaption that may be due to changes in the market or legislation quickly and easily. In particular, starting with a prototype with only a few functions and adding *new features every week* kept the users interested in future features and the end solution. In addition, Generali CEE Holding started with one *pilot project* (i.e., the back office in the Czech Republic) to identify the particular context, challenges, and successes of the project and considered them in taking further steps. The number of back offices in Europe that have started to implement RPA and have learned from this pilot project is steadily rising. At the time of this writing, the new platform includes 51 processes and has been delivered in four countries and five languages.

Be Agile and Involve Users Rather than using the traditional waterfall approach, Generali CEE Holding followed an agile approach (i.e., Scrum) to account for user requirements in the solution. A motivated *project team* that drives the change project should include the IT and business departments to ensure a good overview of and solid foundation for the project (e.g., for mapping business processes and providing information about process frequency). Based on regular workshops, interviews, and briefings, the project captured *user feedback* and *requirements* for the solution. Workshops help to ensure that business and technology users are on the same page. BPM experts should also be connected with RPA experts so all project participants are always informed about every decision and update. Created *prototypes* should be delivered quickly to gain stakeholder commitment and investments in the project. The faster a new version of a prototype exists, the better.

Master Change Implementing a new platform is successful only if future users accept and work with the new platform. Therefore, four easy rules should be followed to minimize resistance to the change. First, the new platform should be *relevant* to users and other employees. Top management should support the new platform and communicate its importance to all levels of the organization. Second, negative views from skeptical employees should be *heard* and taken seriously through training or workshops. The entire project team should always take time to hear feedback in regularly held meetings for user requirements and feedback. If possible, remove the fear of job loss and communicate that employees' capabilities are of value to other units (e.g., customer service). Third, make the new platform *desirable*. If employees understand that the new platform is easy to use and valuable and that it eases their work, it is more likely to be accepted. Fourth, the project team should *stay flexible*. They should have a project plan (e.g., timeline, tasks, responsibilities) in mind but should be comfortable with change and with adjusting the project plan.

References

Aguirre, S., & Rodriguez, A. (2017). Automation of a business process using robotic process automation (RPA): A case study. In *Proceedings of the 4th International Workshop on Engineering Applications* (pp. 65–71). Cartagena.

Aladwani, A. M. (2001). Change management strategies for successful ERP implementation. *Business Process Management Journal, 7*(3), 226–275.

Bostrom, R. P., & Heinen, J. S. (1977). MIS problems and failures: A socio-technical perspective. Part I: The causes. *MIS Quarterly, 1*(3), 17–32.

Dingsøyr, T., Nerur, S., Balijepally, V., & Moe, N. B. (2012). A decade of agile methodologies: Towards explaining agile software development. *Journal of Systems and Software, 85*(6), 1213–1221.

Dumas, M., La Rosa, M., Mendling, M., & Reijers, H. (2018). *Fundamentals of business process management* (2nd ed.). Heidelberg: Springer.

Fung, H. P. (2014). Criteria, use cases and effects of information technology process automation (ITPA). *Advanced Robotics & Automation, 3*, 1–11.

Highsmith, J., & Cockburn, A. (2001). Agile software development: The business of innovation. *IEEE Computer, 34*, 120–127.

Osmundsen, K., Iden, J., & Bygstad, B. (2019). Organizing robotic process automation: Balancing loose and tight coupling. In *Proceedings of the 52nd Hawaii International Conference on System Sciences* (pp. 6918–6926). Maui.

Rosemann, M., & vom Brocke, J. (2015). The six core elements of business process management. In J. vom Brocke & M. Rosemann (Eds.), *Handbook on business process management 1* (pp. 105–122). Heidelberg: Springer.

Schmiedel, T., & vom Brocke, J. (2015). Business process management: Potentials and challenges of driving innovation. In J. vom Brocke & T. Schmiedel (Eds.), *BPM – Driving innovation in a digital world* (pp. 3–16). Heidelberg: Springer.

Simoes, P. M., & Esposito, M. (2014). Improving change management: How communication nature influences resistance to change. *Journal of Management Development, 33*(4), 324–341.

van der Aalst, W. M., Bichler, M., & Heinzl, A. (2018). Robotic process automation. *Business and Information Systems Engineering, 60*, 269–272.

vom Brocke, J., Mendling, J., & Rosemann, M. (2021). Planning and scoping business process management projects and programs with the BPM Billboard. In J. vom Brocke, J. Mendling, & M. Rosemann (Eds.), *BPM cases. Digital innovation and business transformation in practice* (Vol. 2). Springer.

vom Brocke, J., Schmiedel, T., Recker, J., Trkman, P., Mertens, W., & Viaene, S. (2014). Ten principles of good business process management. *Business Process Management Journal, 20* (4), 530–548.

vom Brocke, J., Zelt, S., & Schmiedel, T. (2016). On the tole of context in business process management. *International Journal of Information Management, 36*, 486–495.

Willcocks, L., & Lacity, M. (2016). Service Automation: Robots and the Future of Work, Warwickshire: Steeve Brokes Publishing.

Sensor-Enabled Wearable Process Support in the Production Industry

Stefan Schönig, Andreas Ermer, and Stefan Jablonski

1 Introduction

Business processes are executed within application systems that are part of the real-world, involving humans, cooperative computer systems, and physical objects (Dumas, Rosa, Mendling, & Reijers, 2018; Meroni, Di Ciccio, & Mendling, 2017a; Schönig, Jablonski, Ermer, & Aires, 2017). The Internet of Things (IoT) enables continuous monitoring of phenomena based on sensing devices like wearables and machine sensors. Process execution, monitoring, and analytics based on IoT data can facilitate a comprehensive view of processes. Embedding intelligence by way of real-time data gathered from devices and sensors and consuming them through Business Process Management (BPM) technology helps businesses decrease costs and increase efficiency. In the literature, several concepts related to combining IoT and BPM have emerged (Janiesch et al., 2017; Meroni, Di Ciccio, & Mendling, 2017b; Meroni, Baresi, Montali, & Plebani, 2018; Schönig, Ackermann, Jablonski, & Ermer, 2018; Schönig, Aires, Ermer, & Jablonski, 2018), such as IoT-based process-conformance checking and process execution. Still, many challenges remain (Janiesch et al., 2017; Schönig et al., 2020; Schönig, Jablonski, & Ermer, 2019).

In this chapter, we describe a BPM case implemented in the production industry. We introduced BPM support for several production processes in corrugated-paper plants, where paper is glued together to produce raw material for cardboard boxes.

S. Schönig (✉)
University of Regensburg, Regensburg, Germany
e-mail: sschoenig@maxsyma.de

A. Ermer
Maxsyma GmbH & Co. KG, Floß, Germany

S. Jablonski
University of Bayreuth, Bayreuth, Germany

J. vom Brocke et al. (eds.), *Business Process Management Cases Vol. 2*,
https://doi.org/10.1007/978-3-662-63047-1_3

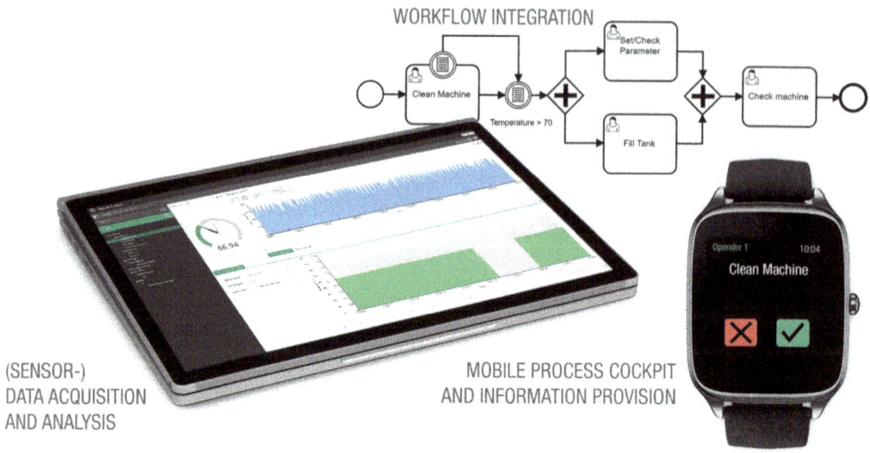

Fig. 1 Overview of the implemented BPM solution

Because of increasing automation and staff reductions, fewer operators are available to control a corrugated paper production line, so users must go to several locations to access the control panels, resulting in delayed information flows. Delayed reaction time is frequently the reason for an increased number of deficient products. Corrugation plants also currently face high turnover, such that process knowledge is lost over time. As a result, new employees frequently have to learn production process control from scratch.

Based on these issues, the project's goals were *(i)* to increase operators' productivity in terms of reduced stop times and increased production speed, *(ii)* to facilitate the education and onboarding of new employees through transparent process knowledge, and *(iii)* to ensure traceability of work steps. These goals were approached in several phases, as visualized in Fig. 1:

1. Introducing and implementing a wearable production-information system that provides up-to-date, sensor-based process information and process control capabilities on a smartwatch interface for production operators.
2. Modeling the existing production processes of the corrugation plants using the Business Process Model and Notation (BPMN).
3. Combining collected sensor data, wearable interfaces and executed BPMN models to realize sensor-enabled, wearable process management in the production industry.

The solution was rolled out in several plants in Germany and the United Kingdom in 2018 and 2019. Forty production operators have been equipped with smartwatch devices and assigned a username in the BPM system. Our approach demonstrates process innovation in three dimensions:

- Feasibility: We introduce an innovative, wearable process-user interface based on smartwatches and a sensor-enabled process-management solution.
- Desirability: The case presented here demonstrates the first process-based, mobile production-information system in the corrugation industry.
- Viability: The case helps organizations to realize an integrated BPM-based solution for machine control and maintenance.

First evaluations carried out with operators showed that the solution improves their understanding of the underlying production process and their certainty regarding how and when work steps should be carried out and reduces the delay between work steps by providing mobile, sensor-enabled, real-time tasks. The case serves as a great example of how to make process data useful for users via mobile devices, and, thus, create a strong value-add through BPM (vom Brocke, Mendling, & Rosemann, 2021).

The rest of the chapter is structured as follows: First, we describe the initial situation that led to the solution explained in Sect. 2. Section 3 describes the actions taken, including technical details and roadblocks that occurred during the solution's introduction. Section 4 describes the first evaluation results and Sect. 5 concludes the chapter.

2 Situation Faced

Because of increasing automation and staff reductions, fewer operators are available to control a corrugated paper production line, so users must go to several locations to access the available control panels, resulting in delayed information flows. These delayed reaction times are frequently the reason for increased numbers of deficient products.

Typically, a corrugation production line is divided into several independent areas (cf. Fig. 2), with well-defined interfaces between them. Each part of the production line has control panels (*CPs*) that operators *O* use to intervene in the production processes when errors occur, but more often because of maintenance tasks. It is also typical that error and maintenance information, as well as other context-related information (*CRI*) is depicted on one (or a few) central information devices. A rule of thumb says that the longer an operator takes to complete an intervention, the worse it is for the production process.

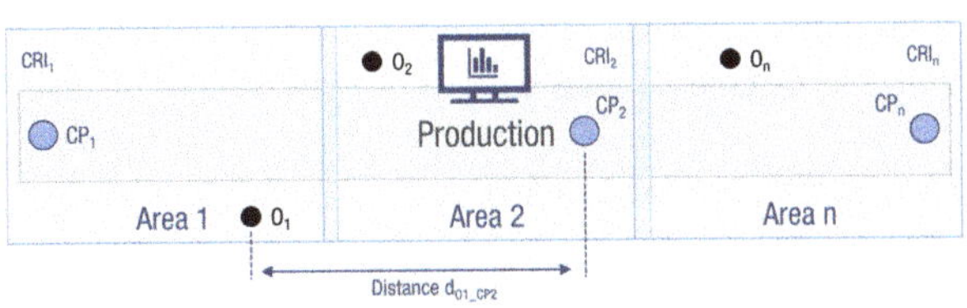

Fig. 2 Conceptual modeling of a production hall

In the traditional setting, the time an operator O_i in area i needs to operate a control panel CP_j is composed of three parts:

(i) The time to find out what, if any, control panel intervention is required—that is, the time to go from the operator's current position to the information device (t_{noti})
(ii) The time to select the relevant information CPI_i from the information device (t_{read})
(iii) The time to go from the information device to the control panel (t_{cont})—that is, to walk a certain distance $d_{O\text{-}CP}$

In sum, $t_{intervene} = t_{noti} + t_{read} + t_{cont}$ is a period of time that is largely determined by physical work—that is, the time it takes for an operator to walk from his or her current position to the information device (t_{noti}) and then from this information device to the control panel (t_{cont}). A third time component is the time the operator needs to select and filter relevant information on the information device since these devices are often heavily overloaded with status information from an entire production line.

Figure 2 illustrates the problem by depicting a situation in a corrugation plant in which the production area is about 140 m long. An operator is located somewhere in that production area. To learn about the potential need for an intervention, the operator has to go to the local information device (t_{noti}), find the relevant status information (t_{read}), and go to a control panel to perform the intervention (t_{cont}). Through observation, we determined that filtering status information takes an average of about 20 s and that an operator covers an average distance of 40 m per intervention, so it takes about 2 min to perform an intervention. During this time, deficient products are produced.

We also noted that corrugation plants face high employee turnover, so new employees frequently must learn the production process from scratch. Thus, we identified two primary needs from which the corrugation production shop floor could benefit:

- The need for individual, wearable production process information and control systems to diminish the time required for the user to get information and provide the required intervention
- The need for transparent process descriptions and active process support to synchronize and guide production operators

3 Action Taken

This BPM case was implemented in two phases, advancing the organization's information technology capabilities (vom Brocke et al., 2021). First, we introduced a wearable production-information system that visualizes current process data and allows operators to control production. Second, we enhanced the solution by realizing process-model-based task coordination for all operators.

3.1 Phase 1: Wearable Production Information Systems

To address the issues we observed, we introduced innovative technology in the form of wearables that allowed the production floor to move from fully centralized information and equipment control to flexible, decentralized production monitoring and control. In particular, we deployed mobile concepts for *(i)* process monitoring in the form of up-to-date, individual production process and equipment information, and *(ii)* process control that allows operators to impact production processes from anywhere in the plant. One of the major advantages of wearables is immediate notification of operators, independent of where the operator is located and where the information originates, as long as it is part of the information system. Such fast notification enhances the operators' situational awareness. A second major benefit is the ability to intervene in production through a wearable device that allows a production line to be controlled remotely. Combining the need for intervention with immediate notification and remote control through wearables saves time that can be calculated easily.

Wearables provide a multiplicity of monitoring functions to operators, including *(i)* visualization and confirmation of alarm and error messages, *(ii)* observation of current status information and process parameters of various production modules, and *(iii)* communication between operators. Thus, responsible operating and maintenance staff are pointed to current alarm messages or instructions from machinery in real time on smartwatches that are right on their wrists. Here, messages and instructions are transmitted to users through visual, acoustic, and, in case of noisy environments, haptic signals like vibration alarms. By means of configurable user roles or user priority groups, production and shift supervisors, equipment operators, and maintenance staff can react to disturbances and changed situations immediately.

In addition to observing process data, users can also use wearable devices to influence production processes and control the functionality that is necessary to operate machinery. For example, production speed can be adjusted by a corresponding operation on the smartwatch. Since the functionality and visual information for process monitoring and process control depend on the user's role, application-specific services and information are accessible only where they are needed, protecting users from information overload.

For example, wearable devices offer diverse functionality to operators at the Dry-End, the area where produced corrugated paper leaves the plant. Such functionality can include *(i)* the remaining time of the current production job, *(ii)* the remaining time to the next stack transport, or *(iii)* the current production speed. Information modules that implement functions *(i)* and *(ii)* are shown in Fig. 3. Users can also influence current process and equipment parameters in real time via certain scroll bars to, for example, adjust the current warp of the corrugated paper. Users at the Wet-End, the area where the paper is brought into the plant, receive continuous

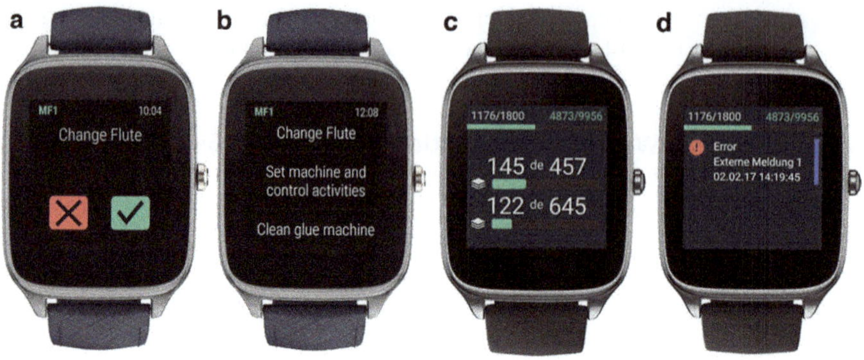

Fig. 3 Wearables: (**a**) unclaimed/complete task; (**b**) tasks; (**c**) and (**d**) context information

information concerning. *(i)* the next necessary roll change or *(ii)* errors and defects in machinery modules.

3.2 Phase 2: Sensor-Enabled Process Support

Despite the introduction of wearable information systems, plant administration still faced the issue of uncoordinated operators: for example, machine alarms that required operator intervention may have been taken care of by either no one or more than the operator. These synchronization problems required a new approach: the introduction of a BPM solution based on well-defined workflows and task assignment and coordination.

Therefore, we defined and modeled all of the production processes over 4 months. We observed and documented production and operator tasks and discussed our observations and model drafts with operators and production supervisors. For example, we described a subprocess that is executed every time paper rolls run empty and new paper rolls need to be spliced with the old paper rolls. To execute this process, several real-time interactions with IoT devices—sensors and operator equipment—are necessary: the process execution system, BPMS, must be "aware" of sensor data that indicates that a splice will happen soon, triggering the splice subprocess. Operators, who are located somewhere along the machinery, must observe the splice process to avoid issues, so they have to be notified in real time to walk to the splicer, which requires wearable interfaces to communicate with the BPMS over the IoT. Depending on the sensor value that indicates the paper type/quality of the next roll, the BPMS must execute one of several paths. If the environment or machine and production parameters change, operators' tasks must be reordered based on priorities or canceled by the BPMS. In addition to the current tasks to be executed, operators require context-specific information, such as the splicer's location and the quality of the next paper roll. Operators must also continuously observe the glue's viscosity and temperature to ensure a successful splice.

The process is initiated by defining internal variables. Then the control flow splits into several branches depending on the priority of tasks and the machine's characteristics. Each task uses the variable Element Documentation, which captures current machine information and is visualized as an additional remark below the task's name. To notify operators directly when human actions are needed, plant personal was been equipped with smartwatches (Fig. 3). Therefore, a user-group model was been defined in the BPMS. Here, available operators were assigned to an area of production for which they were responsible. Thus, depending on the area in which operators are working, the BPMS assigns a different set of tasks. Furthermore, operators are used more effectively because low-priority work is aborted in favor of high-priority work. Concrete and goal-oriented information in error cases and warning messages about supply shortfalls can be transmitted to operators, enhancing the process's transparency and, thus, the quality of task execution.

3.3 Technology Stack and Implementation

The approach described here was implemented based on a four-layer architecture (Fig. 4) that consists of four layers: (i) IoT objects like sensors as data sources, (ii) IoT infrastructure and communication middleware, (iii) the BPMS, and (iv) data sinks in the form of IoT objects of human participants in the process.

The four layers are connected based on standard communication protocols. To connect arbitrary sensor objects, we used IBM's open-source platform Node-RED, which acts as a communication middleware between various IoT protocols and data sources like TCP sensors and the BPMS. A Message Queue Telemetry Transport (MQTT) Broker is used so the IoT objects at layer (i) can communicate with the IoT middleware at layer (ii) and the BPMS. IoT objects like sensors and actuators represent publishers and are connected to an IoT gateway using architectures like Profibus, LAN, WLAN, or Bluetooth. An IoT variable v_x is acquired and published on an MQTT topic/v_x/data. Through an MQTT Broker, the acquired data is sent to an acquisition application at layer (ii) that stores IoT data into a high-performance NoSQL database. Our implementation used the latest version of the Apache Cassandra database.

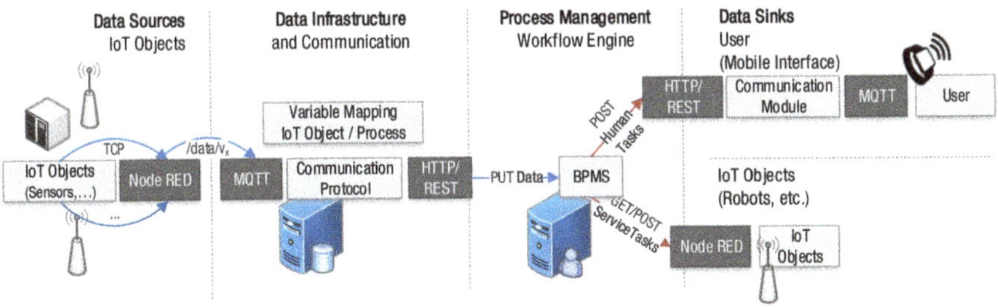

Fig. 4 Integrated communication architecture for sensors and BPMS

A distribution application at layer (ii) keeps the BPMS updated with the latest sensor values, so all running instances of a particular process receive the corresponding data value. The application cyclically acquires the values from the database in a key-value structure and sends them to the BPMS. Our architecture used the latest version of the Camunda BPMS, so communication with the workflow engine was by means of the Camunda Rest API. The tools at layer (ii) ensure that information from the IoT is up to date. The acquisition tool provides IoT data meta information that makes clear where the data comes from. The engine calculates available activities using the current IoT data values.

We implemented as a mobile user interface an Android-based smartwatch application that subscribes to certain MQTT topics. The distribution application cyclically requests from the Camunda API each defined user's current tasks and publishes the information to the correct MQTT topic, given that the mobile device identifier, the smartwatch device, is configured on the BPMS. The application allows users to start and complete tasks and to initiate new process instances. The process by which the device recognizes its configuration is implemented as follows: The distribution application cyclically checks the user configuration in the BPMS. When a change is detected, it publishes the new configuration to the topic /{actor_id}. The assignment of a smartwatch to a specific user is implemented by means of a unique device ID; that is, a certain actor's smartwatch subscribes to the topic of its device identifier. Having established these connections, the smartwatch communicates with the MQTT Broker by subscribing to the current tasks for a specific operator that are published on the topic /{actor_id}/tasks. The device sends operator commands like "complete task" to the topic/{actor id}/command. The content of the message is forwarded straight to the BPMS using a POST request. If there are active interactions with the IoT environment, BPMN Service Tasks are used. Here, we use the Camunda HTTP connector either to communicate directly with IoT objects that support HTTP communication or to send current variable values to Node-RED.

3.4 Roadblocks

We faced several problems and roadblocks during the project, which can be divided into technical issues and social and organizational issues.

As for technical issues, we needed to establish a smoothly working WiFi infrastructure to ensure full coverage of the production floor for real-time communication. Because of blocking machinery and access restrictions, doing so turned out to be difficult and cumbersome, so for some time, we faced connection problems, resulting in delays in task notifications. Finally, a network with nine access points that covered the whole shop floor was installed. A WiFi controller ensured fast roaming and handover, such that each device was always connected to the access point with the best signal.

Social and organizational issues turned out to be even more challenging. Sensor-based event initiation depends heavily on access to sensor and machinery data. A big part of the required data came from external device providers who were asked either to provide their data in an accessible way or to implement an interface so the data could be collected and referenced in executed processes. Both solutions were difficult to realize and took months to establish. Finally, the fundamental modeling of the running shop-floor processes proved difficult as well. There was no written document of activities and work steps, and operators and supervisors on site usually busy. As a result, gathering the necessary process information was a long procedure that occasionally involved unpleasant conversations.

4 Results Achieved

The process solution we established for a German production plant is captured in Fig. 5. The solution significantly reduced reaction time decreased the number of deficient products and improved the overall quality of the corrugated paper produced. The equipment downtime also decreased significantly since problems were avoided or recognized in advance so they could be solved proactively, increasing the overall equipment efficiency improved. To quantify these findings, we analyzed the process execution by tracking the corrugation process (*i*) for 5 days without operators using wearable devices and (*ii*) for another 5 days with operators using smartwatches. We measured the average instance-throughput time for splice processes and the effectiveness of the approach based on machine stop times and waste reduction. On average, 100 splices are executed per 8 h of production. Without the smartwatches, we recorded a total stop time that averaged approximately 12 min per shift. With the smartwatches, the stop time decreased to an average of approximately 4 min per shift. These results show that using the wearable sensor-enabled BPMS led

Fig. 5 Exemplary process-based user interface in a corrugation plant

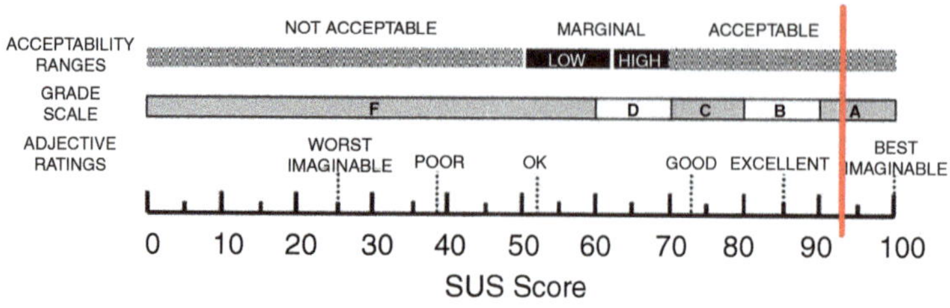

Fig. 6 Qualitative user experience evaluation

to fewer machine stops because users needed less time to recognize the work to be done and to do it.

We also performed a qualitative usability evaluation that involved the operators of two shifts, eight people. A usability evaluation of the wearable user interface was performed by calculating its System Usability Score (SUS). Operators at the Wet-End completed a SUS questionnaire consisting of ten statements that they rated from worst imaginable to best imaginable on a 100-point scale:

1. I would like to use this application frequently.
2. I found the application unnecessarily complex.
3. I thought the application was easy to use.
4. I would need the support of a technical person to be able to use this application.
5. The various functions in this application were well integrated.
6. There was too much inconsistency in this application.
7. Most people could learn to use this application quickly.
8. The application was cumbersome to use.
9. I felt confident using the application.
10. I needed to learn a lot of things before I could get going with this application.

The evaluation resulted in a system usability score of 93.33 out of 100, which is between "excellent" and "best imaginable." Figure 6 visualizes the evaluation results.

5 Lessons Learned

In this chapter, we described an innovative BPM case carried out in the corrugation production industry. We implemented a sensor-enabled wearable process-management device that combines collected sensor data, wearable interfaces, and executed BPMN models, that way strengthening the organization's capability to deliver strategic objectives (vom Brocke et al., 2021), specifically in regard to time and quality.

First evaluations showed that the solution improved operators' certainty about how and when specific work steps should be carried out and reduced the delay between work steps by providing mobile and sensor-enabled real-time tasks. It is highly likely that the solution presented here can be generalized to other industries as well if the most important lessons we learned throughout the project and the factors that contributed to the successful completion of the case are kept in mind.

- BPM technology yields advantages over traditional information systems for production shop floors. User-specific task coordination based on sensor data that a process-oriented solution can provide may be the missing link between production information and operator guidance.
- Modeling processes for production shop floors can be a cumbersome task that requires both deep technical background with regard to the production system and the modeling language used (e.g., BPMN). To establish a working solution that is accepted by users, an expert in both areas should do this job.
- Organizational issues, such as issues with external companies, should be identified at an early stage of the project to reduce waiting time when adjustments are needed.
- Production employees' understanding of BPMN-modeled processes should not be taken for granted. Models were misinterpreted frequently, and repeated explanations were necessary to ensure a common understanding of the notation and the defined processes.
- As a result, BPMN models turned out to be less important as a basis of communication for those who participated in the project. Instead, executed processes and concrete task assignments increased operators' certainty about their tasks, even without knowing the overall flow of work.

References

Dumas, M., Rosa, M. L., Mendling, J., & Reijers, H. A. (2018). *Fundamentals of business process management* (2nd ed.). Berlin: Springer.

Janiesch, C., Koschmider, A., Mecella, M., Weber, B., Burattin, A., Ciccio, C. D., et al. (2017). *The Internet-of-Things meets business process management: Mutual benefits and challenges*. CoRR, vol. abs/1709.03628.

Meroni, G., Di Ciccio, C., & Mendling, J. (2017a). Artifact-driven process monitoring: Dynamically binding real-world objects to running processes. In *CAiSE forum*, 2017.

Meroni, G., Di Ciccio, C., & Mendling, J. (2017b). An artifact-driven approach to monitor business processes through real-world objects. In *ICSOC*, 2017.

Meroni, G., Baresi, L., Montali, M., & Plebani, P. (2018). Multi-party business process compliance monitoring through IoT enabled artifacts. *Information Systems, 73*, 61–78.

Schönig, S., Ackermann, L., Jablonski, S., & Ermer, A. (2018). An integrated architecture for IoT-aware business process execution. *Enterprise, Business-Process and Information Systems Modeling*, 19–34.

Schönig, S., Ackermann, L., Jablonski, S., & Ermer, A. (2020). *IoT meets BPM: A bi-directional communication architecture for IoT-aware process execution*. Software and System Modeling.

Schönig, S., Aires, A. P., Ermer, A., & Jablonski, S. (2018) *Workflow support in wearable production information systems. In Information systems in the big data era.* CAiSE Forum 2018 (pp. 235–243).

Schönig, S., Jablonski, S., & Ermer, A. (2019). IoT-basiertes Prozessmanagement – Mobile Benutzerführung in der digitalen Fabrik. *Informatik Spektrum, 42*(2), 130–137.

Schönig, S., Jablonski, S., Ermer, A., & Aires, A. P. (2017). *Digital connected production: Wearable manufacturing information systems.* In OTM workshops, 2017.

vom Brocke, J., Mendling, J., & Rosemann, M. (2021). Planning and scoping business process management projects and programs with the BPM Billboard. In J. vom Brocke, J. Mendling, & M. Rosemann (Eds.), *BPM cases. Digital innovation and business transformation in practice* (Vol. 2). New York: Springer.

Enabling Financing in Agricultural Supply Chains Through Blockchain

Interorganizational Process Innovation Through Blockchain

Luise Pufahl, Bridie Ohlsson, Ingo Weber, Garrett Harper, and Emma Weston

1 Introduction

Global agricultural industries produce the food, feed, fiber, and many other products that are essential for feeding and clothing the world's population. In 2018, these combined industries had a total production value of US$3.4 trillion (World Bank, 2019). In a globalized world, the production, processing, and distribution methods of agri-commodities, such as crops and livestock, have created long and complex supply chains with networks of farmers, processors, traders, logistics providers, financiers, consumers, and many others, each with its own, sometimes competing, interests.

In a typical agricultural supply chain, farmers provide their harvested crop to a first buyer (exporter, trader, processor, feedlot) but do not receive payment until much later. Commodity buyers usually have limited funds, so that they need financing before they can pay the farmers, which can take weeks to months. Thus, the farmer has to bear challenges like lack of liquidity and the risk that the counterparty will not pay at all. Access to financing for the time between delivering their assets and receiving payment would provide farmers with the liquidity to make sound marketing decisions or to purchase additional inputs to add value to their products. However, financiers are often unwilling or unable to offer financing

L. Pufahl (✉) · I. Weber
Software and Business Engineering, Technische Universität Berlin, Berlin, Germany
e-mail: luise.pufahl@tu-berlin.de; ingo.weber@tu-berlin.de

B. Ohlsson
Geora, Sydney, NSW, Australia
e-mail: bridie.ohlsson@geora.io

G. Harper · E. Weston
AgriDigital, Sydney, NSW, Australia
e-mail: garrett.harper@agridigital.io; emma.weston@agridigital.io

J. vom Brocke et al. (eds.), *Business Process Management Cases Vol. 2*,
https://doi.org/10.1007/978-3-662-63047-1_4

against these assets because they have insufficient visibility on such assets, or obtaining sufficient visibility is too expensive. The impact of this dearth of financing is enormous; farmers are unable to invest in new production equipment and methods that would make them more sustainable by creating efficiencies, supporting a transition to better farming practices, and boosting overall yield. The Food and Agriculture Organization of the United Nations (FAO) estimates that the total investment required to reach the United Nations sustainability goals is US$2.1 trillion annually (FAO 2017).

As grain farmers, the founders of AgriDigital, an Australian-based startup company, experienced these challenges personally and had further insights into the complete supply chain from their experiences in previous businesses. They observed that blockchain technology could help to improve the trust in grain assets and support payment security, as blockchain and distributed ledger technologies allow immutable storage of relevant supply chain information independent of any central authority (Xu et al., 2019). The AgriDigital case, therewith, can be seen as a well-fitting case to demonstrate the effective use of blockchain technology in a BPM initiative and its adaptation to the specific organizational context (vom Brocke, Mendling, & Rosemann, 2021).

Within a year of beginning operations, AgriDigital had developed two workstreams: (1) a commodity management application designed to assist farmers, buyers, and site operators with their contracts, deliveries, payments, inventory management, and export documentation, and (2) a blockchain pilot program to test the application of blockchain across the Australian grains industry. In order to bridge the gap between the user capabilities and requirements and the core technical components of blockchain technology, the foundation *Geora* was spun out of AgriDigital to allow the system, designed and tested as part of the blockchain pilot program, to be rolled out as open-source digital infrastructure for all global agri-supply chains. Geora developed a digital platform to improve trust among supply chain participants, provide secure asset registries, and facilitate payment and financing transactions based on blockchain technology.

The process of getting to a production blockchain system followed the green-fields approach. First, AgriDigital ran three pilots to explore the needs and requirements of stakeholders—farmers, buyers, and financiers—and to determine how each participant could benefit from blockchain technology. Based on the insights these pilots generated, a successful new product was developed, Geora. By architecting a blockchain solution specifically to meet the needs of agri-supply chain participants. Together with AgriDigital, the Geora toolkit now supports cotton and grain farmers with an asset registry and secure payment and provides buyers access to financial products.

Business process management (BPM) supports organizations in reaching operational excellence with regard to their business processes. The traditional BPM lifecycle, which focuses on intraorganizational business processes, structures typical BPM activities into phases that include process identification and discovery, analysis and redesign, implementation, execution, and monitoring (Dumas, La Rosa, Mendling, & Reijers, 2018). This case study addresses an interorganizational process—a collaboration among supply chain participants—which is a typical target of applications of blockchain (Mendling et al., 2018). The next section first identifies the interorganizational process before reporting on the process discovery and analysis: the situation faced by agricultural supply chain participants is described with a special focus on farmers and the uncertainty that surrounds their payments. Section 3 presents the three pilots as three options for process redesign, while Sect. 4 explains the process implementation and execution in terms of the resulting product, the Geora toolkit, along with its design and commercial use in combination with AgriDigital. Section 5 reports on the technological and market-specific lessons learned from this process-innovation initiative for collaboration in supply chains.

2 Situation Faced

Agriculture has not broadly benefited from the "first wave" of digital transformation but is now undergoing a revolution as emergent technologies like the Internet of Things, cloud computing, robotics, and artificial intelligence (AI) are changing farming (Rose & Chilvers, 2018).

Although the industry is driving forward with new technologies and related opportunities, many farms are run by old-school farmers who adhere to traditional farming practices, lack reliable internet access, and have limited touchpoints to the digital economy. In Australia, access to the internet is 8.5 points higher in capital cities (62.4%) than it is in country areas (53.9%) (Thomas et al., 2018), with the northern and western rural areas in Australia facing even poorer internet access. Globally, agricultural supply chains are still largely based on paper records and handshake deals. Information about assets like physical assets, data, and finance is not freely available between participants, as shown in Fig. 1. AgriDigital's founding team includes Australian farmers and agribusiness professionals with more than 80 years of combined experience in the grain industry. They understand the challenges of low transparency in agri-supply chains, where the producers have to burden much of the financial risks.

Traditionally, Australian farmers have seasonal contracts with commodity buyers like exporters, traders, processors, and feedlots that consume, process, or sell the grain. After harvest, many grain farmers elect to transport their grain to a third-party site operator's silo (or elevator), where it is stored on behalf of the farmer pending sale to a trader or other counterparty. This interorganizational process is shown as a BPMN collaboration diagram in Fig. 2. BPMN collaboration diagrams (OMG BPMN, 2011) can be used to visualize interaction partners as pools and the information/asset transfers between them as messages. (We abstract from the detailed internal processes of the single pools, as they are not relevant to illustrating the collaboration.)

Once a truck arrives at such a site, it pulls up at the weighbridge and quality testing station. Based on the quality and the amount of grain, the farmer receives a warehouse receipt, and the grain is stored in a silo of this first buyer, where it is commingled with grain delivered by other farmers. With the warehouse receipt and

Fig. 1 Traditional agri-supply chains, with separate flows for trade, data, and finance. © 2018 AgriDigital. Reprinted with permission

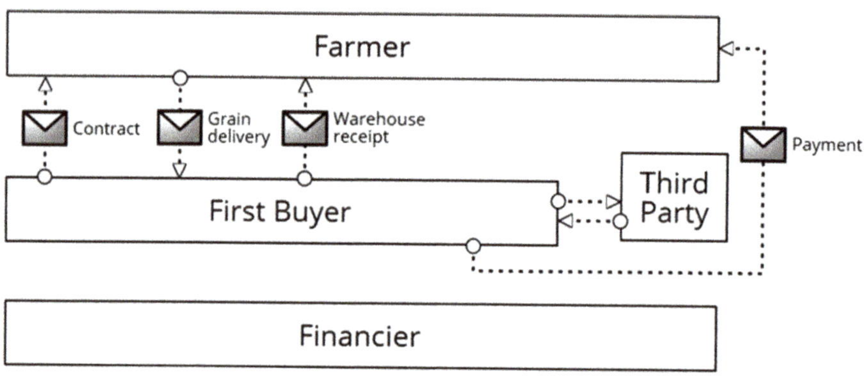

Fig. 2 Collaboration between the farmer and the first buyer without involvement by a financier

the information of the contract to the first buyer, the farmer has indirect title to the delivered products. The farmer has not yet been paid, and his or her grain is not separable from the grain of other farmers. Next, the grain is transported, usually by ship, to a processor that sells the processed grain to a retailer (a third party), who finally sells it to an end consumer. The grain is not sold as a single asset, as the farmers delivered it, but as a bulk commodity, increasing the complexity in transferring the asset and title to it. The farmer has to wait until the first buyer receives financing or payment for the harvested assets before being paid, which can take months.

The main reason for the delayed payment is that the data flow is disruptive and manually handled by the single participants. It requires costly back-office reconciliation processes and manual double data entries burdening the supply chain with additional costs and human errors. Participants have a hard time verifying commodities and matching payments to title and asset transfers. This lack of transparency leads, on the one hand, to the situation that participants only trust a limited number of counterparties, and therefore are hesitant to do business with others, leading to suboptimal market conditions. On the other hand, financiers are not willing to offer necessary financing to the farmers or stockholders to provide liquidity. Financiers have insufficient visibility or insight into the harvested assets, so an investment is a high risk for them. Obtaining the necessary information can entail considerable effort and cost; for instance, sending a representative of the financier to a farmer's remote side of a stockholder might cost $1000 just for travel expenses and time spent, and if the loan is for only $10,000, it is simply not worth it.

With no financial support, farmers have to carry much of the financial risk, which has two key consequences:

- *Lack of liquidity*: With delayed payments, farmers have to use their available funds on short-term investments like the next harvest, so long-term investments that ensure business stability and growth, such as transitioning to sustainable production methods or adapting to climate change, often become impossible.
- *Counterparty risk*: Although the farmer is still the owner of the delivered asset, the physical possession, the ownership, and the payment are misaligned, so the farmer carries the counterparty risk until the grain is finally sold. Often this counterparty risk is connected with the processor at the start of the supply chain. The key challenge is that, as a bulk commodity, grain provides no clear visibility into the commodity's ownership. Manual data-handling systems provide little to no security for the farmer when the payment fails. Thus, the farmer bears the payment security of large parts of the supply chain.

3 Action Taken

After experiencing these challenges, AgriDigital's founders established a blockchain pilot program to test the use of blockchain in agriculture to bring together the physical assets, data, and financial flow. The blockchain, a logically centralized data store that is physically distributed over a network of participants, facilitates the storage of immutable data (Xu et al., 2019). Changes to the state of the data store are limited to appending new data in the form of transactions, and such changes require verification by and consensus among the network's participants. These features of a blockchain can support the grain supply chain participants by having a single source of truth, where information about an asset, title transfers, and corresponding payments are managed, improving the asset's provenance and transparency for the grain commodity. Authorization to read or write data or participate in the consensus of a blockchain can be restricted (*permissioned* or *private* blockchain) or public. For fine-grained access control, some blockchains allow channels, a subset of the blockchain participants who can see transactions that happen in the channel. For commercial confidentiality, it is common to restrict visibility in enterprise applications of blockchain.

AgriDigital followed a green-field approach in determining how they could innovate the existing supply chain with the new blockchain technology. To this end, they ran a pilot program for process redesign, where they tested in constrained environments requirements from three viewpoints: those of farmers, first buyers, and financiers. These three pilots are presented next.

3.1 Pilot 1: Payment Security for the Farmer (December 2016)

In December 2016, AgriDigital executed the world's first settlement of a physical commodity on a blockchain. The wheat farmer, David Whillock from Geurie, NSW, delivered 23.24 metric tons of wheat to Fletcher International Exports, an export business in Dubbo, NSW, and he was paid instantly. The payment was supported by blockchain technology using a private instance of an Ethereum blockchain. As soon as the quality and quantity of wheat was recorded at the silo in Dubbo, a smart contract was auto-executed that valued Whillock's wheat delivery against an existing legal contract and verified that Fletcher International had sufficient funds in its digital wallet to pay him, as shown in the collaboration diagram in Fig. 3, with the blockchain instance as an active partner. If this exchange were successful and the physical delivery were finished, the title of the grain would be transferred from the farmer to the buyer, and the payment would be simultaneously initiated. The payment was done off-chain using traditional banking methods so the farmer could

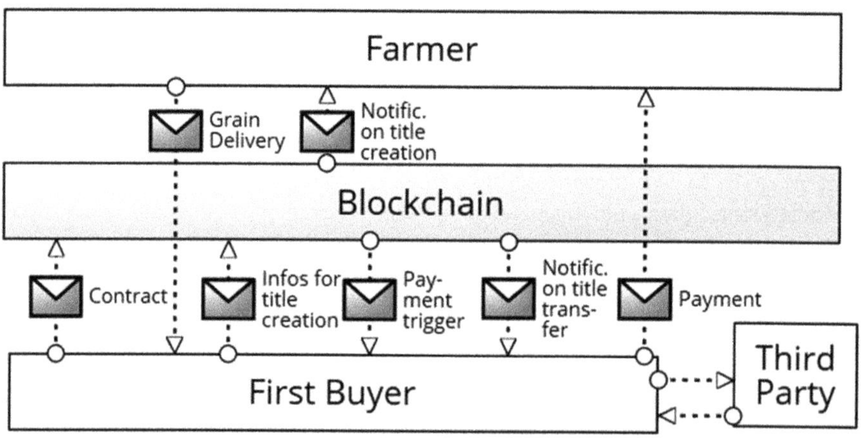

Fig. 3 Collaboration between the farmer and the first buyer with title transfer and immediate payment using the blockchain technology

receive the money in the local currency. Therefore, a message was sent to the buyer as a bank file for uploading and paying on the same day.

Pilot 1 showed that a farmer's risk can be reduced by means of payment and title creation and transfer to the buyer on delivery. However, this pilot ignored the first buyer's financial challenges, which were addressed in Pilot 2.

3.2 Pilot 2: Extended Pilot with a First Buyer (July 2017)

Next, AgriDigital established a partnership with CBH Group, Australia's largest grain exporter, to run a pilot at CBH's subsidiary Blue Lake Milling, an oat processor in Bordertown, South Australia. The first buyer's requirements had two important aspects:

1. Providing longer payment terms (here, 7 days) while providing security over the farmer's asset during that period.
2. Ensuring a level of confidentiality between the participants such that procedures, prices, and details of deals are subject to commercial confidentiality and are not disclosed to all network participants to preserve the buyer's negotiating power.

For this pilot, AgriDigital created a user interface and used a private Quorum instance. Quorum is an Ethereum-based blockchain that allows fine-grained access control through channels. On this blockchain, AgriDigital created the AgriCoin cryptocurrency, pegged 1:1 to Australian dollars, to represent payments. Digital titles for delivered grains were also created on the blockchain to symbolize ownership of the asset (Fig. 4).

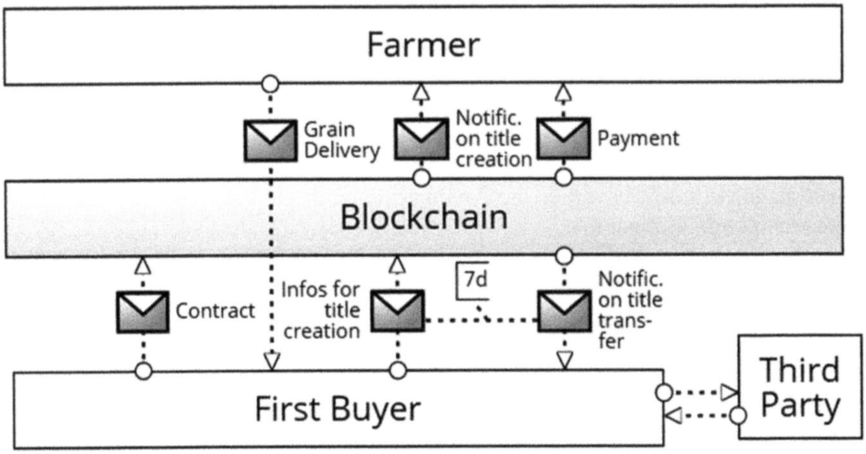

Fig. 4 Collaboration between the farmer and the first buyer with a 7-day payment term and title transfer with the help of blockchain technology (off-chain payments not shown)

As soon as the farmer's delivery was tested and weighed at CBH's site, the quality and quantity of the delivered oats were recorded in the blockchain-based platform. From these inputs, a smart contract on the platform issued a digital title for the delivered oats to the farmer. Thus, the farmer could prove ownership of the asset, even though it was in the first buyer's physical possession. The digital title improved the visibility of ownership and rights, such as the right to obtain a loan against the asset or to sell the asset. The digital title was flagged for payment after seven business days, after which two transfers happened simultaneously: the title was transferred to the buyer, and the requisite number of AgriCoins was transferred to the farmer. At the same time, the payment of AgriCoins was mimicked using traditional banking methods (through a platform called Sybiz) so the farmer received the payment in Australian dollars.

Pilot 2 showed that the challenge of matching delivery to payment can be addressed efficiently and that a trustworthy digital title for grain can reduce the farmer's risk by delaying the title transfer until the moment payment is made. However, 7-day payment term poses liquidity issues for some stockholders, so a financier was involved in Pilot 3.

3.3 Pilot 3: Grain Commodity Financing with a Bank (December 2017)

Pilot 3 demonstrated in a lab environment the purchase and sale of grain commodities on a blockchain with Rabobank, the world's leading agricultural bank. Traditionally, Rabobank finances structured inventory. A grain trader, the first buyer, can enter into an agreement with the bank, under which the bank acts as an entity that buys the grain asset from the farmer. The grain trader then must purchase the grain back from Rabobank within a specific period, and only then can the legal title pass to the trader. Rabobank played the role of financier in the process to test how Rabobank's structured inventory product could be supported with the Quorum blockchain (Fig. 5).

In this process, as soon as the delivery is made, a smart contract auto-executes the digital title transfer from the farmer to the Rabobank and initiates the payment both on and off the blockchain. When the trader is ready to sell the product to a third party, the smart contract settles the payment between the bank and the trader and transfers the title to the trader.

This pilot in the lab environment showed that the blockchain can ease the time-consuming process of handling an inventory-financing product. These kinds of arrangements usually incur substantial back-office costs and are available only to traders that have strong reputations. With blockchain technology, a trustworthy digital representation that is accessible to all participants can be created, transforming grain assets into an investment object. The title transfer and payment initiation can also be streamlined.

The three options for redesigning the traditional agri-supply chain process showed that blockchain technology can increase the trust in the grain supply chain

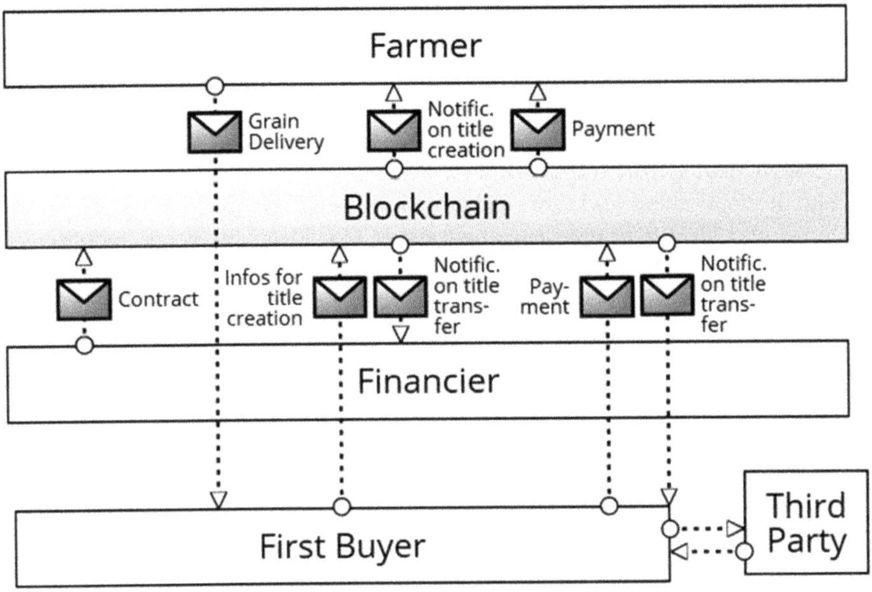

Fig. 5 Collaboration among the farmer, the first buyer, and the commodity financier with the help of blockchain technology (off-chain payments not shown)

by working with digital representations of assets. The ownership and the payments concerning a commodity are visible to the supply chain partners, and there is a clear view of open payments and loans. Furthermore, the digital representation of the asset in a blockchain offers the possibility to involve external financiers by providing them increased visibility on the asset to be financed and streamlining their finance processes so they are more willing to finance lower-value assets. Thus, the availability of financing for grain commodities improves. However, the pilots also showed that data confidentiality is essential to the participants of the supply chain and that data should be shared only with permitted partners.

Next, we report on the resulting production system.

4 Results Achieved

Based on what we learned from these pilots, (1) the blockchain part of the technology was spun out into a foundation, Geora, and generalized for other industries, and (2) a final product was developed by AgriDigital. AgriDigital's product, which is essentially an ERP for participants in agri-supply chains, uses Geora's blockchain technology on the backend to interact with a registry of assets. Integration of other supply chain participants and financiers is established through this backend. This section first presents the production design of the Geora toolkit and then describes how it is commercially used today.

4.1 Production System Design

Geora is technically a permitted Ethereum-based blockchain protocol with an accompanying developer toolkit that allows its users to build solutions for trading, tracing, and financing along agri-supply chains. Aiming to be the world's largest digital registry of agricultural assets, the toolkit consists of a set of smart contracts in support of supply chain workflows and provides a REST API for simple access to the smart contract layer from off-chain applications. Confidentiality is ensured through suitable key management and off-chain data storage that, for example, enhance the digital asset by means of certificates. As shown in Fig. 6, the Geora product consists of three primary layers: the contract layer, the application layer, and the integration layer.

- *The smart contract layer (on an Ethereum blockchain)*: The smart contract layer provides a set of open-source smart contracts and executes the logic on the private Ethereum instance. Smart contracts are available for the creation of digital assets records, their verification, financial creation, and so on. Additional smart contracts can be created and deployed to this layer.

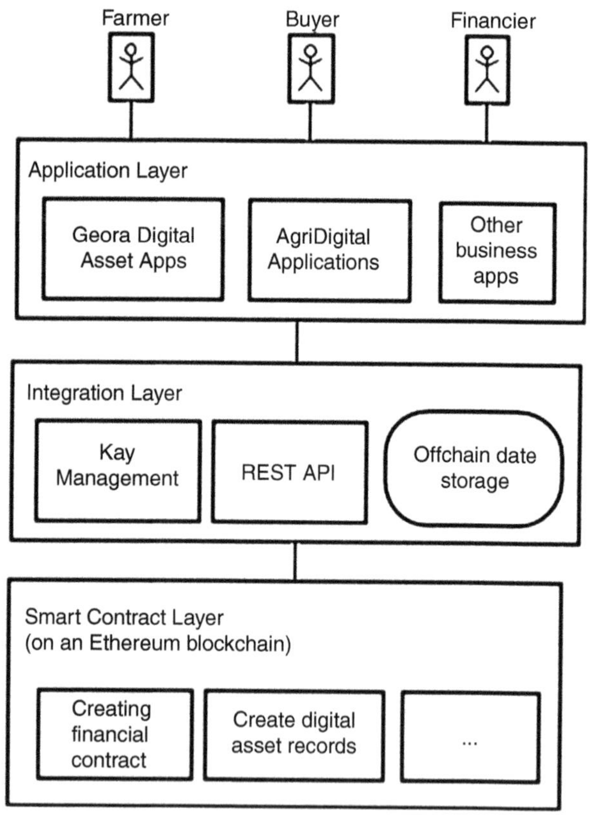

Fig. 6 Conceptual architecture of the Geora toolkit

Geora uses the Ethereum blockchain to power the smart contract layer. A private, permitted network contains nodes that execute and verify all transactions and are operated by both Geora and its customers, creating a consortium chain. The network is secured using the IBFT2 consensus protocol, which provides finality and fault tolerance and prevents bad actors from adding incorrect data or breaking the system's rules. With a current inter-block time of 2 seconds and a large block size, the network can process hundreds of transactions per second.

- *Integration layer*: The integration layer gives access to the smart contract layer through a simplified REST API, which assumes no blockchain knowledge. Further, to keep customers' information secure, it provides the key management functionality needed to manage the business users' cryptographic keys, which are tied to customer identity and used to sign and verify actions in the smart contract layer. Finally, the integration layer provides a fast, query-able database that reflects data stored in the smart contract layer, makes the data available to applications, and stores encrypted certificates attached to assets in the Ethereum smart contracts.
- *Application layer*: The application layer contains tools for building rich workflows on the protocol, including financial contracts and agreements, and provides applications for customer use-cases. AgriDigital is the first customer application to use the Geora protocol.

Customer confidentiality and flexibility of data permission are built into all of Geora's layers. Geora supports *data confidentiality*, making asset and workflow data available only to those with permission, as well as *transactional confidentiality*, which obscures a customer's counterparties and the actions they take within financial contracts. To achieve these goals, Geora uses a four-pronged confidentiality solution:

1. Merkle trees secure asset data at the smart contract layer by compressing all data into a single hash. The protocol can share this hash across all nodes without revealing any of the constituent data. Through Merkle proofs, workflows and contracts can check specific values in the data without revealing the entire asset.
2. When customers upload certificates, the protocol encrypts the data using a unique data key per certificate and stores it on IPFS. Users can share and revoke access to these files using their own private keys via asymmetric encryption.
3. Each user in the system can hide his or her identity using pseudo-anonymous on-demand identities. For each action taken, the user can generate a new identity using a hierarchical deterministic wallet that cannot be traced back to his or her public identity.
4. Within workflows and contracts, state channels hide the details of actions from non-participants. The channels perform the individual steps of a workflow away from public view and reveal only the final outcome.

4.2 Commercial Use

Geora already supports five applications—operating trade and finance solutions across the horticulture, livestock, grain, cotton, and essential oil industries in Australia and Asia.

AgriDigital and Geora combined their development efforts using a joint technical stack to support real-time finance applications in the grain and cotton industries. Since AgriDigital's launch in 2018, its commercial funds have provided finance across cotton, cotton-seed, and grain. Since May 2019, Geora has supported the product suite through its digital asset registry, allowing the product to scale and embed security for the participants. Figure 7 shows that 75 growers and six buyers already use the product and that 122,000 bales of cotton and 34,000 tons of grain have been already financed, with a total value of US$18.5 million. Next, we describe two of the commercial use cases in more detail.

4.2.1 Commercial Use Case 1: Cotton Financing

AgriDigital and Geora designed a system to create a data-rich digital record of a cotton bale, which was then shared with a financier. Having a live view of the asset provides the financier with the oversight needed to offer growers competitive financial products. For cotton farmers, this financing option allows them to delay selling their assets until after they have been ginned, classed, and warehoused, increasing liquidity and allowing farmers to optimize their marketing decisions by knowing the value of their assets after they are classed and by gaining flexibility in decision-making regarding their preferred counterparties and the timing of their sales.

AgriDigital used Geora's toolkit to create digital records of cotton bales in real time as they are ginned, classed, and warehoused. Integrating these records with data pulled directly from various parties along the supply chain can create a robust and shared digital record of the cotton. This bale data was then read through the registry by the AgriDigital special purpose vehicle, giving the company the information it required to deliver invoice financing to the farmer in real time.

4.2.2 Commercial Use Case 2: Real-Time Grain Financing

Following the cotton case, the product expanded into the grains market. Transacting and settling on-chain, creating a more efficient and secure supply chain for farmers

Fig. 7 Number of users, financed assets, and investments with the AgriDigital Finance Product and Geora as blockchain backend

and financiers, and linking digital and physical worlds is a focus of continued innovation. AgriDigital finance software allows the team to manage a massive number of assets without added friction or an increase in operational resources. The application is built to handle all types of assets, including discrete (e.g., a cotton bale) and bulk (e.g., wheat) assets. The application integrates into the Geora digital asset registry to provide live updates of the assets in question and any changes in the quality or quantity of inventory. Drawing from this on-chain data source, each asset is assigned a market value. To ensure price integrity, the AgriDigital financial software integrates with the AgriDigital platform to access live pricing data, a bevy of marketplace web sources via an API, and pricing oracles via the Geora platform.

The Geora registry provides financiers with a summary of all assets and financing sent through the system, thus giving the AgriDigital financial product a streamlined and transparent way of communicating with investors in the fund. Leveraging the Geora engine, M2M calculations, and the AgriDigital platform allows for a financial product that is disruptive in nature. The traditional financial sector in agriculture is primarily driven by PDFs and Excel sheets, which often require manual processes, and this model is challenged by these new digital methods of real-time finance.

5 Lessons Learned

Over the course of developing a commercial product based on blockchain technology from the AgriDigital pilot program to the initial commercial use cases with the Geora toolkit, several lessons were learned. We structure these lessons into technological and market-specific lessons.

5.1 Technological Lessons Learned

5.1.1 Making Blockchain Accessible Through a Digital Toolkit

Over its years of development, one of the clear lessons industries have learned is that launching and managing commercial blockchain solutions is difficult. Commercial applications require confidentiality, scalability, identity-management solutions, and ease of access, each of which demands deliberate design. The base blockchain technology itself is changing rapidly and can be difficult for many users to understand and access. Deep expertise is required to design a blockchain solution, but more widespread adoption of blockchain can be achieved by making design decisions that abstract some of blockchain's components.

By dividing the architecture of this platform into layers, the blockchain can be updated and changed while the technology continues to mature, without disrupting the user's experience through the integration layer. Essentially, the protocol can be designed to "lift and shift" as better base technologies emerge. Geora developed a *generalized set of smart contracts* that can be used for supply chains in various agricultural industries. These contracts are accessed via well-documented developer

APIs, making it easier to launch applications backed by the security- and scale-related benefits of blockchain technology.

5.1.2 Confidentiality

One of the key findings from the pilot program was that agri-supply chain participants require a high degree of data confidentiality when they access the blockchain. The counterparties' identities, transaction values, and production processes are all considered proprietary business knowledge and commercially confidential. Tension between transparency and commercial confidentiality is common in enterprise blockchain use cases (Xu et al., 2019), and full transparency across all data fields has not been accepted. However, where data was disclosed, the recipient had to be able to trust that it was correct and unadulterated. In response to this requirement, Geora focused its development efforts on building out a confidentiality solution, which required compromises to the decentralized nature of the protocol, but that decision was necessary for a commercial solution. Feedback from the customers on the requirements for this solution was essential in making the trade-off design decisions around confidentiality versus decentralization and transparency.

5.1.3 Separation of Concerns

Separating the AgriDigital workstream from the Geora blockchain solution allowed the blockchain solution to be generalized to handle a variety of workflows in supply chains. The Geora team designed the Geora API and digital toolkit to allow users complete flexibility in how they use the product. While AgriDigital is necessarily more focused on providing a SaaS solution and maintaining data quality for customers, Geora provides full flexibility to AgriDigital as a user of the protocol. Everything from key management to permission and data record structures is left to the discretion of the application, giving Geora the opportunity to scale the protocol and serve many applications for a wide variety of use cases.

5.2 Market-Specific Lessons Learned

5.2.1 Low Technical Capabilities

The agri-user typically works off a low technical base. After each pilot and customer launch, the technical documentation and processes were redesigned to improve continuously the simplicity and scalability of such processes as onboarding. The latest launch of the online developer toolkit abstracted many of the blockchain elements to cater to the Geora user's (i.e., the application provider's) level of technical expertise.

Customer onboarding to the protocol can get started with a few devices or systems in operation along the supply chain. As benefits become visible as soon as digital solutions are used on site, customers can integrate and build out a more comprehensive digital solution that accesses other features of the blockchain.

5.2.2 Incent Good Behavior and Prohibit or Reveal Bad Behavior

When building network technology, one must consider the various incentive models for those who interact with the system. One of the key design principles is providing incentives for good behavior and prohibiting (or at least revealing) bad behavior. The system's and the digital asset's designs must meet the realities of the industry and the various relationships involved. One of the most useful tools in enforcing data and transaction integrity is the permission system. When roles and permissions are established within the system, the system itself can ensure that certain actions are prohibited. For example, an asset's owner must be the actor who signs a transaction to sell that asset.

In the same way, separating the creation of a digital asset from the owner (i.e., following the four-eye principle (Russell, van der Aalst, Ter Hofstede, & Edmond, 2005)) ensures that assets in the system reflect what exists in the real world. For example, when a farmer is the owner of a physical asset, the site operator who records the quality and quantity of the delivery provides the data on the basis of which the asset is created and issued to the farmer's digital wallet.

Data contribution is an area in which incentives can encourage or discourage bad behavior. On the one hand, rewarding users for data contributions can encourage spamming the network. On the other hand, requiring a payment for contributing data can prevent the digital assets from becoming data-rich representations of the physical commodity. For this reason, Geora does not charge fees for data reads and writes; smart contracts that incur an execution fee are those that result in an exchange of value (i.e., financing or payments).

Maintaining physical and digital parity is not solved by blockchain technology alone (Lo et al., 2019), but blockchain offers a tool with which users can assess the source of the data. In reality, a comprehensive digital solution, including IoT devices, provides accurate sources of data and helps bridge the physical and digital worlds. Photographs and on-chain certificate registries provide ways of verifying assets and building trust in the data quality and authorship, making the overall digital assets more trustworthy and valuable.

In addition, manual, human data input continues to be a threat to data integrity. Integrating Geora's blockchain solution with platforms and IoT devices, sensors, and machinery like weighbridges and quality testing instruments reduces the need for manual data entry. Removing human data input and increasing the number of such integrations increases data reliability and the integrity of the data stored on the blockchain.

5.2.3 On-Chain Payments Are Still a Challenge

While the Geora protocol itself can be designed to meet many of the user requirements as a commercial solution for asset registries, providing on-chain payment facilities is still commercially limiting. Cryptocurrencies, bank-backed blockchain-based currencies, and other blockchain-based solutions, such as stablecoins, have not met the point of commercial viability for the agriculture use case. The result is that users of the Geora protocol rely on off-chain payment mechanisms for settlement, which is best done through integration with third-party solutions. However, a level of risk is reintroduced by moving onto traditional payment rails, as the counterparty security offered by using atomic swaps to execute payments on-chain is broken. Geora's focus through 2020 and 2021 is on this on-chain alternative financing and decentralized financing (defi) space in hopes of making them widely accessible to agricultural supply chain participants.

In conclusion, blockchain technology can change interorganizational processes markedly by improving supply chain participants' visibility of valuable assets. This case study showed how farmers can get payments faster by improving financing options. However, the application of blockchain technology still has challenges because it requires a specific skill set and the preservation of the confidentiality of business data.

References

Dumas, M., La Rosa, M., Mendling, J., & Reijers, H. A. (2018). *Fundamentals of business process management* (2nd ed.). Berlin: Springer.

Food and Agriculture Organization of the United Nations. (2017). *The future of food and agriculture*. Rome: Trends and Challenges.

Lo, S. K., Xu, X., Wang, C., Weber, I., Rimba, P., Lu, Q., & Staples, M. (2019). Digital-physical parity for food fraud detection. In *International conference on Blockchain* (pp. 65–79). Cham: Springer.

Mendling, J., Weber, I., van der Aalst, W. M. P., vom Brocke, J., Cabanillas, C., Daniel, F., et al. (2018). Blockchains for business process management-challenges and opportunities. *ACM Transactions on Management Information Systems (TMIS), 9*(1), 1–16.

OMG, BPMN. (2011). Business Process Model And Notation Specification Version 2.0. [Online]. Retrived from https://www.omg.org/spec/BPMN/2.0/

Rose, D. C., & Chilvers, J. (2018). Agriculture 4.0: Broadening responsible innovation in an era of smart farming. *Frontiers in Sustainable Food Systems, 2*, 87.

Russell, N., van der Aalst, W. M., Ter Hofstede, A. H., & Edmond, D. (2005). Workflow resource patterns: Identification, representation and tool support. In *International conference on advanced information systems engineering* (pp. 216–232). Berlin: Springer.

Thomas, J., Barraket, J., Ewing, S., MacDonald, T., Mundell, M., & Tucker, J. (2018). Measuring Australia's digital divide: The Australian digital inclusion index 2018. RMIT University, Melbourne, for Telstra.

vom Brocke, J., Mendling, J., & Rosemann, M. (2021). Planning and scoping business process management projects and programs with the BPM Billboard. In J. vom Brocke, J. Mendling, & M. Rosemann (Eds.), *BPM cases. Digital innovation and business transformation in practice* (Vol. 2). Berlin: Springer.

World Bank. (2019). *World Bank national accounts data, and OECD National Accounts data files: Agriculture, forestry, and fishing, value added (current US$)*. Retrieved January 30, 2019, from https://data.worldbank.org/indicator/NV.AGR.TOTL.CD

Xu, X., Weber, I., & Staples, M. (2019). *Architecture for blockchain applications*. Springer. https://doi.org/10.1007/978-3-030-03035-3. ISBN 978-3-030-03034-6.

Digital Transformation of Global Accounting at Deutsche Bahn Group: The Case of the TIM BPM Suite

Fabian Ludacka, Jean Duell, and Philipp Waibel

1 Introduction

Deutsche Bahn Group,[1] a German railway company, is one of the largest transportation companies in the world. With more than 320,000 employees, it is the largest railway operator and infrastructure owner in Europe and the largest employer in Germany. The case serves as an impressive example of how to deliver strategy through BPM by carefully align a BPM program to the organizational context (vom Brocke, Mendling, & Rosemann, 2021).

Deutsche Bahn Group's previously decentralized accounting function (350 locations worldwide, with approximately 70 in Germany) was centralized into three Shared Service Centers (SSCs), using the TIM BPM Suite[2] as a digital request and communication tool. The implementation that was based on TIM is called Service Management (SeMa) as part of the overall program Global Accounting SSC (GASSC). Each SSC serves certain countries: The SSC Germany in Berlin is responsible for the German companies, the SSC Europe/Africa in Bucharest serves the rest of Europe and Africa, and SSC APAC in Manila serves the rest of the world. A tool for decentralized posting requests had to be introduced that digitizes standardized processes for the approval of posting requests and inquiries and their

[1]https://www.deutschebahn.com/

[2]https://www.tim-solutions.de/

F. Ludacka
TIM Solutions GmbH, Garching, Munich, Germany

J. Duell
SeMa Application Owner and Operational Management, Deutsche Bahn AG, Berlin, Germany

P. Waibel (✉)
Institute for Information Business, WU Wien, Vienna, Austria
e-mail: philipp.waibel@wu.ac.at

J. vom Brocke et al. (eds.), *Business Process Management Cases Vol. 2*,
https://doi.org/10.1007/978-3-662-63047-1_5

further management at a global scale. The goal of Deutsche Bahn Group was to become a profitable leader in quality with a return on capital of at least 8%. In addition to the economic component, the company sought to strengthen employee satisfaction by fitting jobs and work activities for the future through digitization and all aspects of work 4.0.

The German organization GFO[3] awarded the SeMa project its "Process Solution Award 2019" in the category of workflow management for its strategic importance, use of methods, creation of acceptance, and measurable qualitative and quantitative benefits.

The remainder of this paper is organized as follows: Section 2 describes the decentralized accounting function before the GASSC project. Section 3 addresses the actions that were taken in the GASSC project to reach a centralized accounting approach. Section 4 presents the results achieved and Section 5 concludes the paper with a summary of the lessons learned.

2 Situation Faced

Deutsche Bahn Group's previously decentralized accounting function was not sustainable in terms of quality and economic aspects, so the drastic step to centralize was taken by means of the GASSC program. Centralization meant that processes had to be changed to ensure transport and approval of accounting requests to the SSCs, not to mention that the heterogeneous system landscape of the 350 accounting locations was a significant roadblock to optimization.

Before the tool was introduced, the as-is processes were documented by a separate team and compared with standards. Held partly in the respective countries and partly at headquarters, workshops that lasted several days sought insights into each global process. Accounting requests were handled through various channels, an approval history could not be found, and it was difficult to track the history of accounting transactions.

Because of documentation requirements regarding Internal Control System (ICS) and tax laws, it was necessary to establish a way of working that was consistent and traceable. Before a digital system was introduced, reporting was not reliable because processes were handled by means of thousands of e-mails written each day.

Without insight into process performance indicators (Van Looy & Shafagatova, 2016) and because of a fragmented accounting system landscape, improving the existing processes was nearly impossible. Handling processes without a centralized accounting platform also meant that there was no transparency about single process instances, which caused delays, inquiries by phone, and unnecessary meetings. Figure 1 summarizes the as-is situation.

The project to address this situation began in 2015. The actions that led to the project's success are described in the following sections.

[3]https://gfo-web.de/

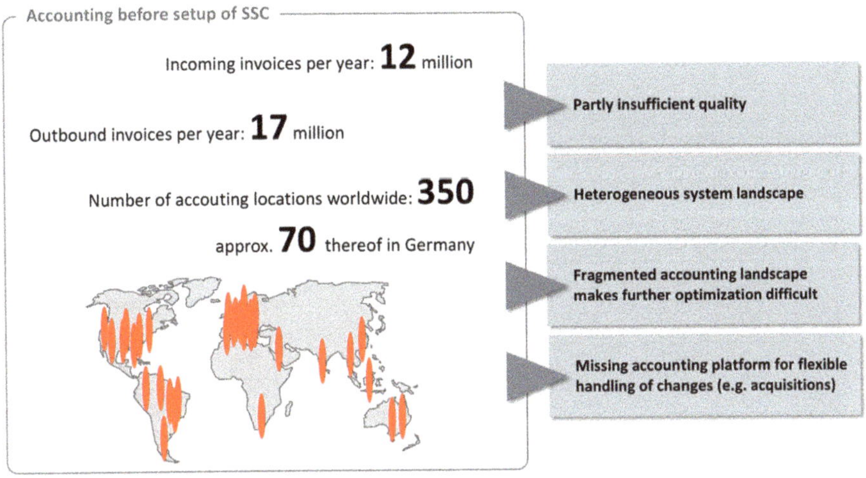

Fig. 1 Global situation and obstacles before the centralization into three SSCs

3 Action Taken

These sections first discuss the SeMa project team and then the actions that were taken to transform the complex, decentralized accounting function into a centralized one.

The structure of the SeMa project team was set up as having one application owner from the Deutsche Bahn Group's accounting systems department at the group's headquarters and two consultants. Other members of the team were developers and a project manager on the product side, as the tool was purchased from an external software company. The development expertise resided directly with the software company, and since the software company was comparatively small, product changes were realized quickly. However, this small project team has to be seen in the larger GASSC project context, as there were more consultants involved in the overall project.

3.1 Actions Taken on the Process Level

As a first step in the transformation, several new processes were created, inspired by the BPM lifecycle (Dumas, La Rosa, Mendling, & Reijers, 2018). The BPM lifecycle describes an approach to improving the use of processes in the daily business. The lifecycle starts with identifying a process and improving it iteratively (see Fig. 2).

Therefore, the process identification, as identified by the BPM lifecycle, took place at the beginning of the SeMa project. In this phase, teams led by Global Process Owners for accounting identified the scope of the individual processes and

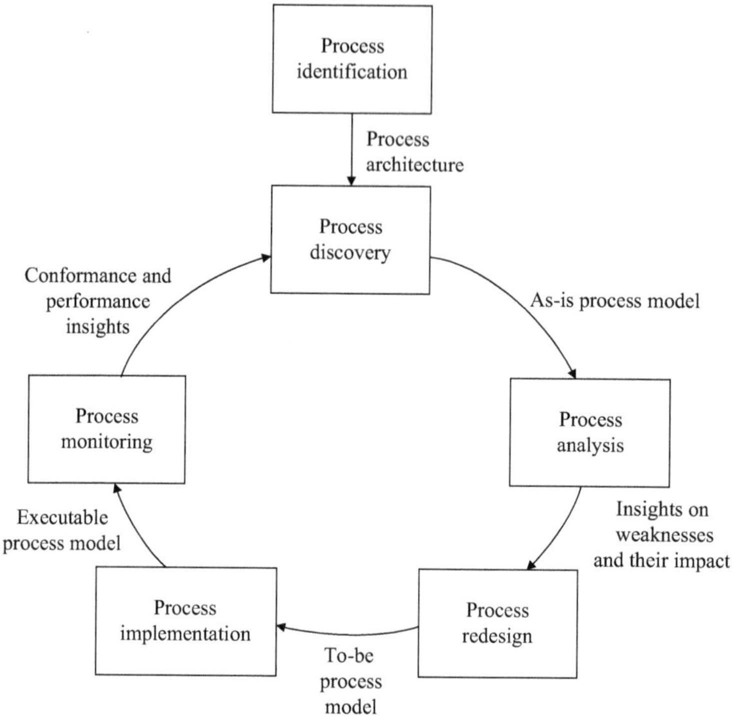

Fig. 2 The BPM lifecycle. Adapted from (Dumas et al., 2018)

defined the relationship between the processes. The processes were modeled using the Business Process Model and Notation 2.0 (BPMN 2.0) (Object Management Group, 2011) standard, and are documented in process manuals. This process documentation then served as a template for user stories in the SeMa project that were then used to analyze the designed processes and to implement and improve them as defined in the BPM lifecycle.

The SeMa project was realized using an agile development approach with the Scrum framework for developing complex and sustainable IT solutions (Schwaber & Beedle, 2002). Using the Scrum framework, the team determined that there would be five sprints that would last 2 weeks each. After each development sprint, a review meeting was held to present the results of the previous sprint and carry out realistic tests that identified various optimization options for the upcoming sprints. Two representatives of two SSCs (Berlin, Bucharest) and one representative of the Global Process Owner Organization acted as product owners.

3.2 Actions Taken on the Process Task Level

The implemented workflows generate all tasks based on the BPMN 2.0 process models and assign them to the corresponding agent at runtime. Thanks to the model-driven approach, each workflow can be changed easily, and tasks may be added or deleted. Since more than 220 companies work with the tool and more are constantly joining, an easy way to integrate new companies, including their users and legal structure, was indispensable. Following this approach, the SSCs were set up as independent tenants in the TIM BPM Suite and put into operation by the Deutsche Bahn Group. Furthermore, in compliance with the BPM lifecycle, constant process monitoring, process analysis, and process implementation are executed to improve the processes.

Another important part of the SeMa project was to integrate third-party systems into the workflows. Using Robotic Process Automation (RPA) (van der Aalst, Bichler, & Heinzl, 2018) was preferred over developing expensive interfaces between the systems. RPAs are software tools that automate repetitive tasks. For instance, a repetitive task that was substituted by RPA in the course of the SeMa project was related to statutory tax requirements. These requirements state that accounting documents must be kept for 10 years, so a History PDF file was created by the TIM BPM Suite to contain all the files and process data related to one request and archived in SAP, attached to the respective SAP posting receipt. This repetitive (and unpopular) process step takes about 3 min when an accountant performs it manually, but because of the high error rate and the loss of time that could be used for qualitatively demanding work, it was an ideal candidate for an RPA improvement. In concert with the human workflow, the robot automatically processes several steps within the TIM BPM Suite and SAP, day and night. After logging into SAP and the TIM BPM Suite, the robot identifies all relevant tasks in the TIM BPM Suite. It downloads the History PDF file for each file and copies the SAP posting number into the clipboard. Then the robot switches to SAP, navigates to the transaction FB03, opens the posting using the number in the clipboard, and uploads the History PDF file. At that point, the task in the TIM BPM Suite is complete, and the same procedure starts for the next request.

Each SSC is responsible for certain countries, each with its own language and accounting requirements, so a posting request must be processed by an employee with the right skills. The SSCs have virtual teams that process the companies' posting requests based on the teams' language and accounting skills. The dynamic allocation of these teams takes place by means of five parameters: company, category, region, a rules matrix, and a decision table that is comparable to the Decision Model and Notation (DMN) standard (Taylor, 2016). The Deutsche Bahn Group can change these rules without further development effort, which allows the individual teams' workloads to be controlled. For instance, there are currently 4433 such rules at the SSC Europe/Africa, and Excel import and export support the administration of these rules.

3.3 Workflow Application Rollout

The TIM BPM Suite is web-based, so the technical rollout focuses primarily on the local IT setup to provide intranet connectivity to the Deutsche Bahn Group network. As the GASSC program has far-reaching consequences for several thousand employees, the organizational rollout was done using an approach in which the software was rolled out gradually by country. Figure 3 shows the rollout over time.

Dedicated rollout teams planned each company's or country's rollout and introduced the new tool. The rollout involved numerous events and discussions that also involved the workers' council. In addition, the project management team was provided monthly information about the project's progress and goals steering committees, a newsletter, and an intranet page. E-lessons and onsite training courses and workshops with the accounting departments were carried out.

After the Go Live, several optimizations to the workflows were implemented, as shown in Fig. 4.

3.4 Process Performance Monitoring

As part of the GASSC program, the separate subproject, Service and Performance Management, is responsible for analyzing process performance (Van Looy & Shafagatova, 2016). To ensure that the subproject system can access the operational data from SeMa, an interface to an existing business intelligence tool was created.

Service Level Agreements (SLAs) between the companies and the SSCs were reviewed as well. Since these SLAs cannot be mapped in the system because of their number and complexity, extensive reports were created so compliance and performance could be monitored. For this purpose, dashboards were created in the TIM BPM Suite that show the time spent by the company and the SSC per single posting

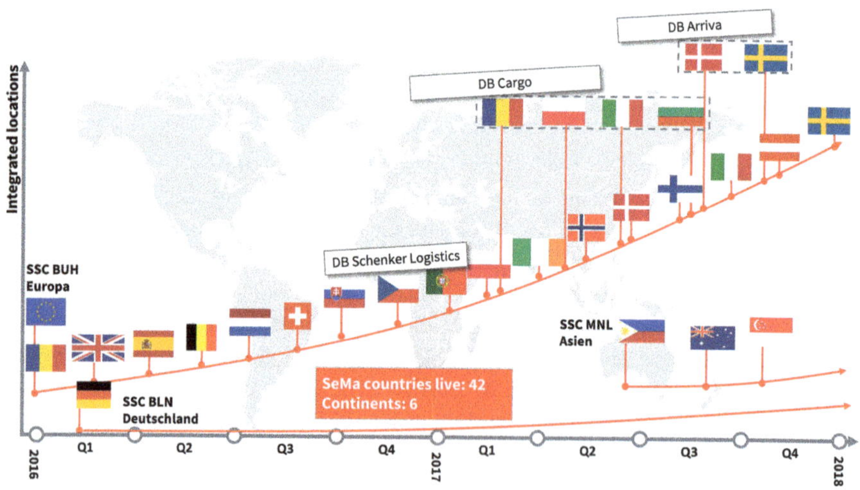

Fig. 3 Global rollout of the workflow application in the Deutsche Bahn Group

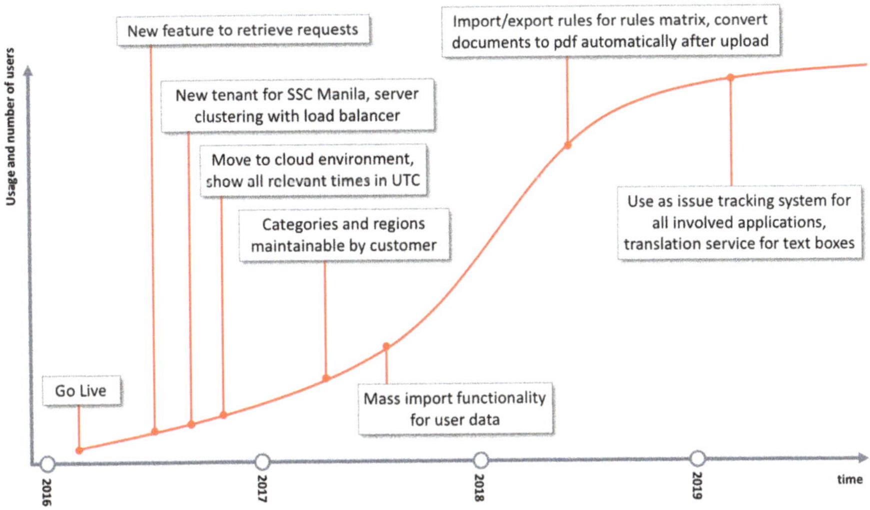

Fig. 4 Number of users and implemented optimizations over time

request. Filter and sorting options and an Excel export make it easy to determine long-running posting requests.

The escalation management is handled by e-mail reminders sent automatically if approval tasks are not completed within 16 business hours to ensure that users who do not complete approvals on time do not delay the processes.

3.5 User Acceptance

Studies have shown that transformation initiatives like the GASSC and the integration of the TIM BPM Suite are far from easy, and projects often fail (Dumas et al., 2018; Reijers, Vanderfeesten, & van der Aalst, 2016). One crucial part of such a transformation initiative is the acceptance of a new approach by the people who are working with it. However, as studies showed, this is always a complex topic (Kegan & Lahey, 2001).

To increase the acceptance of new digital processes, users were integrated right from the beginning. For instance, accountants were involved in the design process at an early stage to ensure that the product that was developed covered all functional requirements. Furthermore, an employee survey on all introduced tools was performed, and national and international pilot programs were carried out. After these pilot programs, the project and tools were recalibrated. In addition, meetings and workshops were held to discuss users' experience with the tool at an early stage so it could be modified if necessary. These actions and the idea of global standardization helped to increase acceptance.

The guidelines that determined which users to include were defined partly by the GASSC project and partly by the project team directly, which was also a driver of success. Testing by main users in the SSC and local companies took place at an early stage so their input could be included right away. In addition, by using the Scrum framework, the developers could react quickly to user feedback during testing.

Section 5 addresses the aspect of project acceptance further.

4 Results Achieved

The SeMa project guarantees global standardized digital processes, has positive economies of scale thanks to its flexible rollout options, facilitates the integration of existing companies and new acquisitions, and meets all legal and compliance requirements. Figure 5 shows the SeMa workflow environment, including all of its components. The workflows are initiated by filling in TIM BPM Suite's forms, at which point a process instance of a particular BPMN 2.0 process is started and the tasks based on the process model are created in the workflow system. After approval, the parameters are sent to the rules matrix to find the right processing team in the SSC. This team receives a new task in its task inbox and executes the posting in the ERP system. After that, the History PDF is automatically archived by an RPA robot. SLAs and other key performance indicators can be monitored in real-time using TIM Business Activity Reporting.

Because of the high number of requests that are processed in the tool and its 24/7 use globally, the project has a high priority in the company. In the event of a failure, the SSCs would not be able to make any postings, the accounting department would come to a standstill. In such a failure, the requests would have to be processed by e-mail, but this approach would not be controllable with the mass of requests and would not be feasible for compliance reasons. Figure 6 shows the key performance indicators of the project as of March 2019.

Several goals that were achieved ensure the efficient running of processes like the integration of third-party systems using RPA and the continuous monitoring of process performance indicators.

For instance, the quality of the task of storing the History PDFs from the TIM BPM Suite to SAP (as described in Sect. 3.1) was improved drastically by using RPA. Instead of an average of 3 min to perform the task manually, the robot needs only 30 s. In addition, it works error-free and is available 24/7. With approximately 60,000 archiving tasks per month, the company saves 3000 man-hours (=20.5 FTEs). At an average hourly rate of 30 €, the company saves 90,000 € per month or 1.08 million € per year.

By centralizing the accounting function, the Deutsche Bahn group could significantly reduce the number of company departments involved in the function. In addition, savings from lower salaries in the SSCs and reallocation of these positions to low-wage countries were achieved. (These advantages are regarded as a general goal of centralizing processes.) While the actual monetary savings of the program cannot be published, it is obvious that the processes are handled by fewer people than before.

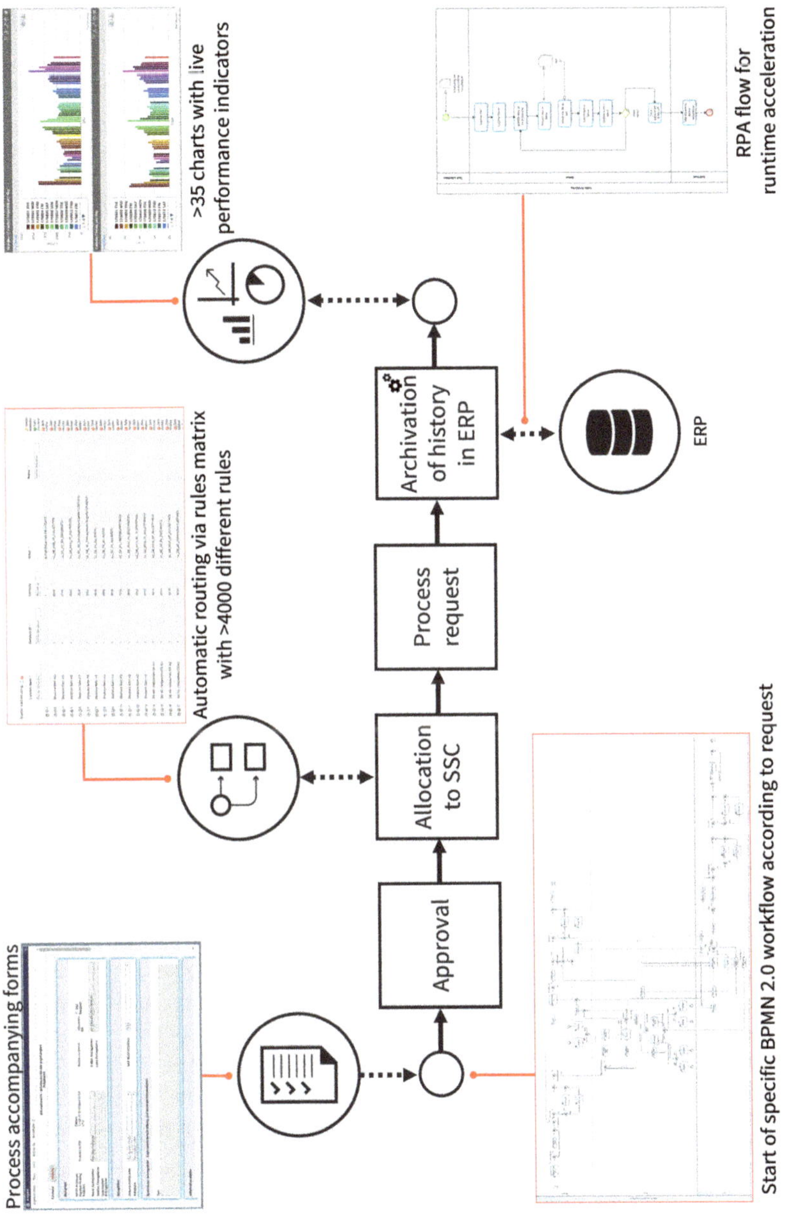

Fig. 5 SeMa workflow with relevant components

Booking requests	Approx. 75.000 per month Up to March 2019: > 1,5 Mio.
Tasks (e.g. approvals, reworks, bookings, etc.)	Approx. 260.000 per month Up to March 2019: > 4,5 Mio.
Users	Approx. 19.000
Active companies	225
Number of involved countries	42
Number of involved continents	6

Fig. 6 Status of project key performance indicators as of March 2019

5 Lessons Learned

Acceptance was one of the most important factors for the whole project. Many actions were undertaken to ensure acceptance of the project and the tools used. The lessons learned deal primarily with this factor.

5.1 Changing Habits: e-mail Inbox

Many users found it difficult to say goodbye to their beloved e-mail inboxes, even though TIM BPM Suite presents their tasks in a similar way. Changing habits generally represents a difficult task (Kegan & Lahey, 2001). Even though employees saw processing accounting requests by e-mail as easier, that approach could not meet legal and ICS-related requirements. Adapting to working without using e-mails remains a challenge for many employees, although ongoing efforts to explain the reasons for introducing an automated workflow tool helped to improve the situation.

A digital process with no e-mails at all may never be achieved, especially since demands for integrating external parties like customers and suppliers into the system are getting louder. For security concerns, these external parties continue to be involved in the processes through e-mail.

5.2 Establishing User Communication Platforms

Many questions came up about how to handle the tool, but most of these questions stemmed from a lack of knowledge about the workflow implementation. To deal with these and other issues, key user meetings and SSC roundtables took place every 3 months and continue today, even after the completion of the transformation, to ensure the project's high level of quality. Organized by the application owner, meetings for the German and international colleagues gave them the opportunity to communicate with power users, and the feedback on problems and features has been helpful. The meetings also help the application owner to see how users actually use the tool so it can be improved.

5.3 Conducting Surveys

Fielding a survey on the global tools that were introduced was another approach to improving acceptance. However, the survey was addressed to the supervisors, most of whom were not hands-on users, so their answers, based on little knowledge about and experience with handling the tool, were not of much use, and issues like compliance and ICS were not taken into consideration at all. However, the problems reported on the survey were discussed and solved where appropriate, and the organizers plan to address future surveys to those who use the system every day.

5.4 Setting up a Standardized Change Request Process

The 19,000 current users can submit suggestions for improvement to their responsible key users. The suggestion must be entered into a template to ensure that all necessary information is included and then submitted by authorized persons in accordance with a globally standardized change request process. The application owner clarifies open questions with the requester, agrees with the final requirements, including the cost offer with the manufacturer, and submits the request to the board for approval. Almost all improvements so far have been initiated by the users. Some exceptions have included conversion to application server cluster operation (JBoss cluster) and administrative issues (mass import of users).

In general, centralization projects of this kind do not have an easy time gaining acceptance, especially when these projects are accompanied by resource optimizations and budgetary constrictions. No matter which tool is used, acceptance may not be achieved in the short term, but it grows with time and continuous support by listening to the system's users and acting on their suggestions. Although full acceptance may be delayed, regular training sessions with key users and discussions with process managers can help to increase acceptance on a global level, however gradually.

References

Dumas, M., La Rosa, M., Mendling, J., & Reijers, H. A. (2018). *Fundamentals of business process management* (2nd ed.). Berlin: Springer.

Kegan, R., & Lahey, L. L. (2001). The real reason people won't change. *HBR's 10 Must Reads on Change, 77*, 297.

Object Management Group (OMG). (2011). Business Process Model and Notation (BPMN) Version 2.0.

Reijers, H. A., Vanderfeesten, I., & van der Aalst, W. M. P. (2016). The effectiveness of workflow management systems: A longitudinal study. *International Journal of Information Management, 36*(1), 126–141.

Schwaber, K., & Beedle, M. (2002). *Agile software development with scrum*. Upper Saddle River: Prentice-Hall.

Taylor, J. (2016). An introduction to decision modeling with DMN. *Decision Management Solutions.*

van der Aalst, W. M. P., Bichler, M., & Heinzl, A. (2018). Robotic process automation. *Business & Information Systems Engineering, 60*(4), 269–272.

Van Looy, A., & Shafagatova, A. (2016). Business process performance measurement: A structured literature review of indicators, measures and metrics. *Springerplus, 5*(1), 1797.

vom Brocke, J., Mendling, J., & Rosemann, M. (2021). Planning and scoping business process management projects and programs with the BPM Billboard. In J. vom Brocke, J. Mendling, & M. Rosemann (Eds.), *BPM cases. Digital innovation and business transformation in practice* (Vol. 2). Berlin: Springer.

Tracking Energy Efficiency Performance at Clean Energy Solutions

Applying Adaptive Case Management to the Building Construction Industry

Antonio Manuel Gutiérrez Fernández, Freddie Van Rijswijk, Christoph Ruhsam, Klaus Kogler, Anna Shadrina, and Gerhard Zucker

1 Introduction

In December 2015, 195 countries adopted the first legally binding climate agreement at the Paris Climate Conference (EU Commission, 2016). The agreement states that meeting the agreement's targets requires mitigating greenhouse gas (GHG) emissions in the buildings sector. Energy efficiency in the building sector is key to supporting the transition to a low-carbon economy and contributing to meeting the goals of the Paris Agreement, as the building and housing sector alone accounts for 40% of European energy consumption and 36% of its GHG emissions (EU Commission, 2018). The European Commission's recent actions show a clear strategy for and commitment to supporting the achievement of the goals defined in the Paris Agreement.

As part of its effort to enforce sustainable principles in the finance industry for financing construction projects, the European Commission plans to develop guidelines for investors and asset managers on how to integrate sustainability and the risks related to it into the areas of organizational requirements, operating conditions, risk management, and target market assessment. To illustrate the

A. M. Gutiérrez Fernández · F. Van Rijswijk · C. Ruhsam (✉)
ISIS Papyrus Europe AG, Brunn am Gebirge, Austria
e-mail: antonio.gutierrez@jku.at; freddie.van.rijswijk@isis-papyrus.com; christoph.ruhsam@isis-papyrus.com

K. Kogler
CES Clean Energy Solutions, Wien, Austria
e-mail: k.kogler@ic-ces.at

A. Shadrina · G. Zucker
AIT Austrian Institute of Technology, Seibersdorf, Austria
e-mail: anna.shadrina@mum.at; gerhard.zucker@ait.ac.at

J. vom Brocke et al. (eds.), *Business Process Management Cases Vol. 2*, https://doi.org/10.1007/978-3-662-63047-1_6

principles of sustainable finance in construction projects, we refer to an example from the Netherlands that was presented in the Sustainable Digital Finance Alliance report (Sustainable Digital Finance Alliance, 2018). ING Real Estate Finance worked with a technology partner to help its borrowers identify the energy-improvement measures for their buildings that provided the most attractive financial returns and the greatest reductions in carbon emissions, after which it offered discounts on sustainable loans. However, what ING did not address is how to ensure that the energy-improvement measures meet the objectives defined in the early project stages and that consequences apply to design teams, contractors, and building operators when the sustainability and energy performance indicators do not meet the initial predictions. The lack of information and information asymmetry have been identified as key constraints and barriers to implementing sustainable financing, mostly because of the lack of information disclosure and analytical capability (EU Commission, 2018).

The heterogeneity in software products, data formats, internal procedures of project participants, and buildings themselves hinder seamless collaboration between the parties and make the management and sharing of information, documents, and models challenging. A significant number of recent software solutions and tools aim to increase the digitalization level in the construction industry, but the McKinsey Global Institute industry digitalization index (McKinsey & Co, 2016) demonstrates that the construction industry remains at a very low digitalization level. Partly because of this, projects' budgets and timelines often deviate between what was planned and what is achieved. However, what is often not addressed is the significant gap in how buildings are designed, built, and operated in terms of energy performance. The lack of information management and process misalignments are among the main obstacles to meeting the challenges outlined above, so we propose an approach built on the digitalization of the construction sector to help bridge the gap between designed and built performance and, thus, support the transition to a low-carbon economy. The case presents an example of a BPM approach designed to meet the context of a specific domain, namely the building industry (vom Brocke, Mendling, & Rosemann, 2021).

Because of the heterogeneity in software products, data formats, companies' internal procedures, and buildings themselves, strict business process models are difficult or even impossible to define and maintain during a building project's life cycle. Our approach uses the adaptive case management (ACM) methodology to support the interorganizational processes and facilitate the building project's management to accomplish goals based on domain-specific business language.

2 Situation Faced

Management of building projects typically suffers from nonintegrated and fragmented construction processes that result from a lack of formalization. Furthermore, task forces are driven by knowledge workers' experience and, if problems are found, these are discussed in small workshops to solve them. There are no formally defined cross-organization or cross-disciplinary software-supported procedures and protocols, and interim information like decisions and reports is tracked manually. This lack of centrally monitored processes hinders the ability to trace responsibilities and decisions made at various stages of a project (Alreshidi, Mourshed, & Rezgui, 2017). Current approaches to design management as it relates to buildings are coupled with existing and widespread engineering software tools that do not support cross-organizational communication among the parties involved, nor do they facilitate transparent project management, where the degree to which the project objectives have been achieved (e.g., energy-related KPIs) can be traced back to the associated decisions, because the project's evolution is usually managed manually by each party, resulting in deviations between the reported project status and the current status.

Clean Energy Solutions (CES), a company and competence center for energy efficiency, renewable energy, and sustainable development, operates worldwide and offers complete solutions to its clients for energy design and management in the building sector. It is a qualified partner according to renowned national and international green building and sustainability rating schemes like Austrian Climate Initiative Certified Designer and BREEAM Assessor, DGNB Certification Expert and Auditor, EUREM European Manager, LEED Accredited Professional, and EU GreenBuilding Endorser. Although the company has successfully implemented BIM tools and processes in its daily work, its project teams are faced with the problems described above and need to address the challenges involved in managing the information represented in its building models. These challenges often lead to inefficiencies and information loss in certain design disciplines and even more in exchange with other design disciplines and stakeholders included in a project. Energy performance depends on parameters like building materials, room topology and occupancy, building envelope, and mechanical equipment, which are interconnected and are highly dependent on other design disciplines, such as architecture and the respective architectural model. As a result, the design information about a certain parameter is influenced and managed by multiple parties, such as the architect or the heating, ventilation, and air conditioning (HVAC) energy designer. Furthermore, the impact of changes among these parties is either not traced or is manually supported, such as with architectural plans on paper or with incomplete digital models.

In an attempt to solve some of these challenges, CES has tried several of the information-exchange platforms that are available on the market, but most of those platforms are limited to simplified document management based on versioning, rather than goal-oriented knowledge management. Missing project information management, BIM cannot deliver the expected benefits or can do so only to a limited extent. The available platforms still do not support effective tracing of decisions and their impact on the project design. The challenges related to software and the process heterogeneity in various project disciplines and teams present additional barriers. Although this problem focuses on the energy aspects that are due to CES's specific experience, the same problems related to sharing information appear in other areas and disciplines as well. By linking this project and operational level barriers to the policy level, a paradigm shift in the development and financing of construction projects is expected to facilitate the introduction of a goal-oriented design approach that is also more transparently integrated.

To achieve this goal, management of such projects requires a method and a platform that support enhanced and more transparent process management horizontally (i.e., through the projects' stages) and vertically (i.e., addressing stakeholders, project participants, and team members). A key element of holistic project governance is the definition of a unique business vocabulary, the formalization of which would support the interconnection of supporting systems and provide a seamless integration of design, construction, and operation processes so the project goals can be assessed in all phases of the project. The integration and interconnection of these systems must make the knowledge-based decisions open to the project stakeholders and participants (e.g., the architects and the planners of HVAC systems) by creating a common data environment (ISO, 2018).

Stakeholders' and project participants' levels of technical understanding often differ, which is another reason for introducing a clear, domain-oriented methodology and a terminology that are based on the principles of *open BIM*, where the information exchange between disciplines is executed "by means of a uniform open interface and common data structure" (Bauer et al., 2017, p. 28). As Rezgui et al. (2013, p. 240) defined it, BIM governance is "the process of establishing a project information management policy across lifecycle and supply chain underpinned by a building information model, taking into account stakeholders' rights and responsibility over project data and information." Energy-related KPIs and design performance are expected to gain importance in overall construction project development, where information flow and transparency, as well as goal-oriented workflows, will be key factors in developing construction projects under predefined target criteria of energy efficiency and sustainability. Based on this definition, the solution proposed in this paper brings to the fore a novel approach that focuses on content-related targets and a platform shared by all stakeholders.

3 Action Taken

The current case is in the context of the "BIM Saves Energy" research project, which is funded by the Austrian Research Promotion Agency FFG under contract no. 861710. The project seeks to manage building projects with sustainable processes where (1) the evolution of KPIs related to energy demand and consumption can be optimized throughout the building project and (2) the impact of decisions made in this regard can be tracked between the parties involved. To seamlessly support the management of energy-related business cases with multiple stakeholders, we consider that the partners' shared knowledge (e.g., architectural models or thermal properties) is a key factor.

With this objective, the ACM paradigm is proposed to solve the identified problems in building projects. As Motahari-Nezhad and Swenson (2013) and Swenson (2010) explained, ACM is a methodology designed to manage knowledge work with ad hoc situations that cannot be modeled with predefined workflows. The methodology proposes that business users (aka knowledge workers) adapt the case execution to each individual business project (e.g., a building). In other words, ACM supports businesses by letting them focus on content rather than task flows when business processes are difficult or even impossible to model in advance or are susceptible to frequent and rapid changes. For the project described in this chapter, we use the ACM platform Papyrus Converse from ISIS Papyrus (Papyrus Converse, 2019), which provides the automation for the designed value streams. Therefore, in this project, we address the process analysis, redesign, and implementation of the business process lifecycle.

3.1 Business Architecture Approach

In ACM, the business behavior is commonly described with business rules, such as "to specify the thermal transmittance, the window properties must be defined." The definition of new rules (with an immediate impact on the case execution) supports the maintenance of business applications. Such behavioral rules are evaluated at runtime by monitoring events in the ACM platform, which avoids defining rules using programming languages that business users seldom understand.

To meet the BIM project management needs discussed above, we propose combining an ACM platform with the business architecture methodology introduced by Open Group (Open Group, 2017) using the business rules concept Ross (2013) suggested. This proposal, presented in Gutierrez Fernandez et al. (2019), defines domain-specific requirements from the business perspective to empower business users and allow them to react to specific needs with minimal IT involvement.

Goals are defined as value streams (VSs), which can contain subgoals (or VS stages, VSSs). VSs are end-to-end flows of activities triggered by a certain business event (e.g., a request for a new building model), which deliver a value to the involved parties after the project's completion (e.g., the new building model). Further, behavioral rules (BRs) are defined either as entrance rules or completion rules to constrain the actions that business users can take. Entrance rules refer to prerequisites to action and completion rules refer to evaluating the accomplishment of a VSS. A business application (BA) is described throughout its VSs, VSSs, BRs, and actions. A summary of the BA for a project is depicted in Fig. 2. To automate the management of the BA, it is formalized using a business ontology that includes all the business concepts (and their properties) involved in the BA, and it is shared by all the partners. This ontology avoids ambiguities and confusing terms while at the same time allowing the BA to be described in natural language with the help of natural language patterns and grammar. Thus, business domain analysts can express a wide range of business rules and actions using a formalized natural business language.

Papyrus Converse provides a conversational user interface where the grammar elements are used to build rules, goals, and actions that support the proposed methodology. This type of user interface allows business users to communicate

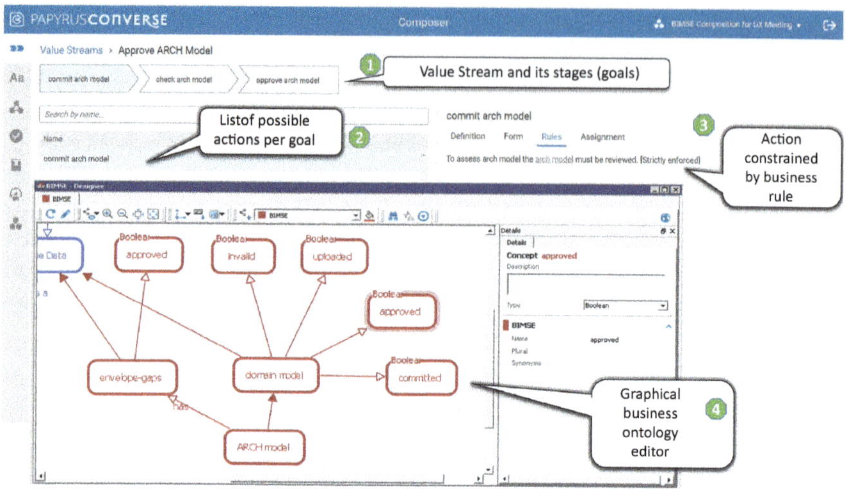

Fig. 1 Papyrus Converse Composer and ontology editor

with the system intuitively to reach a certain goal, guided by the BRs. The platform also provides a business composer that defines all of the business artifacts—that is, VSs, goals, actions, and rules—based on a domain-specific business ontology, as depicted in Fig. 1. The definition and administration of the business ontology by business domain analysts can be addressed with ontology editors (item 4 in Fig. 1) along with data mappings to underlying information systems that depend on the business domain. However, business data structures tend to be stable during the business lifecycle, so they can be developed at the early stages of the domain development. The actions are performed by business users through a user interface based on the rule analysis for business compliance. A number of event-processing engines can analyze rules, as Tran et al. (2015a, 2015b) showed.

3.2 Managing the BIM Project

To address the management of a BIM-based project, we apply the methodology described in the previous subsections. The digitalization of the BIM VSs encompasses the project's various management levels and enables interactions among the project's participants. These management levels are depicted in Fig. 2. Level 1 is where the partners responsible for certain building trades define their own domain models, to meet either the individual goals for each participant (e.g. check the quality of building envelope) or goals that involve other partners (e.g. adding physical parameters to the building elements). With a set of domain models, a complete building model, a so-called coordination model, is created in level 2 and additional goals (e.g. there is no overlapping between pipes and electrical panels) can be defined. Finally, in level 3, the results of the achieved goals are compared

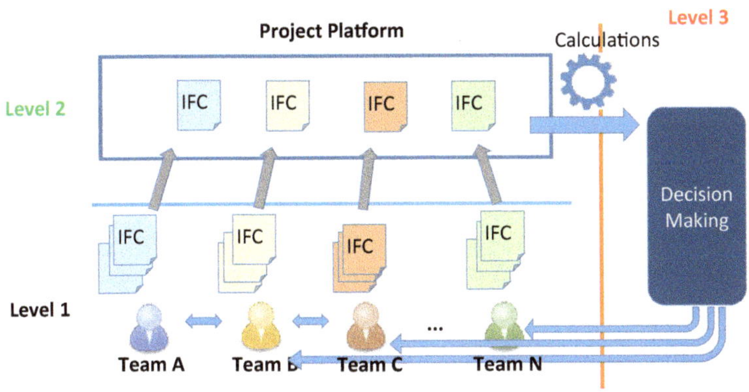

Fig. 2 Building project management. Source: FFG project No: 861710 (BIMSavesEnergy)

with the initially defined KPIs to facilitate decisions for the next iterations (e.g. request for an improvement in building materials to reduce heating energy demand).

This paper focuses on the VSs related to the use cases of the consumption of and demand for energy. These use cases cover the calculation of the building energy demand and the impact of "summerly overheating." The thermal behavior of a building depends on factors like the building's location, its structure, the room topology, and the building materials, while summerly overheating is a special case that corresponds to the dynamic behavior of the materials in response to higher temperatures in summer. Summerly overheating aims to avoid or reduce the size of mechanical cooling facilities. The calculations depend on a proper definition of the architecture model (e.g. without building gaps) and the building material properties (e.g. thermal transmittance), which are considered separate use cases but their evaluation is required to avoid unnecessary, computation-intensive energy calculations.

In an attempt to address the issue of repetitive actions—because if the architectural model does not fulfill a certain model quality, such as nonoverlapping walls, it has to be recreated specifically for the thermal calculations—the model's quality checks include checks for gaps, overlaps, and building materials. Linking the architectural and building physics model with the help of material numbers is planned, and if the checks are successful, also using the architectural model as a basis, enriching it with the necessary parameters, and proceeding to the thermal calculations. We exemplify the use case related to defining an architectural model in the VS *Approve Architectural Model*, depicted in Fig. 3. This VS is composed of three goals, *Commit Model* (i.e. confirm that the version of the architectural model is a final one before further handling of such version), *Check Model* (i.e. perform different checks to evaluate the quality of the architectural model), and *Approve Model* (i.e. evaluate positively the quality of the model in order to share it with the rest of the project teams, such as building physic engineers). The actions that lead to fulfilling these goals depend on BRs like "to commit a model, the model has to be uploaded." The rules are automatically evaluated so the BIM manager can make decisions based on the checks of the current version of the building models. Other

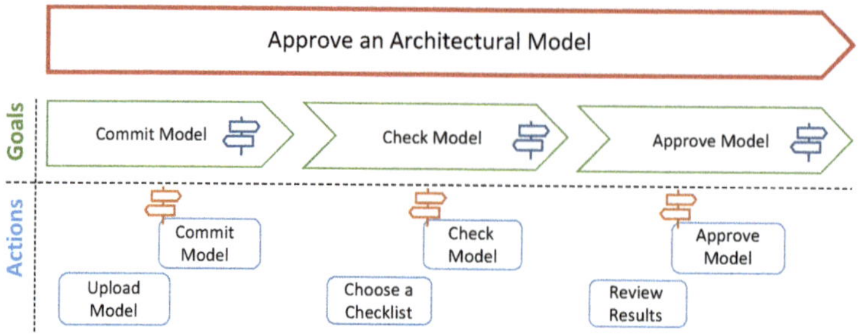

Fig. 3 Creation of business application from action and rules (marked by the rule icon)

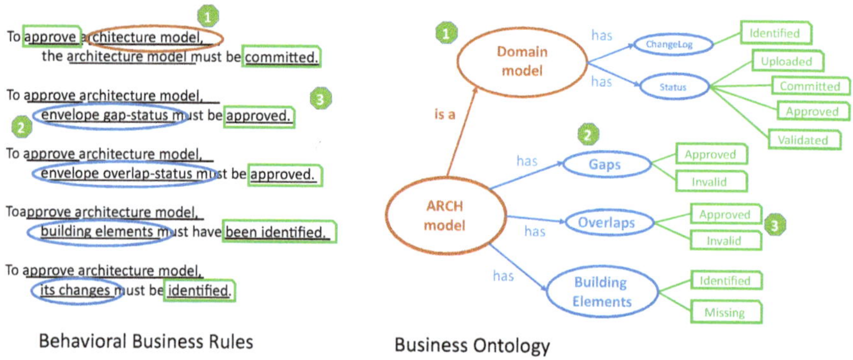

Fig. 4 Defining behavioral rules using ontology

actions involved in the VS are also shown in Fig. 3. To formalize actions and rules, we first design the underlying ontology that allows users to describe each action and rule with concepts in business terminology. Figure 4 depicts this formalization for the VS *Approve an Architectural Model* and shows that BRs in this model constrain the action *Approve architecture model*, along with the related items from the business ontology. The BRs are composed of an action name and a constraint, where the action has a predicate composed of a verb and an object, such as *Commit Model*, and the object is one concept in the ontology (e.g. Model). The constraint describes the business state required to perform the action and is formalized with the concepts and their properties. A dedicated workplace supports the management of the rules through searches, sorting, and version-controlled modifications and deletions, if possible, for the running cases.

4 Results Achieved

Our approach has two main advantages:

1. Although the formalization of the BA for four VSs required the definition of more than 100 entities in the ontology, 30 actions, and 70 rules, the definition of actions and rules could be easily accomplished by knowledge workers using natural language patterns defined in the grammar and applied to the ontology entities. This approach supports business users in their daily work by providing an intuitive, nontechnical application. Rules can be combined using *and/or* operators, although each action rule should be as simple as possible to ensure comprehensibility. With this procedure, the partners share the expected behavior of the building management in a catalog that is understandable by all business users (e.g. architects, BIM managers). The definition of the business actions that are constrained by these rules supports the users in making decisions in the conversational user interface of Papyrus Converse. It also avoids the need for IT implementations of business logic for action flow control. The user receives explicit explanations of requirements, as shown in Fig. 5. In this figure, the next expected action for the current user is *Check Model*, but as it is described, this action is not possible because the model checking requires adding a checklist. This dependency is described along with the suggested action required to fulfill it. In this way, the business user can freely define new actions that may eventually be required to fulfill the goal.
2. The project's life cycle of the content is fully traced throughout the project, providing all of the information required to make decisions about energy-saving measures. The BIM manager can analyze the energy KPI for each project iteration to make decisions and request changes from the architect or building physics to correct deviations. The evolution of the energy KPI can be traced along with other indicators, such as model quality, as depicted in Fig. 6. The analysis of the KPIs can lead to redesigning the case, which is outside the scope of this proposal.

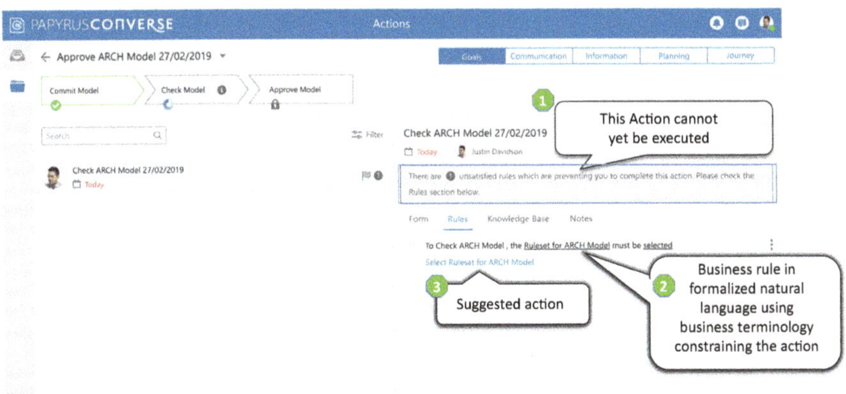

Fig. 5 Papyrus Converse Player for case execution

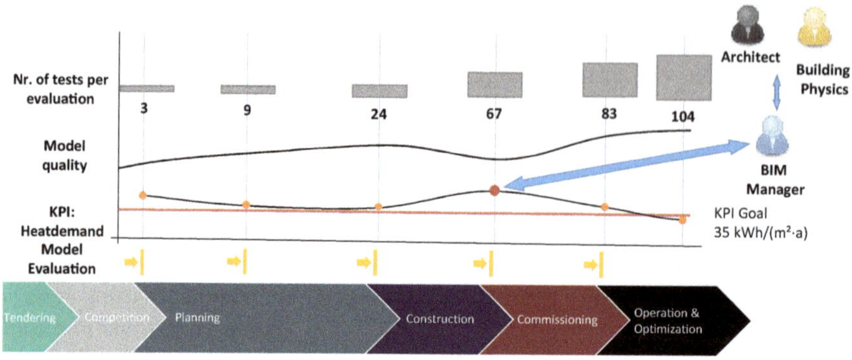

Fig. 6 Evolution of heating demand throughout the project

5 Lessons Learned

One of the first steps in the approach presented here is the formalization of the business information model with a business ontology that describes all entities in terms of the definition of goals, actions, and rules. In our project, business users from the construction industry with many years of experience in their field were asked to define these ontology entities. We realized that identifying the involved entities in an unambiguous way requires several iterations to review the VSs with all stakeholders at CES (and their departments), as well as the Austrian Institute of Technology (AIT). However, we saw these iterations as a benefit in achieving a common terminology and agreeing on "the way we work."

The formalization required a structured approach, which was supported by the business domain analyst using the Papyrus Converse Composer for the definition of actions and rules, as described in Sect. 3. One key element in this iterative process is the modeling tool used, which must support intuitive editing and reviewing of concepts and relationships. To this end, we worked with a graphical editor to facilitate the creation of relationships. As the ontology becomes more complex, the possibility to work with business-specific subdomain definitions provides a valuable mechanism that can help to avoid errors and redundancies. This initial effort was not taken into account in the project management, resulting in delays in the initial phase of the project and in the implementation of cases. Despite the initial definition-related effort, we found that the effort required decreases rapidly once the ontology becomes more complete, as new rules can be formulated by reusing existing concepts and relationships and by adding new items to meet new business requirements. The current version of the ontology's navigation-based grammar causes certain rules to be formulated with unnatural phrases (e.g. *the architectural model must have a check that has filled output* instead of *the architectural model must be checked*) but advanced techniques of natural language processing will be developed in the future. The tracking of energy efficiency requires a flexible integration layer so different tools from different vendors, as well as open-source projects like Solibri and EnergyPlus, can be integrated into the system easily. The iterations of the architecture model and frequent changes in materials until defined energy KPIs are met can be seamlessly executed and verified and can serve as proof of the ease of use by the involved parties. These encouraging results allow us to apply this methodological solution to new projects with a wide range of companies in the construction industry. The initial results also show significant potential for applying a similar approach outside the energy domain.

Acknowledgments This work is co-funded by the Austrian Research Promotion Agency (FFG) within project BIMSavesEnergy (grant agreement number 861710), where ISIS Papyrus delivers the business-architecture-enhanced ACM methodology and CES and AIT delivers the construction industry and energy domain-specific aspects.

References

Alreshidi, E., Mourshed, M., & Rezgui, Y. (2017). Factors for effective BIM governance. *Journal of Building Engineering, 10*, 89–101.

Bauer, K., Dohmen, P., Eichler, C., Hebblethwaite, R., Lah, M., Lajkovic, G., et al. (2017). *Begriffe zu BIM und Digitalisierung*. Vienna.

EU Commission. (2016, 03 02). The road from Paris: Assessing the implications of the Paris agreement and accompanying the proposal for a council decision on the signing, on behalf of the European union, of the Paris agreement adopted under the united nations framework convention. Brussels.

EU Commission. (2018). *Smart finance for smart buildings investment facility*. Retrieved from https://ec.europa.eu/clima/sites/clima/files/docs/pages/initiative_7_smart_en.pdf

Gutierrez Fernandez, A., Van Rijswijk, F., Ruhsam, C., Krofak, I., Kogler, K., Shadrina, A., et al. (2019). Applying business architecture principles with domain-specific ontology for ACM modelling: A building construction project example. In *Business Process Management Workshops – {BPM} 2019 International workshops*. Vienna: Springer.

ISIS Papyrus. (2019). *Papyrus Converse*. Retrieved from https://www.isis-papyrus.com/e15/pages/business-apps/papyrus-converse.html

ISO. (2018). *ISO 19650-1:2018: Organization and digitization of information about buildings and civil engineering works, including building information modelling (BIM)—Information management using building information modelling—Part 1: Concepts and principles.*

McKinsey&Co. (2016, June). *Imagining constructions digital future*. Retrieved from https://www.mckinsey.com/industries/capital-projects-and-infrastructure/our-insights/imagining-constructions-digital-future

Motahari-Nezhad, H., & Swenson, K. (2013). Adaptive case management: Overview and research challenges. In *IEEE 15th Conference on Business Informatics* (pp. 264–269). Vienna: IEEE.

Open Group. (2017). Value streams. *The Open Group Architecture Forum Business Architecture Work Stream*. Retrieved from https://publications.opengroup.org/g170

Rezgui, Y., Beach, T., & Rana, O. (2013). A governance approach for BIM management across lifecycle and supply chains using mixed-modes of information delivery. *Journal of Civil Engineering and Management, 19*(2), 239–258.

Ross, R. G. (2013). *Business rule concepts*. Business Rule Solutions.

Sustainable Digital Finance Alliance. (2018). *Digital technologies for mobilizing sustainable finance*. Retrieved from http://unepinquiry.org/wp-content/uploads/2018/10/Digital_Technologies_for_Mobilizing_Sustainable_Finance.pdf

Swenson, K. (2010). *Mastering the unpredictable: How adaptive case management will revolutionize the way that knowledge workers get things done*. Tampa: Meghan-Kiffer Press.

Tran, T., Weiss, E., Ruhsam, C., Czepa, C., Tran, H., & Zdun, U. (2015a). Embracing process compliance and flexibility through behavioral consistency checking in ACM: A repair service management case. In *Business Process Management Workshops* (pp. 43–54). Innsbruck: Springer.

Tran, T., Weiss, E., Ruhsam, C., Czepa, C., Tran, H., & Zdun, U. (2015b). Enabling flexibility of business processes by compliance rules: A case study from the insurance industry. In *13th International Conference on Business Process Management* 2015, Industry track. Innsbruck.

vom Brocke, J., Mendling, J., & Rosemann, M. (2021). Planning and scoping business process management projects and programs with the BPM Billboard. In J. van Brocke, J. Mendling, & M. Rosemann (Eds.), *BPM cases. Digital innovation and business transformation in practice* (Vol. 2). Berlin: Springer.

Industry 4.0 Integration Assessment and Evolution at EVVA GmbH: Process-Driven Automation Through *centurio.work*

Florian Pauker, Juergen Mangler, Stefanie Rinderle-Ma, and Matthias Ehrendorfer

1 Introduction

Production companies are in a difficult situation, as they face decreasing batch sizes, increasing variants, and reduced throughput time. Digitalization and smart factories (Schuh, Gottschalk, Nöcker, & Wesch-Potente, 2008; Westkämper & Zahn, 2009) are supposed to help solve these problems. Digitalization in particular is intended to increase the transparency of the company's processes, traceability of the products, and productivity because of improved understanding of the processes.

However, in the real world, introducing changes to achieve these increases requires human resources (programmers and domain experts), a detailed action plan, and possibly interrupting production. While the benefits of digitalization can be significant, especially for small and medium-sized enterprises (SME), finding the time, money, and human resources to digitize can be difficult. Another issue concerns the gap between information systems and the shop floor (Rother & Shook, 1999)—the Business Manufacturing Gap (Gifford, 2007)—which is challenging to close, especially for highly customized production, as it requires programmers with intimate domain knowledge.

To overcome these problems the Workflow Systems and Technology (WST) Group at the University of Vienna is working with the CDP Center for Digital

F. Pauker
EVVA Sicherheitstechnologie GmbH, Vienna, Austria
e-mail: f.pauker@evva.com

J. Mangler · S. Rinderle-Ma (✉)
Faculty of Computer Science, University of Vienna, Vienna, Austria
e-mail: juergen.mangler@univie.ac.at; stefanie.rinderle-ma@univie.ac.at

M. Ehrendorfer
CDP GmbH, Vienna, Austria
e-mail: matthias.ehrendorfer@acdp.at

J. vom Brocke et al. (eds.), *Business Process Management Cases Vol. 2*,
https://doi.org/10.1007/978-3-662-63047-1_7

Production (CDP) GmbH on the *centurio.work* framework (Pauker, Mangler, Rinderle-Ma, & Pollak, 2018). In general, *centurio.work* is used to describe processes on the shop floor with BPMN, to enact these processes with a process engine, and to describe a step-by-step integration approach. The goal of the research presented in this chapter is to reduce the effort in integrating machines, humans, and information systems, particularly for SMEs, based on the *centurio.work* framework. The framework's step-by-step integration approach facilitates:

- Assessment of the current level of integration
- A steady build-up of domain knowledge for developers
- A way for developers and domain experts to cooperate through BPMN process models to produce reusable artifacts (process models) for evolving digitalization/automation efforts
- The process of definition of milestones for evolving digitalization/automation efforts and structuring these efforts

The case presented in this chapter introduces the step-by-step integration approach based on the *centurio.work* framework. The chapter shows how the approach was applied to a real-world manufacturing scenario in a pilot factory[1] that closely tracked the requirements of the CDP GmbH[2] partners, especially the EVVA Sicherheitstechnologie GmbH.[3] The chapter, therewith, serves as an example to show how innovative process technology inspires modern BPM approaches and how such technology can be put to action in order to realize important strategic objectives (vom Brocke, Mendling, & Rosemann, 2021).

Figure 1 depicts the layout of a robotized manufacturing cell scenario that consists of a cobot by Universal Robot (UR10e) (2), a Hyperturn65 Powermill (HT65PM) lathe by EMCO GmbH (1) and a custom-designed loading station (3).

This flexible manufacturing cell produces parts for mechanical locking systems. The product's complexity is the result of its small tolerances and the customer-specific changes that lead to small lot sizes.

Section 2 describes challenges, as well as the methodological and technical frameworks that guide the development of our solutions. Section 3 describes the step-by-step plan of action when BPM technology is introduced to our partners and customers so we can have the flexibility to explore various degrees of automation and a safety net while we do so. Section 4 presents a set of process models that realize a subset of the scenario, the machining by a lathe and handling by a robot, including human interactions with the system. We conclude with lessons learned in Sect. 5.

---

[1] http://pilotfabrik.tuwien.ac.at/en/

[2] https://acdp.at

[3] https://www.evva.com/int-en/

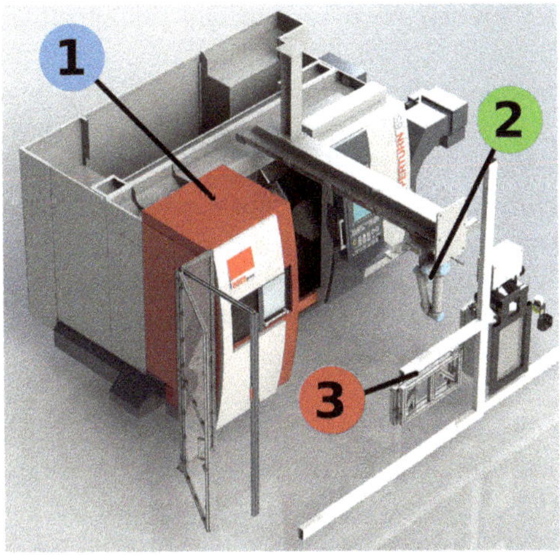

Fig. 1 Scenario layout

2 Situation Faced

EVVA is one of Europe's leading manufacturers of mechanical and electronic locking systems. Custom machines and custom assembly stations are used in producing these systems, as the production process is complex because of the use of proprietary interfaces for each kind of equipment and the high number of small parts that result in complex assembly. Everything is hierarchically structured based on the automation pyramid; that is, there is a strict separation between software that operates the machine, software that controls the sequence in which parts are made, and ERP-level information about orders. We chose a workflow-based orchestration to increase the level of digitalization in terms of seamless data exchange from work order to finished products. Because not all divisions in the company have the same digitalization level, a stepwise approach was needed:

- Introduction of BPM notation and technology to provide a unified way of describing manufacturing orchestrations while not disrupting production, and introduction of stable production procedures
- Expansion of domain knowledge among those who work with information systems (ERP, MES, CAD-CAM) and machines, which are often tailored to fit the items produced
- Closing of digitalization gaps when dealing with human–machine interaction or external partners

This step-by-step approach helps to ensure the natural evolution of how processes and subprocesses are structured, and how the functionality of individual tasks is defined.

This approach is especially important, as digitalization should be seen as a progressive journey, not as a single step a company takes. While one task, such as measuring the quality of a produced part, might at first be performed by a human, it might later be performed fully automatically by a machine, and eventually be replaced by a prediction algorithm that operates based on data collected earlier. In all these cases, the process model stays the same and the label of the task stays the same, but the functionality realized by the task changes. Therefore, the progress in this particular case might be from a human's worklist component, to an OPC UA[4] machine adaptor component to a data analytics component.

The design of a robust system must consider that individual components might fail, such as when a data analysis component has no access to data because of a data collection problem, in which case it might be necessary to switch back to the human. Situations in which over-automation[5] becomes a problem should also be planned for. Thus, addressing digitalization/automation should be a step-by-step journey in which decisions that result in problems can easily be reverted or circumvented until suitable solutions are found.

Our ongoing work seeks to standardize the digitalization journey based on available BPM technology and standard digitalization models and architectures like those in DIN Deutsches Institut für Normung e. V. (2016) and SCE-Cisco-IBM Sgra Team_2011 (2011).

The remainder of this section describes components that are part of the scenario outlined in Sect. 1, along with the technologies, standards, and methods we considered.

2.1 BPMN-Based Automation

As Bettenhausen and Kowalewski (2013) proposed, CPS-based automation architecture will replace the automation pyramid architecture (Fig. 2). This new architecture can be seen as a kind of network in which the functions of the previous layers are connected. In the automation pyramid architecture, only modules on neighboring layers can communicate with each other, which gives it some kind of structure. However, this constraint is not present in CPS-based automation, so there is a need for another kind of system that creates the context between the functions.

As presented in Pauker et al. (2018), BPMN-based automation can be the solution (Fig. 2). Processes that are seen as functions can be coupled, thus granting some context that reduces complexity and increases flexibility, transparency, and maintainability. The result is *centurio.work*,[6] an orchestration framework based on BPMN processes (Pauker et al., 2018) that allows context-based dynamic orchestration of machines, humans, and software services. Highly adaptable manufacturing

[4]https://opcfoundation.org/about/opc-technologies/opc-ua/

[5]https://www.businessinsider.de/tesla-robots-are-killing-it-2018-3

[6]https://centurio.work

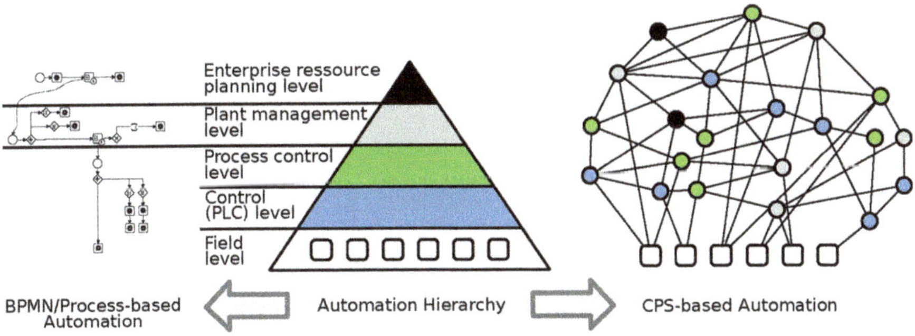

Fig. 2 CPS-based and BPMN-based Automation (Pauker et al., 2018)

processes that are necessary for realizing a production based on cyber-physical production systems are characterized by being:

- Context-based: Information from various software systems (e.g., ERP), sensors, and the manufacturing machines, are used at run-time.
- Dynamic: Different subprocesses can be in place for machines that do the *same* thing, but have different hardware and interfaces.
- Orchestrated: BPMN processes are annotated with all necessary information (i.e., links to interfaces and necessary parameters) so the model can be enacted directly in a process engine.
- Human-involved: Specialized worklist components deal with a variety of settings, such as hazardous environments that can only be operated with protective gear.

2.2 Theoretical Framework

Standardization is key to realizing a modern production process to combat a plethora of competing approaches and technologies. The Reference Architecture Model Industry 4.0 (RAMI) standardized as DIN SPEC 91345 (DIN Deutsches Institut für Normung e. V., 2016) is a three-dimensional map that describes a structured approach to the topic "Industry 4.0." The three dimensions are the product life cycle, based on the IEC 62890; the hierarchy levels, based on IEC 62264 and IEC 61512; and the functional hierarchy.

Our solution, *centurio.work*, is inspired by the design of RAMI, where type and instance correlate with well-known BPM models and instance concepts. *centurio.work* offers services on the business, functional, information, and communication layers. The top three levels are covered by a process engine, while communication is realized by a set of reusable modeling artifacts (tasks) that implement standard protocols like OPC UA, MQTT, and REST, and proprietary protocols like Siemens S7. These tasks can cover all hierarchy levels from "product" to "connected world."

The reason for imagining *centurio.work* in the context of RAMI is that, in modern manufacturing scenarios, experts from a variety of domains have to work together. RAMI provides the common vocabulary so people whose domain knowledge differs can talk about a common goal.

3 Action Taken

We develop a step-by-step integration approach that has four evolution steps: soft integration, process modeling, augmentation, and control. With each step, control over the production process increases, and more domain knowledge is made explicit by BPMN models. Each of the four evolution steps follows the BPM life cycle (Dumas, La Rosa, Mendling, & Reijers, 2013).

The remainder of this section explains how going through these evolutions facilitates the smooth realization of the robotized manufacturing cell scenario outlined in Sect. 1 and shown in Fig. 1. This section also explains the process models discussed in Sect. 4, which are the outcomes of the implemented *centurio. work* scenario.

3.1 Evolution 1: Soft Integration

Evolution step 1, soft integration approach, is intended not to disturb current production but to model and monitor what happens to easy-to-identify resources on the shop floor. This step includes tracking new orders from an Enterprise Resource Planning (ERP) system, sourcing materials and scheduling production resources from a Manufacturing Execution System (MES), and collecting data from all machines, robots, and other equipment used on the shop floor.

This step results in simple, runnable process models that collect and structure data, similar to software like MindSphere[7] and the Predix Platform.[8] Most resources already log data into their private data-tanks, while the MindSphere and Predix provide adaptors with which to collect, combine, and present data from the data-tanks.

A side effect that materializes in evolution step 2 is that the context for the collected data is processed in evolution step 1. The challenge is to connect to custom developed and highly specialized machines and to write the adapter software that realizes something like the "monitoring" depicted in Fig. 3. For this particular task, we experimented with OPC UA interfaces and collected data through the Siemens S7 communication protocol. The result is a set of standard tasks that can be used and parametrized during modeling, and reused for future customers.

[7]https://www.siemens.com/global/en/home/products/software/mindsphere.html

[8]https://www.ge.com/digital/iiot-platform

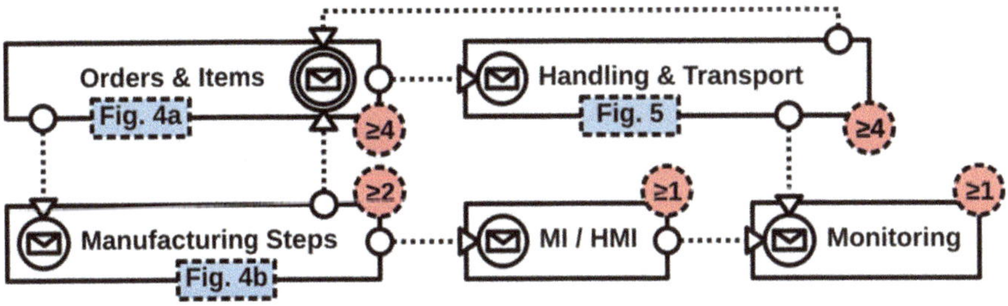

Fig. 3 Process models: connections and evolution (Red Bubble)

3.2 Evolution 2: Process Modeling

Step 2 still avoids disturbing production. The difference from step 1 is that step 2 focuses on how the resources interact with each other by determining how orders are scheduled, how the sourcing of material interacts with its scheduling, and which machines participate in what order in the manufacturing of a part.

The result is extensive information about how things work together. With this step, the contextualization of existing data flows is fully realized through BPM technology. The data in the private data tanks is ignored, as the data flowing through the process engine runs processes like the one shown in Fig. 4b. In this evolution step, the task "manually measure," as illustrated in Fig. 4b, is a placeholder for something that a human does. In this evolution, the process depicted by "AZ32 G2 Turn" in Fig. 4b checks whether a human presses a button that starts the machine and then instantiates the collection process in evolution step 1.

3.3 Evolution 3: Augmentation

Step 3 focuses on digitalization gaps on the shop floor, so it targets mainly interactions between humans and machines. As the processes passively monitor the production of parts, introducing active functionality becomes possible. For example, a machine operator might take notes on a piece of paper about the quality of the produced parts, and later write a document on a computer that is sent to the customer as part of a protocol. Augmentation can take the form of placing a screen at the machine where the user inputs the data for each task using a keyboard or giving the user a connected caliper to avoid keyboard input. The goals are to establish a set of supporting user interfaces (UIs), set up independent scheduling-model logic that shows, for example, machine set-up UIs if necessary, ensuring quality by capturing data (e.g., notes) from part-prototyping and part-production phases, and capturing information about the repair of machines and machined parts (semantic machining). The process models are extended to capture all of these goals. The desired result is to close the existing semantic and digitalization gaps that are typically filled by humans and their knowledge.

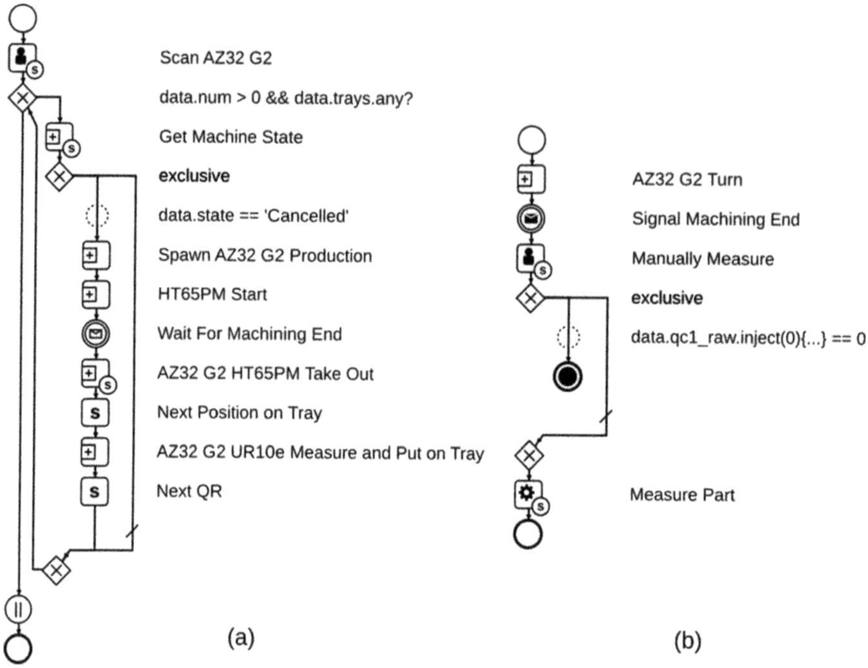

Fig. 4 Part-specific processes. (**a**) Coordinate production and robot handling. (**b**) Producing a single item

In this evolution step, a user interface that can be parametrized from the process model to collect certain indicators (e.g., the diameter of a produced part) replaces the "manually measure" step (cf. Fig. 4b).

3.4 Evolution 4: Control

Step 4 is the final expansion state of *centurio.work*, as it is in this phase that *centurio.work* assumes control of the manufacturing. Typical functions are managing the software artifacts that are necessary for production (e.g., NC-programs) and triggering the execution of production based on scheduling data.

The result is that humans are guided and that they supervise production, rather than driving it with their actions, such as pressing buttons. As the process presented in Fig. 4a shows, humans scan a product code to start production—"HT65PM Start" is a subprocess that starts the machine—while in evolution step 3 the process might have triggered a UI to tell the user to press that start button. (In evolution step 2, no UI existed).

4 Results Achieved

The two main results are that domain knowledge that was available only in nondescriptive form or on software with no source available was made explicit through BPMN process models,[9] and that, instead of each machine having its own data collection and the data being cleaned, transformed, and loaded into a database ex-post, now all data is collected through the process engine, already cleaned, contextualized, and ready for analysis. As data collection is a byproduct of process execution, all changes to the processes automatically yield updated data streams for analysis without requiring additional effort or changes. Thus, in-situ analysis and real-time data presentation can be performed, creating a powerful driver for future innovation efforts.

Figure 3 shows how the process models presented in this section are connected, as well as for which evolution they were created. We also provide a video[10] that demonstrates the interactions depicted in the process models.

Figure 4 shows two examples of how process models can be used to orchestrate a shop floor. Figure 4a depicts a process that was introduced in Evolution 4, showing how a robot chooses produced items out of the machine and puts them on trays to be transported to the measurement station.

Figure 4b shows the steps for producing a single AZ32 G2 item, which is produced on the lathe machine. The process spawns subprocesses for a truing operation, then shows a UI for manually measuring the parts, and finally collects data from an automatic measuring machine. Evolution step 4 spawns a process model like that shown in Fig. 4a. In lower evolution steps, Fig. 4a would not have been possible as, for example, in evolution step 1 no human interaction was modeled. Instead "MI/HMI" detects that the start button was pressed on the lathe and then spawns "monitoring," as depicted in Fig. 3.

Figure 5 shows the interaction between the process and a low-level robot-interface. Robot programs, including programs for taking the part out of the machine and placing it on a tray, as shown in Fig. 4a, are managed and loaded from a GIT repository. After the programs have been assembled, they are loaded and started, and the robot is monitored until successful completion of the tasks. The robot-handling is always triggered after the step "AZ32 G2 Turn" (in Fig. 4b), so "signal machining end" sends a message back to the process shown in Fig. 4a.

---

[9]Please note the two differences from standard BPMN in Figs. 4 and 5: (1) the diagrams are drawn by our designer using the auto-layout to improve comparability between versions of the model versions, so the labels are to the right of the task, not on the task itself; (2) conditions for decisions are depicted by a dashed circle on the edge to improve usability on touch screens.

[10]https://centurio.work/casts/gv12.mp4, Evolution 3.

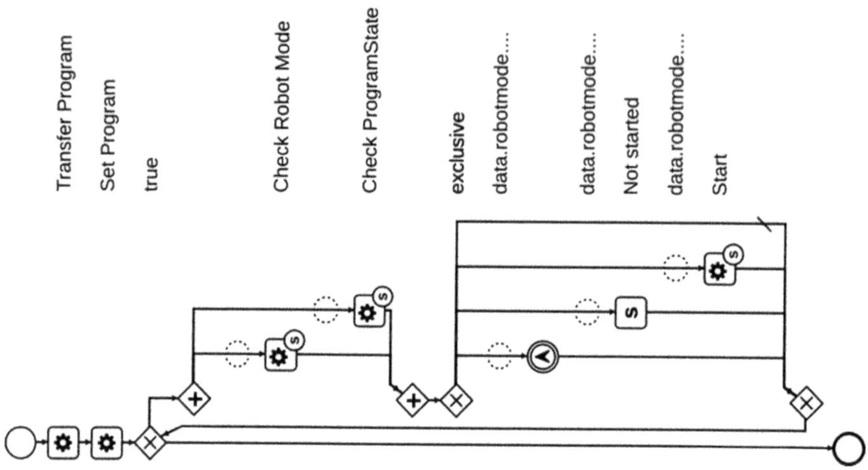

Fig. 5 Generic universal robot process

5 Lessons Learned

After using the stepwise approach, we learned three main lessons: (a) using BPMN as modeling notation provides a better understanding of the processes on the shop floor, (b) increasing the degree of automation does not mean developing everything new because many artifacts can be reused, and (c) the stepwise approach offers a fallback mechanism from less automated process execution.

BPM technologies proved efficient for driving digitalization and automation efforts on the shop floor. Its strategic value is the high level of flexibility achieved when technologies are combined (as required by a heterogeneous shop floor) while retaining maintainability and understandability in the resulting system. Therefore, maintainability and understandability are direct results of the expressiveness of the BPMN notation and the use of a process engine that allows domain experts to try to modify models directly so they can see the effects in the real world.

While an exploratory digitalization and automation approach proved successful, it became clear that streamlining the exploration can have advantages:

- Structured assessment of the current situation regarding the integration of machines can highlight problem areas.
- Monitoring the progress in terms of the proposed evolution steps gives a quick situation overview and allows efficient allocation of human resources. For example, evolution steps 1 and 2 may require more software-development resources and domain experts than the other steps do.
- After achieving evolution step 1, data analytics efforts can start.

As Fig. 3 suggests, many processes have not changed much since they were created. “MI (Machine Interface)” was first directly linked to “Monitoring.” Since for each order or item, a specific NC Program is started, it is necessary only to monitor the start of that program, so “Monitoring” never changed again. The introduction of “Order and Items” did free the user from pressing the button on the lathe, as the lathe is started automatically based on input from an ERP, but the “MI” part is unchanged because pressing the button physically and triggering the machining through software are the same. “Order and Items” evolved over multiple iterations with the introduction of new hardware.

Particularly useful was proving that versions of the functionality developed for tasks in evolution steps 1–4 still have their purpose as fallback mechanisms if problems occur during production. Easily switching individual tasks from full automation back to human work proved to be transparent and simple to achieve while introducing no additional complexity for the factory operators or the process models. While switching back to manual processes is time-consuming, it can be done through logic in the process, such as when the lathe cannot be started automatically (error-detection logic), in which case the old UI-driven subprocess can be spawned.

Acknowledgment This work was supported and funded in part by the Austrian Research Promotion Agency (FFG) via the Austrian Competence Center for Digital Production (CDP) under contract number 854187.

References

Bettenhausen, K. D., & Kowalewski, S. (2013). Cyber-physical systems: Chancen und Nutzen aus Sicht der Automation. *VDI/VDE-Gesellschaft Mess-und, Automatisierungstechnik*, 9–10.

DIN Deutsches Institut für Normung e. V. (2016). DIN SPEC 91345:2016-04 Referenzarchitekturmodell Industrie 4.0 (RAMI4.0).

Dumas, M., La Rosa, M., Mendling, J., & Reijers, H. A. (2013). *Fundamentals of business process management* (Vol. 1). Berlin: Springer.

Gifford, C. (2007). *The Hitchhiker's guide to manufacturing operations management: ISA-95 best practices book 1.0*. Research Triangle Park, NC, ISA.

Pauker, F., Mangler, J., Rinderle-Ma, S., & Pollak, C. (2018). centurio.work – Modular Secure Manufacturing Orchestration. In *Business process management workshops* (pp. 649–661).

Rother, M., & Shook, J. (1999). *Learning to see: Value-stream mapping to create value and eliminate Muda*, Spi. Cambridge, MA: Lean Enterprise Institute, US.

SCE-Cisco-IBM Sgra Team_2011. (2011). Smart grid reference architecture. *International Business, 1*, 1–118.

Schuh, G., Gottschalk, S. F., Nöcker, J. C., & Wesch-Potente, C. (2008). Flexible Vernetzung statt starrer Integration: die Zukunft der digitalen Fabrik. *wt Werkstattstechnik online, 98*(3), 127–131.

vom Brocke, J., Mendling, J., & Rosemann, M. (2021). Planning and scoping business process management projects and programs with the BPM Billboard. In J. van Brocke, J. Mendling, & M. Rosemann (Eds.), *BPM cases. Digital innovation and business transformation in practice* (Vol. 2). Berlin: Springer.

Westkämper, E., & Zahn, E. (Eds.). (2009). *Wandlungsfähige Produktionsunternehmen: Das Stuttgarter Unternehmensmodell*. Berlin: Springer.

Managing Agile Business Processes at N-DECT

Development of a Process-Aware Information System for Agile Business Processes

Jens Geiger, Stefan Jablonski, Sebastian Petter, Louis Püschel, and Maximilian Röglinger

1 Introduction

Process orientation is a key driver of corporate success. Organizations of all sizes and from all industries use process-aware information systems (PAIS) like modeling tools and workflow management systems to control and execute their processes (e.g., planning and controlling of production, processing of incoming customer requests) efficiently. However, most PAIS that are available on the market based on the assumption that processes have only a few variants and that these variants can be planned prior to execution. However, this assumption is no longer valid because of increasing economic complexity, which is further intensified by digitalization.

Small and medium-sized enterprises (SMEs) in particular are affected by the risks associated with changes in their business models toward a digital business model and by the risks associated with an increasingly complex environment. As SMEs tend to have lower budgets, limited resources, and a significantly lower capability to take over risks compared to those of large corporations, SMEs may lose the ability to react and adapt to environmental influences. Because of the lack of appropriate IT support, the planning and control of complex business processes that feature both planned and unplanned events in an increasingly complex environment are often

J. Geiger
N-DECT, Pretzfeld, Germany
e-mail: jens.geiger@n-dect.de

S. Jablonski · S. Petter (✉)
University of Bayreuth, Bayreuth, Germany
e-mail: stefan.jablonski@uni-bayreuth.de; sebastian.petter@uni-bayreuth.de

L. Püschel · M. Röglinger
Project Group BISE of the Fraunhofer FIT, University of Bayreuth, Research Center FIM, Bayreuth, Germany
e-mail: louis.pueschel@uni-bayreuth.de; maximilian.roeglinger@uni-bayreuth.de

J. vom Brocke et al. (eds.), *Business Process Management Cases Vol. 2*,
https://doi.org/10.1007/978-3-662-63047-1_8

carried out manually, without considering internally or externally available key figures or key performance indicators (e.g., order-specific, profit-specific, or product-specific delivery date). Such manual processes are time-consuming and prone to error, causing SMEs to tie up scarce resources that are then available for neither value-creating tasks nor innovation.

The ability to handle planned and unplanned events like delayed shipments, machine breakdowns, and changes in customer requirements and orders in a continuously changing environment can be defined as agility or, more precisely, operational agility (Conboy & Fitzgerald, 2004; Hinsen, Jöhnk, & Urbach, 2019; Jöhnk, Roeglinger, Thimmel, & Urbach, 2017). Planned events can be predicted prior to execution and captured via process models, while unplanned events are not modeled but can be handled by reprioritizing or re-sequencing tasks. However, agile processes would enable organizations to respond to customers or suppliers individually and faster, which would increase customer satisfaction and competitive advantage. Nevertheless, most available PAIS do not support the design and enactment of agile processes, do not meet the high demands of agile processes, and neglect the impact of organizational key figures for process management. Specifically, practical concepts and implementations that go beyond research prototypes are lacking.

Against this backdrop, the development of a PAIS that addresses these challenges is sorely needed. To realize such a system, we structure the PAIS architecture along the common three-layer architecture, extended by a novel component for handling agile processes. This component prioritizes process instances that are relevant to an organization's internal and external key figures (e.g., the profit from an order or a product's delivery date) and to plan for the processing of instances or activities that vary in importance. As a result, the PAIS architecture comprises three layers: data storage (i.e., data related to process model, runtime data, and historical data), application logic (i.e., a modeling component and an execution and monitoring component with a workflow engine, a worklist, and a prioritization component), and user interface (i.e., for modeling agile processes and worklist processing).

To realize the PAIS for the execution and monitoring of agile processes, an interdisciplinary consortium consisting of the University of Bayreuth's Chair for Databases and Information Systems, the Professorship for Information Systems and Business Process Management, and four SMEs—three application partners and one implementation partner—collaborated in a joint project funded by the Bavarian Ministry of Economic Affairs, Regional Development and Energy. The project's goal was to design, demonstrate, and evaluate an agile PAIS in the form of a software prototype that supports the modeling and key-figure-based monitoring and execution of agile processes. Demonstration and evaluation took place by testing the prototype at the operational level at the SMEs' sites. The proposed PAIS helps make these organizations' processes adaptable, increases their ability to react to unexpected customer requests, and increases their competitiveness. The case serves as a rich example of how the various components of a successful BPM approach interlink (vom Brocke, Mendling, & Rosemann, 2021), specifically in regard to the IT capabilities role to enable agile practices and the organization's ability to deal with change.

In the following, we describe the case of N-DECT, a producing SME that provided one of the most complex scenarios in our project consortium. This case focuses primarily on the monitoring, execution, and improvement of business processes (Dumas, La Rosa, Mendling, & Reijers, 2018; Rosemann & Vom Brocke, 2010). We examine N-DECT's core processes, which are highly variable and can be improved with the addition of expertise (vom Brocke, Zelt, & Schmiedel, 2015).

2 Situation Faced

N-DECT develops and produces customer-specific solutions for materials testing with a particular focus on eddy current and ultrasonic testing. With the company's investigation procedures, materials and components can be tested for purity, accuracy, and robustness. For this purpose, testing machines are integrated into customer-specific machine constructions. Thus, N-DECT's processes handle up to 20 orders in the form of projects, resulting in agile processes of varying complexity that result from variations in customer requirements. For most orders, a new testing machine has to be developed that corresponds to the customer's requirements. It is not possible to exactly predict the duration of single activities in the process, and as the risk of changes in the customer's requirements is high, N-DECT must often reschedule its processes. N-DECT's core process can be divided into three main steps (Fig. 1): processing a customer's request, setting up the project, and carrying out the customer's order.

Existing methods and tools for process execution and monitoring do not cover such agile development, construction, and assembly processes satisfactorily. The decision process to select which customer orders are most important for N-DECT is carried out manually, which requires considerable effort and can be subjectively biased. To process customer requests and related orders more efficiently, a software prototype of an agile PAIS was used at N-DECT as an execution and monitoring component. In this system, customer orders are instances of an agile process that must be prioritized depending on N-DECT's strategic key figures, which are either order-related (e.g., delivery date and delivery volume, turnover, profit, replacement time of goods for assembly) or customer-related (e.g., importance of the customer, history with the customer). Based on the prioritization of customer orders, an initial feasibility check, concerning which customer orders can be postponed and which cannot, is visualized on a dashboard. Furthermore, a worklist for processing orders is created to ensure integrated monitoring and control of customer orders across all

Fig. 1 Overview of N-DECT's manufacturing process

departments. Based on this prioritized worklist, employees select the most important activities. To consider the real conditions at N-DECT, the process steps and the related effort (e.g., working hours) are compared with the available capacities (e.g., in the design and production process). The available capacities can be taken, for example, from the project hours booking system. In addition, unplanned events like human error and machine failures that require customer orders to be rescheduled must be considered. The solution must also be integrated with existing (e.g., MS Project) and future (e.g., ERP system, CRM system) information systems, as they are important sources for key figures.

The additional requirements focus primarily on refining the simulation of various project constellations because the prioritization of projects based on key figures already provides reliable results. For example, N-DECT needed to describe the employee as a central resource more precisely, including whether employees are assigned to the project according to their capabilities, whether they can perform particular tasks (e.g., construction of mechanical or electronic components), and whether several employees work simultaneously on a process step. Additional data sources, such as personnel, project, and customer data, had to be considered so feasibility checks are carried out not only with regard to available employees but also with regard to further process parameters, such as cost.

3 Action Taken

In developing the agile PAIS, we started with a planning and structuring process that revealed that the research project should be carried out along five development phases: (1) Requirements engineering, (2) designing, (3) development, (4) evaluation of the prototype, and (5) specification of the system.

Phases 1 and 2 focused on the requirements analysis and the technical specification and software design of the agile PAIS. In Phases 3 and 4, the results of the preceding phases were first implemented as an IT artifact in the form of three software prototypes—one per application partner. Then the prototypes were evaluated at the application partners' sites to ensure that changes that were relevant to the application partners had been incorporated. After the evaluation of the prototypes and the incorporation of changes in Phase 4, a detailed system specification was developed in Phase 5. Figure 2 shows the five phases of the research project.

Fig. 2 Phases of the project

Phase 1: Requirements Engineering

Phase 1 focused on the identification and cataloging of requirements to produce a requirements catalog. To cover all important requirements, a broad range of sources was used to identify requirements: (1) application partners' use cases, (2) analysis of software solutions the application partners had used, (3) a literature review with a focus on execution and monitoring of business processes, key figure-based process monitoring, and agile processes, and (4) an analysis of publicly accessible and scientific PAIS implementing agile approaches. Both sources (1) and (2) are described in the *Situation faced* section. Steps (3) and (4) are discussed in more detail in the following.

Searches in scientific databases like EBSCOhost, Google Scholar, and ScienceDirect, along with contributions from practitioners and other Internet sources were carried out continuously during the research project. In particular, the review of the relevant literature served as a starting point for the requirements catalog (e.g., optimization of process instances, determination of process instances including risks, prediction of the execution of process instances, and prediction of the process result) (Di Francescomarino, Ghidini, Maggi, & Milani, 2018). The results of the literature review showed that requirements for agile PAIS are widely distributed in the literature and that there is no holistic approach that meets all requirements. In particular, the literature review revealed that the prioritization of process instances (i.e., activities) based on organization-specific key figures is all but missing. In addition, existing work usually addresses small application scenarios or does not use extensive real-world data. As a result, one of the goals of the research project was to combine the extant approaches to develop a more holistic system.

Here the research project came into play, as the process management software has to enable organizations to prioritize their processes on the basis of organization-specific key figures and to compose the various approaches from the literature to provide a holistic approach that can deal with a large amount of real-world data. However, the available literature provides only part of the requirements, so the requirements the literature provided were supplemented by an analysis of publicly accessible and scientific process-management systems that use agile approaches. Reflecting these parameters in one system is the key challenge of this project.

The Department of Databases and Information Systems at the University of Bayreuth developed the Process Navigator, a declarative PAIS that can be used to execute declarative process models. The Process Navigator evaluates whether a process's activities violate the rules defined in the process model, so only valid activities are provided to the user during the process execution. However, the Process Navigator does not prioritize process instances based on key figures, which is an essential differentiation of our research project. Furthermore, the Process Navigator covers little of the subareas derived from the literature (e.g., optimization of process instances, determination of process instances, including risks).

Camunda BPM is another publicly available workflow management system that makes it possible to define and execute business processes, although it uses different modeling notations (e.g., BPMN 2.0, CMMN, DMN). Camunda BPM is relevant to the research project, as it provides a comprehensive IT architecture, the Camunda

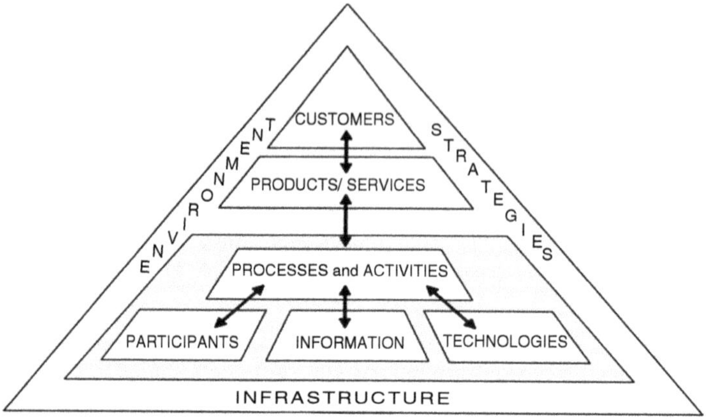

Fig. 3 Work system theory (Alter, 2013)

stack, a three-layer architecture that is similar to the architecture of our agile PAIS. In addition, the system can be extended using self-developed plug-ins like our prioritization component. Camunda BPM also provides both imperative (i.e., BPMN 2.0) and declarative (i.e., CMMN, DMN) modeling notations.

In addition to Process Navigator and Camuda BPM, PAIS like ADONIS, Axon Ivy, Bizagi, KiSSFLOW, Signavio, ARIS, and ProcessMaker are also based on the process modeling language BPMN 2.0.

The identified requirements were systematized in a multi-perspective catalog, which was used in Phase 2 as a basis for the conception and in Phase 4 for evaluation of the software prototype. In the following, the requirements catalog and its underlying structure are described in more detail.

A useful framework for classifying requirements is the Work System Theory (Alter, 2013). Alter (2013) describes a work system as one in which participants like employees, machines, and application systems act together in performing processes by using information, technologies, and other resources to create products or services for internal or external customers. The work system is influenced by the environment (e.g., laws, technology trends, the organization's culture), the infrastructure (e.g., technologies, available information), and stakeholders' strategies (e.g., strategies of organizations or departments) (Fig. 3) (Alter, 2013).

Since Work System Theory describes an organization's internal and external drivers of an organization at various levels, this classification can also be applied to classifying the requirements of a PAIS. To classify the requirements we gathered, the research, application, and development partners used an iterative process to assign the requirements to the dimensions derived from the Work System Theory. However, we found that the dimensions "customer," "products and services," and "technologies" deviated from Alter's (2013) work, so they were not considered. The reasons for this choice are that the "customer" is assigned to the environment (i.e., external dimension), as the customer influences the organization's processes primarily through external specifications. The dimension "products and services" is less

Table 1 Excerpt of the requirements catalog

Dimension	Description	Example
Environment	Key figures and specifications of customers and suppliers (external)	The delivery of production lots should be carried out within a certain period (e.g., within 4 weeks)
Environment	Key figures and specifications of the environment (external)	To comply with emission standards, certain products may be produced only on weekdays
Strategy	Key figures and restrictions of the organizations (internal): *Resources*: The limited number of resources in the organization influences the ability to carry out a process. *Organization's strategic goals*: The organization's strategic goals influence the process flow	*Resources*: Only a certain number of employees are available for the execution of a production process. *Organization's strategic goals*: A customer request has to be answered within 24 h
Strategy	Weighting of key figures according to their importance	The requirement that the response to a customer request may not take longer than 24 h is in contrast to the requirement that two important customers have made a request simultaneously
Processes and activities	Simulation and assessment of process instances (also at the run time)	For a complex manufacturing process, instances are simulated with regard to throughput time and resource requirements to determine which instances are feasible

relevant for the research project, as the focus lies on the SME's processes. Therefore, requirements with a relation to "products and services" are subsumed under other dimensions (e.g., delivery of products within a certain time as a restriction from the customer as part of the environment). Furthermore, the dimension "technology" was removed, as the project does not focus on technologies (i.e., tools for operating processes) other than our developed PAIS. Instead of the technology dimension, we added the new dimension "application systems" with the goal of capturing requirements that result from the user's interaction with the PAIS, an aspect that was missing from the requirements catalog.

We gathered a total of 30 requirements and assigned them to the dimensions of environment, strategy, processes and activities, process participants, application systems, information, and infrastructure. Table 1 shows an excerpt of the catalog, focusing on key figures and the simulation of process instances.

Phase 2: Designing the Prototype

Based on the requirements catalog developed in Phase 1, Phase 2 focused on both the technical concept and the agile PAIS's software design. In on-site meetings, application, development, and research partners discussed the processes and information systems related to the application partners' use cases to achieve a common understanding. In these use cases, we considered only the core processes that had a significant need for flexibility. The actual design took place afterward in the context of workshops with application and development partners and guided by the research partners. Here, the key challenge was to develop a PAIS architecture that copes with all the requirements of the project partners.

Figure 4 illustrates the structure of the PAIS for the use case of N-DECT. As N-DECT does not use information or process management systems that provide an appropriate architecture, the use case was realized using Camunda BPM.

Data Storage Layer

The data management in the use case of N-DECT was challenging since the data for key figures (e.g., order-related and customer-related) are stored mainly in Microsoft Office applications like Excel and MS Project. Therefore, the data was extracted from N-DECT's Office applications and transposed into a form that can the PAIS could process. The import functionality was especially useful for the initial filling of the PAIS. After extraction, the prepared data was buffered for further processing and prioritization. The data extracted was stored as execution data during and after the prioritization step. Data related to the process flow also had to be considered, as the process model data was used in defining the process flow in Camunda BPM. Thus, certain activities (e.g., construction of a component) and related information (e.g., information on components) were assigned to the right employees (e.g., construction and assembly) in the right order.

Application Logic Layer

The modeling component and the execution and control component of Camunda BPM were used in the application layer. The execution and control component comprised a workflow engine and a worklist as an integrated part of Camunda BPM, which was extended by a self-programmed component for the prioritization of processes based on key figures. The prioritization component stored the prioritized key figures and matched them with the characteristic values of the key figure from N-DECT's information systems. Therefore, management must

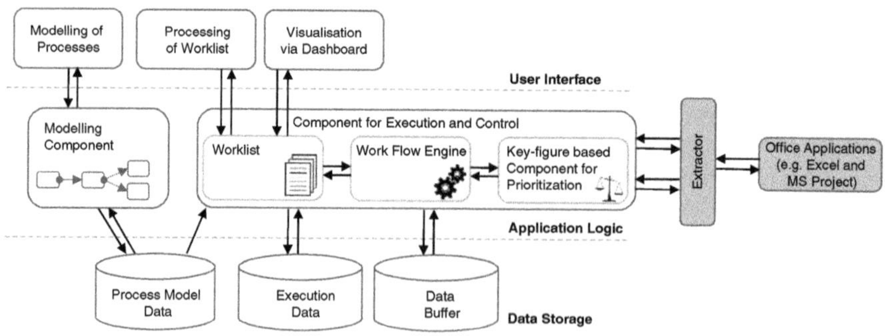

Fig. 4 Technical concept and software design—N-DECT

periodically evaluate the prioritization of the key figures with regard to their topicality and update the prioritization if necessary.

The prioritization component works on the basis of multi-criteria decision-making approaches, which enable the evaluation and prioritization of alternatives (e.g., number of customer orders to be processed) based on such criteria as order-related key figures. A well-known multi-criteria decision-making approach is the Analytic Hierarchy Process (AHP). The AHP evaluates several alternatives using pair-wise comparisons. This procedure is carried out for all decision criteria, resulting in a sequence of all alternatives (e.g., sequence of customer orders to be processed depending on their importance) (Saaty, 1990).

To use the AHP, N-DECT first uses AHP to weight key figures as they relate to their customer orders, resulting in a list of prioritized key figures that are then stored as reference in the prioritization component. Then the Workflow Engine assigns the corresponding key figure characteristic value to each customer order, which originates from the Office applications of the N-DECT. For example, if the key figure characteristics of two customer orders are equal except for the values of the sales volume, then the customer order with the higher sales volume is prioritized. As a result, the Workflow Engine creates a list of prioritized customer orders whose individual tasks (i.e., activities) are provided to the employees across all departments (e.g., construction, assembly) via the Camunda Tasklist.

The modeling component provided by Camunda BPM via the Camunda Modeler is also considered in the application layer. By defining the process model in the modeling component, the process flow and its rules are defined, so the process model ensures that certain activities and related information are assigned to the right employees.

User Interface Layer

The user interface for N-DECT deviates from the generic three-layer architecture. In addition to the worklist component realized by the Camunda Tasklist (i.e., employees can accept, process, and confirm the execution of activities), a dashboard for the management has been developed. The purpose of the dashboard is to visualize and carry out an initial feasibility check (i.e., which customer orders are really necessary) on the one hand and to track the progress of customer orders on the other. Furthermore, the weighting of the relevant key figures can be adjusted here. The Camunda Modeler is used for modeling N-DECT's business processes. In addition to the modeling of the process flow, activities with a high degree of agility can be defined (i.e., activity in which a large number of alternatives have to be prioritized).

Phase 3: Developing the Prototype

In Phase 3, the developed technical concept and the software design along the three-layer architecture were implemented in the form of a software prototype. The implementation was used as a feasibility study to evaluate whether these manifold requirements could be implemented within a single PAIS. The functionality of software available on the market was examined regarding its suitability for the implementation of our agile PAIS. Camunda BPM and its architecture in particular served as an ideal starting point, as they had only to be extended by a prioritization component. Based on this existing architecture, the individual components of the technical concept and the software design were prioritized and implemented. The software prototypes were realized based on the use cases of the three application partners involved in the project. Furthermore, the interfaces to other information systems (e.g., Office applications, ERP, QM system) defined in Phase 2 were realized as far as was reasonable. An iterative development of the software prototype in the form of an agile development process had the advantage of the continuous involvement of the application partners, whom we asked for feedback after each iteration. This development process also enabled an iterative evaluation of the prototype and the identification and elimination of technical risks in early iterations.

Phase 4: Evaluating the Prototype

In Phase 4 the software prototypes implemented at the application partners' sites were evaluated with a focus on the prototype's functional correctness, practicability, and integration with other information systems, as well as whether it delivers valid results despite a high number of decision parameters (i.e., key figures). In particular, we examined whether the execution and control component delivered valid results based on the application partners' real-world data.

The evaluation was carried out at the partners' sites in tests that lasted several weeks. The evaluation was accompanied by semi-structured interviews based on a questionnaire. In the case of N-DECT, the prototype was evaluated by using real-world data. With the help of a sensitivity analysis, it was possible to determine whether the AHP's calculations remained stable even after the input parameters changed. We found that adjusting the weighting of the key figures improved the results. Furthermore, the prototype began to be used in the project managers' weekly meetings to validate the results.

In another step, the requirements catalog from Phase 1, which served as an evaluation template, was compared with the application partners' software prototypes. The requirements' coverage was assessed with Harvey balls, round ideograms that can be completely, partially, or not filled. The aim is to indicate whether a requirement is completely fulfilled, partially fulfilled, or not fulfilled. An excerpt of the evaluation based on the requirements catalog is shown in Table 2.

Phase 5: Specifying the System

The goal of Phase 5 was to define a detailed concept for the agile PAIS's system. In addition to collecting additional functional requirements, the prerequisite for the development of a system is to collect nonfunctional requirements, which are implemented in the follow-up to the project. To implement a specification across every use case, additional functional and nonfunctional requirements were identified in Phases 4 and 5 and classified in addition to the requirements catalog for functional requirements.

The literature already provides a good overview of nonfunctional requirements that should be considered in the context of software development. These

Table 2 Excerpt of the evaluation based on the requirements catalog

Description	Coverage	Explanation based on use cases
Environment: Key figures and specifications of customers and suppliers (external)	●	Because of the analytic hierarchy process (AHP), key figures of any type can be used. For example, in the use case of N-DECT, customer- and supplier-related key figures can be considered
Environment: Key figures and specifications of the environment (external)	●	Because of the AHP, key figures of any type can be used. For example, in the use case of N-DECT, working hours that are specified by laws can be considered
Strategy: *Key figures and restrictions of the organizations (internal):* *Resources*: The limited number of resources in the organization influences the ability to carry out a process. *Organization's strategic goals*: An organization's strategic goals influence the process flow	●	A limited number of resources is considered. For example, in the case of N-DECT, projects are always dispatched depending on available resources (i.e., employees and their available working hours). Organizations' strategic goals are considered. Although none of the application partners has a strategic guideline in its use cases (according to the definition), consideration of strategic goals like answering a customer's request within 24 h could be implemented with the help of the AHP
Strategy: Weighting of key figures according to their importance	●	Based on the AHP, key figures of any type can be weighted and prioritized, even across several hierarchy levels. For example, one of the application partners uses five super-thematic categories for key figures, and each of the super-categories has corresponding key figures on a second hierarchy level
Processes and activities: Simulation and assessment of process instances (also at the run time)	◑	Simulation and evaluation based on key figures is partly fulfilled. For example, in the case of N-DECT, the dispatching of new customer orders can be simulated with regard to feasibility (e.g., based on resource requirements and lead time) and their effect on other projects. However, the prototype should be extended to include other parameters, such as effects on costs

requirements relate to dimensions like the system's performance and usability or the validity of its results (Robertson & Robertson, 2013). These and other dimensions form the framework for the nonfunctional requirements, which were discussed with the application and development partners in interviews. The result of the interviews along the three use cases were 25 nonfunctional requirements.

4 Results Achieved

The goal of the research project was to develop a PAIS that supports the execution and monitoring of agile business processes based on company-specific key figures. Demonstration and evaluation took place at three SMEs using a software prototype at the operational level. The main finding of our project enables companies to prioritize process instances objectively and automatically based on company-specific key figures. During the execution of our project, we did not find a similar approach either on the market in the form of an available product, or in the literature in the form of a (research-) prototype. The agile PAIS we developed helps to make organizations' processes adaptable, increases their ability to react to unexpected customer requests, and increases their competitiveness. In the case of N-DECT, we estimate that the software prototype can significantly decrease the time required to select the most important projects and allocate the available resources.

Generic Three-Layer Architecture

To realize a PAIS for executing and monitoring agile processes, we developed a three-layer architecture in line with common systems, extended by an innovative component for key-figure-based process prioritization (Fig. 5). A major result of our project is that the requirements with respect to the application partners' agility can be addressed by one generalized PAIS architecture. As a result, this PAIS architecture comprises three layers: data storage, application logic, and user interface.

The data storage layer comprises a database for process models (declarative, imperative, or hybrid) and a database for execution-related data like currently running and historical instances. The application logic comprises a modeling component and an execution and monitoring component. The modeling component enables the specification of agile processes in the form of process models, as well as key figures, relationships among key figures, preferences of the individuals involved in the process, and relationships between key figures and the process model. The execution and monitoring component comprises a workflow engine, a

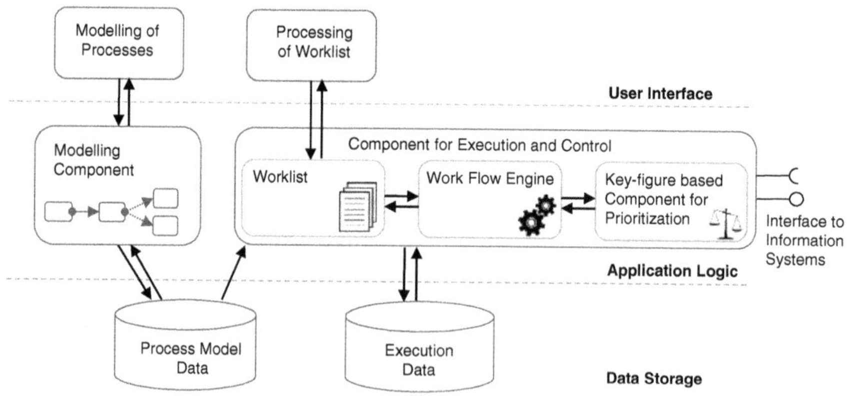

Fig. 5 Generic three-layer architecture

key-figure-based prioritization component, and a worklist. The component for key--figure-based prioritization, as an entirely new approach compared to other PAIS, has the task of prioritizing all process instances based on company-specific key figures. After prioritizing, the workflow engine enables the generation of valid process instances based on the defined process flow and the rules contained in the process model.

Relevant process instances and their activities are assigned to a user via a worklist. The user interface has a modeling component (i.e., modeling of processes with different modeling notations such as hybrid, imperative, or declarative) and a component for processing the worklist (i.e., individual activities based on the user's role in the organization). Based on evaluation of its generic and modular architecture in various organizational contexts (e.g., manufacturing and service processes), the PAIS and its components can be applied to other contexts and information system landscapes. For example, some organizations may be interested only in the prioritization component, as they have information systems already that provide the necessary infrastructure.

Key Figure-Based Prioritization

The project demonstrates that it is possible to identify sets of criteria for process prioritization in a highly agile and heterogeneous application domain. We developed an innovative prioritization component based on multi-criteria decision-making with the goal of objective and automated prioritization of strategically relevant and agile processes. Multi-criteria decision approaches enable the prioritization of alternatives based on various criteria. We used the AHP to evaluate several alternatives (e.g., number of customer orders to be processed) with regard to various decision criteria (e.g., key figures like sales related to a customer order, the importance of the customer) by means of pair-wise comparisons (Saaty, 1990). As an important result, we showed that our prioritization component can handle a huge amount of external (e.g., customer-, supplier-, or law-related) and internal (e.g., the organization's strategic goals and restrictions) key figures and related data. For example, one of the application partners gathered 55 key figures for prioritizing technicians that process customer orders. Our result shows that companies have only to determine the weighting of their key figures.

Then the PAIS calculated process instances from a pool of possible process instances using data from a variety of sources, including Office applications, ERP, and QM systems. As a result, the prioritization and selection of important activities based on key figures helps organizations to make the prioritization more structured, transparent, objective, and efficient based on, for example, increasing customer satisfaction or making decisions easier for employees to trace. For example, in the use case of N-DECT, we used the PAIS to prioritize customer orders with the goal of determining which customer orders are important and can be managed under restrictions like employee and machine capacity and time (e.g., delivery date). Thus, the PAIS with its prioritization component uses data from nearly all sources to give recommendations.

In the future, we expect that the PAIS can significantly decrease the time required for selecting important projects and allocating the available resources. This in turn leads to better communication with customers, since N-DECT now can determine more valid delivery dates based on well-prioritized processes and the optimal allocation of its resources.

5 Lessons Learned

To cope with the increasingly complex environment surrounding SMEs and the impact on these organizations' business processes, the project team developed, implemented, and evaluated software prototypes for an agile PAIS at three SMEs, one of them N-DECT. The agile PAIS was based on a three-layer software architecture and extended by an innovative key figure-based prioritization component for monitoring and executing agile processes. During the project, the project team gained first-hand experience that has important implications for practice and research.

Learning 1: There Are Different Kinds of Agility

One main finding was that there are different kinds of agility, depending on the SME's use case. A common feature across all of our application partners' use cases is that process agility can always be traced back to a certain activity, a decision point for the prioritization of process instances. A decision must be made based on a large number of key figures, which are used to prioritize and select relevant process instances. Examples are the prioritization of incoming customer orders, the selection of a technician to handle a customer order, and the selection of articles with critical manufacturing defects to determine which should be processed first.

The application partners' use cases had substantial differences. In one partner's use case, the agility step focused exclusively on the selection of an alternative based on a high number of key figures. The subject of the use case was the selection of a technician for processing customer orders based on key figures like the distance to the customer or the customer's importance. Approximately 55 key figures were gathered for the prioritization of technicians. However, the selection of the technician is not followed by a complex process. While the technician must carry out certain activities to process the customer order, the activities for solving the customer problem are always the same (e.g., organization of materials). In contrast, the use cases of N-DECT and those of a third application partner not only focus on agility within an individual activity, but the selection and prioritization of alternatives always affects subsequent processes. Based on the selection and prioritization, the organizations know which process steps or activities must be processed next (e.g., in the case of N-DECT an organization-wide worklist is created). Furthermore, both agility types can be combined since there can be several decision points in the process. For example, the procurement of materials can be a decision point, as the selection and prioritization of a supplier can be based on a large number of key figures. Finally, depending on their complexity, the processes can be modeled with an imperative, declarative, or hybrid process modeling language. Processes with few execution alternatives can still be modeled with an imperative language.

Learning 2: Prioritization Can Be Realized Through Key Figures
The results of the research project enabled the application partners to prioritize activities and the associated process instances based on internal and external key figures in a new way. Because of the AHP's functionality, the number of key figures and organization uses can be almost arbitrary. Since one of the application partners gathered approximately 55 key figures, the company decided to define categories (i.e., super-categories) for the key figures (e.g., technician, logistics, and customer). In accordance with the AHP, the categories were initially prioritized against each other on the first hierarchy level. In the hierarchical approach are key figures that correspond to each super-category. These are also prioritized against each other on a second hierarchy level. Multiplying the two levels results in a weighting for each key figure. In addition to defining thematic categories, the application partner also classified key figures according to their importance. With this alternative, there is no thematic classification of the super-categories (the first hierarchy level), but the super-categories differ based on their importance. Within the super-categories (the second hierarchy level) are thematically mixed key figures, which are weighted against each other. As a result, our approach can handle a large number of strategically important key figures in different ways.

Learning 3: Methodological Support Is Needed
The findings from the use cases show that the adoption of an agile PAIS in organizations has many aspects, ranging from the identification of decision points and the associated type of agility in the process to the selection and weighting of relevant key figures to the linking of both findings with operational processes and information systems. To make this procedure manageable for organizations, a method, e.g., based on the situational method engineering approach, should be developed in the future (Braun, Wortmann, Hafner, & Winter, 2005; Denner, Püschel, & Röglinger, 2018; Vanwersch et al., 2016). Methods of this kind consist of various substeps and aim to support organizations in establishing a PAIS for agile business processes. This would allow organizations to act independently from external partners and to be able to design their business processes more efficiently on their own.

References

Alter, S. (2013). Work system theory: Overview of core concepts, extensions, and challenges for the future. *Journal of the Association for Information Systems, 14*, 72–121. https://doi.org/10.17705/1jais.00323.

Braun, C., Wortmann, F., Hafner, M., & Winter, R. (2005). Method construction – a core approach to organizational engineering. In H. M. Haddad, A. Omicini, R. L. Wainwright, & L. M. Leibrock (Eds.), *Proceedings of the 2005 ACM symposium on applied computing – SAC '05* (p. 1295). New York: ACM Press.

Conboy, K., & Fitzgerald, B. (2004). Toward a conceptual framework of agile methods. In N. Mehandjiev, P. Brereton, K. Bennett, D. Budgen, & P. Layzell (Eds.), *Proceedings of the 2004 ACM workshop on interdisciplinary software engineering research – WISER '04* (p. 37). New York: ACM Press.

Denner, M.-S., Püschel, L. C., & Röglinger, M. (2018). How to exploit the digitalization potential of business processes. *Business & Information Systems Engineering, 60*, 331–349. https://doi.org/10.1007/s12599-017-0509-x.

Di Francescomarino, C., Ghidini, C., Maggi, F. M., & Milani, F. (2018). Predictive process monitoring methods: Which one suits me best? In M. Weske, M. Montali, I. Weber, & J. Vom Brocke (Eds.), *Business process management* (pp. 462–479). Cham: Springer International.

Dumas, M., La Rosa, M., Mendling, J., & Reijers, H. A. (2018). *Fundamentals of business process management* (2nd ed., 527pp). Berlin: Springer.

Hinsen, S., Jöhnk, J., & Urbach, N. (2019). Disentangling the concept and role of continuous change for IS research – A systematic literature review. In *40th International Conference on Information Systems (ICIS)*.

Jöhnk, J., Roeglinger, M., Thimmel, M., & Urbach, N. (2017). How to implement agile IT setups: A taxonomy of design options. In *25th European Conference on Information Systems (ECIS)*.

Robertson, S., & Robertson, J. (2013). *Mastering the requirements process: Getting requirements right* (3rd ed., 541pp). Upper Saddle River, NJ: Addison-Wesley.

Rosemann, M., & Vom Brocke, J. (2010). The six Core elements of business process management. In J. Vom Brocke & M. Rosemann (Eds.), *Handbook on business process management 1* (pp. 107–122). Berlin: Springer.

Saaty, T. L. (1990). *The analytic hierarchy process: Planning, priority setting, resource allocation* (2nd ed., 287pp). Pittsburgh: RWS.

Vanwersch, R. J. B., Shahzad, K., Vanderfeesten, I., Vanhaecht, K., Grefen, P., Pintelon, L., et al. (2016). A critical evaluation and framework of business process improvement methods. *Business & Information Systems Engineering, 58*, 43–53. https://doi.org/10.1007/s12599-015-0417-x.

vom Brocke, J., Mendling, J., & Rosemann, M. (2021). Planning and scoping business process management projects and programs with the BPM Billboard. In J. vom Brocke, J. Mendling, & M. Rosemann (Eds.), *BPM cases. Digital innovation and business transformation in practice* (Vol. 2). Berlin: Springer.

vom Brocke, J., Zelt, S., & Schmiedel, T. (2015). *Considering context in business process management: The BPM context framework.*

Part III

Cases on Process Analysis and Monitoring

Analysis of the Customer Journey at the Pension Provider APG Using Self-Service and Data Hub Concepts

J. C. A. M. Buijs, R. F. M. Bergmans, and R. El Hasnaoui

1 Introduction

Customers expect transparency, freedom of choice, and accountability from all companies, but from the financial sector in particular. Increasing digitization and computerization has an impact on work methods and service provision. Pension funds and their customers, the participants in the funds, face the problems of reduced pension value, so there is ongoing pressure to lower execution costs to minimize these reductions while at the same time increasing customer satisfaction. Clearly, the pension system will have to gradually but drastically change to make room for individual consumer choice.

Algemene Pensioen Groep (APG), a financial services provider, focuses on asset management, pension administration, pension communication, and employer services. APG performs these activities on behalf of pension funds and employers in a variety of sectors, but mainly education, government, and construction. As of August 2019, APG managed 529 billion euros in pension assets for pension funds and customers. APG works for more than 21,000 employers, providing the pension for one in five families in the Netherlands (more than 4.5 million customers) (APG website, 2019). APG foresees major changes in pension schemes in the Netherlands, particularly the possibility that customers will be able to choose their own pension funds.

Therefore, APG is focusing on understanding its customers better, mainly through its "intense customer focus" strategic program. In addition to user-group studies, customer conversations, and so on, APG also used process mining (van der Aalst, 2016) to analyze customer journeys, such as customer retirement.

J. C. A. M. Buijs (✉) · R. F. M. Bergmans · R. El Hasnaoui
Data Intelligence Department, APG Algemene Pensioen Groep N.V, Heerlen, The Netherlands
e-mail: joos.buijs@apg.nl; rick.bergmans@apg.nl; rachied.elhasnaoui@apg.nl

J. vom Brocke et al. (eds.), *Business Process Management Cases Vol. 2*,
https://doi.org/10.1007/978-3-662-63047-1_9

This chapter presents APG's application of process mining as a process-analysis methodology (Dumas, La Rosa, Mendling, & Reijers, 2013) in the customer journey of retirement, APG's key customer journey. That way, the case serves as a great example to link innovative process technology to strategy via the development of BPM capabilities (vom Brocke, Mendling, & Rosemann, 2021). Section 2 explains the reason for the analysis: an expected change in the Dutch pension market, combined with changing customer expectations. Section 3 presents the actions taken, such as the use of a multidisciplinary approach to data analysis. The section also discusses our use of a central data store that gives APG employees access to analytical insights. The results achieved by these actions are presented in Sect. 4. The main results suggest concrete actions to be taken to increase customer satisfaction. The lessons learned during the project are detailed in Sect. 5, and Sect. 6 concludes the chapter.

2 Situation Faced

One of APG's key processes is the retirement process, which takes several months, from orientation to proactive mailing, calling, and other activities to make sure the customer enjoys his or her well-earned retirement. Following the BPM context framework (vom Brocke, Zelt, & Schmiedel, 2015), the retirement process is a knowledge-intensive core process with a repetitive nature (once per participant). It depends on many other processes and on data quality. Given that multiple triggers can start the process and because repetitions are possible, variability in the customer journey is high. The current execution of the process has been well documented and is supported by workflow management systems, but for customers, retirement is an uncertain landscape, where they do not know whether retirement benefits are sufficient, which choices to make, and whether everything is arranged correctly. Hence, customer satisfaction is key to this process.

Since APG wants to be the first choice in controlling its customers' financial future, "intense customer focus" is one of its key values, and customer satisfaction is one of its key performance indicators. However, one out of four calls to the call center are about the retirement process, and many of these calls involve complex questions about the status of the retirement process that are difficult for the call agents to resolve, resulting in many of the calls being forwarded to the experts in the back-office. Several departments and channels are involved in this retirement process, so what the next steps in the process were and what the customers could expect of each phase of the process are not always clear. What is more, communication from APG during the retirement process was not aligned with other areas of activities. In addition, as the insights in Sect. 4.1 show, customers called more than three times during the process, expending an average of more than half an hour on these calls. Naturally, all of these factors had a negative impact on customer satisfaction. The lack of detailed insight into the success of process automation, combined with poor customer satisfaction, triggered several internal initiatives to improve customer satisfaction.

One of these initiatives was the use of process mining, an innovative exploration technique, to improve the process. Since the overall process used several channels and systems, we soon realized that we needed to take the end-to-end customer journey as our scope. An early version of APG's central data hub concept (called the "Data Core" internally) was available (cf. Sect. 3.4) and contained all necessary process data from the various source systems. This data was combined with data from three customer-contact systems, one administration system, and our customer survey system.

3 Action Taken

The project's overall goal was to increase customer satisfaction, as measured through the Net Promotor Score (NPS). We needed to gain insights from the APG's many contact points with the customer over time and relate them to each other to "connect the dots" between the activities that take place in the customer journey. By correlating high or low customer satisfaction with certain characteristics of the customer journey, we found several opportunities to adjust. We were not familiar with taking the end-to-end customer journey as our scope, so we chose to apply process mining to bring the end-to-end customer journey into view. After a successful proof of concept, which we undertook to investigate the feasibility of analyzing a customer journey with Celonis (Celonis website, 2019), APG's process-mining tool, we started the analysis in 2017, scaling up to the intense customer-focus program in 2018.

3.1 The Objective

The main objective was to increase customer satisfaction, as measured through APG's NPS. This score is determined by asking our customers to use a scale from 1 to 10 to indicate how likely they are to recommend APG to their friends and families. People who give a rating of 6 or lower are labeled "detractors," and those with scores of 9 or higher are "promoters." The overall NPS is then calculated as the percent of promotors less the percent of detractors, so it has a range of −100 (everyone is a detractor) to +100 (everyone is a promotor).

To improve the NPS, we looked for correlations between high or low customer satisfaction and the customer journey's characteristics. This approach resulted in suggestions for improvement that spanned systems and processes, so it was necessary to combine business knowledge (i.e., process and customer knowledge) with data insights based on process mining of the end-to-end customer journey. To ensure the project would not have a one-off character, we sought to achieve some degree of self-service in the business, so we set up a program for the business with which we jointly went through four steps:

1. Identify the data needed for the analysis
2. Interpret the data to derive insights and results
3. Formulate actions for improvement based on these insights and results
4. Evaluate and monitor the effects of these actions

3.2 Setting Up a Multidisciplinary Team

The initiative to set up a multidisciplinary team was the first in which the improvements were set up chain-wide instead of focusing on one department. In 2017, we set up a multidisciplinary agile team consisting of data engineers, data scientists, and marketeers: the Data Insights Team (the DIT). The DIT prepared the data, tools, and analysis and obtained initial insights. When the Intense Customer Focus initiative started in 2018, the DIT was responsible for the data track. The team worked closely with the retirement and process experts and employees from the front-office, such as the call center, to obtain insights from the data analysis. One of the goals became to teach the business experts to use and interpret the dashboards so they could access the data themselves through self-service. This step is part of the Data Intelligence (DI) Department's objective of "making APG data-driven."

3.3 Data Collection

During the first Intense Customer Focus data session, we jointly identified the customer journey and then identified the customer's touchpoints. Using the touchpoints and processes, we built a list of data sources to be included in the process-mining analysis.

The main data challenge was to align the definitions of "case" and "event" in all systems. Although it seems logical to take a customer as a case, customers can also retire twice by retiring only part-time or by taking early retirement from one job and then retiring from another later. However, splitting the data over the two retirements was not feasible, as it would be difficult, for example, to assign a call to one retirement instance. Having the customer as the case notion, we were able to extract data from several systems and connect them together. Another issue related to choosing the correct level of detail. For instance, we could include each individual process step in the customer journey or only the executed processes, without the individual steps. Alternatively, we had each click in the myFund environment available. We decided to use as events the executed processes (not process steps) and myFund sessions (not individual clicks). Other aspects of the initiative, such as the expected insights and the performance of Celonis, were also considered.

In the initiative's scope were nearly 75,000 customers who retired between January 6, 2015, and January 6, 2017. Customer data, collected from 1 year before retirement (if known) to half a year after retirement, includes:

1. Customer behavior on channels like the online portal (myFund) (685,000 visits), telephone (171,000 calls), and e-mail (7000 e-mails)
2. Data about the retirement life event (75 k life events)
3. One-to-one conversations (3000 appointments)
4. Process logging of the pension administrative system (360,000 process instances)
5. Demographic data like income, gender, marital status, employment sector (20+ facts for each customer)
6. Pension choices like part-time retirement (77,000 choices)
7. Customer satisfaction data (3000 completed surveys)

Collecting this customer data resulted in 75,000 cases with more than 20 case attributes and more than 1.3 million events. This project marked the first time APG collected such a large amount of data at once using process mining.

3.4 The Data Core

This project again showed the usefulness of the data core, which is the DI Department's ongoing data hub implementation. As shown in Fig. 1, the Data Core provides one canonical data-access layer to data in the company's systems; it copies data from the source systems and translates it to objects in the presentation layer that tools like Celonis then access. The presentation layer contains data from

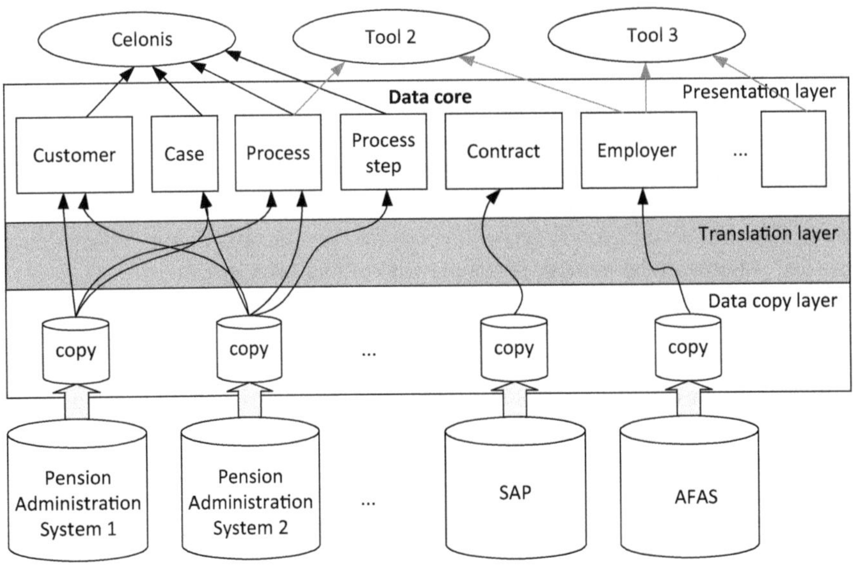

Fig. 1 The setup of the Data Core that is currently under construction at APG. In the Data Core, data is copied from source systems, translated, and presented as one canonical data source, including clear definitions of objects and attributes

several systems, presented in well-documented objects (client, case, process, employer, etc.).

When we executed this analysis phase, an early version of the process part of the Data Core was available, which allowed us to extract all executed processes for the customers that were in our scope, irrespective of the systems in which these processes ran. As a result, we saved considerable data-preparation time and effort, which we then spent analyzing the rich dataset we obtained.

3.5 Identifying the Customer Journey: Exploration of Facts and Figures Through Self-Service

We created a dashboard that shows the real customer journey and delivers general facts and figures. Eschewing the traditional approach, where data scientists analyze the data and build the dashboards, which are then shown to the business, we sought to make a co-creation through self-service. Therefore, we delivered the data and then built the dashboard together with the business to deliver the insights they needed. In this self-service approach, we prepared the data and a first version of the dashboard, which was then improved upon with the business users, so the business received practical training in how to interpret the Celonis dashboard and in what Celonis was capable of.

We had four meetings in which we gained several insights from the dashboards. During one meeting we worked short-cyclically and incrementally: The business identified what it wanted to see on the dashboard, and most of the insights were developed "live" in the dashboard during the meeting, with the business watching and steering. The more difficult dashboard elements were prepared for the next meeting. This setup allowed quick hypothesis testing, leading to new hypotheses that could be tested.

The dashboards present facts and figures from several angles. Figure 2 shows telephone statistics, such as the number of calls per customer and (average) call times, statistics that are closely related to customer satisfaction. Figure 3 shows clear seasonal patterns in the number of people who retired each month.

The seasonal pattern helps us to interpret process performance statistics correctly, since we know that the process contains more or fewer cases, depending on the season. Figure 4 shows the complex customer-journey process. For example, the complexity is shown in how the old and new processes are triggered, as well as when telephone, myFund, and mail contact occurs. Other developed dashboards show demographic data (gender, salary range, working sector, etc.), contact channel use (comparing phone, e-mail, and myFund usage), customer satisfaction, throughput-times, costs, and so on.

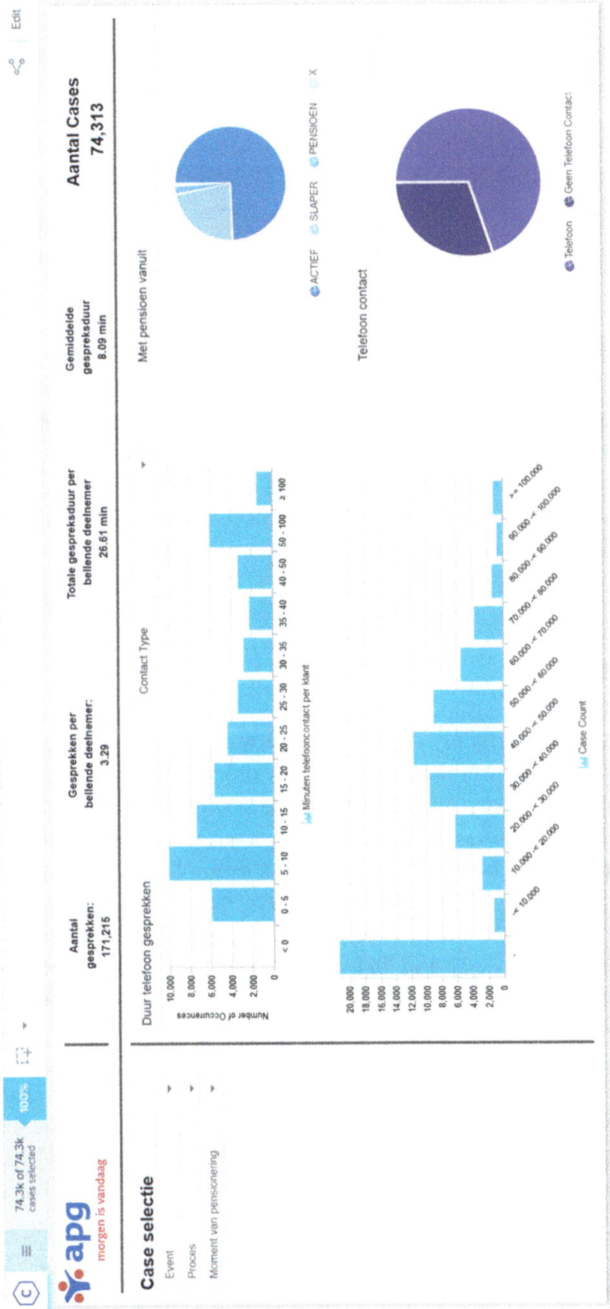

Fig. 2 Celonis dashboard layout showing telephony statistics, a key aspect of customer satisfaction

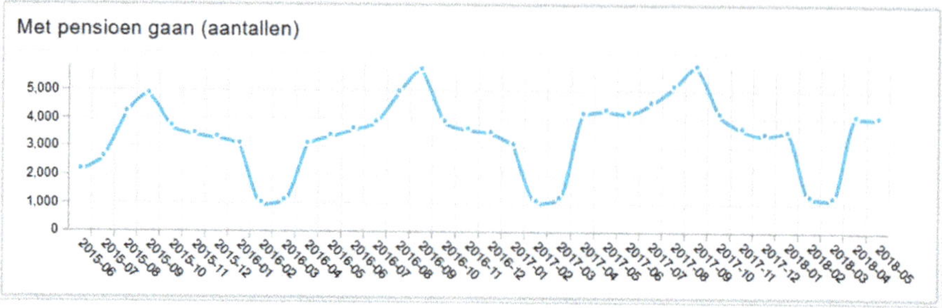

Fig. 3 Seasonality in retirement

4 Results Achieved

Together with a broad delegation of the business, marketing, back-office, and front-office employees, we identified possible points in the process where improvement was possible, based on the obtained insights. We presented our main findings in a final session with the business, where we identified two key improvements. The business took the lead in implementing these improvements.

4.1 Insights

Our analysis made immediately clear that there was not one customer journey but many: more than 10,000 unique journeys (i.e., orders of processes, letters, phone calls), in fact. One of the key findings (partly based on Fig. 2) is that around 70% of the customers called the call center for help at least once, and 21% of these customers were passed along to the back-office. More than 80% of customers used the portal (their personal myFund), and about a third retired before their expected retirement date. The average customer calls 3.29 times, with a total call duration of 27 min per customer. Another observation was that 49% of visitors to the myFund environment call immediately after their visits to the website, largely because of a (known) bug in the website. The data showed the actual impact of the bug, which was far larger than expected. We also identified unclear letters sent to customers that resulted in a call, with as much as 45% of recipients calling after receiving a letter. We also observed that 27% of customers called after receiving a requested offer from the back-office.

These insights were the starting point of useful discussions about whether calling three times on average is good or bad and why so many visit myFund but so few use the site's digital retirement process.

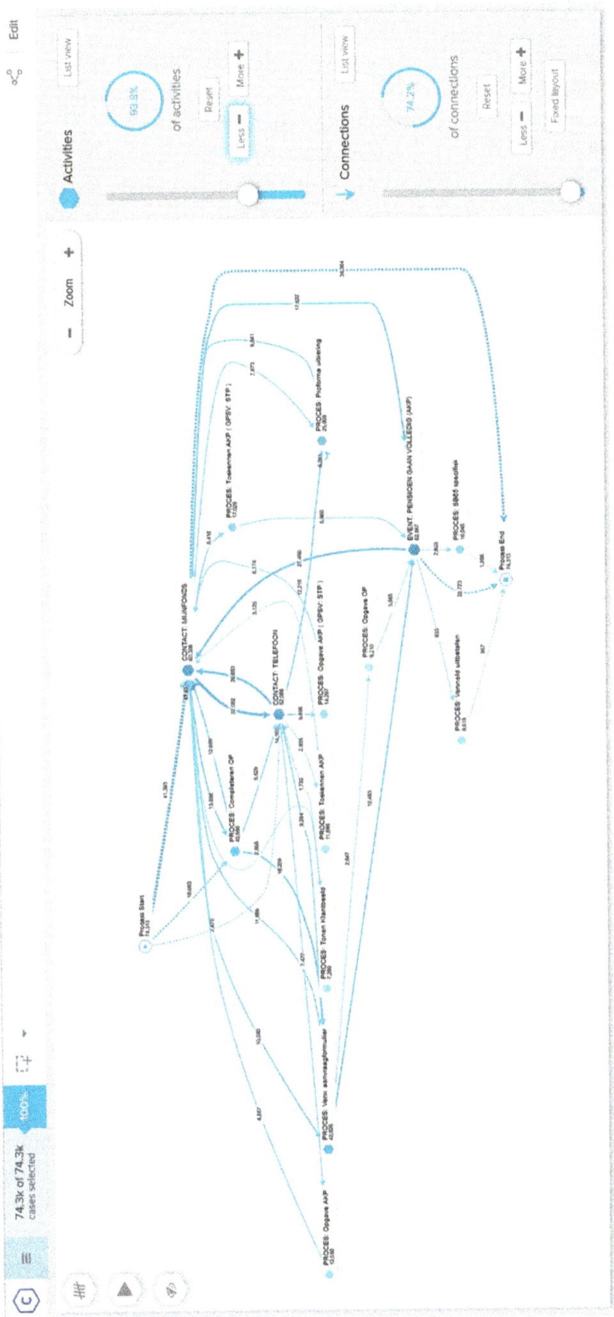

Fig. 4 Dashboard showing the complexity of the customer journey

4.2 Improvements in Communication and in the Customer's Retirement Journey

One of our surprises was that many people call after they complete the retirement process. The administrative part of the retirement process is usually completed 3–5 months before the retirement date, during which time there is no communication with our customers. The data showed that 18% of customers call us after the completion of the retirement process, usually because they are worrying about whether everything is really arranged and when they can expect the first payment. Therefore, we changed the process so an e-mail is sent 30 days before the first payment:

1. Welcoming them to their retirement life and recognizing that a new phase in their life has begun
2. Assuring them that everything is arranged for their retirement
3. Answering common questions, such as when they can expect their first payment

We measured whether our customers appreciated this e-mail using A/B testing. Almost 90% of those to whom we sent the e-mail opened it, and 94% of this group gave the e-mail a "thumbs up." Customer satisfaction with the end-to-end process, that is, the transactional NPS, increased by 16 points. Therefore, the e-mail was considered a success and was implemented.

We also noticed that our customers usually start to explore the possibilities of retirement 9 months before the expected retirement age, although we wait until 6 months before to send an information-package about retirement possibilities. As a result, 20% of our target group of 35,000 customers nearing retirement call before they receive the first information letter. Sending the letter earlier could avoid up to 7000 calls, so we changed to process to send the information package 9 months before the expected retirement age.

4.3 Self-Service Introduction to the Business

The self-service concept was first applied in the retirement case. We saw that internal clients of the DI Department wanted to create their own insights and did not want to be dependent on the DI Department. Therefore, we taught the business how to create their own insights by using or adjusting Celonis' process-mining dashboards themselves. However, this approach was, at least for now, too ambitious for this novice group, as we assumed a one-size-fits-all approach. (See also lessons learned in Sect. 5.1.)

Even so, these educational sessions did create awareness of the usefulness and power of process mining and of taking a data-driven approach to defining improvements, resulting in several instances of using process mining in the business. One of these instances was the creation of a Celonis taskforce in the business to get actionable insights and define process improvements. This effort contributed to the DI Department's goal of making APG more data-driven.

4.4 A Vision of Process Mining in APG

The retirement case created a pull from the business. The usefulness of process mining is now well known throughout APG, as we receive increasing numbers of process-mining requests to improve processes or solve other types of problems. For example, the customer journey to becoming a new customer and the journey to divorce are currently being analyzed. Process mining, including self-service training, is now also used for purposes like SLA-monitoring, consistency checks, and fraud (risk) detection.

This broad interest led us to develop a vision of and roadmap to 2025, including what operations research (OR) could bring to APG, in addition to our other analytics domains of visualization and machine learning. The roadmap provides a clear vision of APG and DI because data analytics experts and data scientists commit to one of the three roadmaps to build their expertise. The OR roadmap currently recognizes four dimensions in which we want to grow:

1. From offline analysis via prediction to recommendation of the best actions to take
2. From operational process analysis via tactical analysis to strategic-level analysis
3. From data on process steps via more detailed case data to rich data
4. From one-off analysis to continuous self-service

The case study presented in this chapter was offline and focused on operational processes, but it used rich data and had the goal of becoming a continuous analysis. The ideal setting is one in which all of APG, from domain experts to the board of directors, uses the same (set of) dashboards, builds on the same data, and so are aligned with one another.

To achieve this goal, we take both a top-down approach and a bottom-up approach. By organizing regular, open, non-project-related community sessions, we foster bottom-up interests. During these sessions, we discuss the latest features and techniques but also encourage people to experience process-mining themselves on real data (although not directly in a project context) with the goal of increase the internal client's self-service ability. About 20 employees join these bimonthly sessions on their own time, which often leads to one or more process-mining analysis projects.

4.5 Follow-Up Data Science Analysis

The analysis showed that there is a relationship between customer satisfaction and the number and length of phone calls and/or visits to the myFund environment. Van der Steege (2018) focused on combining process mining and data science methods to make this observation actionable by applying a newly developed methodology to the customer journey's data. This approach revealed, for instance, that customers who call two or more times provide a statistically significant lower customer satisfaction score. The approach also provided a structural approach in the Celonis tool, so it was accessible to the business users who wanted to repeat the analysis to gain other findings.

5 Lessons Learned

From this first large customer-journey process-mining project, we learned two key lessons: self-service is not a one-size-fits-all approach, and our Data Core approach requires attention to detail. (We also learned that we underestimated the complexity of an analysis project.)

5.1 Self-Service Is Not One-Size-Fits-All

What we learned with the first workshops was that self-service training goes beyond providing such "hard" things as data, tools, and tool-training, as we must also take the "soft" aspects of self-service into consideration. Our colleagues have different work backgrounds, learn at different speeds, have different goals, levels, and interests, and can be overly critical of the data and technology. Therefore, our initial one-size-fits-all approach did not fit everyone in the group, and we lost some people during the training, especially at the dashboard-building part. We now use a level-based maturity approach in which, together with the business, we first determine the desired level of training. Then we take it step by step, and at each level assess whether the required level of maturity is met before moving on. The maturity levels, each of which includes all the skills of the preceding maturity levels, focus on:

1. Correctly using and understanding the dashboard
2. Modifying the dashboard
3. Building a dashboard from scratch
4. Checking the data quality
5. Gathering and combining data

Each level is first performed with the trainee and the data scientists, and then gradually with less and less help from the data scientists. Note that we are currently setting up learning goals and a curriculum to streamline the self-service sessions and monitor who has been trained and to what level.

A positive side effect of the self-service approach is that we regularly discuss the current results with the business. We were used to analyzing the data and creating cool dashboards to present to the business, but it is better to get results step by step than to present a big design upfront. Our initial analysis contained more than 100 insights, of which only four resulted in concrete improvements. Turning insights into actionable insights takes a lot of follow-up and traction. Unfortunately, we realized too late that the self-service concept also allowed us to focus on the hypotheses we wanted to investigate, as the business was present to indicate which line of investigation it was interested in—and which it was not. Although this realization came too late in this project, we are now applying it more often in follow-up projects.

5.2 Data Core Requires Attention to Detail

This project was also the first large project in which the early version of the Data Core was applied. As such, with respect to certain aspects of implementation, we learned that the unified process view across systems was a considerable help. However, a current issue relates to how to handle diversity between the systems, such as in their level of detail and presence or absence of certain attributes.

The ability to connect different objects/concepts from different systems showed the strength of the Data Core, but we must also continuously allow these connections to be made by noticing that objects can be linked in a concise way.

6 Conclusion

APG applied process mining to analyze the full customer journey in the process of retiring. During this analysis we applied our self-service and Data Core concepts to build the dashboards jointly, teaching users to interpret and use them along the way and to extract most of the data from one database that combined and aligned multiple source systems.

Based on the insights we gained, two concrete improvement actions were undertaken: First, after the administrative process is completed but before the customer retires, we send a welcome e-mail that congratulates him or her on retirement and answers some common questions, such as when to expect the first payment. This informative letter increased NPS by 16 points in a small test setting, which signaled a significant increase. Second, we moved the time we send the initial preretirement letter from 6 months before the expected retirement date to 9 months, which could save thousands of calls to our customer contact center per year.

From this large customer-journey project we learned that our self-service approach needed fine-tuning, as the training cannot be one-size-fits-all, as we assumed at the start. We also noticed the value of the Data Core concept but realized that considerable care must be taken in its implementation. In the end, increased awareness of the value of process mining at APG resulted in a significant increase in the number of process-mining project requests.

Acknowledgments The authors thank all of the colleagues who were involved in this intense customer-focus project for their efforts and participation. Our thanks also go to Celonis, which provided us with a tool that was suitable for self-service and provided outstanding support and collaboration on certain topics. All authors contributed equally to this chapter.

References

APG website. (2019). About APG. https://www.apg.nl/en/who-is-apg. Last Accessed 2019-11-25.

Celonis website. (2019). Celonis website. https://www.celonis.com. Last Accessed 2019-11.

Dumas, M., La Rosa, M., Mendling, J., & Reijers, H. A. (2013). *Fundamentals of business process management*. Berlin: Springer.

van der Aalst, W. (2016). *Process mining: Data science in action* (2nd ed.). Berlin: Springer.

van der Steege, J. P (2018). *Optimizing aggregated performance indicators in service processes using process mining*. Master's thesis, Eindhoven University of Technology, the Netherlands.

vom Brocke, J., Mendling, J., & Rosemann, M. (2021). Planning and scoping business process management projects and programs with the BPM Billboard. In J. van Brocke, J. Mendling, & M. Rosemann (Eds.), *BPM cases. Digital innovation and business transformation in practice* (Vol. 2). Berlin: Springer.

vom Brocke, J., Zelt, S., & Schmiedel, T., 2015. Considering context in business process management: The bpm context framework. *bptrends.com*, 12.

Enabling Process Mining in Airbus Manufacturing

Extracting Event Logs and Discovering Processes from Complex Data

Álvaro Valencia-Parra, Belén Ramos-Gutiérrez, Ángel Jesús Varela-Vaca, María Teresa Gómez-López, and Antonio García Bernal

1 Introduction

Process mining helps organizations understand their business processes. It usually involves analyzing process event logs and discovering the process models behind them (de Murillas, 2019). Several approaches can be used to discover them (Banziger, Basukoski, & Chaussalet, 2019; Calvanese, Kalayci, Montali, & Santoso, 2017; Van Der Aalst, Weijters, & Maruster, 2004).

One of the challenges in process mining is related to *the ability to extract suitable events* (van der Aalst, 2016). Moreover, obtaining event logs produced by the systems is becoming more complex, as the systems tend to produce massive, distributed, heterogeneous, and complex data in new Internet-of-Things (IoT) and Cyber-Physical Systems (CPS) environments and to derive chaotic combinations of elements (Lira et al., 2019; Tax, Sidorova, & van der Aalst, 2019) without structured schema. These issues bring about an extra level of complexity to be managed by the current process mining solutions that involve the use of event logs because they focus primarily on structured homogeneous data.

The main issue this chapter addresses concerns how the complex data structures that are typically generated in IoT environments can be transformed to create an event log that the existing process-mining tools can manage. In this regard, the chapter provides a rich case on how to put process mining to practice in order to

Á. Valencia-Parra (✉) · B. Ramos-Gutiérrez · Á. J. Varela-Vaca · M. T. Gómez-López
Universidad de Sevilla, Seville, Spain
e-mail: avalencia@us.es; brgutierrez@us.es; ajvarela@us.es; maytegomez@us.es

A. García Bernal
Airbus Defence and Space, Seville, Spain
e-mail: antonio.garcia.bernal@airbus.com

J. vom Brocke et al. (eds.), *Business Process Management Cases Vol. 2*,
https://doi.org/10.1007/978-3-662-63047-1_10

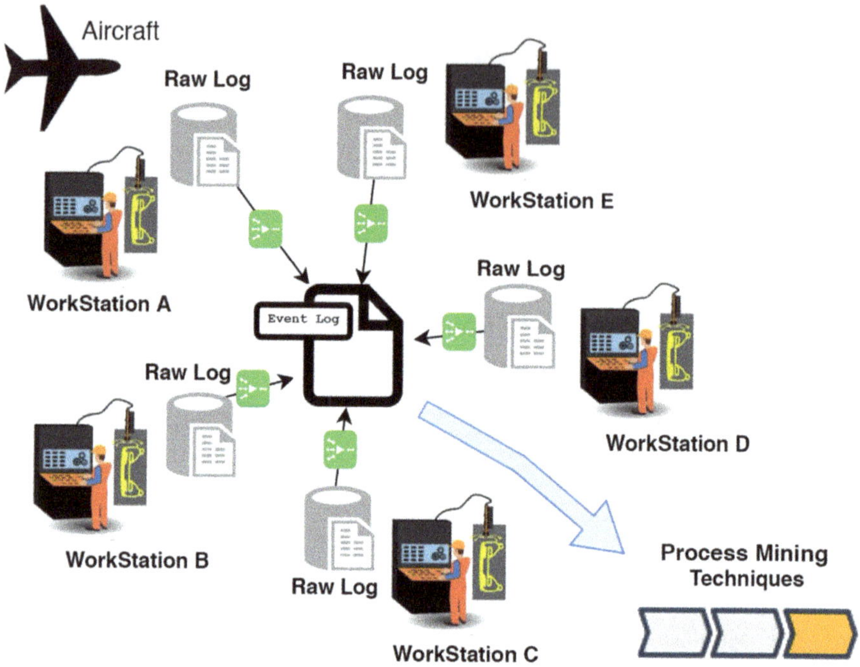

Fig. 1 Example of IoT scenario

deliver the strategy in a real-world organizational context (vom Brocke, Mendling, & Rosemann, 2021). Figure 1 shows a scenario of log extraction in the aeronautic industry that is based on the data produced by workstations in an aircraft-assembly process. In this scenario, several workstations perform tests and produce logs of their execution. The information, which follows a complex data structure, is stored in a NoSQL database (i.e., MongoDB). The challenges involve aggregating such complex data and extracting from them event logs in XES format, at which time process discovery techniques can be applied.

The objective of this work is to develop an approach that enables the extraction of event logs in XES format from complex data and to integrate this solution into a tool that non-experts can use to can benefit from the solution.

2 Situation Faced

This section describes the situation faced by the company.

2.1 Challenging Scenario

IoT and CPS environments are becoming highly relevant to organizations' (Lee & Lee, 2015) efforts to monitor their operations. However, a challenge concerns how to manage and analyze the recovered information so it is useful. The project *Clean Sky 2: A-24 One step beyond on automated testing technologies*, which was developed in collaboration with *Airbus Space & Defence*, inspired the notion of improving data extraction in IoT and CPS scenarios for the creation of event logs. The example is based on the assembly and testing processes of aircraft. Figure 1 illustrates a complex process that is executed in several of Airbus Space and Defence's locations without guidance from a Business Process Management System (BPMS) (Dumas, La Rosa, Mendling, & Reijers, 2013).

In this context, the main process in the organization is the assembly and testing of aircraft in accordance with an assembly chain of workstations. In this process, an aircraft with an identifier (*accode*) is located at a *workstation*, where a set of instructions is carried out (*gticode*). The instructions are validated by an operator (*executor*), and they begin and finish at a specific time (*start_date*, *final_date*). The moment when the test succeeds is specified (*successdate*). Each instruction might generate a set of incidents (*incidentcode*, *incidenttype*, *start_date*, *resolution_date*, and *label*).

The workstations, which are physically distributed, generate complex data structures depending on the tests that are executed. To generate logs that can be consumed by process-mining techniques, extraction of the logs from the structure in Fig. 2 must be defined. The figure shows a set of datasets formed of complex structures (lists and nested structures), but the event logs must fit the schema that is also shown in the figure.

Using this data, several trace logs can be generated that depend on the type of process that must be discovered, such as the evolution of the aircraft per workstation, the evolution of tests, or the life-cycle of incidents. These perspectives of the data can be used as the input from the process-discovery techniques to ascertain the actual process and to enable the analysis and improvement of the processes of assembly and testing.

2.2 Problems to Be Faced

The main problem to be faced in this scenario is the lack of a reliable approach to extracting event logs from complex semi-structured data. Many of the extant approaches were developed using relational databases as a starting point. The main idea in these cases is that events leave "footprints" by changing the underlying databases that are registered in the database system's redo logs (de Murillas, 2019; de Murillas, van Der Aalst, & Reijers, 2015; van der Aalst, 2015). This approach has

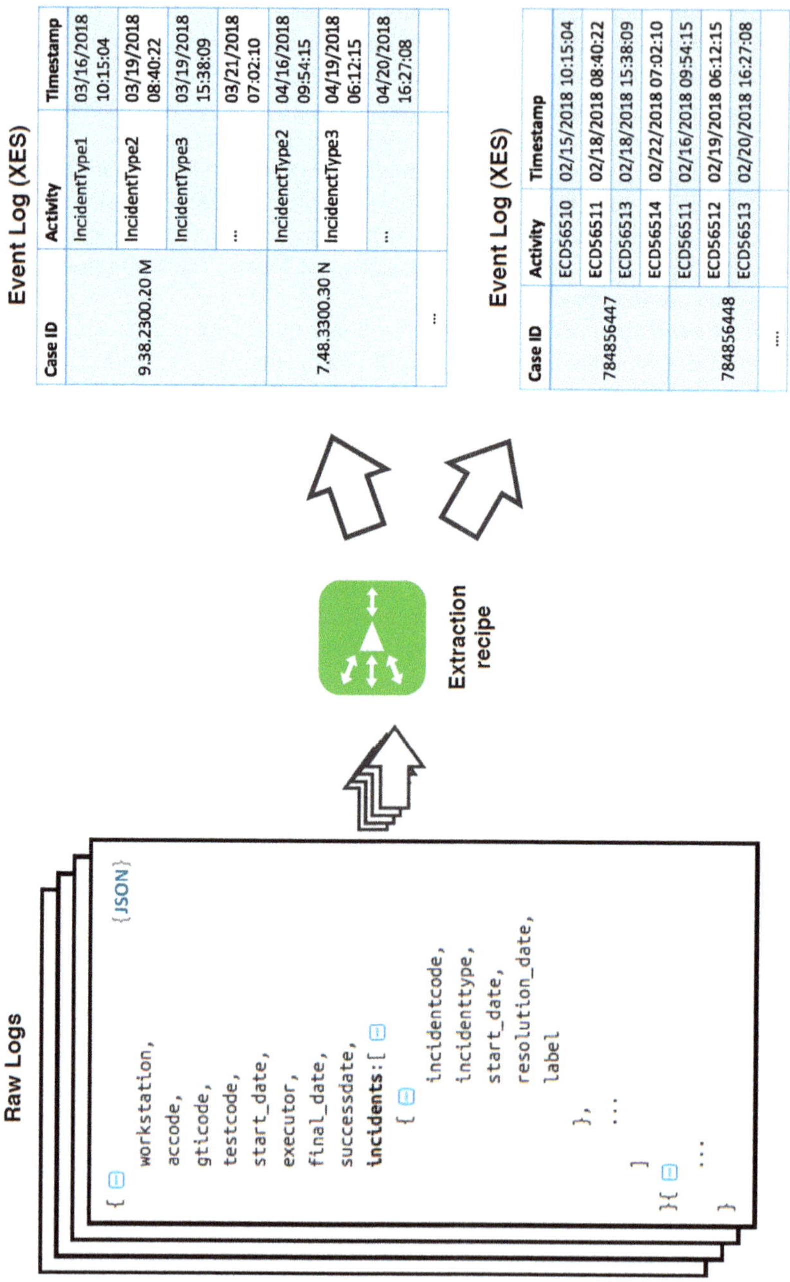

Fig. 2 Scenario of event log extraction

been supported by tools like XESame and PromImport plugin[1] (Günther & Van Der Aalst, 2006; Verbeek, Buijs, van Dongen, & van der Aalst, 2011), which transform information from relational databases into XES event logs. Data extraction from relational databases has been analyzed in general contexts that are not oriented toward process mining (Valencia-Parra, Varela-Vaca, López, & Ceravolo, 2019) but also from the perspective of ontology-based data access (Calvanese et al., 2017; Calvanese, Montali, Syamsiyah, & van der Aalst, 2016) by using metamodels as intermediaries (Gómez-López, Reina Quintero, Parody Núñez, Pérez Álvarez, & Reichert, 2018), supported by the *onProm* tool.[2]

Nonetheless, as the IoT scenario confirms, relational databases are not considered unique sources of events. Gupta and Sureka (2014) present an approach that shows how data is extracted from bug report histories, which are XML, JSON, or log files, although nested and complex structures are excluded. That work shows that the need to extract event logs from unstructured sources is a real issue, but there are no frameworks that facilitate it. In the same study, quasi-manual mapping of the report's attributes and those of the process is carried out, and these attributes are stored in a relational database from which the log of events will be extracted. In the context of Customer Relationship Management (CRM), Banziger et al. (2019) studied the possibility of transforming unstructured data into a log of events in XES log format (IEEE Computational Intelligence Society, 2016). In that case, the proposal involved a framework with which to discover business process models from semi-structured data that applies various preprocessing steps to CRM activities and then uses Latent Dirichlet Allocation (LDA) to classify and label all activities automatically by constructing a log of XES events.

We conclude that extracting event logs in a usable format for process-discovery purposes is a key step in the context of business process management and that such extraction is not properly supported in IoT contexts with semi-structured data. As described in *The Six Core Elements of Business Process Management* (Rosemann & vom Brocke, 2010), among the core elements in this framework are the methods and information technology. While the first is intended to provide tools and techniques to enable activities along the process life-cycle, the second provides technical solutions for this purpose. The proposal described in this chapter is intended to help in the *process design and modeling* stage. Our proposal will help organizations by providing a methodological approach for extracting event logs from semi-structured data sources so they can discover the processes and inefficiencies in their manufacturing. This methodology is supported by an IT solution.

[1]PromImport plugin: http://www.promtools.org/promimport/

[2]onProm tool: https://onprom.inf.unibz.it/

Table 1 Characteristics of the raw log

Description	Values
Number of aircraft	15
Number of workstations	52
Number of GTIs	1110
Number of executions	9397
Number of incidents	3049

3 Action Taken

The first action was to depict the characteristics of the dataset (i.e., raw logs) for the real scenario. To address the problems of event log extraction, we developed a domain-specific language (DSL)[3] to enable XES event log extraction from complex semi-structured data. The DSL fulfills the main objective since it removes the need to transform complex data with nested and recursive structures when generating event logs in XES format. In short, the proposal is based on specifying the paths to the attributes to be employed as *case_id, activity_id, timestamp* and other optional parameters of XES event logs. The underlying framework then infers the transformations to be performed so as to reach the desired schema, in this case, an XES event log with the attributes indicated by the user.

3.1 Understanding the Data

To measure the scenario's complexity, the characteristics of the datasets (i.e., raw logs) that are used as the input in our approach must be ascertained. As shown in Table 1, the dataset contains *9367* sets of tests, provided by *52* workstations. *Fifteen* aircraft were tested in these workstations, with a total of *1110* tests (i.e., GTI). The tests can be executed more than once for each aircraft, which is why there are *9397* executions of these tests. These repetitions occur when a test execution is unsuccessful, thereby causing an incident, so there are *6049* incidents in the raw log. Some statistical data has been extracted (e.g., the average of GTI per aircraft) to complement this information and provide a greater level of detail. The dataset we use here is a subset of the real data obtained in the project *Clean Sky 2*; our dataset is a small part of the information generated and is made up of *9397* raw logs, filtered and modified.

Considering the IoT scenario, each workstation periodically provides a raw log of the execution of a test on an aircraft, which may also contain incidents.

[3]Our tool can be found at https://github.com/IDEA-Research-Group/ELE

3.2 Example of Event Log Extraction

Example 1.1 illustrates a use of the DSL in *the process of the assembly of aircraft for each of the workstations in which the tests are evaluated*. The aircraft production follows a process in which each part of the aircraft is assembled and tested in accordance with the engineers' design. Each step of the assembly process is performed in a workstation, where the resulting event log is made up of a set of traces with the following information: (i) ***case_id***: *accode*, the aircraft identifier; (ii) ***activity_id***: *workstation*, the workstation in which the test was conducted; and (iii) ***timestamp***: *start_date*, the date when the aircraft passed through the workstation.

Example 1.1 Piece of code for extracting event logs in XES format.

```
  extract(
 define trace id("accode"),
 define trace event(
  activity = "workstation",
  criteria =
   orderBy(t"start_date"->toDate("MM/dd/yyyy HH:mm:ss")),
   timestamp = t"start_date"->toDate("MM/dd/yyyy HH:mm:ss")
 )
) from ("mongodb://mongo-instance:27017/db/logs")
```

4 Results Achieved

This section describes how the results we obtained help to improve the aircraft-assembly process.

4.1 Extraction of Event Logs

A set of test cases is outlined first, followed by the results are discussed in the next subsections.

Test Case A. Process according to the workstation that executes the test This test case has been described in Sect. 3.1 (cf. Example 1.1).

Test Case B. Process according to the GTI execution A set of test instructions must be carried out during the aircraft-assembly process. In this test case, the processes related to the tests applied to the aircraft (*gticode*) are extracted. Hence, the resulting event log has the form: (i) ***case_id***: *accode*, the aircraft identifier;

(ii) ***activity_id***: *gticode*; and (iii) ***timestamp***: *start_date*, the first time the test was applied to the aircraft.

The piece of code that allows this test case to be carried out is shown in Example 1.2.

Example 1.2 Test Case B

```
 extract(
define trace id("accode"),
define trace event(
 activity = "gticode",
 criteria =
  orderBy(t"start_date"->toDate("MM/dd/yyyy HH:mm:ss")),
timestamp = t"start_date"->toDate("MM/dd/yyyy HH:mm:ss")
)
) from ("mongodb://mongo-instance:27017/db/logs")
```

Example 1.3 Test Case C

```
 extract(
define trace id("gticode"),
define trace event(
 activity = "incident.incidenttype",
 criteria =
  orderBy(t"start_date"->toDate("MM/dd/yyyy HH:mm:ss")),
timestamp = t"start_date"->toDate("MM/dd/yyyy HH:mm:ss")
)
) from ("mongodb://mongo-instance:27017/db/logs")
```

Test Case C. Process according to the type of incident If the tests (*gticode*) report a set of incidents with an (*incidenttype*), the resulting event log must be in the following form: (i) ***case_id***: *gticode*, the test identifier; (ii) ***activity_id***: *incidents.incidenttype*; and (iii) ***timestamp***: *start_date*, the first time this type of incident occurred.

The piece of code that corresponds to this extraction is shown in Example 1.3.

4.2 Analysis of the Extracted Event Logs

Once the event logs (i.e., XES files) are obtained, certain studies on the data that they contain can be performed to discover the processes. Table 2 describes the features

Table 2 Extracted logs features

Description	Test case A	Test case B	Test case C
CaseId	15	15	673
Events	369	5771	1777
Activities	52	1110	10
Median case duration	75.8 days	50.2 days	0 ms
Mean case duration	76.1 days	67.1 days	20.8 days
Activities' minimal frequency	1	1	16
Activities' maximal frequency	15	15	424
Activities' median frequency	6	3	108
Activities' mean frequency	7.1	5.2	177.7
Activities' standard deviation	3.45	4.58	144.3

attained for each example of data extraction. A process-discovery tool, Disco,[4] was employed to analyze these logs.

The resulting processes discovered are shown in Fig. 3. These processes help to clarify and identify information that could not be analyzed manually. For instance, the process for *Test Case A* helps to clarify the flow of the aircraft through the various workstations, so we can see how certain workstations can perform tests in parallel with other workstations. *Test Case C* helps to clarify the flow of the incidents by showing how the incidents evolve.

4.3 Effects of Actions Taken

The event logs and the discovered process help to clarify the aircraft-assembly process:

Test Case A In some cases, an aircraft was in two workstations simultaneously because, for some tests, it is easier to move the station than to move the aircraft. Some workstations have assumable transition values between them (hours or days) while in others the time the aircraft is there is always 0 s. Therefore, we can assume that they are intermediate states in which nothing is done. There are also workstations in which the aircraft has been only once or not at all. The time spent in the workstations ranges from 0 ms to 55 days. Knowing the average time aircraft spend in each workstation and which workstations aircraft of the same type must pass through, experts can know whether deviations are occurring and compare the current state to the desired state.

Test Case B This case helped experts to see the sequence of tests that must be carried out and the time that must be spent on each one. It also allowed the experts to

[4]Disco by Fluxicon: https://fluxicon.com/disco/

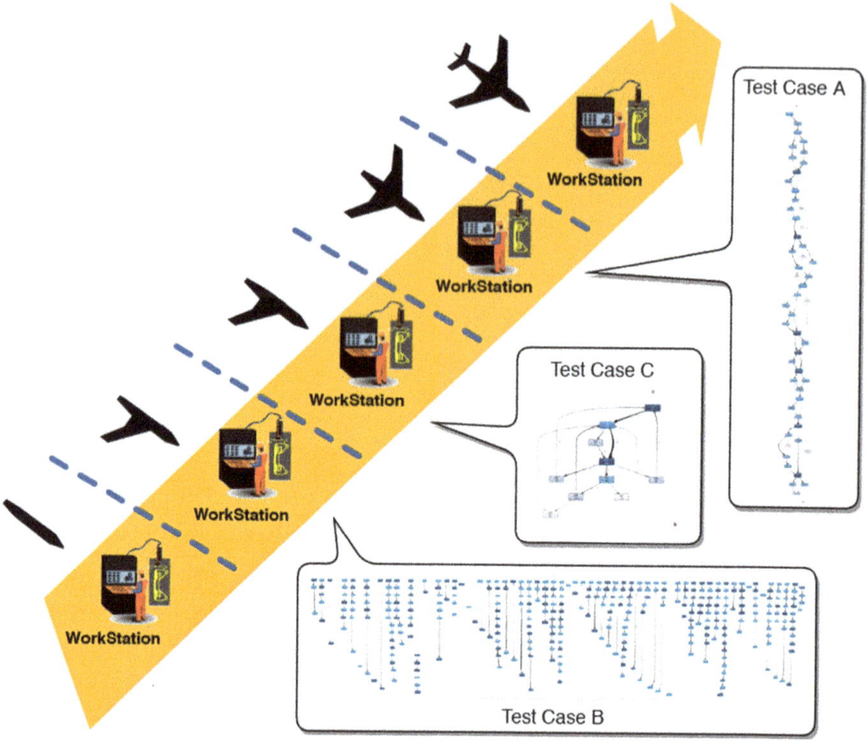

Fig. 3 Result of the process discovery for the extraction of each test case

make decisions about improvements that could be made to the tests performed at the workstations.

Test Case C The Discovery of the incident process by type helps experts see which types of incidents are most likely to occur after another incident occurred. Discovery of the incident process by type helps them see the average time that is likely to be required to resolve the same incident and how it will affect the entire assembly and testing process. The most frequent type of test is on the first incident and the last one. Other issues are detected, such as incidents that occur after a shift change of operators, which occurs in more than 30% of cases. These incidents are always of two: *Aircraft Configuration Failure* or *Test Edition Failure*.

4.4 Tool and Technical Details

The implemented tool is based on three main components: (1) the DSL language, which specifies the recipes for extraction from NoSQL databases, such as MongoDB, and the generation of event logs in XES format; (2) a prototype of

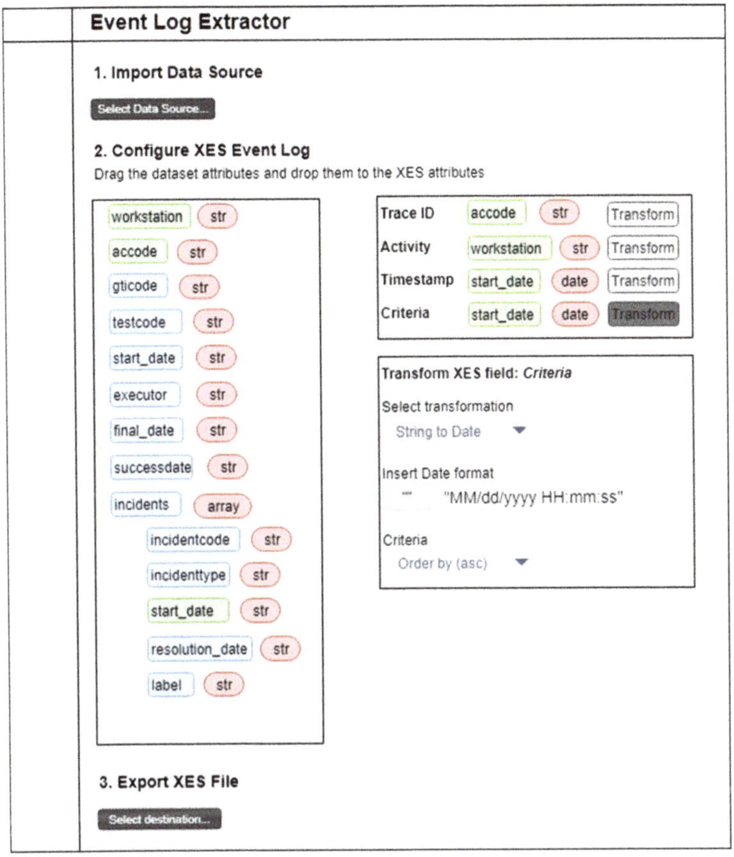

Fig. 4 Prototype of UI for transformation

application (cf., Fig. 4) in which the transformation can be defined in a user-friendly way; and (3) a connector that allows the generated XES logs to feed the ProM™ (see footnote 2) tool automatically during the discovery of process models. All the resources that have been were employed in this work are freely available (see footnote 3). The raw log used in the paper was stored in a MongoDB database, and the extraction recipes were implemented in the DSL language, based on Scala, and developed using a model-driven engineering approach. The current implementation of the connector uses only *Inductive Miner* (Tax et al., 2019), but other tools, such as Disco from Fluxicon, have also been employed to illustrate the discovery process.

5 Lessons Learned

This chapter presents an industrial approach to the extraction of data from complex semi-unstructured databases for the generation of an event log that can be used by process-mining tools. The solution includes a DSL and a prototype that enable non-expert users to extract event logs from NoSQL sources. The solution was applied to a real case study based on the aircraft-assembly process, thereby showing the applicability of our proposal to a real scenario after using the extracted data for process discovery. The proposed approach was also supported by the implementation of an instrument that is connected to process-mining tools.

The proposed approach contributes to the need for methods and IT solutions for process design and modeling. Both the methodology, which consists of matching the dataset attributes with an XES event log template, and the IT solution, which frees users from dealing with flattening and aggregating operations, fulfill the objectives of these areas in *The Six Core Elements* framework (Rosemann & vom Brocke, 2010).

Four lessons have been learned in the development of the approach:

1. *Extraction of event logs in IoT and CPS scenarios*. The complexity of the data in IoT scenarios increases the complexity in the extraction of event logs that require intensive analysis.
2. *Massive data production and processing*. An environment in which data is continuously being generated could require integration with Big Data architectures.
3. *Selection of case analyses that are useful to the organization*. The selection of the case analysis and the activity-filtering criteria can influence the results of the selected case, so it is not always an easy task since it involves considerable pre-analysis of the data and a significant understanding of the organization.
4. *Risk factors of discovery of spaghetti-like processes*. Depending on the data and the case, the discovery process can retrieve a spaghetti-like process that increases the complexity of analyzing the discovery process.

Acknowledgment This work was been partially funded by the Ministry of Science and Technology of Spain through ECLIPSE (RTI2018-094283-B-C33), the Junta de Andalucia via the METAMORFOSIS project, and the European Regional Development Fund (ERDF/FEDER). The authors thank the Cátedra de Telefónica "Inteligencia en la Red" of the Universidad de Sevilla for its support.

References

Banziger, R., Basukoski, A., & Chaussalet, T. (2019). Discovering business processes in CRM systems by leveraging unstructured text data. In *Proceedings – HPCC/SmartCity/DSS 2018* (pp. 1571–1577). Institute of Electrical and Electronics Engineers Inc. https://doi.org/10.1109/HPCC/SmartCity/DSS.2018.00257

Calvanese, D., Kalayci, T. E., Montali, M., & Santoso, A. (2017). OBDA for log extraction in process mining. In *Lecture Notes in Computer Science (including subseries Lecture Notes in Artificial Intelligence and Lecture Notes in Bioinformatics)*. Springer (pp. 292–345). https://doi.org/10.1007/978-3-319-61033-7_9

Calvanese, D., Montali, M., Syamsiyah, A., & van der Aalst, W. M. P. (2016). Ontology-driven extraction of event logs from relational databases. In *Lecture Notes in Business Information Processing* (pp. 140–153). Springer. https://doi.org/10.1007/978-3-319-42887-1_12

de Murillas, E. G. L. (2019). *Process mining on databases: Extracting event data from real-life data sources*. Eindhoven: Technische Universiteit Eindhoven.

de Murillas, E. G. L., van Der Aalst, W. M. P., & Reijers, H. A. (2015). Process mining on databases: Unearthing historical data from redo logs. In *Lecture Notes in Computer Science* (pp. 367–385). New York: Springer. https://doi.org/10.1007/978-3-319-23063-4_25

Dumas, M., La Rosa, M., Mendling, J., & Reijers, H. (2013). *Fundamentals of business process management, fundamentals of business process management*. Berlin: Springer. https://doi.org/10.1007/978-3-642-33143-5.

Gómez-López, M. T., Reina Quintero, A. M., Parody Núñez, M. L., Pérez Álvarez, J. M., & Reichert, M. (2018). An architecture for querying business process, business process instances, and business data models. In *Lecture Notes in Business Information Processing* (pp. 757–769). Springer. https://doi.org/10.1007/978-3-319-74030-0_60

Günther, C. W., & Van Der Aalst, W. M. P. (2006). A generic import framework for process event logs. In *Lecture Notes in Computer Science* (pp. 81–92). Springer. https://doi.org/10.1007/11837862_10

Gupta, M., & Sureka, A. (2014). Nirikshan: Mining bug report history for discovering process maps, inefficiencies and inconsistencies. In *ACM International Conference Proceeding Series*. Association for Computing Machinery. https://doi.org/10.1145/2590748.2590749

IEEE Computational Intelligence Society. (2016). Standard for eXtensible Event Stream (XES) for achieving interoperability in event logs and event streams. In *Proceedings of the IEEE* (pp. 1–50). https://doi.org/10.1109/IEEESTD.2016.7740858

Lee, I., & Lee, K. (2015). The Internet of Things (IoT): Applications, investments, and challenges for enterprises. *Business Horizons, 58*(4), 431–440. https://doi.org/10.1016/j.bushor.2015.03.008.

Lira, R., Salas-Morales, J., Leiva, L., de la Fuente, R., Fuentes, R., & Delfino, A., et al. (2019). Tailored process feedback through process mining for surgical procedures in medical training: The central venous catheter case. In *Lecture Notes in Business Information Processing* (pp. 163–174). Springer. https://doi.org/10.1007/978-3-030-11641-5_13

Rosemann, M., & vom Brocke, J. (2010). The six core elements of business process management. In *Handbook on business process management* (pp. 105–122). https://doi.org/10.1007/978-3-642-00416-2

Tax, N., Sidorova, N., & van der Aalst, W. M. P. (2019). Discovering more precise process models from event logs by filtering out chaotic activities. *Journal of Intelligent Information Systems, 52* (1), 107–139. https://doi.org/10.1007/s10844-018-0507-6.

Valencia-Parra, Á., Varela-Vaca, Á. J., López, M. T. G., & Ceravolo, P. (2019). CHAMALEON: Framework to improve Data Wrangling with Complex Data. In *ICIS 2019 proceedings*. Retrieved November 14, 2019, from https://aisel.aisnet.org/icis2019/data_science/data_science/16

van der Aalst, W. M. P. (2015). *Extracting event data from databases to unleash process mining* (pp. 105–128). Cham: Springer. https://doi.org/10.1007/978-3-319-14430-6_8.

van der Aalst, W. (2016). Data science in action. In *Process mining* (pp. 3–23). Berlin: Springer. https://doi.org/10.1007/978-3-662-49851-4_1

Van Der Aalst, W., Weijters, T., & Maruster, L. (2004). Workflow mining: Discovering process models from event logs. *IEEE Transactions on Knowledge and Data Engineering, 16*(9), 1128–1142. https://doi.org/10.1109/TKDE.2004.47.

Verbeek, H. M. W., Buijs, J. C. A. M., van Dongen, B. F., & van der Aalst, W. M. P. (2011). XES, XESame, and ProM 6. In *Lecture notes in business information processing* (pp. 60–75). New York: Springer. https://doi.org/10.1007/978-3-642-17722-4_5.

vom Brocke, J., Mendling, J., & Rosemann, M. (2021). Planning and scoping business process management projects and programs with the BPM Billboard. In J. vom Brocke, J. Mendling, & M. Rosemann (Eds.), *BPM cases. Digital innovation and business transformation in practice* (Vol. 2). New York: Springer.

Improving the Arthrosis Care Process at Maastricht UMC+: Unraveling Complex and Noncomplex Cases by Data and Process Mining

K. F. Canjels, M. S. V. Imkamp, T. A. E. J. Boymans, and R. J. B. Vanwersch

1 Introduction

Osteoarthritis is one of the largest causes of disability among the elderly. Patients experience pain, instability, and limitation of movement (Doherty, Abhishek, Hunter, & Ramirez Curtis, 2017). Because of the chronic character of osteoarthritis, care crosses the boundaries of primary care (i.e., GPs), secondary care (e.g., general hospitals), and tertiary care (e.g., university medical centers). Since the population of patients with osteoarthritis in the Netherlands is expected to grow by 92% over the next 25 years (Rijksinstituut Volksgezondheid en Milieu, 2018), the complete inter-organizational care process must be organized to operate efficiently.

This initiative focuses on improving the inter-organizational care process for patients at the Maastricht University Medical Center+ (MUMC+) who have knee osteoarthritis. The case sets a great example of how to link BPM to important strategic objectives of real-world relevance (vom Brocke, Mendling, & Rosemann, 2021). Currently, noncomplex knee osteoarthritis patients (e.g., patients who follow a short treatment trajectory with only standardized, routine activities like X-rays, consultations, and injections) and complex knee osteoarthritis patients (e.g., patients who follow a long trajectory during which many diagnostic and treatment options must be considered and executed) use the same costly facilities and highly specialized staff. Substantial gains in efficiency can be expected from using resource substitution (especially for noncomplex trajectories). To identify and quantify this

K. F. Canjels (✉) · R. J. B. Vanwersch (✉)
Maastricht University Medical Center+, Maastricht, The Netherlands

Eindhoven University of Technology, Eindhoven, The Netherlands
e-mail: rob.vanwersch@mumc.nl

M. S. V. Imkamp · T. A. E. J. Boymans
Maastricht University Medical Center+, Maastricht, The Netherlands

J. vom Brocke et al. (eds.), *Business Process Management Cases Vol. 2*, https://doi.org/10.1007/978-3-662-63047-1_11

improvement's potential, in-depth insights into the existing noncomplex and complex trajectories are necessary. Which patient trajectories can be considered noncomplex, so the patient trajectory can be done outside the university medical center at less costly facilities, and which cannot? What is the size of these patient trajectories in terms of the number of patients? By investigating these questions, the potential for improvement can be operationalized and quantified in such a way that concrete implementation steps can be taken with the full support of the staff involved.

An accurate view of the current processes from beginning to end can be obtained with process mining, a method by which to discover process models based on data from event logs (e.g., billing data). Process mining has been shown to be useful to optimize, for example, an emergency department (Mans, Schonenberg, Song, van der Aalst, & Bakker, 2009) and stroke care (Mans et al., 2008). Although process mining has been demonstrated to be valuable, it also faces some difficulties in producing practical models for complex processes. Patient flows have a heterogeneous character because patients follow various trajectories in the hospital, which leads to "spaghetti" models (Song, Günther, & van der Aalst, 2009). Typically, this problem is exacerbated in the context of inter-organizational care processes, such as the knee osteoarthritis care process. Spaghetti models are difficult to interpret and do not facilitate the unraveling of complex from noncomplex trajectories. Hence, analytics options beyond process mining have to be considered in the context of the knee osteoarthritis care process.

In particular, ways to divide the patients into homogenous subgroups should be sought, as this division reduces data complexity before process mining, enabling the care process to be unraveled and improved. Previous studies on health care processes have used clustering techniques prior to process mining (Mans et al., 2009; Song et al., 2009; Song, Yang, Siadat, & Pechenizkiy, 2013), but we are, to the best of our knowledge, the first to report on a comprehensive technique consisting of data preparation, clustering, and data reduction techniques prior to process mining, and all applied to a process that spans the boundaries of a single organization.

In this report, we show how an innovative, three-step methodology can be used to unravel and improve an inter-organizational care process. This methodology provides guidelines on how to preprocess and integrate multiple data sets and outlines data clustering and reduction techniques that can be applied prior to process mining. In this way, this methodology offers support to the process discovery and analysis phase in the BPM life cycle model (Dumas, La Rosa, Mendling, & Reijers, 2016). We also show how applying this innovative methodology led to substantial potential for improving the efficiency of the knee osteoarthritis care process as part of the BPM life cycle's process redesign phase.

The remainder of this chapter is structured as follows. Section 2 describes the situation faced. Section 3, which explains the approach and actions taken, is followed by a discussion of the results in Sect. 4. Finally, Sect. 5 closes with lessons learned.

2 Situation Faced

Given the large expected growth in osteoarthritis patients and the scarcity of resources, the MUMC+ is looking for opportunities to improve the process efficiency of the inter-organizational care of knee osteoarthritis. The knee osteoarthritis process is complex in nature since the patients follow multiple care paths. A patient's individual care path starts with an appointment with his or her general practitioner (GP). A GP who decides to refer the patient to an orthopedic medical specialist can choose the outpatient city clinic, which is partially owned by the hospital, or the hospital itself. Orthopedic medical specialists at the city clinic perform consultations with patients outside the hospital, which allows GPs to refer patients about whom they have doubts regarding diagnosis and treatment without referring them to hospital care. The orthopedic medical specialist at the city clinic decides on the required nonsurgical or surgical treatment plan. The GP may also refer the patient directly to the hospital, where a final diagnosis is made and a nonsurgical or surgical treatment can be started.

In the current situation, knee osteoarthritis patients who are undergoing a noncomplex trajectory (i.e., a short path that consists only of standardized, routine activities like X-rays, consultations, and injections) and those who are undergoing a complex trajectory (i.e., a long path during which many diagnostic and treatment options must be considered and executed) may start their trajectory at either the city clinic or the hospital. It is expected that even patients who start their trajectory directly at the hospital often follow a noncomplex trajectory with a small number of standardized, routine activities. The care provided to this category of patients, as well as the care provided to noncomplex patients who start their trajectory at the city clinic, might be organized more efficiently substituting more costly staff at the university medical center with less costly staff at the city clinic. Patients' trajectories must be visualized to quantify the potential gain in efficiency, gain insights into the complexity of patient trajectories, determine which facilities and staff are involved in the most common trajectories, and evaluate whether these facilities and staff match the complexity of care. Subsequently, opportunities for organizing noncomplex trajectories outside the university medical center can be identified and quantified.

3 Action Taken

To analyze the various patient trajectories, data was collected from both the MUMC + and the outpatient city clinic. Patient data from the MUMC+ was extracted from the hospital's information system, while that from the city clinic was obtained from a list that describes the consultations held with each patient. The patient data from the hospital information system consisted of all the activities recorded for billing purposes for 2600 patients treated for knee osteoarthritis between January 2016 and October 2018. This data extraction resulted in 634,972 recorded events and 1262 unique event classes (activities). The city clinic data consisted of all event classes executed at this clinic, of which there were only three. The two data sets were

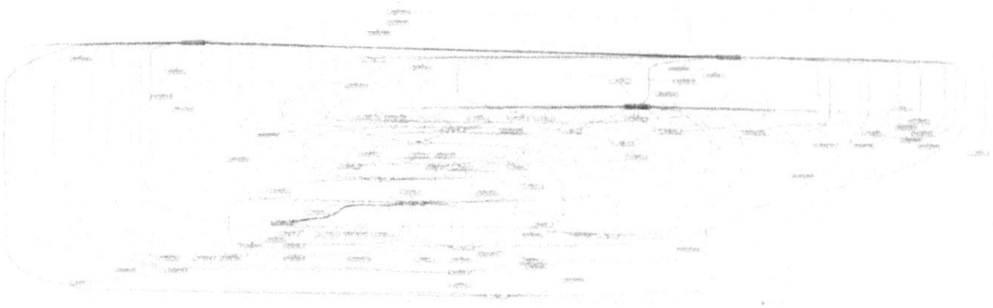

Fig. 1 The complete process model

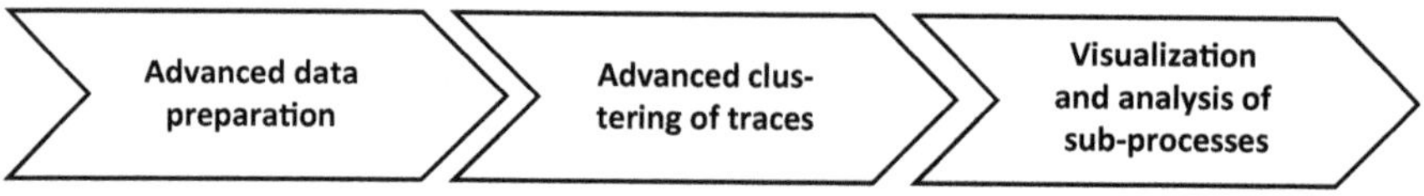

Fig. 2 A three-step methodology for analyzing complex healthcare processes

integrated and served as input for the analysis. Our first analysis of the process using process mining resulted in a spaghetti model (Fig. 1).

The process model shown in Fig. 1 is difficult to read and does not facilitate the unraveling of complex and noncomplex patient trajectories. Hence, other analytics options were considered in the context of the knee osteoarthritis care process. In particular, we developed a three-step methodology that includes guidelines on how to preprocess and integrate multiple data sets and outlines data clustering and reduction techniques that can be applied prior to process mining. This methodology is shown in Fig. 2.

In the first step, data is preprocessed and integrated into multiple datasets so data and process-mining techniques can be used later on to identify and visualize subgroups of patient trajectories. In the second step, data mining techniques are selected and applied to cluster traces of the complete event log. These data-mining techniques enable visualization and analysis of homogenous subprocesses by means of process-mining in the third step. During this initiative, all steps were executed by a data scientist, and all decisions were made and outcomes discussed with an expert team consisting of three orthopedic specialists and a process analytics expert.

3.1 Advanced Data Preparation

The first step, "advanced data preparation," contains five sub-steps: (1) filter the relevant diagnosis, (2) merge the data, (3) exclude irrelevant activities, (4) cluster the activities, and (5) exclude patients with incomplete processes.

Filter the relevant diagnosis: Care organizations collect data on all care activities related to individual patients. When the care organization is interested in the process applied in response to a particular disease, only one or a couple of diagnoses must be analyzed. In this case, we selected *knee osteoarthritis* and/or *loosening of the knee prosthesis* because these diagnoses are relevant in the context of knee osteoarthritis patients.

Merge the data: With the focus on cross-organizational processes, files from multiple organizations must be analyzed and files must be merged. Therefore, an identifier to link the patients from the various databases must be found. We selected the patient number as the identifier with which to combine the hospital data and city clinic data.

Exclude irrelevant activities: To prevent the generation of a spaghetti-like model, irrelevant activities were excluded through discussion with experts. An example of an irrelevant activity in our situation was the *telcode*, which is a code required for billing purposes, indicating a consultation by phone. However, since this activity is also separately registered as *consultation by phone*, we excluded it.

Cluster activities: Some activities are useful on a more abstract level. For example, for many diseases, the lab tests that are executed are not relevant when one needs only to know whether one or more lab tests were performed at a certain laboratory, so the detailed activities can be clustered and mentioned once in the model. In addition, when multiple activities take place together, the main activities can be selected and others excluded from the model. For example, on the day of a surgery, multiple activities take place (e.g., anesthesia and surgery preparation). Only the main activity can be selected and the other activities can be excluded from the model while still maintaining the activity *surgery*. We also indicated whether patients received physiotherapy during their stays in the hospital by changing the activity *admission to hospital* to *admission to hospital with physiotherapy*. For these patients, the activities that correspond to physiotherapy were excluded from the analysis because they were indicated in the renamed activity.

Exclude patients with incomplete processes: To obtain valid insights into the patient trajectories, we first included only completed patient trajectories. However, selecting only completed trajectories leads to a bias toward short trajectories that were completed in recent years because trajectories that began only recently are not likely to have been completed by the end of our time horizon for data analysis (October 2018). We analyzed the percentage of patients who underwent knee surgery (long trajectories and found that 86% of the patients in 2016 and 2017 finished their trajectories within 10 months after knee surgery, so to include only completed patient trajectories without engaging a substantial bias toward short trajectories, we considered only patients who started their care process before January 2018.

After these data-preparation activities are executed, the resulting data should be in the form of an event log that reflects all time-ordered activities for each patient.

3.2 Advanced Clustering of Traces

In the second step, advanced trace clustering divided the data set into multiple groups of patients with similar care activities. This clustering was done to unravel the patient trajectories/subprocesses and increase the comprehensibility of the subprocess models. Clustering was performed with the trace clustering plug-in of the Process Mining Framework (ProM) version 5.2.

Clustering algorithms

Clustering algorithms are a form of unsupervised learning that clusters the data in multiple groups of similar patients to obtain partial, more comprehensible process models. The four trace clustering algorithms used in this case were K-means, Qualitative Threshold Clustering (QTC), Agglomerative Hierarchical Clustering (AHC), and Self-Organizing Maps (SOM), as described in Song et al. (2009). As the distance measure that was required for calculating the dissimilarity between cases, we employed the often-used Euclidean distance measure (Song et al., 2009) for all algorithms. While the four algorithms are well known in the data mining area and have been widely applied in various domains, their application in the context of process mining (i.e., discovering process models) has been limited, so we compared them to identify the most useful one for the present case.

We also looked at whether the clustering algorithms might profit from dimensionality-reduction techniques. The dimensionality of the data refers to the number of unique events, which describe every record in the data (Song et al., 2013). Trace clustering can become computationally expensive when the number of dimensions is high. Reducing the dimensions could reduce processing time and have a positive influence on the clustering results by reducing noise in the dataset. We applied three well-known dimensionality-reduction techniques—Singular Value Decomposition (SVD), Random Projection (RP), and Principal Component Analysis (PCA)—which gave us 16 different combinations for trace clustering.

No preprocessing SVD Random Projection PCA	✖	Clustering algo-rithms: - K-means clustering - Quality threshold - AHC - SOM	= **16 combinations**

In addition to trace clustering, we applied the sequence-clustering algorithm to the data set. Sequential clustering performs clustering based on traces' sequential behavior (Veiga & Ferreira, 2010), so, in contrast to the other techniques, sequence clustering takes the sequence of activities in the event log into account while clustering. This inclusion leads to 17 combinations used to cluster the data.

Performance Measures for Cluster Algorithms

Four performance measures were used to compare the clustering algorithms: average fitness, complexity of the model, variance within clusters, and processing time.

Average fitness and complexity are specifically designed to measure the subprocess models' performance, but average fitness also describes the gap between the behavior observed in the log and the behavior described by the subprocess models. We replayed the process model in a Petri Net to calculate the average fitness (Rozinat & van der Aalst, 2008). The complexity of the model is indicated by the size of the model in terms of nodes, arcs, and the relationships between them. We used HeuristicMiner in ProM to derive a process model for every cluster (Thaler, Ternis, Fettke, & Loos, 2015) for which the complexity was calculated. The total variance within the cluster indicates whether the clustering algorithm reduces the variance within the clusters to less than the total variance in the data. As a final performance measure, processing time measures the total time required to cluster the data, so it measures the clustering algorithm's efficiency. All of the algorithms' performance was compared using all four performance measures to identify those that perform best.

Subsequently, the process-mining results (in the form of visual subprocess models) of the best-performing algorithms were presented to the expert team of three orthopedic specialists and a process analytics expert so they could select the clustering algorithm that led to the easiest-to-interpret grouping of patient trajectories.

3.3 Visualizations and Analyses of Subprocesses

After the best-performing clustering algorithm was selected, the final subprocess models were visualized and analyzed with the expert team by means of the process-mining tool Disco. We identified and quantified the patient trajectories that can be considered noncomplex, so the patients can be seen outside the university medical center by less costly staff and in less costly facilities.

4 Results

4.1 Results Regarding Advanced Data Preparation

The advanced data-preparation steps outlined in the previous section (e.g., selecting the diagnosis and clustering the surgery activities), performed in consultation with the orthopedic specialists, reduced the number of event classes from 1262 to 90.

4.2 Results Regarding Advanced Clustering

In the advanced clustering of traces, the AHC, AHC with PCA, and K-means clearly outperformed the other algorithms in terms of the various performance measures. However, when we compared the three best-performing clustering algorithms (Table 1), we observed that each algorithm has its strengths and weaknesses.

Table 1 Comparison of the three best clustering algorithms

Performance measures	AHC	AHC with PCA	K-means
Average Fitness	0.584	0.594	0.557
Average |A|	131.530	113.580	119.100
Average |N|	46.200	38.110	41.790
Average CNC	2.010	2.140	2.030
Average CN	86.330	76.470	78.310
Average Δ	0.091	0.102	0.095
Within Cluster Variance	10,737.510	13,169.740	10,803.730
Processing time	00:04:55	00:22:30	00:33:35

Note: Darker blue colors indicate better scores. $|A|$ = number of arcs (number of transitions between activities); $|N|$ = number of nodes (number of activities); CNC = $\frac{|A|}{|N|}$ (connectivity coefficient); CN = $|A| - |N| + 1$ (cyclomatic number); $\Delta = \frac{|A|}{|N|*(|N|-1)}$ (density). Processing time is in hrs:min:sec. Note that, for reasons of comparison, we forced all algorithms to generate five clusters. A higher number of clusters did not result in more clearly distinguishable clusters

To select the final clustering algorithm, we compared the resulting subprocess models for each of the three algorithms and discussed the results with the experts. The discussion revealed that K-means performs best in coming up with easy-to-interpret groups of complex and noncomplex patient trajectories. The algorithm is also markedly better than the others in unraveling the nonsurgical and surgical trajectories.

4.3 Results Regarding Visualization

The K-means algorithm's output is five clusters. Cluster 1, *consultation at the city clinic*, consists of patients who have only one consultation at the outpatient city clinic. Cluster 2, *consultation at MUMC+*, consists of patients who have only one consultation in the hospital, after which their trajectory is finished. Cluster 3, *consultation at MUMC+ with X-ray*, consists of patients who have an X-ray and consultation in the hospital. Cluster 4, *conservative treatment at MUMC+*, consists of patients who follow a conservative treatment path in the hospital; the patients in this cluster have an average of 3.94 activities. Finally, cluster 5, *surgical treatment at MUMC+*, is the most complex group and consists of patients who have surgery in the hospital; these patients have the most extensive treatment path, with an average of 24.32 activities.

As an example, clusters 3 and 4 are visualized and explained in Figs. 3 and 4, respectively. Cluster 3 represents patients with a noncomplex care path, as they enter the hospital with an X-ray of the knee (X-Knie in Dutch), after which they finish their trajectory with a single consultation (1e consult algemeen). Patients in cluster 4 have a longer conservative treatment path that usually begins with an X-ray of the knee (X-Knie), followed by the first consultation (1e consult algemeen). After this consultation, many patients continue with a follow-up consultation (Vervolgconsult

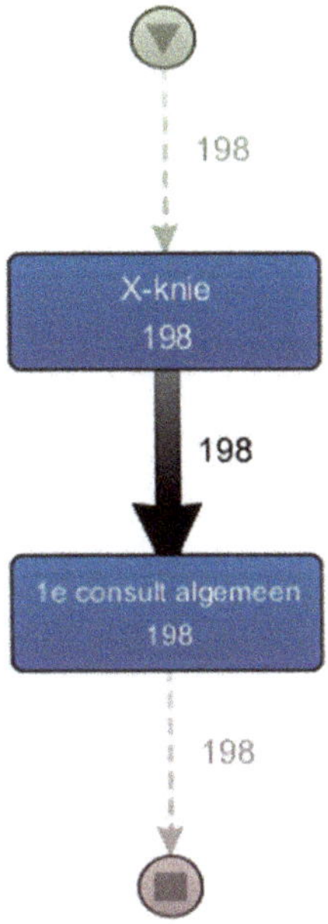

Fig. 3 Cluster 3: consultation at MUMC+ with X-Ray

algemeen; 47.2%), but they might also have an injection (injectie kenacortinspuiting; 33.7%) or a knee MRI (mri knie; 19.1%). After the first follow-up consultation, a slight majority of patients leave the hospital, but others come back for multiple follow-up consultations or injections before finishing their trajectory.

4.4 Improvement Opportunities

Analyzing the subprocess models of the five clusters reveals that clusters 1, 2, and 3 can be classified as noncomplex patient trajectories because they represent patients who have, at most, one X-ray and one consultation at the outpatient city clinic or hospital. All three of these trajectories can be completely executed at the city clinic, where patients can be seen less expensive staff (i.e., physician assistants, specialized GPs, physiotherapists under supervision of medical specialists). Cluster 4 is more complex because it consists of patients who have a longer conservative treatment path in the hospital. However, the visualization of the process model reveals that the majority of the group (65.4%) has only standardized, routine activities (consultations, X-rays, and injections) that can be completely executed at the city clinic. Patients in cluster 4 who do not follow a complete standardized routine trajectory could at least start their trajectory (i.e., X-ray and consultation) in the city clinic. The most complex care is given to patients in cluster 5. Despite the complexity of this group's treatment, visual inspection leads us to conclude that these patients can also start their trajectory (i.e., X-ray and consultation) at the city clinic. The effects of the redesign options discussed here are presented in Table 2.

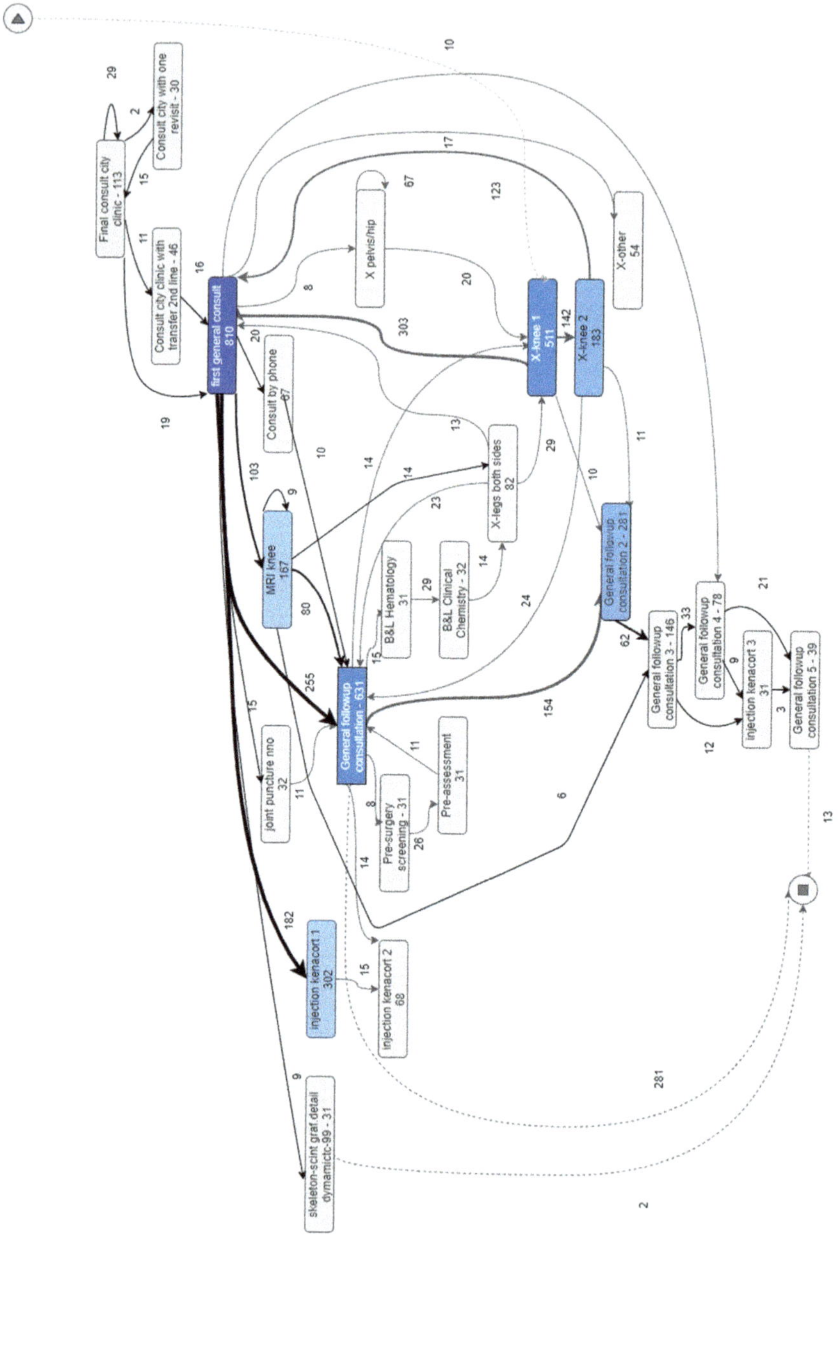

Fig. 4 Cluster 4: conservative treatment at MUMC+

Table 2 Impact of redesign

	Current facility			Potential facility	
	Full trajectory at city clinic	Start in city clinic, follow-up at MUMC+	Full trajectory at MUMC+	Full trajectory at city clinic 2.0[a]	Start in city clinic, follow-up at MUMC+
Cluster 1—*Consultation at the city clinic*	151 (9.4%)	0	0	151 (9.4%)	0
Cluster 2—*Consultation at MUMC+*	0	0	163 (10.1%)	163 (10.1%)	0
Cluster 3—*Consultation at MUMC+ with X-ray*	0	0	198 (12.3%)	198 (12.3%)	0
Cluster 4—*Conservative treatment at MUMC+*	43 (2.7%)	55 (3.4%)	793 (49.1%)	583 (36.1%)	308 (19.1%)
Cluster 5—*Surgical treatment at MUMC+*	0	9 (0.6%)	201 (13%)	0	210 (13%)
Total	194 (12.0%)	64 (4.0%)	1355 (84.0%)	1095 (67.9%)	518 (32.1%)

[a]Note: In the city clinic 2.0 resource substitution is introduced such that patients will be seen by less expensive staff than is the case with the current situation

As Table 2 shows, the percentage of patients who undergo their full (noncomplex) care trajectory at the city clinic is expected to grow from 12.0% to 67.9%, while the percentage of patients who undergo the initial, noncomplex start of their trajectory at the city clinic is expected to grow from 4.0% to 32.1%. In the new situation, resource substitution is introduced at the city clinic, where patients are seen by less expensive staff (i.e., physician assistants, specialized GPs, physiotherapists under the supervision of medical specialists). Given the annual forecast of patient numbers, these percentages, and the average number of activities per cluster that can be moved out of the hospital context, approximately 1250 patient sessions (consultations and/or injections) can be moved out of the hospital and done more efficiently at the city clinic, leading to an expected yearly efficiency gain of at least 75,000 €. Moreover, patients are likely to benefit from reduced average waiting times when noncomplex (fast queue) and complex (slow queue) trajectories are unraveled and when they are seen more often in the more patient-friendly setting of a city clinic.

5 Lessons Learned

Healthcare organizations increasingly face pressure to improve the efficiency of their care processes by providing adequate care for patients at reduced costs. One way to meet this goal is to ensure that the complexity of patient care matches with the facilities and resources used. By applying a comprehensive data-mining and process-mining approach, we unravel the noncomplex and complex trajectories of knee osteoarthrosis patients and pinpoint opportunities for improvement. Our study identified five clusters of patient trajectories: three clusters of noncomplex care (*consultation at the city clinic*, *consultation at MUMC+*, and *consultation at MUMC+ with X-ray*), one of mostly noncomplex care (*conservative treatment at MUMC+*), and one of complex care (*surgical treatment at MUMC+*).

In keeping with our expectations, the resulting models showed that care for a large group of patients was possible outside the university medical center by less expensive resources and staff. We found that many activities can be moved out of the hospital context if all patients who can undergo their full or partial (noncomplex) care trajectory in an efficient city clinic context do so. Besides the substantial efficiency gain that can be realized, a reduction in average waiting times (especially for noncomplex patients) is expected, along with an increase in patient satisfaction, that way delivering highly important strategic objectives through BPM (vom Brocke et al., 2021). The results revealed that the identification and quantification of complex and noncomplex patient groups can improve the healthcare process as long as it is supported by the involved staff's willingness to change.

> Now, we finally see the size of the noncomplex patient group and the possible impact of reorganizing our care processes (Orthopedic surgeon, MUMC+)

From a methodological perspective, this study shows the value of the data-driven three-step methodology for unraveling and improving care processes. The results show the potential of thorough preprocessing of data and using data mining tools prior to process mining to transform a spaghetti-like mined model into easy-to-interpret subprocess models. Other parties might benefit from the applied methodology to analyze and improve similar cross-organizational healthcare processes. This methodology could also be extended to complex processes outside the healthcare setting, but to foster such use, future research should focus on developing guidelines for selecting the best-performing clustering algorithm in various settings.

References

Doherty, M., Abhishek, A., Hunter, D., & Ramirez Curtis, M. (2017). *Clinical manifestations and diagnosis of osteoarthritis* (UpToDate).

Dumas, M., La Rosa, M., Mendling, J., & Reijers, H. (2016). *Fundamentals of business process management*. Heidelberg: Springer.

Mans, R., Schonenberg, H., Leonardi, G., Panzarasa, S., Cavallini, A., Quaglini, S., et al. (2008). Process mining techniques: An application to stroke care. *Studies in Health Technology and Informatics, 136*, 573–578.

Mans, R. S., Schonenberg, H., Song, M., van der Aalst, W. M. P., & Bakker, P. J. M. (2009). Application of process mining in healthcare: A case study in a Dutch hospital. *Communications in Computer and Information Science, 25*, 425–438.

RIVM. (2018, June 20). *RIVM: Aandoeningen Welke aandoeningen hebben we in de toekomst?* Retrieved from volksgezondheidtoekomstverkenning: https://www.vtv2018.nl/aandoeningen#:~:text=In%202040%20zijn%20er%20bijvoorbeeld,in%20overgewicht%20in%20de%20bevolking

Rozinat, A., & van der Aalst, W. (2008). Conformance checking of processes based on monitoring real behavior. *Information Systems*, 64–95.

Song, M., Günther, C. W., & van der Aalst, W. M. P. (2009). Trace clustering in process mining. *Lecture Notes in Business Information Processing, 17*, 109–120.

Song, M., Yang, H., Siadat, S. H., & Pechenizkiy, M. (2013). A comparative study of dimensionality reduction techniques to enhance trace clustering performances. *Expert systems with Applications, 40*(9), 3722–3737.

Thaler, T., Ternis, S., Fettke, P., & Loos, P. (2015). A comparative analysis of process instance cluster techniques. In *International conference of Wirtschaftsinformatik* (pp. 423–437). Osnabrück.

Veiga, G. M., & Ferreira, D. R. (2010). Understanding spaghetti models with sequence clustering for ProM. *Lecture Notes in Business Information Processing, 43*, 92–103.

vom Brocke, J., Mendling, J., & Rosemann, M. (2021). Planning and scoping business process management projects and programs with the BPM Billboard. In J. vom Brocke, J. Mendling, & M. Rosemann (Eds.), *BPM cases. Digital innovation and business transformation in practice* (Vol. 2). New York: Springer.

Ensemble Deep Learning for Proactive Terminal Process Management at the Port of Duisburg "duisport"

Andreas Metzger, Johannes Franke, and Thomas Jansen

1 Introduction

Big data offers tremendous opportunities for innovation of transport processes and will have a profound economic and societal impact on mobility and logistics. As an example, with annual growth rates of 3.2% in passenger transport and 4.5% in freight transport in the EU (DG MOVE, 2018), transforming the current transport and logistics processes into processes that are significantly more efficient will have a major impact. Improvements in operational efficiency empowered by big data are expected to save as much as EUR 440 billion globally in terms of fuel and time, as well as 380 megatons of CO_2 emissions (OECD, 2013). The transport and logistics sector is ideally placed to benefit from big data technologies, as it already manages massive flows of goods and people while generating vast amounts of data (DHL, 2014).

One important big data technology that will deliver innovation in transport is *predictive analytics* (Metzger, Thornton, Valverde, Lopez, & Rublova, 2019). Predictive analytics is the next step from descriptive analytics (Khatri & Samuel, 2019): Where descriptive analytics aims to answer the question "what happened and why?" predictive analytics aims to answer the question "what will happen and when?" Predictive analytics in the form of predictive process monitoring supports business process management by facilitating proactive adaptation of running processes

A. Metzger (✉)
paluno (The Ruhr Institute for Software Technology), University of Duisburg-Essen, Duisburg, Germany
e-mail: andreas.metzger@paluno.uni-due.de

J. Franke · T. Jansen
duisport (Duisburger Hafen AG), Duisburg, Germany
e-mail: johannes.franke@duisport.de; thomas.jansen@duisport.de

J. vom Brocke et al. (eds.), *Business Process Management Cases Vol. 2*,
https://doi.org/10.1007/978-3-662-63047-1_12

(Francescomarino, Ghidini, Maggi, & Milani, 2018; Márquez-Chamorro, Resinas, & Ruiz-Cortés, 2018; Metzger et al., 2015).

Such adaptation can help prevent problems and mitigate the impact of those that do occur by dynamically replanning a running process instance (Mehdiyev, Emrich, Stahmer, Fettke, & Loos, 2017; Nunes, Santoro, Werner, & Ralha, 2018; Poll, Polyvyanyy, Rosemann, Röglinger, & Rupprecht, 2018). As an example, a delay in the delivery time for a freight transport process may incur contractual penalties (Gutierrez et al., 2013). If a delay is predicted during the execution of such a process, faster transport services (e.g., air delivery instead of road delivery) can be proactively scheduled to prevent the delay.

We present an industry case that employs big data for innovation in process management at duisport, the world's largest inland container port. The case presents one of the rare examples of how to apply deep learning in practice to develop a next-generation BPM approach that significantly contributes to strategy (vom Brocke, Mendling, & Rosemann, 2021). We focus on how ensemble deep learning facilitates proactive management of port terminal processes by delivering a predictive process monitoring system that provides decision support to the terminal operators. Deep learning entails artificial neural networks with many neurons and layers (Goodfellow, Bengio, & Courville, 2016). Ensemble deep learning combines many of these neural networks into more powerful prediction models (Polikar, 2006). Applying ensemble deep learning became feasible with the availability of large volumes of data, recent breakthroughs in learning algorithms, and the advent of powerful hardware. In particular, we customize and apply the ensemble deep learning approach presented in Metzger, Neubauer, Bohn, & Pohl (2019) to this industry case.

Referring to general business process management (BPM) terminology, our case focuses on the aspects of using information technology (Rosemann & vom Brocke, 2015) for process monitoring and control (Dumas, La Rosa, Mendling, & Reijers, 2018).

In what follows, Sect. 2 describes the situation faced in managing terminal processes. Section 3 elaborates on the actions taken to exploit ensemble deep learning for such management. Section 4 presents our results with respect to the impact on terminal operations, and Sect. 5 provides our lessons learned.

2 Situation Faced

Context and Challenges for Management of Terminal Processes The case we present is located at duisport, an inland container port that handles over four million containers per year. Duisport is situated in the middle of a large city, with close to a half-million inhabitants, and at the center of Germany's largest metropolitan region, the Rhine-Ruhr metropolitan region, with close to 10 million inhabitants. A multitude of roads, tracks, and waterways serve as entry and exit points for containers to and from the terminals and ports, and this transport infrastructure is shared with the metropolitan region.

Given duisport's location, any increase in container volumes that is due to growth in freight transport cannot be captured by a growth in space but requires improvement in terminal productivity. The duisport case focuses on improving the productivity of port terminals, which typically offer rail connections, trans-shipment tracks, and gantry cranes. The terminals are connected with other port areas and with more than 80 destinations in Europe and Asia, including daily rail and barge shuttles to the seaports of Antwerp and Rotterdam and more than 30 trains per week between China and duisport.

We developed the duisport case as part of the EU-funded Big Data Lighthouse project, TransformingTransport (Castiñera & Metzger, 2018). The project ran from January 2017 to July 2019 and brought together the knowledge and solutions of major European information technology and big data technology providers with the competence and experience of key European industry players and public bodies in the transport and logistics domain. TransformingTransport developed 13 pilot cases that demonstrated how various transport sectors can benefit from big data solutions and the increased availability of data.

Big Data as an Opportunity for Innovation in Process Management The main driver of the decision to explore big data technologies for innovative process management at duisport was the increased availability of data that resulted from the terminal equipment's instrumentation and digitization. To illustrate, the gantry cranes that move containers between trains and towing vehicles (trucks) produce data on about 100 variables in 5-s intervals. These variables include information on each crane's current state, position, speed, energy consumption, observed faults, as well as whether it transports a container.

We explored eight data sets and more than 30 million data entries from nine devices. Figure 1 illustrates some of the available data.

The figure shows a terminal and its equipment and a visualization of the integrated and aggregated data in the form of a heat map depicting the density of containers over the last 96 h (ranging from low density to high density). Density here refers to the number of containers that were positioned (including stacked over one another) at a particular geolocation during a particular timeframe.

With respect to the usefulness of predictions as input for proactive process adaptation, we had to address two important requirements: prediction accuracy and prediction earliness.

Requirement 1: Prediction Accuracy Informally, prediction accuracy characterizes the ability of a prediction technique to forecast as many actual problems as possible while generating as few false alarms as possible (Salfner, Lenk, & Malek, 2010). Accurate predictions forecast more actual problems, so they trigger more proactive process adaptations. Each missed prediction of an actual problem means one less opportunity to prevent or mitigate the problem. Accurate predictions also mean fewer false alarms and fewer unnecessary process adaptations that incur additional costs while not addressing actual problems (Metzger et al., 2012). In addition, a high

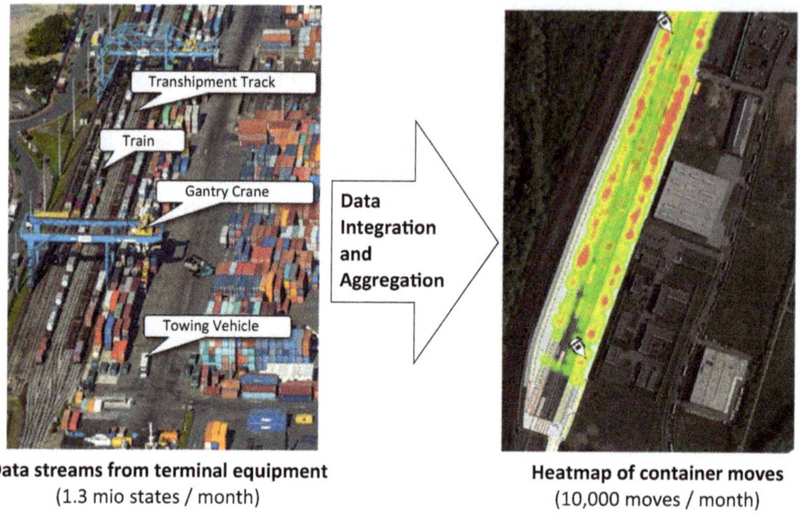

Fig. 1 Illustration of terminal data availability. The heatmap shows the container density (low density = "green"; high density = "red")

rate of false alarms will cause a terminal operator to distrust the predictions and so will not use them for decision-making.

Requirement 2: Prediction Earliness Predictions should be produced early during process execution to leave adequate time to make necessary adaptations. A process adaptation typically has a non-negligible latency; that is, it may take some time to make an adaptation and for it to take effect (Leitner, Ferner, Hummer, & Dustdar, 2013; Moreno, Cámara, Garlan, & Schmerl, 2018). For example, dispatching additional personnel to mitigate delays in container transports may take several hours. In addition, the later a process is adapted, the fewer options may be available, and if an adaptation made late in the process turns out to be ineffective, not much time remains for remedial actions. For example, while at the beginning of a transport process one may be able to transport a container by train instead of ship, once the container is aboard the ship, such a change is no longer feasible.

There is an important tradeoff between these two requirements for accuracy and earliness. Later predictions typically have greater accuracy because more information about the ongoing process instance is available, but the number of options for effective adaptations typically decreases. This tradeoff is depicted in Fig. 2.

3 Action Taken

Exploiting Advanced Analytics for Decision Support One of the main actions in leveraging the data availability described in Sect. 2 was to employ advanced

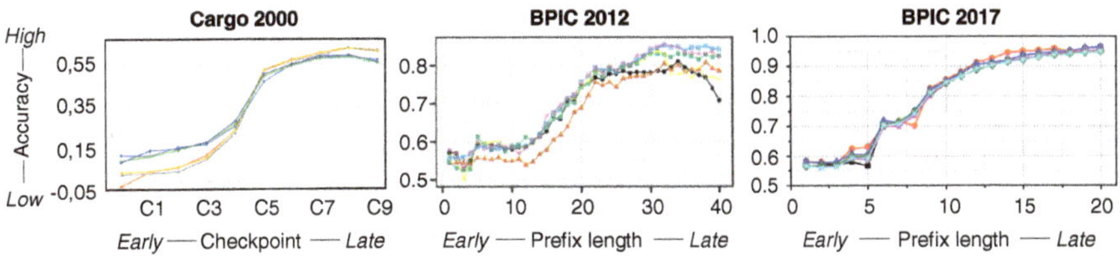

Fig. 2 Earliness vs. accuracy. The *y*-axis gives the accuracy for all predictions made at the indicated point; given as the MCC metric for Cargo 2000 (Metzger & Neubauer, 2018) and as the AUC metric for BPIC2012 (Teinemaa, Dumas, Rosa, & Maggi, 2019) and BPIC 2017 (Wang, Yu, & Sun, 2019). The different curves represent different concrete configurations of the prediction models

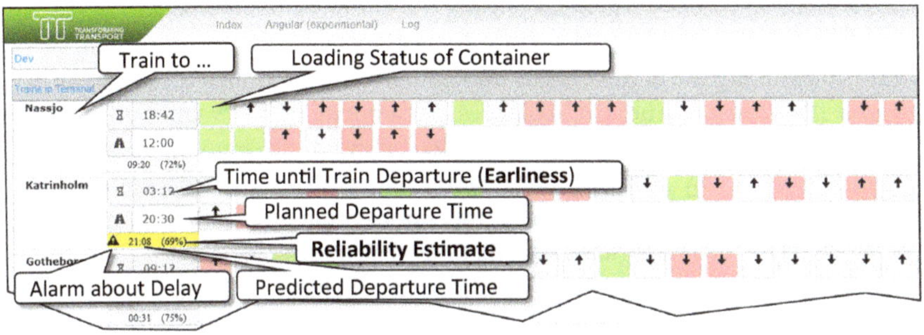

Fig. 3 Screenshot of Terminal Productivity Cockpit (TPC) prototype (excerpt)

analytics to provide decision support for terminal operators in managing terminal processes.

The key concept we prototypically developed in the duisport case is the *Terminal Productivity Cockpit* (TPC). The TPC exploits advanced data-processing and predictive analytics capabilities to support terminal operators in proactive decision-making and process adaptations. In particular, the TPC leverages ensemble deep learning techniques for predictive monitoring of business processes. The concrete processes that the TPC monitors involve the loading and offloading of containers onto trains. In its current application, the TPC predicts the overall outcome of these processes (and not single tasks, as proposed by Cabanillas, Ciccio, Mendling, and Baumgrass (2014)) and monitors these processes separately (and not in batches, as proposed by Pufahl and Weske (2016)).

Figure 3 shows a screenshot of the TPC prototype, which visualizes the current and predicted situation of three running processes in the duisport terminal (trains to Nassjo, Katrinholm, and Gothenburg).

The TPC shows the following information for each train that is in the terminal (in one of the seven trans-shipment tracks):

- *Loading status of container:* Each train can carry multiple containers, so the TPC shows the status for each of the containers scheduled to be on a train: An upward-facing arrow indicates that a container is to be offloaded, a downward-facing arrow indicates that a container is to be loaded onto the train, a green box around an arrow means a container has been successfully loaded onto the train, while a red box around an arrow indicates a potential problem in container loading.
- *Planned departure time:* A train's scheduled departure time is essential information, as fixed time slots are imposed by the use of the public train infrastructure, and the train may have to meet fixed departure windows of sea vessels if it connects to a seaport.
- *Time until train departure:* The TPC shows the time until the train is scheduled to depart so operators know how much time remains for any necessary adaptations in the running processes thus addressing the earliness requirement.
- *Predicted departure time:* The TPC shows the predicted departure time for the train considering the current status and data from the terminal's equipment.
- *Alarm about delay:* The TPC balances the amount of information displayed to satisfy the operators' need for information without causing cognitive overload (Endsley, 2011) by showing information about all trains and containers in a general overview and highlighting the information that indicates a problem. Thus, the TPC visibly indicates predictions that forecast a delay.
- *Reliability estimate:* The TPC also shows a reliability estimate (in %) for the predicted delay. Reliability estimates help operators distinguish between more and less reliable predictions on a case-by-case basis.

Together with the earliness indicators, reliability estimates can help operators decide whether to trust an individual prediction enough to adapt the running process (Metzger, Neubauer, et al., 2019; Teinemaa, Tax, de Leoni, Dumas, & Maggi, 2018). For example, in the situation visualized in Fig. 3, a terminal operator is informed that there is a 69% probability that the train to Katrinholm scheduled for 20:30 may be delayed until 21:08 and that there are 3:12 h remaining for any proactive action. Given the relatively low probability that the prediction is correct and the little time remaining for taking proactive actions (e.g., rescheduling the terminal workforce may take around 3 h), the terminal operator may decide not to act here.

Ensemble Deep Learning for Predictive Process Monitoring We compute the aforementioned predictions and reliability estimates using ensembles of deep learning models. Ensemble prediction is a meta-prediction technique in which prediction models' predictions are combined in to a single prediction (Polikar, 2006), which helps to increase prediction accuracy (Zhou, 2012). In our case, we measured a prediction accuracy for our ensemble of 0.884 (F1-Score), which was 40% more accurate than the best-performing single deep learning model in the ensemble. In addition to delivering increased accuracy, ensembles are used to compute reliability estimates for predictions (Bosnic & Kononenko, 2008; Metzger, Neubauer, et al., 2019).

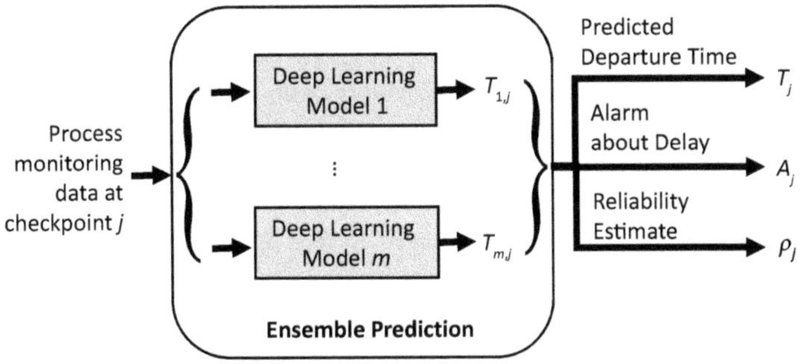

Fig. 4 Deep learning ensemble for predictive monitoring of transport processes

To build the ensembles, we use bagging (bootstrap aggregating (Dietterich, 2000)), which generates new training data sets by sampling from the whole training data set uniformly, so an individual deep learning model is trained for each of the new training data sets. We use bagging with a sample size of 60% of the whole training set to increase the diversity of the ensemble. Bagging facilitates the scalability of our approach, as training the individual models can happen in parallel.

Figure 4 provides an overview of our approach for predictive monitoring of transport processes, which we customized based on (Metzger, Neubauer, et al., 2019). Each of the ensemble's individual deep learning models predicts the train's departure time at any step in the process, called a *checkpoint*. These individual predictions are used to compute the three main pieces of information shown in the TPC: (1) the predicted train departure time T_j, (2) the alarm about a potential delay A_j, and (3) the reliability estimate for the alarm ρ_j.

In computing the predicted departure time, we follow the recommendations of Breiman (1996) and compute the mean value of the individual predictions $T_{i,j}$:

$$T_j = 1/m \cdot \sum\nolimits_{i=1, \cdots m} T_{i,j}$$

In computing the alarm A_j, we first determine for each of the individual predictions whether they indicate a delay by comparing the prediction with the scheduled departure time. Thus, $A_{i,j}$, = true indicates a predicted delay. Then, A_j is computed as a majority vote over $A_{i,j}$:

$$A_j = \{\text{true if } | i : A_{i,j} = \text{true}| \geq m/2; \text{false otherwise}\}$$

The reliability estimate ρ_j for A_j is computed as the fraction of predictions $A_{i,j}$ that predicted the delay, i.e.,

$$\rho_j = 1/m \cdot \mid i : A_{i,j} = \text{true} \mid$$

Deep Learning Models We used RNN-LSTMs (Recurrent Neural Networks—Long Short-term Memory) as the individual deep learning models in the ensemble.

LSTM cells allow the RNN to capture long-term dependencies in the data (Mehdiyev, Evermann, & Fettke, 2017; Tax, Verenich, Rosa, & Dumas, 2017), which is particularly important in the duisport case, as the processes may be long (up to 274 process steps). We used a shared multitasks layer architecture, as presented by Tax et al. (2017), because doing so provided good prediction accuracy for the individual RNN models. Our implementation is available online.[1]

RNN-LSTMs offer two key advantages to our approach: the ability to handle sequences of arbitrary lengths and scalability.

- *Sequences of Arbitrary Length:* RNNs can handle sequences of input data of any length (Goodfellow et al., 2016) and therefore can be used to make predictions for business processes that have any number of process activities. In contrast, other prediction models (e.g., random forests or multilayer perceptrons) may require special encoding of such sequences (Márquez-Chamorro et al., 2018; Metzger et al., 2015; Teinemaa et al., 2019), which requires additional manual engineering steps when building a predictive monitoring system. In addition, some of these encodings entail information loss that may limit prediction performance.
- *Scalability:* RNNs facilitate the scalability of our approach. If we have c checkpoints in the business process, a single RNN model can make predictions at any of these c checkpoints (Camargo, Dumas, & Rojas, 2019; Evermann, Rehse, & Fettke, 2017; Tax et al., 2017). If we want to avoid information loss, other prediction models (e.g., random forests or multilayer perceptrons) require training a prediction model for each of the c checkpoints. Performance measurements using a benchmark data set indicate a training time of about 8 minutes per checkpoint for multilayer perceptrons on a standard PC, while the training time for an RNN was 25 min in total.[2] RNNs provide better scalability if the process has many checkpoints.

4 Results Achieved

Feedback from Terminal Operators Demonstrations and structured interview sessions with terminal operators provided a qualitative assessment of the TPC with respect to its usefulness and usability. The general feedback was positive, although terminal operators initially felt overwhelmed by the amount of information displayed in the TPC and suggested providing only the information that could indicate a problem and its cause. As a result, the current version of the TPC shows only the information that is relevant to a problem and visibly highlights such alarms.

[1]https://github.com/Chemsorly/BusinessProcessOutcomePrediction

[2]Further performance increases are possible via special-purpose hardware and RNN implementations, reducing RNN training time to 8 min on GPUs and to 2 min on Tensor Processing Units (TPUs).

While terminal operators were interacting with the TPC, they became aware of the broad range of existing data about the terminal and the possibilities that data may provide in finding answers for hitherto unanswerable questions.

Potential Improvements in Terminal Operations To quantify the usefulness of the TPC, we analyzed the potential improvements in terminal operations with respect to terminal productivity and costs.

Productivity. To assess the improvement in the productivity of terminal operations, we measured the improvement in one business KPI: "Number of trains leaving the terminal on time." This KPI is a critical success factor since trains have designated time slots, and if a train misses its time slot, rescheduling is necessary and penalties for late deliveries can be levied. Using historic data about terminal operations, we estimated that the use of the TPC may increase the rate at which trains leave the terminal on time by up to 4.7%.

Costs. To estimate cost savings from using the TPC, we performed controlled experiments following the experimental design presented in (Metzger, Neubauer, et al., 2019), in which simplified cost models that considered various combinations of adaptation costs and penalties were used to represent situations that may be faced in practice. Experimental results from using the simplified cost models indicated that proactive process adaptations may lead to cost savings in 85% of the situations and average cost savings of 19%. Considering reliability estimates when deciding whether to initiate a proactive process adaptation delivered cost savings in another 10% of the situations, with additional average cost savings of 3.5%. Thus, the TPC can help terminal operators address the tradeoff between prediction accuracy and prediction timeliness.

5 Lessons Learned

To complement the qualitative and quantitative results from above, we present our two main lessons learned in developing the TPC.

Ensemble Deep Learning Contributed to Efficient Engineering of Data Analytics Solutions If enough good quality data is available—see also the second point, below—we experienced that ensemble deep learning techniques provide high prediction accuracy without the need for extensive hyper-parameter tuning. In addition, RNNs did not require special encoding of the sequential input data, which is needed if prediction models (e.g., multilayer perceptrons or random forests) are to be used.

Understanding, Integrating, and Cleansing Data Required Major Effort in Delivering Useful Data Analytics Solutions Data quality is an important concern in data analytics (Rahm & Do, 2000). We had to do extensive data cleansing because of missing data (e.g., because it was not available in digital form or because of network outages), lack of precision (caused by imprecise measurements), and timeliness (caused by delays in data collection). With respect to data integration, we often did not have control over the data from third parties (e.g., equipment manufacturers), or data collection and semantics drifted over the course of development. Other examples were telemetry data that used different coordinate systems (e.g., GPS vs. an internal coordinate system) and timestamps that were based on non-synchronized clocks. We estimated that understanding, integrating, and cleansing data consumed around 80% of the resources spent in the duisport pilot case. This high level of effort can be attributed to the TPC having been developed by integrating the required data sources in a somewhat ad-hoc fashion and using off-the-shelf machine-learning libraries. Using domain-specific data platforms and domain-specific machine learning components could significantly increase productivity in developing and deploying data analytics solutions (Zillner, Gomez, Garcia, & Curry, 2018).

6 Summary

The duisport case shows how ensemble deep learning can deliver profound innovations in transport processes. We demonstrate the feasibility of our deep learning approach by implementing it as part of a Terminal Productivity Cockpit prototype that provides decision support to terminal operators for proactive process adaptations. Our approach's viability is demonstrated by (estimated) improvements in a key business KPI and (experimentally measured) cost savings compared to terminal operations without using proactive adaptation. The desirability of our approach is confirmed by the positive feedback received from terminal operators.

Acknowledgments This research received funding from the EU's Horizon 2020 R&I program under grant agreements no. 731932 (TransformingTransport), 871493 (DataPorts), and 732630 (BDVe).

References

Bosnic, Z., & Kononenko, I. (2008). Comparison of approaches for estimating reliability of individual regression predictions. *Data & Knowledge Engineering, 67*(3), 504–516.

Breiman, L. (1996). Bagging predictors. *Machine Learning, 24*(2), 123–140.

Cabanillas, C., Ciccio, C. D., Mendling, J., & Baumgrass, A. (2014). Predictive task monitoring for business processes. In S. W. Sadiq, P. Soffer, & H. Völzer (Eds.), *Business Process Management – 12th International Conference, BPM* 2014, *Haifa, Israel, September 7–11, 2014. Proceedings*. Vol. 8659: Lecture Notes in Computer Science (pp. 424–432). Springer.

Camargo, M., Dumas, M., & Rojas, O. G. (2019). Learning accurate LSTM models of business processes. In T. T. Hildebrandt, B. F. van Dongen, M. Röglinger, & J. Mendling (Eds.), *17th International Conference on Business Process Management (BPM* 2019*)*. Vol. 11675: LNCS (pp. 286–302). Springer.

Castiñera, R., & Metzger, A. (2018). The transforming transport project – Mobility meets big data. In *7th Transport Research Arena (TRA* 2018*), Vienna*, April 16–19, 2018. Elsevier Transportation Research Procedia.

DG MOVE. (2018). EU transport in figures: Statistical pocketbook 2018, Directorate- General for Mobility and Transport (European Commission).

DHL. (2014). *Big data in logistics: A DHL perspective on how to move beyond the hype.*

Dietterich, T. G. (2000). *Ensemble methods in machine learning* (pp. 1–15). Berlin: Springer.

Dumas, M., La Rosa, M., Mendling, J., & Reijers, H. A. (2018). *Fundamentals of business process management* (2nd ed.). New York: Springer.

Endsley, M. R. (2011). *Designing for situation awareness: An approach to user-centered design* (2nd ed.). Boca Raton: CRC.

Evermann, J., Rehse, J., & Fettke, P. (2017). Predicting process behaviour using deep learning. *Decision Support Systems, 100.*

Francescomarino, C. D., Ghidini, C., Maggi, F. M., & Milani, F. (2018). Predictive process monitoring methods: Which one suits me best? In M. Weske, M. Montali, I. Weber, & J. vom Brocke (Eds.), *BPM, Sydney, Australia, September 9–14, 2018.* Vol. 11080: LNCS (pp. 462–479). Springer.

Goodfellow, I., Bengio, Y., & Courville, A. (2016). *Deep learning.* Cambridge, MA: MIT.

Gutierrez, A., Cassales Marquezan, C., Resinas, M., Metzger, A., Ruiz-Cortés, A., et al. (2013). Extending WS-Agreement to support automated conformity check on transport & logistics service agreements. In S. Basu, et al. (Eds.), *ICSOC*, Berlin, December 2–5, 2013. Vol. 8274: LNCS (pp. 567–574). Springer.

Khatri, V., & Samuel, B. M. (2019). Analytics for managerial work. *Communications of the ACM, 62*(4), 100.

Leitner, P., Ferner, J., Hummer, W., & Dustdar, S. (2013). Data-driven and automated prediction of service level agreement violations in service compositions. *Distributed and Parallel Databases, 31*(3), 447–470.

Márquez-Chamorro, A. E., Resinas, M., & Ruiz-Cortés, A. (2018). Predictive monitoring of business processes: A survey. *IEEE Transactions on Services Computing, 11*(6), 962–977.

Mehdiyev, N., Emrich, A., Stahmer, B. P., Fettke, P., & Loos, P. (2017). iprodict – Intelligent process prediction based on big data analytics. In Brambilla & T. Hildebrandt (Eds.), *BPM 2017 Industry Track, Barcelona, Spain, September 10–15, 2017.* Vol. 1985: CEUR Workshop Proceedings (pp. 13–24). CEUR-WS.org.

Mehdiyev, N., Evermann, J., & Fettke, P. (2017). A multi-stage deep learning approach for business process event prediction. In *Conference on Business Informatics (CBI* 2017*)*, Thessaloniki, July 24–27, 2017.

Metzger, A., Leitner, P., Ivanović, D., Schmieders, E., Franklin, R., Carro, M., et al. (2015). Comparing and combining predictive business process monitoring techniques. *IEEE Trans. on Systems Man Cybernetics: Systems, 45*(2), 276–290.

Metzger, A., & Neubauer, A. (2018). Considering non-sequential control flows for process prediction with recurrent neural networks. In *44th Euromicro Conference on Software Engineering and Advanced Applications (SEAA 2018), Prague, August 29–31, 2018.* IEEE Computer Society, 2018.

Metzger, A., Neubauer, A., Bohn, P., & Pohl, K. (2019). Proactive process adaptation using deep learning ensembles. In P. Giorgini & B. Weber (Eds.), *CAiSE* 2019, *Rome, June 3–7, 2019.* Vol. 11483: LNCS. Springer.

Metzger, A., Sammodi, O., & Pohl, K. (2012). Accurate proactive adaptation of service- oriented systems. In J. Camara, R. de Lemos, C. Ghezzi, & A. Lopes (Eds.), *Assurances for self-adaptive systems* (pp. 240–265). New York: Springer.

Metzger, A., Thornton, J., Valverde, F., Lopez, J. F. G., & Rublova, D. (2019). Predictive analytics and predictive maintenance innovation via big data: The case of TransformingTransport. In *13th Intelligent Transport Systems - European Congress (ITS Europe),* Brainport-Eindhoven, June 3–6, 2019.

Moreno, G. A., Cámara, J., Garlan, D., & Schmerl, B. R. (2018). Flexible and efficient decision-making for proactive latency-aware self-adaptation. *ACM Transactions on Autonomous and Adaptive Systems, 13*(1), 3:1–3:36.

Nunes, V. T., Santoro, F. M., Werner, C. M. L., & Ralha, C. G. (2018). Real-time process adaptation: A context-aware replanning approach. *IEEE Transactions on Systems, Man, and Cybernetics: Systems, 48*(1), 99–118.

OECD. (2013). Exploring data-driven innovation as a new source of growth – Mapping the policy issues raised by 'big data.

Polikar, R. (2006). Ensemble based systems in decision making. *IEEE Circuits and Systems Magazine, 6*(3), 21–45.

Poll, R., Polyvyanyy, A., Rosemann, M., Röglinger, M., & Rupprecht, L. (2018). Process forecasting: Towards proactive business process management. In M. Weske, M. Montali, Weber, & J. vom Brocke (Eds.), *BPM* 2018, *Sydney, Australia, September 9–14, 2018*. Vol. 11080: LNCS (pp. 496–512). Springer.

Pufahl, L., & Weske, M. (2016). Batch processing across multiple business processes based on object life cycles. In W. Abramowicz, R. Alt, & B. Franczyk (Eds.), *Business Information Systems – 19th International Conference, BIS* 2016, *Leipzig, July, 6–8, 2016, Proceedings*. Vol. 255: Lecture Notes in Business Information Processing (pp. 195–208). Springer.

Rahm, E., & Do, H. H. (2000). Data cleaning: Problems and current approaches. *IEEE Data Engineering Bulletin, 23*(4), 3–13.

Rosemann, M., & vom Brocke, J. (2015). The six core elements of business process management. In *Handbook on business process management 1* (pp. 105–122). New York: Springer.

Salfner, F., Lenk, M., & Malek, M. (2010). A survey of online failure prediction methods. *ACM Computing Surveys, 42*(3), 10:1–10:42.

Tax, N., Verenich, I., Rosa, M. L., & Dumas, M. (2017). Predictive business process monitoring with LSTM neural networks. In E. Dubois & K. Pohl (Eds.), *CAiSE* 2017, *Essen, June 12–16, 2017*, Vol. 10253: LNCS. Springer, 2017.

Teinemaa, I., Dumas, M., Rosa, M. L., & Maggi, F. M. (2019). Outcome-oriented predictive process monitoring: Review and benchmark. *ACM Transactions on Knowledge Discovery from Data (TKDD), 13*.

Teinemaa, I., Tax, N., de Leoni, M., Dumas, M., & Maggi, F. M. (2018). Alarm-based prescriptive process monitoring. In M. Weske, M. Montali, I. Weber, & J. vom Brocke (Eds.), *BPM Forum* 2018, *Sydney, September 9–14, 2018*, Vol. 329: LNBIP (pp. 91–107). Springer.

vom Brocke, J., Mendling, J., & Rosemann, M. (2021). Planning and scoping business process management projects and programs with the BPM Billboard. In J. vom Brocke, J. Mendling, & M. Rosemann (Eds.), *BPM cases. Digital innovation and business transformation in practice* (Vol. 2). New York: Springer.

Wang, D. Yu, C. L., & Sun, X. (2019). Outcome-oriented predictive process monitoring with attention-based bidirectional LSTM neural networks. In E. Bertino, C. K. Chang, P. Chen, E. Damiani, M. Goul, & K. Oyama (Eds.), *IEEE International Conference on Web Services, ICWS 2019, Milan, July 8–13, 2019* (pp. 360–367). IEEE.

Zhou, Z.-H. (2012). *Ensemble methods: Foundations and algorithms*. London: Chapman and Hall/CRC.

Zillner, S., Gomez, J., Garcia, A., & Curry, E. (Eds.). (2018). *Data for artificial intelligence for European economic competitiveness and societal progress*. BDVA Position Statement.

Accurate Predictions, Invalid Recommendations: Lessons Learned at the Dutch Social Security Institute UWV

Marcus Dees, Massimiliano de Leoni, Wil M. P. van der Aalst, and Hajo A. Reijers

1 Introduction

Process-aware recommender systems ("PAR systems" hereafter) are a new breed of information systems that predict how the executions of processes will evolve in the future and determine those that are most likely to fail to meet desired levels of performance (e.g., costs, deadlines, customer satisfaction). Recommendations are provided regarding effective contingency actions that should be enacted to recover from risky executions. PAR systems are expert systems that run in the background and continuously monitor the execution of processes, predict their future, and sometimes provide recommendations. Conforti, de Leoni, Rosa, van der Aalst, and ter Hofstede (2015) and Schobel and Reichert (2017) discuss examples of PAR systems.

A substantial body of research on process monitoring and prediction includes the surveys by Teinemaa, Dumas, Rosa, and Maggi (2017) and Márquez-Chamorro, Resinas, and Ruiz-Cortés (2018), but as Márquez-Chamorro et al. (2018) indicate,

M. Dees (✉)
Uitvoeringsinstituut Werknemersverzekeringen (UWV), Amsterdam, The Netherlands
e-mail: marcus.dees@uwv.nl

M. de Leoni
University of Padova, Padova, Italy
e-mail: deleoni@math.unipd.it

W. M. P. van der Aalst
RWTH Aachen University, Aachen, Germany

Eindhoven University of Technology, Eindhoven, The Netherlands
e-mail: wvdaalst@pads.rwth-aachen.de

H. A. Reijers
Utrecht University, Utrecht, The Netherlands
e-mail: h.a.reijers@uu.nl

J. vom Brocke et al. (eds.), *Business Process Management Cases Vol. 2*,
https://doi.org/10.1007/978-3-662-63047-1_13

"little attention has been given to providing recommendations. [p. 17]" In fact, how process participants would use these predictions to recover from those executions that cause problems is often overlooked. It seems that process participants are tacitly assumed to make the "right decision" about the best corrective actions for each case. This view also holds for approaches based on mitigation/flexibility "by design" (Lhannaoui, Kabbaj, & Bakkoury, 2013). Unfortunately, the assumption that an effective corrective action will be chosen is not always met in reality. Interventions are often selected based primarily on human judgment, which naturally relies on the subjective perception of the process instead of objective facts.

In particular, an organization will profit from using a PAR system only if the system makes accurate decisions and the organization bases its decisions on the system's decision. Considerable attention is paid to making accurate predictions—particularly the proper use of data, measuring accuracy, and so on—but we show that the approach to making effective decisions is just as important as making accurate predictions. Both parts are essential ingredients of an overall solution.

This case study reports on a field experiment that we conducted at UWV, a Dutch governmental agency. The case study is inspirational in that it outlines how to enrich BPM programs through PAR systems (vom Brocke, Mendling, & Rosemann, 2021), and it also serves to study challenges in leveraging the value of PAR systems for decision-making.

UWV provides, among other things, financial support to Dutch residents who lose their jobs and seek new employment. Several subjects ("customers" hereafter) unintentionally receive more unemployment benefits than they are entitled to. Such errors are eventually detected—usually after several months—triggering a "reclamation" event. To retrieve the amount of excess support from a customer is difficult, time-consuming, and, often unsuccessful—not to mention upsetting for the customer, who may not have the necessary funds, given his or her joblessness. In this context, an effective recommender system should be able to detect the customers who are most likely to cause a reclamation event, thus providing operational support for UWV in preventing the provision of excess benefits.

Research at UWV has shown that the main cause of a reclamation event lies with the customer making a mistake when informing UWV about his or her other income. Therefore, interventions should be aimed at preventing customers from providing incorrect income information. To follow up on this idea, we developed a predictor module that relies on machine-learning techniques to monitor and identify the subjects who are most likely to receive excess support.

UWV's stakeholders considered several interventions to prevent reclamation events and chose to send an e-mail to the subjects who were suspected of being at higher risk as a field experiment. The contents of the e-mail were determined by previous research at UWV showing the types of errors customers make filling in the form. The e-mail is sent just before the customers would need to provide information about their income to UWV. The results showed that risky customers were detected well, but no significant reduction in the number of reclamations occurred, so the intervention did not achieve the desired effect of preventing reclamation events. Our findings show the importance of conducting research on the interventions themselves, even before they are tested.

2 Situation Faced

UWV is the social security institute of the Netherlands and is responsible for the implementation of a number of employee-related types of insurances. One of the processes that UWV executes is the unemployment benefits process. When residents in the Netherlands become unemployed, they file a request with UWV, which then decides whether they are entitled to benefits. When requests are accepted, these customers receive monthly benefits until they find new jobs or the maximum period for their entitlements is reached. However, sometimes the customers make errors on their other-income forms, resulting in overpayment of benefits until the errors are discovered.

The process for paying unemployment benefits is bound by legal rules. UWV's customers and employees are required to perform certain steps for each benefit month. Figure 1 depicts a typical scenario of a customer who receives benefits for a particular benefit month, along with the steps that are executed in each month until the process is complete and any errors are discovered. Before a customer can receive a payment of benefits for a benefit month, he or she must send an income form to UWV that specifies whether the customer has received income of any kind for that benefit month and, if so, how much. The benefits are adjusted as a function of such income, up to no benefits if the customer's income exceeds the amount of benefits to which he or she is entitled.

Figure 1 shows that, in August, when any error related to the benefit month of June is discovered, 2 months of benefits (June and July) have already been paid based on erroneous information. Although the amounts to be reclaimed are often comparatively small—usually, a few hundred Euros—about 12,000 customers per month are subjects of reclamations, leading to significant losses if the overpayments are not reclaimed.

The main cause of reclamation events is customers' failing to fill in the correct amount of other income earned on the income form. If the customer has not received a payslip, he or she estimates this income. Even with a payslip, customers often make mistakes, as the required amount is the social security wages, not the gross salary or the salary after taxes. Customers who receive their payslips every 4 weeks, rather than every month, may also err in calculating the monthly amount, which,

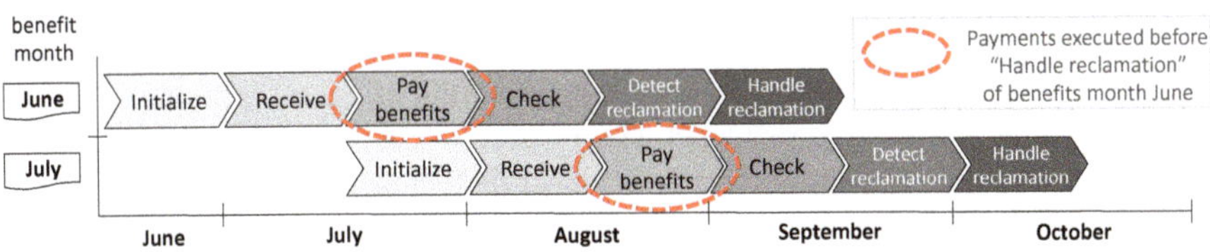

Fig. 1 An example of the activities UWV executes related to providing unemployment benefits to a customer for the months of June and July. (The year is irrelevant.) Each row is related to the activities that must be performed to handle an income form for the month for which benefits are to be paid ("benefit month"). The work for each benefit month takes several months to complete; for example, the work for the benefit month of June is finally completed in September

except for February in most years, is higher than the amount for 4 weeks. Other factors, like vacation money or pension-related income, can also make it difficult to determine the correct amount.

Since the reclamations are caused by customers filling in income forms incorrectly, UWV's only recourse is to prevent customers from making mistakes when they fill in the income form. UWV determined that targeting only the customers who were most likely to make an error on the form was the most fiscally responsible approach, along with the approach least likely to irritate or over-communicate with customers who were unlikely to make errors. Therefore, a recommender system that could identify customers who had a high risk of making an error and could propose interventions would be helpful.

3 Action Taken

Figure 2 shows our approach to the development and testing of a PAR system for UWV. The approach is in line with the BPM Lifecycle Dumas, Rosa, Mendling, and Reijers (2018) presented. Steps 1a and 1b of the approach are to analyze and identify the organizational issue (i.e., process analysis), which, as described in Sect. 2, was related to needless reclamation events.

The second step was to develop a recommender system consisting of a predictor module (Step 2a) and a set of interventions (Step 2b) (i.e., process redesign). The predictor module identifies the cases on which the intervention should be applied, that is, those with the highest likelihood of leading to a reclamation event. (Section 3.1 describes the predictor module setup.) Then a set of interventions is selected in concert with stakeholders to ensure the stakeholders' support, not only for the intervention but also for the changes necessary to implement it. Of several possible interventions put forward, one was chosen (Step 3) that did not strain the limited availability of resources at UWV for executing an experiment. Section 3.2 elaborates on the process of collecting ideas for interventions and selecting the intervention for the field experiment.

Step 4 was to design a field experiment (i.e., process implementation). The field experiment was set up as an A/B test (Kohavi & Longbotham, 2017).

In an A/B test, one or more interventions are tested under the same conditions, to find the alternative that best delivers the desired effect. In our field experiment, the intervention could be tested in the natural setting of the process environment. The objective of the field experiment was to determine the effect of applying an intervention to cases at a specific risk level with respect to whether a customer triggers a reclamation event (the process metric). All other factors that could play a role in the field experiment were controlled as far as possible in our business environment. Under these conditions, the field experiment would show whether a causal relationship existed between the intervention and the change in the values of the process metrics. Section 3.3 describes the setup for the UWV study.

Analysis of the results of the field experiment (Step 5) determined whether the intervention had the desired effect (i.e., process monitoring). Sections 4.1 and 4.2

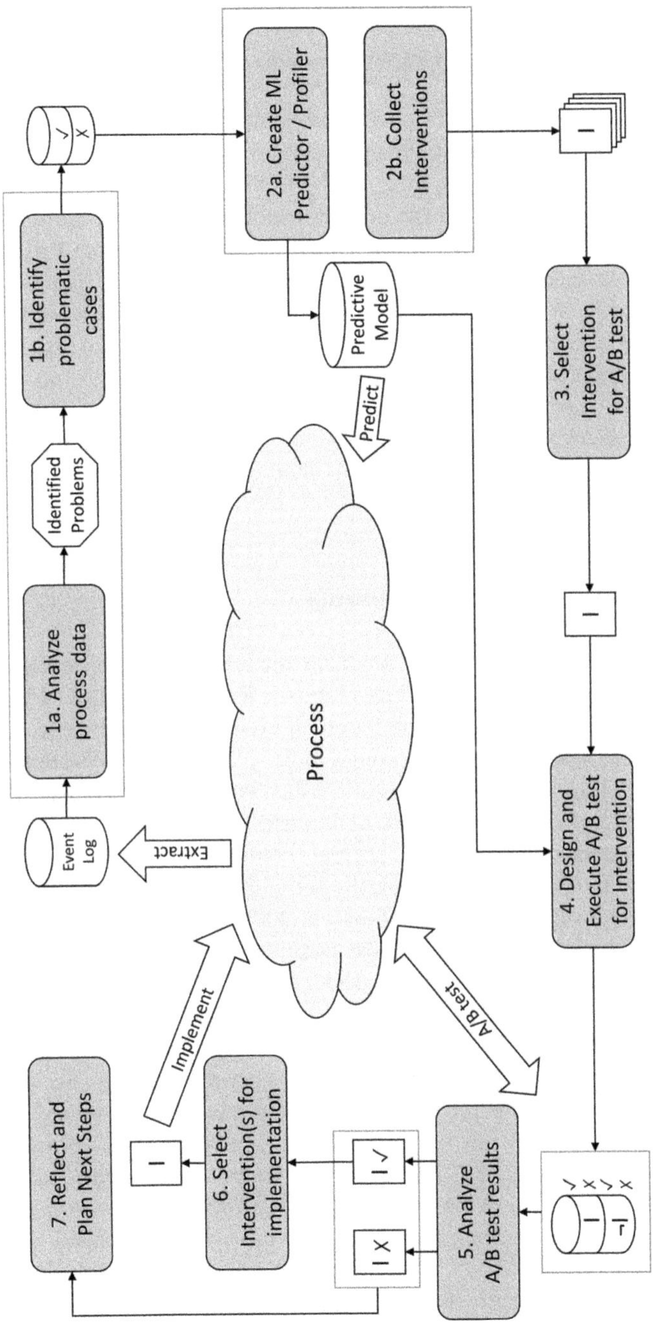

Fig. 2 Overview of the steps that make up the research method for one improvement cycle. "I" refers to "Intervention"

contain the analysis of the intervention and the predictor module, respectively. If the intervention had an effect, then both the direction of the effect (i.e., whether the intervention leads to better or worse performance) and the size of the effect must be calculated. If the intervention had the desired effect, it would be implemented as part of the process (Step 6).

The final step (Step 7) is the reflective phase in which the lessons learned from the execution of the approach are discussed. Section 5 contains the lessons learned for the UWV case.

The interventions, along with the predictor module from Step 2a, make up the PAR system. After the decision to implement an intervention, the PAR system's predictor module must be updated. Changing the process also implies that the situation under which the predictions are made has changed, so a period of time after the change takes effect should be reserved to gather a new set of historic process data on which the predictor module can be retrained.

This research method requires that many choices be made, such as which organizational issues will be tackled and which interventions will be tested. Prior to making a choice, the research participants should be aware of any assumptions or biases that could influence their choices.

3.1 Building the Predictor Module

The prediction is based on training a predictor module that uses historical data, for which we used the data-mining techniques Logistic Regression and ADA Boost. The choice to use these two techniques was based on experience with these techniques at UWV. Both techniques were tuned through hyper-parameter optimization (Claesen & Moor, 2015). To this end, UWV historical data was split into a training set with 80% of the cases and a test set with 20% of the cases. The models were trained with a fivefold cross-validation that used several configurations of the algorithm's parameters. The models were tested on the set of 20% of the cases. The Receiver Operator Characteristic (ROC) curve (Fawcett, 2006), which measures the model's quality, shows for every percentage of false-positives the percentage of true positives that the model finds. The area under the ROC curve (AUC) summarizes a model's total performance. The models are ranked using the AUC, and the models with the highest AUC value were selected for the predictions to be used for the experiment.

The most important features of the predictive models such as the number of occurrences of a first income form and whether the most recent payment was done automatically or manually are process-related. Leaving out all process-related features would reduce the AUC value by 8%, so ignoring the process nature of cases would be detrimental to the predictive models' quality.

The predictor module, implemented as a stand-alone application in Python, leveraged the sci-kit learn library (Pedregosa et al., 2011) to access the data-mining functionality. In the UWV case, the historical data was extracted from the company's systems related to the execution of every activity for 73,153 customers who concluded the reception of unemployment benefits between July 2015 and July

2017. Space limitations prevent us from providing details on how the prediction module was built, but details are available in the technical report (Dees, de Leoni, van der Aalst, & Reijers, 2019) that accompanies this case description.

3.2 Collecting and Selecting the Interventions

After three brainstorming sessions with 15 of UWV's employees and two of its team managers, the choice of the intervention was made based on the experience and expectations of these stakeholders. The goal of the intervention was to prevent customers from putting the wrong amount on the income form. The sessions initially put forward three types of interventions based on the actors who are involved in the intervention (i.e., the customer, the UWV employee, the last employer):

1. An intervention that supports the customer in advance of filling in the income form
2. An intervention in which the UWV employee verifies the information provided by the customer on the income form, and, if necessary, corrects it after contacting the customer
3. An intervention in which the last employer of the UWV customer is asked to supply relevant information more quickly so the UWV can promptly verify the accuracy of the information the customer provides on the income form

An intervention can be executed only once a month, between receipt of the two income forms for two consecutive months. In the final brainstorming session, the stakeholders opted for option 1—supporting the customer in fill out the income form correctly. In the stakeholders' experience, their support with filling out the form helps customers reduce the chance of incurring reclamations.

Only one intervention was selected for the experiment as a result of the limited availability of resources at UWV that arose from temporary under-staffing and an uneven capacity demand throughout the month. The selected intervention entails proactively providing customers, whom the predictor model identified as being most likely to make errors, with information about how errors are often made in filling out the income form. The UWV employees indicated that most mistakes were made regarding topics related to the definition of social security wages, the definition of unemployment, and receiving pay every 4 weeks instead of monthly.

Next, the medium through which the customer would be informed had to be determined: a physical letter, an e-mail, or a phone call from a UWV employee. To keep costs low, sending the information by e-mail was chosen. An editorial employee of UWV determined the phrasing, and the e-mail contained hyperlinks to pages on the UWV website to allow customers to access additional information if they needed it. The customers who received the e-mail were not informed about the experiment. A tool UWV uses to send e-mails to large numbers of customers at the same time provided the functionality to determine whether the e-mail was received—that is, without bouncing—and whether the e-mail was opened. Since the timing of sending the message can influence its success, it was sent on the day preceding the last workday of the calendar month in which the predictor module marked the customer as risky. This approach increased the likelihood that the customer would read the message before filling in the income form for the subsequent month.

3.3 Setting Up and Executing the Field Experiment

The field experiment was used to determine whether using the PAR system's design for prediction and intervention would reduce the number of reclamation events. Specifically, we first determined the number and the nature of the customers who were to be monitored. Then these customers were split into two groups: one on which the PAR system was applied (the experimental group) and one on which the PAR system was not applied (i.e., the control group).

We conducted the experiment with 86,850 cases handled by UWV's Amsterdam branch. These customers were receiving benefits and were not the 73,153 customers who were used to train the predictor module. Of the 86,850 cases, 35,812 were part of the experimental group. The intervention was executed on 30 August 2017, 28 September 2017, and 30 October 2017 by sending the e-mail. The predictor was used to compute the probability of a reclamation event for the 35,812 cases of the experimental group. The probability was higher than 0.8 for 6747 cases, and the intervention was executed for those cases.

4 Results Achieved

The intervention did not have a preventive effect, even though the risk prediction was reasonably accurate. Sections 4.1 and 4.2 describe the results achieved.

4.1 The Intervention Did Not Have a Preventive Effect

Figure 3 shows the results of the field experiment in terms of the percentage of reclamations observed in each group. The number of reclamations did not significantly decrease when the system was used, as they decreased from 4.0% without the intervention to 3.8% with the intervention. The effectiveness of the system as a whole is therefore 0.2%.

The PAR system deemed 6747 cases as risky and were sent the e-mail. Out of these 6747 cases, 4065 (60%) received and opened the e-mails and 2682 (40%) either did not receive it (i.e., the e-mail "bounced") or did not open it. Since there were almost no bounces, most of the 40% did not open it. Among the customers who did receive the e-mail, only 294 clicked on the links and accessed UWV's website, and 10.9% of those had a reclamation event in the subsequent month, which is more than 2.5 times the average and around 1.7 times the frequency among customers who

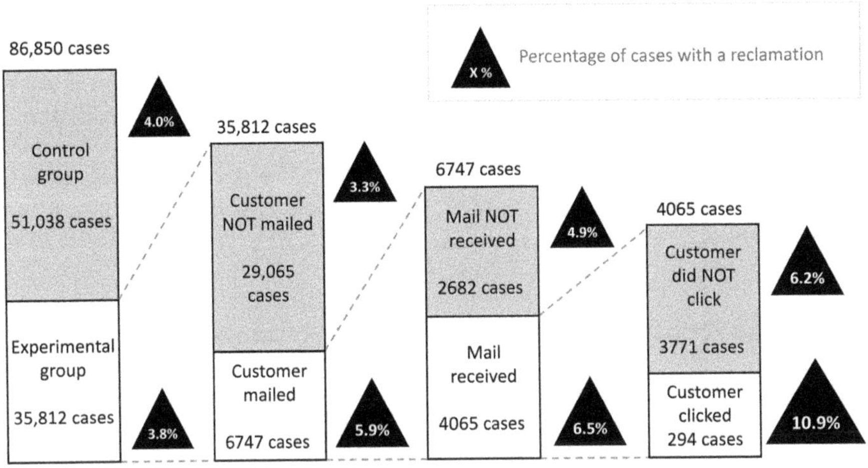

Fig. 3 The number of cases and the percentage of cases that had a reclamation event for all groups. The results show that risky customers were identified, but the intervention did not solve the problem

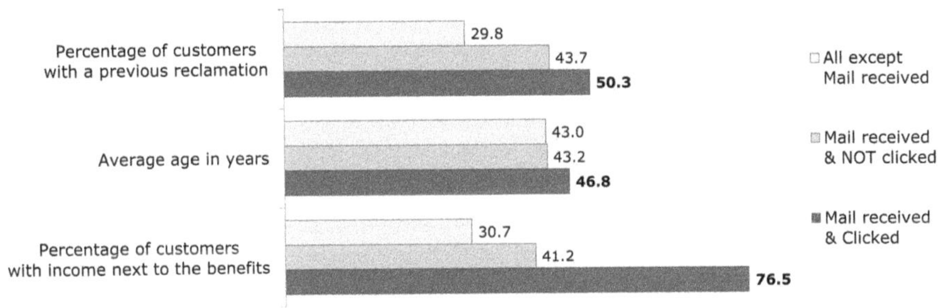

Fig. 4 Comparison of the characteristics of customers who did not receive the e-mail, those who received it but did not click the link, and those who accessed UWV's website through the e-mail's link

opened the e-mail but did not click the links. Therefore, accessing additional information seemed to increase the chances of error!

We conducted a comparative analysis among the customers who did not receive the e-mail, i.e., the e-mail bounced, those who received it but did not click the links, and those who clicked on the links and reached the website. The results of the comparative analysis, shown in Fig. 4, indicate that 76.5% of the customers who clicked the e-mail's links had income in addition to the benefits. (Recall that customers can receive benefits even while employed if their income is reduced, in which case they receive benefits for the difference.) Our results are reasonable, as mistakes are more frequent when filling the income form is more complex, as when there is some other income instead of none. Among the customers who clicked on the e-mail's link, 50.3% had a previous reclamation, and they are on average

3.5 years older than those who did not click on the link, which is a statistically significant difference.

The results suggest that e-mailing is counterproductive or at least that there was a positive correlation between exploring the additional information provided and being involved in a reclamation in the subsequent month. To a smaller extent, 6.2% of the customers who received the e-mail but did not click the links had reclamations versus a mean of 3.8–4.0%. Clearly, the intervention did not achieve the intended goal.

4.2 The Predicted Risk Was Reasonably Accurate

The analysis shows that the intervention did not lead to improvement. We sought to determine whether this result was caused by inaccurate predictions, an ineffective intervention, or both. This section reports on our analysis of the quality of the predictor module, for which we use the cumulative lift curve (Ling & Li, 1998). We chose this measure because of the imbalance in the data, as Ling and Li (1998) advised. As mentioned in Sect. 2, every month only 4% of UWV's customers are involved in reclamation events.

In cases of unbalanced data sets (e.g., between customers who experience reclamation events and those who do not), precision and recall are generally unsuitable for assessing the quality of predictors. In addition, because of the low cost of sending an e-mail, false-negatives, referring to customers with undetected reclamations during the subsequent month, occur more often than false-positives, that is, customers who are incorrectly predicted as having reclamations during the subsequent month.

Figure 5 shows the cumulative lift curve for the case study at UWV. The rationale is that, in a set of *x*% of randomly selected customers, one expects to observe *x*% of the total number of reclamations. The figure shows that, in our case, the predictions are better than random. For example, the 10% of customers with the highest risk of having a reclamation accounted for 19% of all reclamations, which is roughly twice what could be expected in a random sample.

In summary, although the prediction technique can certainly be improved, the prediction was reasonably effective (cf. Sect. 3.1). However, because the system as a whole did not bring about a significant improvement, we conclude that the lack of a significant effect was likely caused by the ineffectiveness of the intervention.

5 Lessons Learned

The experiment proved to be unsuccessful. While the predictions were reasonably accurate, the intervention of sending an e-mail to predicted high-risk customers did not reduce the number of reclamations. In fact, the group of customers who received the e-mail and clicked on its link to more information had twice as many reclamations as the average population. Section 5.1 elaborates on the reasons the

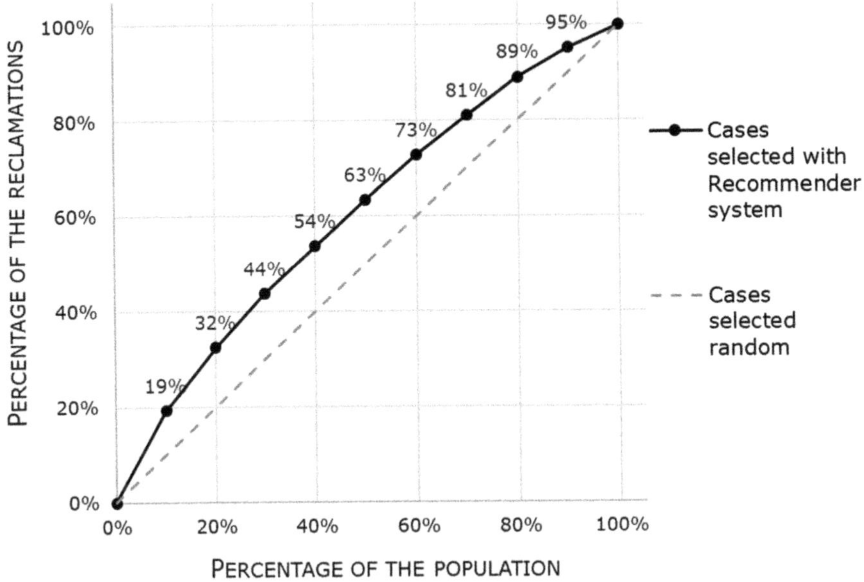

Fig. 5 The cumulative lift curve shows that using the recommender system is superior to using a random selection of cases to predict reclamation events

intervention did not work, while Sect. 5.2 focuses on the lessons learned and explains how the research methodology should be updated.

5.1 Why Did the Intervention Fail to Work?

One of the reasons the intervention was not successful could be related to the timing of sending the e-mail, as different timing during the month could have been more appropriate. However, timing does not explain why only 294 of the 6747 cases acted on the e-mail by clicking the links. Other reasons may be that the customers found the e-mail's message unclear or that the links in the e-mail body pointed to confusing information on the UWV website, as among the group of 294 cases who clicked the links to get more information, reclamations actually occurred 2.5 times as often.

The communication channel could also be part of the cause. Sending the message by letter or by calling the customer might have worked better. We heard several comments from stakeholders to the effect that they did not expect the failure because, for example, "after speaking to a customer about how to fill in the income form, almost no mistakes are made by that customer." In this regard, the UWV case sets a very valuable example that technology does not deliver value to a process per se but that it needs to fit the context to support specific objectives and that it needs close alignment with other capability areas (vom Brocke et al., 2021).

5.2 What Should Be Done Differently Next Time?

We learned that the A/B testing is beneficial in assessing the effectiveness of interventions. The involvement of stakeholders and other process participants, including UWV's customers, helped to achieve our goal of testing an intervention, even though the results did not achieve the expected results. We learned a number of lessons about how to adjust our approach that we will put in place for the next round of testing:

1. Creating a predictor module requires the selection of independent features as inputs to build the predictive model. Our analysis of the reasons for the intervention's failure will help us to derive new features to be incorporated when training the predictor. For instance, the features presented in Fig. 4 can be used to train a better predictor, such as, for the UWV case, a Boolean feature for whether a customer has income other than the benefits.
2. The insights derived from the analysis can also be useful in putting forward other possible interventions. For instance, an intervention could be a manual check of the income form when a customer has had a reclamation in the previous month. This intervention is derived from the feature representing the number of executions of Detect Reclamation, as discussed in Sect. 4.1.
3. The interventions for the A/B test (Step 3 in Fig. 2) should be pre-assessed. The intervention used in our experiment provides information to the customers related to filling the income form, but, before running the test, we could have checked historical event data on whether the average number of reclamations decreased when customers were provided information and support in completing the income form. If we had done this, we could have avoided running a test that was destined to fail.
4. Since a control group was compared with an experimental group on which the system was employed, and the comparison was measured end-to-end, it is impossible to state the reason for the intervention's failure beyond just observing it. For instance, we should have used questionnaires to assess the reasons for the failure: the customers who received the e-mail should have been asked why they did not click on the links or, if they did click on them, why they still made mistakes. Clearly, questionnaires are not applicable to all kinds of interventions, but some methods could have been used to acquire the information needed to analyze reasons for the intervention's ineffectiveness.
5. It is unlikely that the methodology in Sect. 3 provided complete results after one cycle. The methodology should be reiterated in multiple cycles. In fact, this finding is compliant with the principle of action research, which is based on the idea of continuous improvement cycles (Cronholm & Goldkuhl, 2003; Rowell, Riel, & Polush, 2017).
6. Although multiple cycles are useful, just one cycle took a few months to be carried out, so the cycle needs to be repeatable at a higher speed with multiple interventions tested at each cycle. In addition, if an intervention is clearly ineffective, its testing should be stopped without waiting for the cycle to end.

All the lessons learned share one theme: *Accurate predictions are crucial, but their effect is nullified if it is not matched by effective recommendations that are based on evidence from historical and/or experimental data.*

5.3 Conclusion

When one builds a process-aware recommender system, both the predictor module and the recommender parts of the system must be effective for the whole system to be effective. In our case, the predictor module was sufficiently accurate, but the intervention did not have the desired effect. The lessons learned from the field experiment have been used in building an updated research method that uses high-speed iterations with multiple interventions. Systematic support will be needed for each step of the approach to meet these requirements.

We plan to improve the predictor module by using different techniques and leveraging contextual information about the customers and their history. Our analysis showed that, for example, the presence of some monetary income next to the benefits is strongly related to reclamations. We want to use evidence from the process executions and insights from building the predictor module, to select one or more interventions to be tested in a new experiment.

We aim to devise a new technique that finds the best intervention based on the specific case. Different cases might require different interventions, and the choice of the best intervention should be automatically derived from the historical facts recorded in the system's event logs. In other words, the system will rely on machine-learning techniques that (1) reason about past executions to find the interventions that have generally been effective in the current case and (2) make recommendations accordingly.

References

Claesen, M., & Moor, B. D. (2015). *Hyperparameter search in machine learning*. CoRR abs/1502.02127.

Conforti, R., de Leoni, M., Rosa, M. L., van der Aalst, W. M. P., & ter Hofstede, A. H. (2015). A recommendation system for predicting risks across multiple business process instances. *Decision Support Systems, 69*, 1–19. https://doi.org/10.1016/j.dss.2014.10.006.

Cronholm, S., & Goldkuhl, G. (2003). Understanding the practices of action research. In *The 2nd European conference on research methods in business and management*.

Dees, M., de Leoni, M., van der Aalst, W. M. P., & Reijers, H. A. (2019). *What if process predictions are not followed by good recommendations?* arXiv e-prints arXiv:1905.10173, 1905.10173.

Dumas, M., Rosa, M. L., Mendling, J., & Reijers, H. A. (2018). *Fundamentals of business process management* (2nd ed.). New York: Springer. https://doi.org/10.1007/978-3-662-56509-4.

Fawcett, T. (2006). An introduction to roc analysis. *Pattern Recognition Letters, 27*(8), 861–874.

Kohavi, R., & Longbotham, R. (2017). *Online controlled experiments and a/B testing* (pp. 922–929). Boston, MA: Springer US.

Lhannaoui, H., Kabbaj, M. I., & Bakkoury, Z. (2013). Towards an approach to improve business process models using risk management techniques. In *2013 8th international conference on intelligent systems: Theories and applications (SITA)* (pp. 1–8).

Ling, C. X., & Li, C. (1998). Data mining for direct marketing: Problems and solutions. In *Proceedings of the fourth international conference on knowledge discovery and data mining (KDD-98)* (pp. 73–79). New York City, New York, USA, August 27–31.

Márquez-Chamorro, A. E., Resinas, M., & Ruiz-Cortés, A. (2018). Predictive monitoring of business' processes: A survey. *IEEE Trans Services Computing, 11*(6), 962–977.

Pedregosa, F., Varoquaux, G., Gramfort, A., Michel, V., Thirion, B., Grisel, O., et al. (2011). Scikit-learn: Machine learning in Python. *Journal of Machine Learning Research, 12*, 2825–2830.

Rowell, L. L., Riel, M. M., & Polush, E. Y. (2017). *Defining action research: On dialogic spaces for constructing shared meanings* (pp. 85–101). New York: Palgrave Macmillan US.

Schobel, J., & Reichert, M. (2017). A predictive approach enabling process execution recommendations. In *Advances in intelligent process-aware information systems – Concepts, methods, and technologies* (pp. 155–170). Cham: Springer International. https://doi.org/10.1007/978-3-319-52181-7.

Teinemaa, I., Dumas, M., Rosa, M. L., & Maggi, F. M. (2017). Outcome-oriented predictive process monitoring: Review and benchmark. CoRR abs/1707.06766, 1707.06766.

vom Brocke, J., Mendling, J., & Rosemann, M. (2021). Planning and scoping business process management projects and programs with the BPM Billboard. In J. vom Brocke, J. Mendling, & M. Rosemann (Eds.), *BPM cases. Digital innovation and business transformation in practice* (Vol. 2). New York: Springer.

Realizing the Benefits of Process Improvement: The Case of Queensland University of Technology

Imesha Denagama Vitharanage, Denise Toman, Wasana Bandara, and Rehan Syed

1 Introduction

Globalization of education providers and the new business models that are emerging with disruptive technologies are rapidly changing the shape of the higher education industry. Coaldrake and Steadman (2013) suggest that universities should not depend on the market or the government but should take the initiative by adapting to the changing environment. Such organizational transformations can be achieved through business process management (BPM).

Organizations invest substantial resources in process improvement projects (Bradley, 2010; Braun, Mohan, & Ahlemann, 2010) as a way to survive, thrive, and develop a competitive advantage in rapidly changing environments. When managed and delivered appropriately, process-improvement projects can have significant benefits. However, there is little guidance on how to capture these benefits or even how to identify how the benefits materialize. Moreover, many projects still fail when project managers do not ensure that strategic objectives are achieved (Doherty, Ashurst, & Peppard, 2012; Serra, 2017).

Serra (2017) argues that a project's success depends on two factors: project management performance and the creation of or failure to create business value. Project management performance refers to adhering to budgetary and scheduling

Supplementary Information The online version of this chapter (https://doi.org/10.1007/978-3-662-63047-1_14) contains supplementary material, which is available to authorized users.

I. Denagama Vitharanage (✉) · W. Bandara · R. Syed
Information Systems School, Queensland University of Technology, Brisbane, QLD, Australia
e-mail: denagama@qut.edu.au; w.bandara@qut.edu.au; r.syed@qut.edu.au

D. Toman
Business Process Improvement Office, Queensland University of Technology, Brisbane, QLD, Australia
e-mail: denise.toman@qut.edu.au

J. vom Brocke et al. (eds.), *Business Process Management Cases Vol. 2*,
https://doi.org/10.1007/978-3-662-63047-1_14

goals and delivering the desired project output. Creation of business value refers to delivering the expected return on investment (ROI), managing and monitoring undesirable outcomes, and ensuring that the project outcomes align with the business strategy and are the same outcomes the business case planned to deliver. Organizations lose money when projects fail to deliver business value, even when they do well in terms of project management performance (Braun, Ahlemann, & Riempp, 2009).

New capabilities and changes from project outputs fill the "value gap" between an organization's current status and its target future status. Improvements that result from these capabilities and changes are the benefits organizations gain through running projects, and these benefits increase projects' business value. Therefore, delivering benefits is necessary for value creation. As Serra (2017, p. 11) defines them, "benefits are measurable and quantifiable improvements, which are normally expressed in financial terms, so they can justify any investment that may be required from the business." Benefits can be tangible or intangible (Braun et al., 2009).

According to Serra (2017, p. 11) "Benefits Realization is a process to make benefits happen and also to make people fully aware of them throughout the entire process." The Project Management Institute (2019, p. 8) defines *benefits realization (BR)* as the "integration of gains resulting from the use of outputs of portfolios, programs, and projects" and *benefits realization management (BRM)* as "the day-to-day organization and management of the effort to achieve and sustain planned benefits arising from investment in portfolios, programs, and projects." BRM, a BPM method, consists of a "set of tools and techniques that support and enable activities along the process lifecycle and within enterprise-wide BPM initiatives" (vom Brocke & Rosemann, 2014, p. 111).

However, there is little guidance on or examples of current BPM BR methods and tools. BR is often reported as a major challenge organizations face (Project Management Institute, 2019), and failing to realize the benefits of process improvement can be harmful to the reputation of the BPM discipline.

This case study captures the experiences of an Australian University, Queensland University of Technology (QUT), and explains how organization-wide process-improvement efforts emerged as a call for cost-efficient and effective provision of services. BR became a central theme in presenting the value of process improvement to get the buy-in of a complex mix of stakeholders. Given the minimal guidelines available, QUT embarked on its own journey to building and deploying the process-improvement BRM framework that is presented in detail here.

This chapter first presents the context of the case study, introducing the case and the as-is situation, before describing the actions taken and concluding with a summary of the results achieved and the lessons learned. The case serves as a great example of how to demonstrate and communicate value-creation through a comprehensively developed BPM approach (vom Brocke, Mendling, & Rosemann, 2021). Additional information to supplement this case study's content is provided as Ancillary Material (available at https://drive.google.com/open?id=1zIcAiWcfv2tl9fipyThrJw5MNeZY3k-c).

2 Situation Faced

2.1 Introducing the Case Context

Located in Brisbane, Queensland, Australia, QUT was founded in 1989. It is an established university with more than 48,000 students and more than 13,000 staff members. QUT is among the top 20 young universities in the world in two international rankings, the Times Higher Education (THE) Young University Rankings and the QS Top 50 under 50 rankings.

As an outcome of its periodic corporate reviews, QUT recognized the need to address operational inefficiencies as part of required organizational transformation. Administrative business processes at the university contributed to increased costs of resources, time delays, diminished services, inefficiency, duplication, parallel effort across faculties and divisions, and re-work. As a result, in November 2016, Peter Coaldrake, the Vice Chancellor and President of QUT at the time, proposed and laid the foundation for the eForms and Workflow Project to improve business processes. This project was implemented with the expectation of delivering significant savings and a rapid ROI.

However, as the project progressed, the objectives evolved from the automation of forms to adding value to services, reducing risk, and improving overall quality and the user's experience. QUT was aware that the challenges could not be solved with technology solutions alone; a new governance structure was needed to identify, map, and propose holistic, university-wide approaches to key business processes. To address this requirement, the project became the Enterprise Business Process Improvement (EBPI) Project in October 2017, and later the EBPI Program. In December 2018, the Business Process Improvement Office (BPIO) was established as a BPM Centre of Excellence to support continuous process improvement and automation across QUT.

The BPIO creates a range of benefits, including improving users' experience, visibility, and control and reducing, for example, effort, cost, and risk through the process-improvement initiatives. However, like every other organization that practices BPM, QUT struggled in positioning and communicating these benefits and their impacts to the university. Therefore, it needed a mechanism to identify specific, measurable, achievable, realistic, and timely benefits that would contribute to the university's objectives. A BRM approach was introduced to meet this requirement.

2.2 The Commencing Status

QUT uses a "transactional" approach to business process improvement (BPI) that ensures transactional excellence by focusing on reducing net costs and improving service (Weatherhead, 2015). Even though every project should have a strategy and a plan for realizing benefits, QUT did not have a BRM process for process improvement projects prior to implementing the EBPI program. It was not common for the university to develop business cases for projects, so the business cases that were available on completed and ongoing projects were limited in number, and there were few benchmarks, no benefits-reporting mechanism, and no categorizations of benefits put in place.

The BPIO faced other challenges as well, such as a lack of BRM frameworks that support a continuous process-improvement methodology and a lack of guidance for implementing BRM in the higher education context. After an environmental scan seeking guidance, which revealed no actionable guidance, QUT BPIO established a BRM process that would (1) manage projects to align project benefits and outcomes with the organization's strategy; (2) identify benefits and benefit categories during the project design/redesign phase (planned benefits); (3) measure, benchmark, and report project outcomes and benefits; (4) determine the scale of process transformation required to achieve the planned benefits; (5) communicate with top management about the projects' progress and gain their support; and (6) establish the background required to deliver successful project outcomes.

3 Action Taken

QUT's BPIO developed and implemented a BRM approach using an in-house BRM framework to ensure its process-improvement projects and programs delivered the outcomes that would realize the anticipated benefits. A BRM framework is "an integrated set of governance and management practices designed to define, develop, deliver, and sustain planned benefits derived from the outputs of portfolios, programs, and projects" (Project Management Institute, 2019, p. 25). The QUT BRM framework captures the action steps required as a multi-staged process and outlines the resulting artifacts and resources required to deliver the outcomes at each stage.

These BR stages are well aligned with the well-established and well-institutionalized continuous BPI lifecycle at QUT (Fig. 1), which follows the BPM lifecycle stages of discovery, analysis, redesign, implementation, and monitoring (Dumas, La Rosa, Mendling, & Reijers, 2018). (See Ancillary Material Part B.) QUT's BPM life cycle was designed to align with core QUT strategy by focusing on the key performance indicators of "Graduates, learning and teaching," "Research and innovation," and "People, culture and sustainability." (See Ancillary Material Part I.) The lifecycle guides QUT in process improvement, from identifying benefits to delivering them and sustaining the realized benefits through monitoring.

As Fig. 2 shows, the QUT BRM framework has four stages: identify, measure, execute, and sustain. It also has clear governance wrapped around it that aligns with the BPM governance and corporate governance already institutionalized at the university. (See Fig. 2 for an overview of BRM governance, and see Ancillary Material Part A for detailed descriptions of roles.) The roles, responsibilities, and accountabilities are assigned throughout the BR life cycle using Responsible, Accountable, Consulted and Informed (RACI) matrices. This approach also ensures the identification and alignment of stakeholders' involvement across organizational

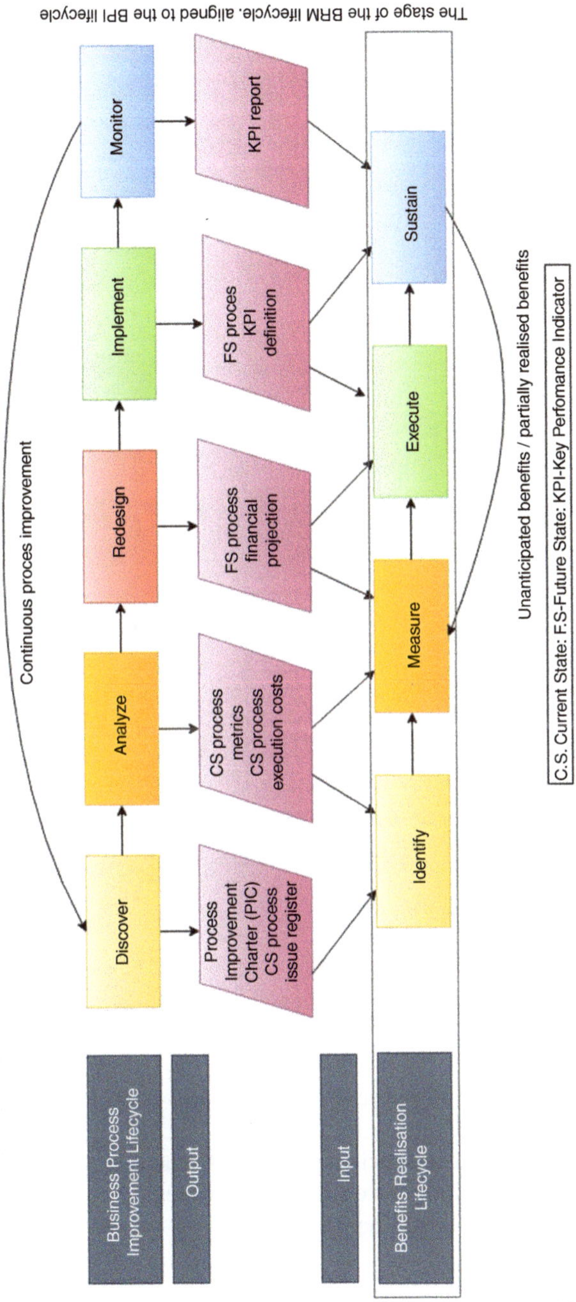

Fig. 1 Alignment of the BR life cycle with the BPI lifecycle

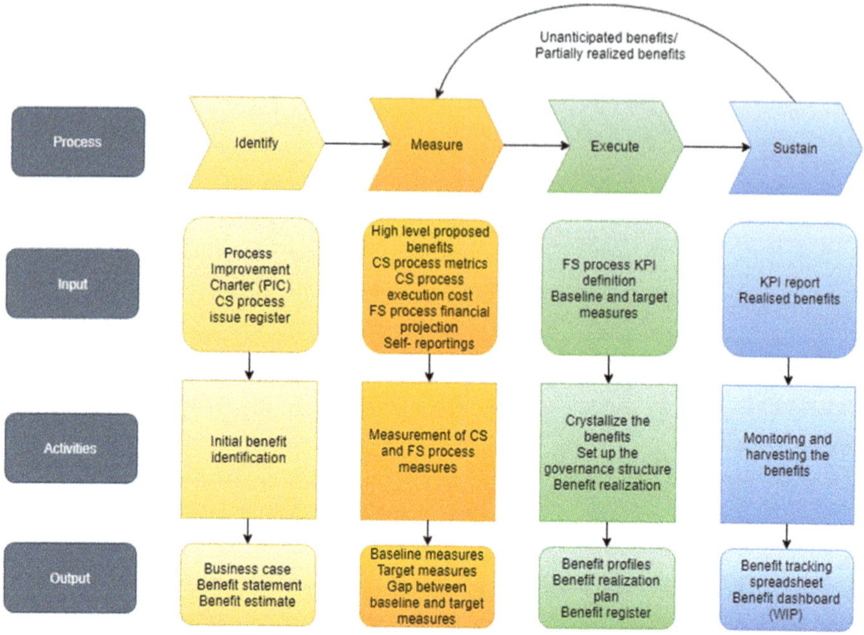

	Identify R	Identify A	Identify C	Identify I	Measure R	Measure A	Measure C	Measure I	Execute R	Execute A	Execute C	Execute I	Sustain R	Sustain A	Sustain C	Sustain I
Process Manager	X															
Process Owner		X														
Sponsors			X	X							X	X				
Beneficiaries			X	X							X	X				
Process Analyst			X		X	X	X								X	
Associate Director - BPIO				X				X				X				X
Operations Manager - BPIO				X				X				X				X
Benefit Manager									X				X			
Change Manager											X					
Benefit Owner										X				X		

CS - Current State: FS - Future State: KPI - Key Performance Indicator: WIP - Work In Progress
BPIO - Business Process Improvement Office
R - Responsible: A - Accountable: C - Consulted: I - Informed

Fig. 2 Overview of QUT's BRM framework

hierarchical levels and areas. BRM involves a variety of roles, each with its own level of engagement.

Governance roles: Process Manager, Process Owner, Associate Director–BPIO, Operations Manager–BPIO
Stakeholder roles: Sponsors, Beneficiaries, Benefit Owners
Managerial roles: Process Coordinator, Benefit Manager
Specialist roles: Process Analyst, Change Manager

Stage 1: Identify

The first stage of the BRM framework is to identify at a high level the benefits a process-improvement process or project is expected to deliver. This identification is heavily engaged in the discovery and analysis stages of process-improvement methodology, particularly in relation to the process-improvement charter (PIC). (See Ancillary Material Part C.) The PIC, a mandatory document for any process-improvement initiative, consists of a business case for which the BPIO captures the anticipated benefits and the sponsors sign off.

Hence, in the identify stage the BPIO creates a business case that describes the benefits and the ROI in sufficient detail to demonstrate the process improvement's impact. The business case ensures that the intended benefits are delivered and the funds are spent appropriately. It also facilitates the communication that is needed to align the diverse interests among diverse stakeholders and provides a clear explanation of the project to all stakeholders and beneficiaries so they can make informed decisions on how to realize these benefits.

Benefits are identified in this stage in relation to the issues to be addressed, a step that is closely related to the transactional/incremental process-improvement paradigm QUT follows. Insights into the issues are gained from the early analysis performed as part of the process-improvement discovery and analysis, and the need to address these issues is then converted into anticipated benefits. Benefit identification is done in a collaboration between the BPIO and the business unit. As part of the business case, a benefits statement and a benefit estimate are documented. The benefit statement details the issues faced by the process and provides a consolidated view of the benefits that can be gained by resolving those issues, while the benefit estimate states the financial and nonfinancial evaluations of the process benefits.

Once completed, the BPIO operations manager, the process coordinator, and the change manager review the business case, which is then approved by the associate director on behalf of the BPIO and the process owner on behalf of the business unit. Business cases are prioritized according to impact and effort, and a basic readiness assessment is conducted to ensure the business unit is capable of committing to the initiative.

Stage 2: Measure

Once the benefits have been identified, the EBPI team embarks on quantifying the benefits. The process analyst collects the baseline and target measures, and the gaps between the current-state measures and future-state measures are calculated. The measurement method, frequency of measurement, and tools needed to measure the benefits (if any) are also determined at this stage.

First, the insights from the analysis stage of the process improvement methodology are used. (See Ancillary Material Part B.) The output of the analysis stage, current-state process metrics, and current-state process execution costs are employed to derive the current-state measures and key performance indicators (KPIs), all of which are the baseline measures.

In the absence of comprehensive KPI data for process-execution timescales and costs, self-reported estimates are obtained from process participants by running workshops and baselined during the capture of the current-state (as-is) process model. KPIs can use varying units of analysis for different roles, transactions, departments, faculties, divisions, or the organization as a whole. Therefore, benefit quantification takes place on multiple levels and can be interrelated. For example, an individual's KPI can impact a KPI of the department in which he or she works. The lack of baseline measures has been an ongoing challenge at QUT. This can impact the data quality and the end-to-end BRM process, and adds to the overall BRM effort and resourcing (e.g., running workshops).

Next, the future-state (to-be) process model, process documentation, and the financial projection from the redesign stage of the process-improvement methodology are used to quantify the target benefits, and the future-state measures and KPIs are collected. For financial benefits, volume data is collected over a 3-year period to identify and account for trends; rather than attempting to capture the variety of pay rates for each participant in a process, an average rate is estimated by role.

Stage 3: Execute

At this redesign stage of the process-improvement methodology, the future-state process models are created, and the process-related changes are decided. The objectives of this stage are to crystallize the benefits and to set up the appropriate governance structure around BR. A clear governance structure with designated roles for accountability and responsibility for realizing the planned benefits and investing appropriate resources is essential, as is communication.

First, the change manager, the process analyst, the process owner, and the process manager define and organize the planned benefits and categorize them (primarily) as financial and nonfinancial benefits for reporting purposes. Nonfinancial benefits are further classified according to business drivers, which are aligned with QUT's organization strategy. (See Ancillary Material part E.)

The change manager then liaises with the business unit to assign the BPM governance roles. A benefit manager responsible for BR is selected for each benefit, while the benefit owner is accountable for the benefit. The process analyst and the benefit owner create a benefit profile for each benefit. (See Ancillary Material part F.) Benefit profiles, which include the measurements of current-state and target-state KPIs, the method of measurement, risks and mitigations, and so on, describe the benefits in detail and record the information needed to analyze the planned benefits, define the extent of the benefit to be delivered, ensure an appropriate person is accountable for the delivery of the benefit, prioritize benefits, clarify the project outputs that are needed to enable the benefit, ensure strategic alignment, and monitor the progress of realizing benefits.

All the benefit profiles are recorded in a benefit register, a single spreadsheet that supports monitoring by filtering information across all the benefit profiles.

Next, the project change manager conducts a readiness assessment with the business unit—see Ancillary Material part D—to assess the feasibility of achieving the targets. The business unit negotiates with the analyst on a target benefit that the unit is comfortable delivering, and if the BPIO feels more is achievable, it sets a stretch target. Then a final decision on the target benefit is made, and the benefit owner and the benefit manager sign off on the benefit profile.

Some of these benefits are realized immediately after go-live. For example, benefits like increased accuracy are derived as soon as a manual process is automated. However, most benefits take longer to manifest, so change management initiatives must be in place to gain the expected outcomes. The process analyst and the benefit manager agree on a detailed BR plan—see Ancillary Material part G—and the benefit manager executes the plan with support from the change manager in the implementation stage of the process-improvement methodology.

To ensure the BR plan is monitored and addressed appropriately, both discrete process risks and overall risks that can impact the organization must be identified. Risks can also be "disbenefits," negative impacts that occur to some stakeholders as a consequence of implementing a solution that realizes benefits for other stakeholders.

Factors like engagement and acceptance of the plan by the key stakeholders and beneficiaries, the planned benefits' impacts on the project's funding, business problems to be resolved, operational obstacles and risks, potential disbenefits a management plan to minimize or avoid disbenefits, prerequisites for change to occur, timeframes for delivery and harvesting, methods of measurement, monitoring and reporting mechanisms, development of communication materials, adequate documentation of benefits, and assignment of roles, responsibilities, and accountabilities for benefit delivery are addressed in the development of the BR plan.

Stage 4: Sustain

Once the redesigned process is implemented, the process analyst in charge of the process monitors the progress of all process benefits. Monitoring is a checkpoint activity conducted at agreed stages, which varies according to the benefit (ideally every 3 months) until the BR plan ends. The analyst and the benefit owner collect the data regularly to review against the targets and determine whether the benefits are on track to be delivered. If an unanticipated benefit emerges as the initiative develops, is deployed, or is implemented, it is captured and directed to the BRM measure stage and discussed with the process owner at the monitoring meeting. These unanticipated benefits can be direct causal results of anticipated benefits or qualitative benefits like improved customer satisfaction and risk reduction. If a disbenefit is captured, the best course of action to avoid or mitigate it is taken as a support case or as a new process-improvement activity.

Monitoring provides insights and trends that can forecast the process's performance and provide new directions for performing incremental process improvements. It also helps in identifying and addressing unanticipated issues, optimizing the process to improve the degree of benefit, realizing the potential to make new modifications that can lead to additional process improvements, and fully realizing partially realized benefits in the next iterations of the process improvement.

At every stage of monitoring, the BPIO attends to the benefits-tracking process, benefit measurement, and budget concerns and to identifies appropriate, measurable, and clear metrics that can address both tangible and intangible benefits during benefits tracking and achieve successful outcomes from benefit monitoring.

Once delivered, the actual benefit achieved can be harvested. Each benefit plan contributes to an overall project BR plan. Identified financial benefits (where relevant) are harvested after implementation at either the triennial budget forecast or mid-year forecast. Some anticipated benefits will not materialize until after the process improvement has been delivered in its entirety (e.g., a technology solution that enables workflows and automation). Therefore, the BR plan should be maintained beyond the initial (non-tech) solution-delivery phase through to complete realization so secondary benefits are harvested when the opportunity is next available. As each process is re-engineered and each benefit is identified and profiled, they are included in a benefit-tracking spreadsheet.

The BPIO develops a benefit dashboard using the spreadsheet data to report progress against the predicted benefits in a way that suits various stakeholders' needs. The dashboard identifies the status of a benefit using a red–amber–green "traffic light" system. For example, if during a review a benefit is recognized as unachievable, it will be flagged in red so mitigations can be identified that can get it back on track. The dashboard helps the BPIO monitor the process performances, discover the reasons anticipated benefits are not fully realized, and ensure that BRM is planned and managed holistically to achieve QUT's objectives and strategic goals.

4 Results Achieved

The concept of creating a business case for every project, which was introduced as a result of the BR process, led to the identification of likely benefits early in the process-improvement lifecycle, creating awareness of the benefits for all process stakeholders, increasing receptivity of unanticipated benefits, and conducting a benefit estimation. Current-state measures and baseline KPIs are now readily available for university-wide processes because of BRM's supporting the university in improving its process analyses. BRM has also ensured that benefits are aligned with QUT's strategy and objectives.

The benefit-reporting mechanisms are now well established, and the transparency of various types of benefits derived by QUT process-improvement initiatives has increased. Benefits categories formed by grouping the benefits support management of their realization and effective communication to stakeholders about project outcomes. These mechanisms have increased understanding of both financial and nonfinancial benefits and efforts to recognize and quantify nonfinancial benefits.

Process efficiency has also improved, so employees can move to more value-adding activities, improving employees' morale. Process stakeholders and beneficiaries are aware of the benefits from the beginning, and they have designated roles and responsibilities in the BR life cycle. This sense of responsibility has an indirect positive impact on employee satisfaction.

The monitoring process tracks the benefits and provides insights into process performance. It has also assisted in identifying new directions for performing incremental process improvements and identifying unanticipated issues. BRM has paved a road for QUT to harvest project benefits and contribute to the university's objectives.

5 Lessons Learned

- *BRM framework for continuous process improvement*
  Although there are many BRM frameworks, most are associated with the project management discipline and report benefits at project delivery. However, BPM is a continuous process-improvement initiative, often with multiple ongoing process-improvement projects, rather than a single project where the work's start and end are known. Therefore, benefits should be tracked and monitored frequently. QUT BPIO was challenged to find a framework that supports BR and reporting for continuous process improvements, where benefits are a growing entity that derives insights into the incremental stages of the BPI life cycle.
- *BRM framework for the higher education industry*
  BR approaches are widely used in manufacturing, the transport industry, the health industry, and elsewhere, but resources for the use of BR are limited in the higher education industry. Even though many universities have implemented process-improvement initiatives, there is a dearth of guidance on how to harvest the benefits from these initiatives.
- *Collecting current-state measures*
  As QUT did not have a proper measurement system prior to the EBPI program, collecting the current-state measures and KPIs that are used as the baseline measures was challenging. In the absence of comprehensive KPI data for process-execution timescales and costs, self-reported estimates were obtained from workshop participants and baselined to capture the current-state process model. Self-reported estimates are not always reliable, as the time spent executing a task depends on many factors, such as individual performance and knowledge. It was a challenge to extrapolate accurate measures from self-reported data.
- *Quantifying qualitative benefits*
  Apart from the financial benefits—cost reduction, increased income, and so on—many nonfinancial benefits are harvested from process-improvement initiatives, but quantifying such benefits in terms of a monetary value can be challenging. For example, if a re-engineered process reduces risk by improving adherence to rules and regulations, the process may have a considerable impact on the business. For example, quantification of the risk reduction could be done in terms of the funds saved by not having to pursue legal actions, but such decisions are made by the business (top management), not the EBPI service. Benefits like saving employees time by reducing reworks allow employees to engage in higher-value-added activities, but reporting it in terms of dollar savings is complicated. In the case of QUT, the money saved is calculated as the product of hours saved and salary per hour. Harvesting this money is the responsibility of the business (division heads and top management), not the BPIO.
- *Institutionalizing the BRM*

Although the EBPI team develops the BR plan, individual business units are responsible for ensuring the benefits are realized. It can be a challenge to get business units to own a process and be responsible and accountable for deriving its benefits. It can also be a challenge to get business units to settle for the target measures the BPIO says are achievable. QUT has embraced flexibility in negotiating the planned benefits and realizing them by addressing variations in planned timelines and unexpected changes. Sometimes resistance to adopting the changes in a process and new frameworks emerges. In response, BPIO introduced the idea of displaying flyers—see Ancillary Material Part H—about the process improvements and their impacts to encourage and reinforce their adoption and to build a BRM culture. Change management and communication play significant roles in the process of institutionalizing BRM.

- *Accumulating project benefits to overall university objectives*
  Individual business units harvest the benefits of process-improvement initiatives, but the BPIO must accumulate these benefits and report their overall outcome to QUT's objectives and strategic goals. Reporting and communicating about the cumulative impact of process improvements that have been carried out across the university provide a rationale for the funded investments and encourage the organization to continue the investments. BPIO plans to implement a dashboard to address this challenge.

References

Bradley, G. (2010). *Benefit realisation management a practical guide to achieving benefits through change* (2nd ed.). Farnham: Ashgate.

Braun, J., Ahlemann, F., & Riempp, G. (2009). *Benefits management-a literature review and elements of a research agenda.* Paper presented at the Wirtschaftsinformatik (1).

Braun, J., Mohan, K., & Ahlemann, F. (2010). *How benefits from is/IT investments are successfully realized: The role of business process know how and benefits management practices.* Paper presented at the ICIS.

Coaldrake, P., & Steadman, L. (2013). *Raising the stakes* (2nd ed.). St. Lucia: University of Queensland Press.

Doherty, N. F., Ashurst, C., & Peppard, J. (2012). Factors affecting the successful realisation of benefits from systems development projects: Findings from three case studies. *Journal of Information Technology, 27*(1), 1–16. https://doi.org/10.1057/jit.2011.8.

Dumas, M., La Rosa, M., Mendling, J., & Reijers, H. A. (2018). *Fundamentals of business process management.* New York: Springer.

Project Management Institute. (2019). *Benefits realization management : A practice guide.* Pennsylvania: Newtown Square.

Serra, C. E. M. (2017). *Benefits realization management : Strategic value from portfolios, programs, and projects.* Boca Raton: Taylor & Francis Group.

vom Brocke, J., Mendling, J., & Rosemann, M. (2021). Planning and scoping business process management projects and programs with the BPM Billboard. In J. vom Brocke, J. Mendling, & M. Rosemann (Eds.), *BPM cases. Digital innovation and business transformation in practice* (Vol. 2). New York: Springer.

vom Brocke, J., & Rosemann, M. (2014). *Handbook on business process management 1: Introduction, methods, and information systems.* New York: Springer.

Weatherhead, D. (2015). *Ambidextrous BPM: An interview with Prof Michael Rosemann*. Retrieved from https://blog.leonardo.com.au/ambidextrous-bpm-an-interview-with-prof-michael-rosemann

Part IV

Cases on Governance and Strategic Alignment

Successful BPM Governance: Insights from Commonwealth Bank of Australia

Wasana Bandara, John C. Merideth,
Angsana A. Techatassanasoontorn, Paul Mathiesen, and Dan O'Neill

1 Introduction

Business process management (BPM) governance refers to the guiding principles that define roles and responsibilities in decision-making (Rosemann & vom Brocke, 2015). BPM governance often entails mechanisms like vertical structures, which are used to organize and manage activities, lateral relationships, processes, and rules for coordination and control of activities related to business processes (Markus & Jacobson, 2015). Although BPM governance is challenging to develop and implement, its importance to the long-term effectiveness of business process initiatives should not be underestimated. In addition to governing the processes, BPM governance also governs the improvement efforts undertaken to improve processes.

This case takes place at the Commonwealth Bank of Australia (CBA). CBA is an Australian multinational bank and one of Australia's leading providers of integrated financial services, including—in addition to retail, business, and institutional

Supplementary Information The online version of this chapter (https://doi.org/10.1007/978-3-662-63047-1_15) contains supplementary material, which is available to authorized users.

W. Bandara (✉) · P. Mathiesen
Information Systems School, Queensland University of Technology, Brisbane, Australia
e-mail: w.bandara@qut.edu.au; p.mathiesen@connect.qut.edu.au

J. C. Merideth
JCManagement Consulting, Ltd, Jensen Beach, FL, USA

A. A. Techatassanasoontorn
Faculty of Business, Economics and Law, Auckland University of Technology, Auckland, New Zealand
e-mail: angsana@aut.ac.nz

D. O'Neill
OpExtion Pt Ltd, Sydney, Australia

J. vom Brocke et al. (eds.), *Business Process Management Cases Vol. 2*,
https://doi.org/10.1007/978-3-662-63047-1_15

banking—funds management, superannuation, life insurance, general insurance, brokerage services, and finance company activities. Founded in 1911 by the Australian government and fully privatized in 1996, CBA is one of the "big four" Australian banks and one of the largest Australian companies listed on the Australian Securities Exchange, along with brands like Bankwest, Colonial First State Investments, ASB Bank (New Zealand), Commonwealth Securities (CommSec), and Commonwealth Insurance (CommInsure). CBA's operations are conducted primarily in Australia, New Zealand, and the Asia Pacific region, but CBA also operates in a number of other countries, including the United Kingdom, the United States, China, Japan, Singapore, Indonesia, and South Africa.

Underpinned by the four capabilities of technology, people, productivity, and strength, CBA gives customers its highest priority and seeks to provide them with the best possible products and services. Recognizing that business processes are at the core of deriving and sustaining this goal, CBA places considerable value in an enterprise-wide process-management paradigm, which the company supports with a multilevel, multifaceted BPM governance effort. The case sets a great example of how to develop the governance-related capabilities in a BPM program, specifically considering a scale organizational context (vom Brocke, Mendling, & Rosemann, 2021). CBA continuously evolves its practices, so this case presents what was current as of August 2018. Additional information to supplement this case study is provided as ancillary material (available at https://drive.google.com/file/d/1X14OA7uSuCyHzQZEnruKBkE0hoOz2JoJ).

2 Situation Faced

CBA has applied many methodologies over the last century to sustaining its growth, often with a close eye to improving operations by enhancing current business processes and/or procedures. The complex, siloed, and hierarchical functional operating model that CBA once used rendered some of its earlier approaches to process management unsuccessful in addressing costly delays in services, high rates of rework/poor quality, non-value-adding tasks within processes, and overall poor customer service. While the firm made many ad-hoc improvements, especially product and technology enhancements, not until the dawn of the twenty-first century did CBA start to think about process management as a whole-organization initiative.

While BPM traditionally focuses on improving or optimizing single processes, one process at a time, CBA's enterprise-wide paradigm for BPM extended the focus to the entire organization by aligning initiatives with the firm's strategy, which provided a systematic way to improve processes across the organization through informed decision-making. This approach meant breaking down the silos that had been the product of functional and organizational hierarchies. In particular, this effort forced CBA to look across these functions and departmental hierarchies to assess end-to-end processes and find opportunities for standardization and scalability. The goal was "process-centricity" so CBA could use its processes consciously to achieve business results.

Recent changes in the sector, along with events at CBA, highlighted the need for adequate oversight and assessment of emerging risks and for clear accountabilities and simple, clear, holistic decision-making processes. Governance in relation to individual processes and how processes are managed was called for, so existing governance approaches had to be extended to include process governance.

3 Action Taken

CBA is *not* unfamiliar with governance, but the addition and integration of a horizontal BPM layer to entrenched vertical (functional) governance frameworks required careful design and application. Governance is applied at CBA to ensure that processes, strategy, process designs, and changes work in concert. In general, it is designed to: (1) oversee and steer process performance management and future states, (2) approve and prioritize process improvement initiatives to ensure that end-to-end processes drive toward the firm's business strategy, and (3) ensure that process decisions are in line with simplification and standardization goals.

BPM governance at CBA evolved through iterative efforts (see ancillary material Part A presents a time-stamped overview of the company's journey). We summarize these efforts into two broad categories as: (a) BPM governance within the specialist BPM team and (b) BPM governance at the organizational level.

3.1 BPM Governance Within the Specialist BPM Team

In 2015, with support from CBA's executive committee (ExCo), the role of the Chief Process Officer (CPO) was created along with the first process architecture governance team (see ancillary material Part B for sample position descriptions). These moves were the start of the top-down structural changes at CBA that were undertaken to drive a process-centric organization with a focus on deriving an enterprise-wide process architecture. The lessons from the first process architectures showed the need for more work to enhance the governance of processes. Although general managers were supportive of a common future-state process and roadmap to work toward for their business units, it was clear that, without top-down support in their businesses or a clear process owner from the senior executive team, the roadmap would not be followed.

At the start of 2017, another structural change resulted in the creation of a General Manager for Process Management and Improvement (GM PM&I) and the four teams that would report to this GM: Process Architects, Process Office, Process Innovation, and Productivity (see Fig. 1). These teams became the main catalysts for all BPM initiatives at CBA. The overarching PM&I team provided 15 services (12 customer-facing and 3 support services), which was clearly communicated via a service catalog (see ancillary material Part C for an overview).

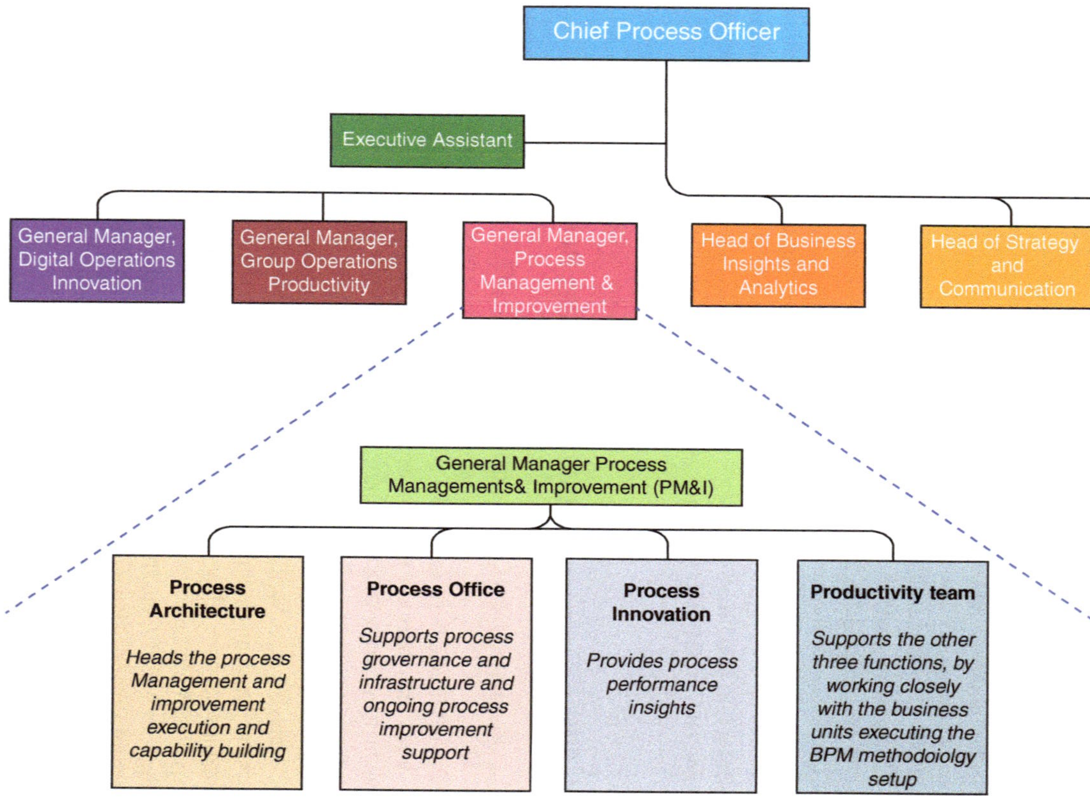

Fig. 1 Positioning of the CPO, GM PM&I, and PM&I team within the overall CBA organization structure

3.2 BPM Governance at the Organizational Level

The key goals of BPM governance at CBA were to elevate process as a strategic asset, protect the integrity of CBA processes, and guide improvement investments so process goals exceed functional goals. The ongoing, stable practice of process governance at CBA required the design of a holistic and multifaceted governance framework, including governance of the processes, the process taxonomy, and related process changes.

3.2.1 Governing the Processes

CBA's mechanisms for governing its processes can be summarized into two targets: (1) the establishment of process owners and subprocess owners and (2) the establishment of process improvement and governance charters.

Process owners and subprocess owners at CBA: To set up the required governance for core processes, the role of the process owner was defined and profiled. The goal was to create consistency in decision-making, with clear roles and responsibilities chartered. Cross-functional decision rights for end-to-end processes were agreed in principle, and clear decision, dispute, and escalation processes were set up. The memberships and decision rights in process governance forums were also articulated, as were decision rights for process owners whose responsibilities span multiple group functions, along with their accountabilities and responsibilities (see Table 1).

Process owners at CBA hold the title of general manager or higher level and are responsible for managing the performance of their end-to-end processes. Each process owner chairs a Governance Forum, at which representatives from the areas that are impacted by the process owner's end-to-end process discuss the performance of and proposed changes to the process to clarify the impact of any changes to the process.

Most end-to-end processes, which are also referred to as the horizontal core processes (e.g., home-buying), also have a number of subprocess areas, which are referred to as vertical processes (e.g., payments and assessments). Subprocesses are a section of the end-to-end process and may be shared by a number of core processes. Each subprocess has its own subprocess owner, who also joins the related governance forums of the end-to-end processes. The various accountabilities and responsibilities allocated to process owners and subprocess owners are consistent with the Banking Executive Accountability Regime (BEAR).[1]

Process improvement and governance charters: All high-impact processes (HIPs) have process governance charters that outline their purpose, membership, inputs, and outputs (see ancillary material Part D, Fig. D.1). Process owners of other

[1]The BEAR regime is part of the Banking Act of 1959, which establishes accountability obligations for authorized deposit-taking institutions and their senior executives and directors. The regime is administered by APRA, an independent statutory authority that supervises institutions across banking, insurance, and superannuation and promotes the stability of Australia's financial system. See https://www.apra.gov.au/banking-executive-accountability-regime for additional details.

Table 1 Process owners' accountabilities and responsibilities

Accountability	Responsibility
• Process Performance: Achievement of process performance targets in line with forecast and actual volumes, as prescribed by, but not limited to, the endorsed Process Future State aligned with group strategy. • Process Design and Improvement: Processing of improvement results with authority to approve process changes • Process Resourcing: Resourcing at levels required to meet process performance targets. • Decision Rights: as outlined in the Quick Reference Guide (QRG)	• Establish a governance body (cross-functional team if required). • Work with and engage the governance body. • Establish and manage appropriate controls to facilitate the process's future state vision, medium- and long-term, ensuring alignment with business and group strategic goals. • Provide visibility for and report on the performance of the process with respect to customer experience and process strategy. • Facilitate identification of opportunities to initiate and drive continuous process improvement, and act as sponsor. • Ensure that the recording of process documentation is current, accurate, accessible, and adhered to. • Deliver the process to external customer requirements and the current Customer Value Proposition. • Maintain relationships with stakeholders who participate in the customer-to-customer process. • Remove barriers to and facilitate collective learning and collaboration across functional boundaries. • Benchmark process performance. • Manage change across projects, people, prioritization, and sequencing of change.

processes were also encouraged to set up a governance forum. When a Process Reference Architecture (PRA) is developed, a PRA charter is also created for each process (see ancillary material Part D, Fig. D.2). The PRAs are governed by the Process Architecture Review Board (PaRB), which has its own charter. The membership of the Process Governance Forum is comprised of permanent or extended members (or their delegates[2]). Permanent members include:

- The Process Owner: The process owner is accountable for the end-to-end process. He or she is typically associated with the product or product family and owns the strategy (or reference architecture) that guides decision-making related to the process.
- Shared Subprocess Owners: Subprocess owners are accountable for the primary business services provided to the end-to-end process that enables the process'

[2]Delegated authority imparts full empowerment to the delegate to act on behalf of the regular attendee in performing the full responsibilities and decision-making rights of forum members.

purpose to be achieved. Examples of subprocess owners are operations, digital, credit decisioning, and customer management.

- Supporting Subprocess Owners: Supporting subprocess owners are accountable for the supporting business services that they provide to a process. These services support the process but are not necessarily critical for day-to-day operations. Examples of supporting subprocess owners are risk, IT, and finance.
- Process Architects: Process architects provide insights, expertise, and guidance to the forum regarding the processes' performance and potential impacts of requested change initiatives.
- Solution Architects (as deemed relevant): Solution architects provide insights, expertise, and guidance to the forum regarding the performance of the technology and potential impacts of requested change initiatives.
- Process Governance Secretary: The secretary provides general administration of the Governance Forum, including sending the agenda, taking and communicating minutes, tracking actions, and performing other associated tasks.
- Extended members are representatives of other processes that may consume the services provided by a process within the scope of the forum. This group may be materially impacted by the decisions of the Process Governance Forum. For example, a credit card process owner may sit on the forum for the payments process.

Decision-making at the Process Governance Forum is clearly specified (see ancillary material, Part E, for details). The Process Governance Forum has the right to make decisions for its process in the best interests of the groups' endorsed business unit strategies and risk and regulatory obligations, including decisions related to endorsing all strategy and initiatives, introducing new capabilities that may impact the process's future state, mobilizing resources to address process performance gaps with respect to progress toward the future state and/or the deterioration of current performance.

3.2.2 Governing the Process-Centric Taxonomy

A BPM taxonomy was designed at CBA to have a clear set of standardized BPM terminology used throughout the whole group (Bandara, Harmon, & Rosemann, 2011). The taxonomy sets the governance rules around how the process architecture can be modified.

The taxonomy also set standards to ensure that the decomposition and leveling are consistent with the process hierarchies, and it provides guiding principles for modeling processes. CBA used these standards for modeling processes with the ARIS tool, which was used to maintain the process architecture (the Process Knowledge Warehouse, or PKW, at CBA). The standards were also used in the process change control and maintenance activities associated with the process architecture and PRAs.

3.2.3 Governing Process-Centric Change

CBA's main goal in governing process-centric change was to integrate BPM governance into existing investment forums to ensure clear process management controls and that required metrics and standards for making and measuring decisions about the impacts of process changes were in place. Specific "process questions"[3] were set up to explain the benefits of change, and a number of governance forums were established to add a process lens to the groups' investment prioritization and strategic planning processes. Examples include the process governance forums, the pre-investment committee(s), and the PaRB.

The purpose of a process governance forum was to facilitate the strategic and operational decisions around an end-to-end process and to oversee the actionable outcomes. The forum assumes responsibility for decisions that affect the end-to-end process in terms of:

1. Endorsing and providing recommendations for the strategy of the end-to-end process and understanding and tracking the impact of a change in strategy to the current metrics and associated business outcomes.
2. Verifying alignment of changes to the process strategy, managing exceptions (reviewing options and making risk management recommendations or escalations to the appropriate governance forum if necessary), consulting/advising on how changes to the scope of an initiative may impact the end-to-end process; and
3. Managing the process's performance by understanding and driving process performance toward defined targets, endorsing targeted process reviews/focus areas, and setting actions to address outcomes (e.g., process KPIs, customer documentation process).

A quick reference guide (QRG) that describes the process governance forums is available to all stakeholders on CBA's intranet via the Process Management and Improvement portal. Extracts from this reference guide that explain how the forums are run are presented in ancillary material Part F. They are meant as a guide and not as prescriptive terms of reference.

The current-state process architecture with performance metrics is a key input to these forums. The delivery of process architecture for HIPs is facilitated by the PM&I team, which is sponsored by the process owner of the end-to-end process. The PM&I team ensures that the members of the Process Governance forum, individually and collectively, have the data for a documented and maintained end-to-end process so they can understand the end-to-end process, including its inputs, outputs, risks, and policies, analyze process performance to enable informed decision-making and identify and drive process improvement.

The PaRB at CBA has the purpose of overseeing and steering the process performance management and future states. PaRB was set up to: (1) endorse process performance targets, process taxonomies, and process future states; (2) understand

[3]These questions concerned seven factors. See ancillary material Part G.

process performance and drive performance to at least a minimum level toward defined targets; (3) endorse targeted process reviews/focus areas and set actions based on the outcomes (e.g., process KPIs, customer document process); (4) endorse recommendations for process-improvement initiatives, ensuring that the initiatives drive toward the targeted future state; (5) reduce complexity across process domains and portfolios; (6) provide immediate recommendations for programs/projects to address process architecture problem spaces; (7) communicate clearly and consistently to ensure the collaboration of stakeholders; and (8) approve process architecture artifacts, products, and processes to drive the right customer outcomes.

This BPM governance approach had to consider CBA's existing governance frameworks and current business operating model. Corporate governance at CBA shifted with the introduction of process governance forums. More recently, process governance has also been aligned with risk and compliance governance at CBA, with the process office at CBA partnering with the group's operational risk and compliance risk functions to create a disciplined, centralized approach to standardizing the end-to-end view of process, obligations, risks, and controls. For example, CBA's process architecture was closely aligned with CBA's risk incident repository (RiskInSite[4]). This collaboration and the integration of the BPM framework with group risk enhanced the value of the process-centric taxonomy to the business by providing a shift from a portfolio–/business-unit risk view to a process view of risk (PvOR). This powerful view enabled the process owner, and delegates in the forums to have a clear line of sight to the inherent risks and controls in the processes they manage and to understand their processes' true health while identifying gaps in their current reporting and management of the processes. The PvOR metrics can be used in combination with other visualization tools for key process-performance metrics, such as Process View of Technology (PvOT) and Process View of Cost (PvoC), all of which enhances process owners' and forums' ability to target ineffective process with initiatives while monitoring the impact of initiatives to the health of end-to-end processes.

4 Results Achieved

CBA's BPM-related steps resulted in mature process governance that supports CBA's corporate governance, which led to more accountable and efficient customer experiences. Table 2 presents a summary of the companywide results achieved through the company's BPM governance practices.

[4]RiskInSite is based on IBM's OpenPages Operational Risk Management system.

Table 2 Summary of BPM governance efforts and results achieved

Governance mechanisms	Results achieved
Establish an executive-level role in charge of processes (the CPO role).	• Signaled the strategic significance of "process" (process as a strategic asset). • Drove process-related activities and delivered an organization-wide process architecture.
Create a special unit (the PM&I team) dedicated to supporting process management activities for the whole organization.	• Created a highly experienced and accredited team with the required process-management capabilities in house. • Provided a one-stop service on process-related activities ranging from training to redesigning a process. • Developed organization-level and individual-level capabilities in process practices. • Brought the CPO and PM&I team together resulting in a clear "BPM home" with the right authority and resources. • Enabled "push" process goals that exceed individualized functional goals (especially those that were disintegrated with corporate goals).
Have an effective engagement model: the PM&I team acting as in-house consultants that can be called upon. The service catalog enabled this engagement.	• Created a service catalog that clearly outlines the process and end-to-end engagement between the business units and the BPM team, setting clear expectations and efficiency of the engagement. • Enabled BPM upskilling across other business units (at both operational and strategic levels) through the engagement model. • Added BPM skills in diverse units and at diverse levels with experiential learning through the actioned projects.
Create process owner (and subprocess owner) roles at senior managerial levels, and design and communicate responsibilities and accountabilities, consistent with national, sectorial standards (i.e., BEAR regime in this case).	• Created consistency in decision-making with clear roles and responsibilities. • Established an agreement on cross-functional decision rights for the end-to-end processes. • Set up clear decisions, disputes, and escalation processes.
Establish horizontal governance mechanisms with cross-functional decision rights.	• Established clear rights to make decisions for a process in the best interests of the groups' endorsed business unit strategies (overruling single functional interests). • Provided guiding principles to adhere to when modeling processes. • Created a rich, well-integrated process architecture, which enabled them to derive reliable process information for critical decision-making.
Establish a horizontal coordination mechanism (i.e., Process Governance Forum) to govern process-centric change.	• Process identification, improvement, and continuous improvement were well guided and resourced with clear roles and responsibilities. • Facilitated both the strategic and operational

(continued)

Table 2 (continued)

Governance mechanisms	Results achieved
	decisions surrounding an end-to-end process and how to oversee the actionable outcomes.
Set up a horizontal coordination mechanism (i.e., Process Architecture Review Board) to govern overall process performance for the entire organization.	• Endorsed process performance targets, process taxonomies, and process future states, providing clear guidance to current and future BPM work. • Ensured that process improvement initiatives are aligned with strategic targets and drove process performance toward defined targets. • Ability to orchestrate effective and well-aligned diverse initiatives to ensure cohesion, appropriate metrics, decision-making and standardization.

5 Lessons Learned

The development of effective enterprise-wide BPM governance is an ongoing process that requires a collaborative effort across the entire organization. CBA's BPM governance mechanisms enabled it to instill a process mindset across the business areas of adopting a new way of looking at how CBA operates and getting all to understand the upstream and downstream implications of process changes. Several lessons can be derived from this case study.

Multilevel governance mechanisms: CBA's experience points to the need for the implementation of governance mechanisms at both the whole-organization and specialist BPM team levels simultaneously. It also illustrates the strong links between BPM governance and an organization's strategic goals. In CBA's case, the process governance was closely aligned with the firm's risk management goals and strategies. The strong process governance complemented the risk-management mechanisms in place and helped CBA achieve better risk outcomes for itself and its customers.

Organization-level governance: A holistic governance framework at an organization level ensures that processes and process improvement projects are aligned with the organization's strategic goals. In particular, a process taxonomy as a standardized BPM terminology throughout an organization and a process architecture (PA) are prerequisites to a holistic view of the organizational processes.

Process governance: Process governance with clear roles and responsibilities is essential to maintaining accountability for and decision rights related to process performance and improvement initiatives.

Process performance: Governance mechanisms around process change help organizations to establish process-performance targets and to prioritize process-improvement initiatives.

BPM center of excellence: A strong and visible BPM team can drive a sweeping process-centric transformation throughout an organization. To communicate the importance of "process," organizations must establish a C-level role for BPM, along with a BPM team that has the capabilities needed to offer a range of services to educate employees, execute process changes, assess process performance, and offer advice and other support necessary.

Notwithstanding the applicability of lessons learned from CBA, organizations should be mindful that BPM governance must be designed in conjunction with current organizational contexts and strategic goals.

Acknowledgments We greatly appreciate input from the members of CBA's Process Management and Improvement team, especially (in alphabetical order), Karen Allen, Max Cardew, Steven Conlon, Anthony Deeb, Cathy Farrugia, Daina Fraser, Liza Holmes, Ayssor Joukhador, Kristin Kow, Bobby Sharma, Pavan Veerapaneni, and Amanda Wickett, who attended a Strategic BPM workshop with QUT staff in March 2018, and whose resulting workshop contributions and discussions provided significant input to this case study.

References

Bandara, W., Harmon, P., & Rosemann, M. (2011). *Professionalizing business process management: Towards a body of knowledge for BPM*. Berlin: Springer.

Markus, M. L., & Jacobson, D. D. (2015). The governance of business processes. In J. vom Brocke & M. Rosemann (Eds.), *Handbook on business process management* (Vol. 2, 2nd ed., pp. 311–332). Berlin: Springer.

Rosemann, M., & Vom Brocke, J. (2015). *Handbook on business process management 2: strategic alignment, governance, people and culture*. Berlin: Springer.

vom Brocke, J., Mendling, J., & Rosemann, M. (2021). Planning and scoping business process management projects and programs with the BPM billboard. In J. vom Brocke, J. Mendling, & M. Rosemann (Eds.), *BPM cases. Digital innovation and business transformation in practice* (Vol. 2). Berlin: Springer.

On the Role of BPM Governance at "System Group". The BPM Journey of an Iranian Software Solution Provider

Ahmad Alibabaei

1 Introduction

The System Group is a leading enterprise resource planning (ERP) solution provider in Iran. The organization's portfolio includes more than 40 integrated solutions and covers 22 industries. With the goal of addressing the diverse information technology (IT) needs of their customers nationwide, the organization, a holding of 24 regional subsidiary companies and 6 specialized companies, also works with 30 licensed, dedicated business partners. Each of these companies has its own valuable characteristics and strengths to contribute to the conglomerate's overarching goal. Established more than 30 years ago, The System Group provides more than 100 application modules. With its performance having improved each year, the company is today at the forefront of its industry in Iran, with more than 57,000 customers and more than 1400 associates. Its revenue is more than 53 million USD annually. The organization targets global standards and uses best practices to adjust as it grows.

Even though the organization has been successful in expanding its market, its future success must be earned through hard work, not by resting on its past successes. The case serves as an example of using a BPM approach to strengthen the fitness of an organization in meeting new challenges (vom Brocke, Mendling, & Rosemann, 2021). New internal and external challenges that have arisen must be addressed to retain its leading position. From an external perspective, the System Group faced changes in Iran's political situations in 2014 (e.g., decreasing sanctions), and many new start-ups entered the market that were agile enough to use new technologies to satisfy customers' needs faster than The System Group could. In addition to these challenges, opportunities like new access to the market in

A. Alibabaei (✉)
Shahid Beheshti University of Medical Sciences, Tehran, Iran
e-mail: a.alibabaei@sbmu.ac.ir

J. vom Brocke et al. (eds.), *Business Process Management Cases Vol. 2*,
https://doi.org/10.1007/978-3-662-63047-1_16

neighboring countries and new demand in the internal market arose. From an internal perspective, the company faced issues in its support processes and improvement opportunities in its sales processes.

To master this situation and act in accordance with its motto, "Smart solutions, wise management," the System Group decided to strengthen and improve its business processes, which can influence operations, services, and performance, by implementing BPM in such a way as to increase customer satisfaction and the organization's agility and continue its success in the market. The centerpiece of this BPM initiative is a new BPM office to govern the huge initiative. As The System Group has many departments and companies, the BPM initiative is divided into many small improvement projects while the BPM office acts as "head" of the BPM initiatives and supports the smaller projects. As a first step, the office designed process architectures, appointed process owners, pushed a shared understanding of the process among employees through communication and workshops, and identified seventeen end-to-end processes. Next, the company identified 5 of the 17 end-to-end processes to address in the first round. Rosemann and vom Brocke's (2015) six capability areas of BPM helped the System Group to undertake actions and understand BPM as a holistic management discipline.

The rest of the chapter is constructed as follows: The situation that the System Group faced is described in Sect. 2, while the actions taken to establish the BPM office and improve processes are elaborated in Sect. 3. Section 4 describes the results achieved, and Sect. 5 discusses the lessons learned.

2 Situation Faced

The System Group has flourished and its revenue has seen exponential growth since it was established. Despite the sanctions in Iran in recent years, the organization has grown rapidly. One key success factor has been keeping the quality high in all areas. While quality always has been one of the company's primary concerns, experiences with improving quality, such as implementing TickIT (i.e., certification program), assessing the organization based on the Capability Maturity Model Integration (CMMI), implementing an IT infrastructure library (ITIL) in the support division, and defining improvement projects differed. In 2015, the System Group wanted to increase quality in several aspects of the business and considered using ISO certification, EFQM-based evaluation, or BPM improvement initiatives. It began a three-step diagnosis project to decide which of these quality-improvement approaches was best for its particular needs.

Step 1: Identify the Main Issues The diagnosis project identified four main issues. First, delivering support services is one of the organization's core activities in the value chain, but customer satisfaction with after-sales services had decreased. Second, emerging technologies had forced the organization to introduce new products to the market, so the organization substituted its previous products with new ones, which required considerable resources, effort, and financial investment.

Third, although the sales rate was good, the success ratio in sales initiatives (sales contract to sales opportunity) did not meet executives' expectations. Since competition would soon become more intense because of market saturation and the entrance of new rivals, it was clear that the success rate would only decline if changes were not made. Fourth, clients wanted some changes in their existing software packages, and even continuous development of software package functions was not enough to meet their needs, so some customizations must be made specifically for some clients and therefore many customers had to wait until their requirements were developed.

Step 2: Identify New Organizational Conditions In addition to these issues, the company was faced with several new conditions in the industry. First, many start-ups and new entrants entered the market that were highly agile and that worked with new technologies, allowing them to satisfy customers' developing needs in a short time. Second, the organization received new project offers that were not completely consistent with the organization's mission. Initially, the System Group focused on providing software packages, but some large companies were requesting unique software solutions that were specific to their needs. Since the financial volume associated with these projects was highly attractive, The System Group had to find a way to realize this opportunity. Third, the political situation in Iran changed as sanctions were going to be eliminated and foreign competitors like SAP, Oracle, and Microsoft were going to enter the market, creating a significant threat for The System Group.

Step 3: Agree on an Improvement Initiative To tackle the challenges and, most importantly, keep its quality standards high, The System Group considered many proposals on how to proceed with the process-improvement project. None of the proposals that would have outsourced the project were attractive, so the organization decided to have consulting experts handle the initiative. These experts proposed BPM as the most suitable method for quality management. A small test with an important customer process was conducted prior to starting the company-wide BPM initiatives. The results were promising, and the organization proceeded to establish a BPM office.

3 Action Taken

The six core elements of BPM—strategic alignment, governance, methods, IT, people, and culture—helped the organization structure its next steps and enlarge its understanding of BPM from a mere technical concept to a holistic management approach (Rosemann & vom Brocke, 2015). In other words, BPM is not a destination but a journey. To achieve its goal of process improvement, The System Group undertook 12 actions.

1. **Establish a BPM office.** To start the BPM journey, the organization started from the enterprise level with the support of the management. The first step,

according to Rosemann and vom Brocke's (2015) capability areas of strategic alignment and governance was to establish a BPM office where employees were responsible for guiding and governing the overall BPM initiative. Relying on best practices (e.g., AlKharashi, Jesus, Macieira, & Tregear, 2010; Dumas, La Rosa, Mendling, & Reijers, 2013), the company established the BPM office with six employees under the direct supervision of the CEO: two senior employees with more than 10 years of experience in the organization, one employee with a software engineering background, one with an industrial engineering background, an expert with more than 5 years of experience in the planning department, and a new employee with 3 years of experience outside the company. In addition to these full-time employees, a senior expert and a BPM consultant worked part-time on the BPM office team. In many organizations, BPM is conducted by the IT department and is the CIO's responsibility, but The System Group separated the BPM office from the IT department and made it a department unto itself.

2. **Identify the BPM initiative's scope.** The scope of the entire BPM initiative included functional departments, regional subsidiary companies, and specialized companies. Since the central BPM office could not fulfill all of its responsibilities and conduct all projects in all departments and companies properly on its own, all departments and companies were involved in the BPM initiative, resulting in many smaller BPM initiatives. Each department and company assigned at least one employee, preferably one with an industrial engineering background, as a focal point for BPM. Most of these approximately 35 employees were familiar with some basic concepts of BPM, so the BPM office functioned as supporter and coordinator of these small BPM initiatives. Thus, the BPM office took on a serving role instead of a directing role; in fact, based on the scope that was defined, the BPM office had a role between serving and coaching (AlKharashi et al., 2010).
3. **Develop a project plan**. Once the scope was clear and BPM representatives of all departments and companies had been appointed, a project charter and a detailed project plan were prepared. To plan the activities related to BPM, previous work related to processes like ISO and ITIL implementations in the organization was reviewed to explicate the history of BPM in the organization. Best practices and managers' ideas were reviewed, and other stakeholders were interviewed about what they thought was important for the BPM initiative to address. Employees were involved to ensure a common understanding of the project (Rosemann & vom Brocke, 2015), and the project plan was discussed in and approved by the board.
4. **Develop a shared understanding.** After the final approval from the management board was announced, everyone who was part of the journey (e.g., BPM office, stakeholders) was informed about the detailed plan and the mission. Then the preparation phase started. Building BPM awareness in the organization and developing internal capabilities and process knowledge were next on the agenda (AlKharashi et al., 2010). A seminar and courses were designed to develop a full understanding of what was planned and why it was important for all

stakeholders. The seminar, held three times, described the BPM concept and its application in organizations for managers and process owners. A short course introduced process maturity evaluation and the plan for conducting such an evaluation. In addition, a modeling course was held based on BPMN for the BPM office experts and the representatives of each department. To build the internal process-management capabilities, a range of methodologies was discussed with the BPM consultant, and one, Lean Six Sigma, was customized for the organization's implementation of the BPM projects. The BPM office team members were briefed about Lean Six Sigma, and a course about Lean Six Sigma was conducted for employees who would be involved in BPM projects. The capability area of IT (Rosemann & vom Brocke, 2015) was covered using tools for process modeling, simulation, and document management that were acquired and provided by the BPM office. However, The IT department had full authority over the tools for automating or monitoring processes.

5. **Work transparently.** After process knowledge was acquired, The System Group sought to ensure it was transparent in the implementing the BPM project. Organizational transparency refers to visibility in how an organization operates. Many operational processes organizations were not so much designed as having evolved based on day-to-day organizational requirements, so getting the same understanding of the organization's processes can be useful in redesigning and improving them. Transparency in processes specifies how data is consumed and produced along a process, what products and services are the result of a process, where customer interfaces are needed, and where the organization is exposed to risk. Designing the process architecture is the start of transparency.
6. **Document processes.** To conceptualize the various views of the organizational processes, a process architecture was designed to show the relationships among the company's processes (Dumas et al., 2013). One challenge in defining process architectures lies in capturing the processes on a highly abstract level on the first level, "level one," of the architecture, which should be clear to the entire organization. The first process landscape model and 17 end-to-end processes—level one of the process architecture—was designed based primarily on a stakeholder analysis technique.
7. **Identify process maturity levels.** One task of the BPM office was to identify the status of BPM inside The System Group, so the BPM office investigated several maturity models and, based on organizational conditions and ease of handling and understanding, chose the Process and Enterprise Maturity Model (PEMM). The PEMM model has two parts, process maturity and enterprise maturity (Hammer, 2007). To identify a status (i.e., government capability) and use the PEMM, a questionnaire was distributed among BPM contributors ($n = 100$) who were selected from among the managers and employees involved in the various processes. All participants completed the first part of the questionnaire (i.e., enterprise maturity) but only those who were involved in or related to a particular process also completed the second part (i.e., process maturity).

Unfortunately, during the time that the maturity assessment was conducted, some problems appeared: Some parts of the questionnaire were not easy to interpret and needed more explanation, and the questionnaire provided three levels for evaluating enablers and capabilities, levels that were too broad to account smaller differences in enablers and capabilities. As a result, important information that could help the BPM office might have been lost. The results of the PEMM questionnaire showed that the organization is in the first stage, although the results showed that the condition in some parts of the organization was better than in others.

8. **Prioritize processes.** Once most processes were documented and the maturity level was identified, the 17 processes were prioritized using a "pain and gain matrix" (Dumas et al., 2013). As the name implies, the matrix had two dimensions: The *pain* dimension reflects the dysfunction in the process ("which process is in more trouble?") and was extracted from reviewing the results of PEMM and the evaluation of the managers' perspectives. The *gain* dimension shows the importance of the processes in the organization's value chain ("which process has the greatest impact on the company's strategic goals?"). To evaluate the gain in each process, 26 managers divided $1000 individually among the 17 end-to-end processes based on their evaluations of the processes' impact on the organization's goals.
9. **Appoint process owners.** Once the highest-priority processes were selected, a process owner was assigned to each one (i.e., governance capability). For end-to-end processes whose activities were all performed in only one department, the manager of that department was selected as process owner. For other processes, the process owners were chosen among managers who had a high level of authority in the organization.
10. **Identify causes of process problems.** With clear responsibilities set (i.e., BPM office, process owners), the reasons for the processes' performing weakly should be identified. Process simulation was used to reveal the processes' bottlenecks and opportunities for improvement. Additional data were gathered from multiple sources, including interviews with stakeholders, process owners, and unit managers who were involved in the processes. After the bottlenecks and other issues were clear, the causes behind each issue were identified (Dumas et al., 2013) by means of interviews and brainstorming sessions with managers and stakeholders (i.e., people capability). To visualize the relationships among the issues and their roots, the BPM office used "Fish Bone" diagrams.
11. **Define process measures.** Ways of measuring the processes were defined (i.e., strategic alignment capability) with two criteria: First, the relationship between the process measures and business KPIs should be clear so the process measures show how the processes affect business outcomes. The balanced scorecard (BSC) can be a useful tool with which to show the relationships, as it defines process measures based on an internal process perspective that includes customer and financial perspectives. The System Group's project used the BSC to clarify the effects of process improvements on business outcomes that had been defined from customer and financial perspectives based on the company's

strategies. Second, both efficiency and effectiveness measures should be considered, not one or the other. The lack of reliable data for evaluating the measures was one of the problems that the BPM group faced during the projects, so designing a procedure using IT tools to gather and analyze data was considered one of the most important activities.

12. **Communicate with employees.** When the overall BPM project started, The System Group wanted to ensure that all employees were up-to-date with its progress, so the company provided information on the intranet and set up a social network system to communicate the vision of the BPM office and its goals. The company used these channels, to announce required activities and progress so as to create an internal BPM community. The social network offered two-way communication with employees, so not only were the employees well-informed but a process-aware culture in the organization was enabled (i.e., people, culture capability).

4 Results Achieved

Based on the many actions The System Group undertook, three key results emerged. Some of the actions are also considered achieved results, as The System Group had to start almost from scratch, and everything they established will be in effect even after the BPM implementation project is over.

4.1 Documentation of End-to-End Processes

The first result was the documentation of 17 end-to-end processes, some of which are contained in one department, but most span multiple departments. An end-to-end process may include one or more intra-department processes. Figure 1 shows four end-to-end processes, three of which include more than one process.

The processes were modeled based on BPMN using the Visual Paradigm software. Table 1 provides an overview of the 17 end-to-end processes.

4.2 Process Priority

The results of the "pain and gain" matrix showed that all of the end-to-end processes had some issues and needed to be improved and that their impacts on management's strategies differed. Figure 2 shows the results of the "pain and gain" matrix.

Based on the results, the 17 processes were divided into three categories: The *first category* consisted of the five processes that had the most impact on the company's strategies and value chain, so they had the highest priority: from hire to retire, from sales contract to support contract, from lead to sales contract, from campaign to lead, and from software issue to resolution. The *second category* consisted of three end-to-

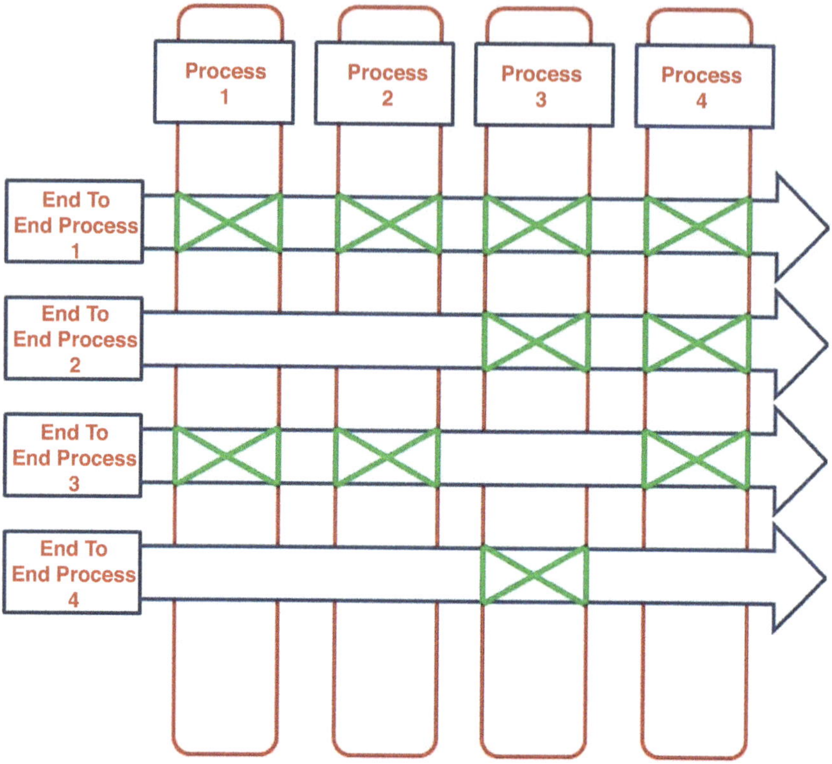

Fig. 1 End-to-end process vs. intra-department processes

end processes: from complaint to solution, from support contract to cash, and from idea to proposal. The other nine processes made up the *third category*.

4.3 Process Improvement Results

In the first round of process improvement activities, The System Group started with the five processes in the highest-priority category.

From Hire to Retire This process's scope was limited to one of the main departments of the company that had other problems. The project started with some difficulties and progressed slowly, but as the project team members worked on their tasks, they came more closely together, and new ideas for future steps emerged. The team around the process achieved 90% of their targets, which included the number of resumes the company received, the number of candidates who passed primary criteria and got to the interview, and the number of candidates who were hired.

Table 1 End-to-end processes

Number	End-to-end process	Description
1	Procure to Pay process	From receiving an office equipment request to paying for the equipment (includes delivering the equipment to the department)
2	Campaign to Lead process	From receiving a request for a campaign to getting sales leads
3	Lead to Sales Contract process	From receiving a sales lead to signing the contract
4	Sales Contract to Support Contract process	From receiving a signed software sale contract to signing a software-support contract (which includes software implementation)
5	Support Contract to Cash process	From receiving a signed software-support contract to receiving the payment from the customer
6	Sales Return process	From receiving a customer request to return software to returning the payment to the customer
7	Software Issue to Resolution process	From receiving a software issue (software bug or new requirement) from a customer to providing a solution
8	Complaint to Solution process	From receiving a customer complaint to providing a solution
9	Quote to Cash process	Issuing a software sale quote to receive the payment
10	Financial Plan to Report process	From starting financial planning operations to providing financial reports for government agencies
11	Forecast to Inventory process	From receiving a tools and equipments forecast to receiving tool and equipment in inventory
12	Idea to Proposal process	From receiving an idea for a product to providing a product proposal
13	Agency Request to Cancel Agency process	From receiving a request for partnership to canceling the partnership
14	Assess to Acquire process	From receiving an acquisition proposal to acquiring (includes assessing)
15	Acquire to Retire process (Fixed Assets)	From receiving a fixed asset request to retiring the fixed asset
16	Hire to Retire process	From receiving a candidate's resume to retiring the employee (includes hiring and human resource services)
17	Proposal to Product process	From receiving a product (software solution) proposal to producing the product (software solution)

From Sales Contract to Support Contract This end-to-end process had the greatest effect on organizational performance and had to be handled carefully. Because of a lack of resources, especially with regard to the BPM office, the redesign of this process was not yet possible and was postponed to the next iteration of process improvement.

From Lead to Sales Contract At the beginning of the preparation phase, during initial meetings with managers and stakeholders, the BPM office found out that the IT department was focused on a parallel project titled "CRM." The BPM office team

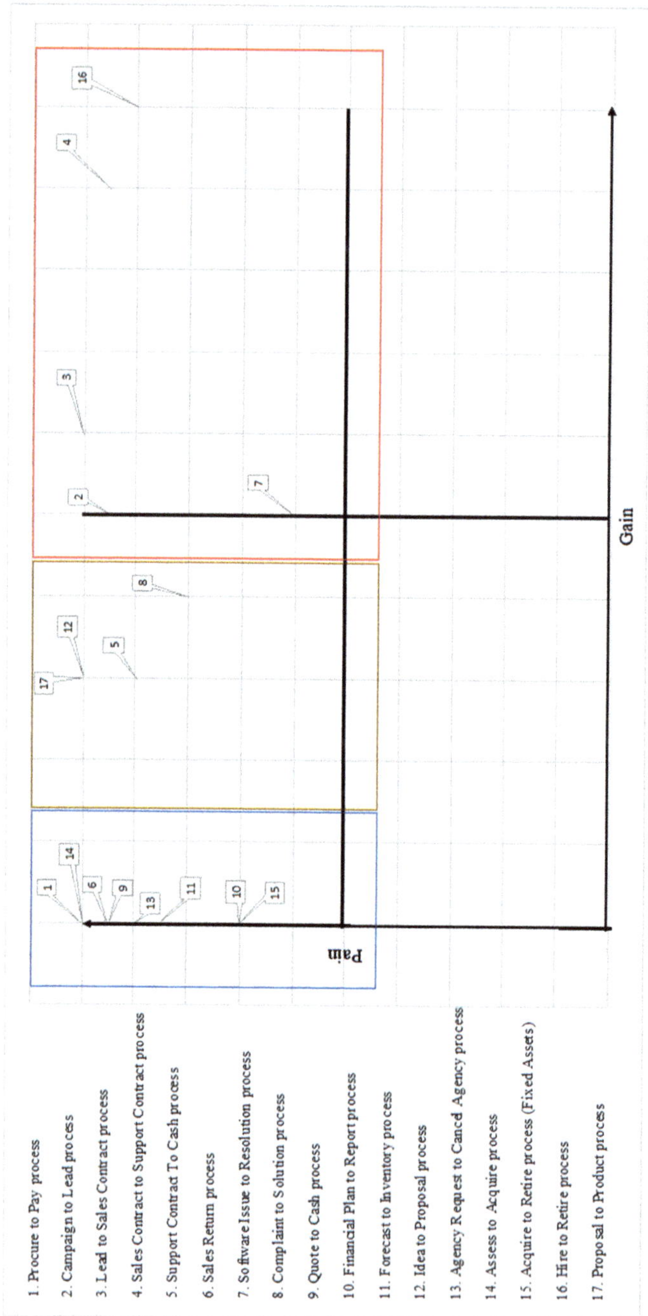

Fig. 2 Pain and gain matrix

provided the IT department some recommendations to consider during the CRM implementation, but the recommendations could not be included because of software solution constraints. As a result, the targeted improvements for this process were not met and the results were far from remarkable.

From Campaign to Lead The marketing department owned this improvement project, but the incompletely transparent marketing strategy and various procedures for running marketing campaigns made this project more difficult. The main achievement of this project was a new approach to conducting the campaigns on which all stakeholders agreed. However, the effects of marketing campaigns on sales leads, as one of the project targets, were not clear and remained for the project's next iteration.

From Software Issue to Resolution This project was the BPM office's first one. The process visualization was done perfectly. Data cleaning, filling in missing data, and implementing IT tools for monitoring the process were the time-consuming parts of the project. However, two members of the BPM office had software engineering backgrounds, which helped the office conquer the obstacles and sped up the project. The process-monitoring IT tools made visible the process bottlenecks, such as software bugs that resulted from inconsistencies between departments and issues related to strategic clients. This process was an inter-departmental process, but many improvements were achieved because of management's commitment.

5 Lessons Learned

The lessons learned from this case are described in five categories, which refer to Rosemann and vom Brocke's (2015) capability areas.

5.1 Methods

Not only a technique, BPM is a discipline that must use multiple methods to be implemented in an organization. In The System Group's case, different methods were used in different phases of the BPM initiative. The process-identification phase used a stakeholder analysis technique, while data was gathered in the process-discovery phase by means of interviews and observations; processes were modeled in BPMN with Visual Paradigm software. Simulation was used in the process-analysis phase to recognize the bottlenecks, followed by the "Fish Bone" diagram technique, which was used for the root-cause analyses of the problems and issues. Implementation of a process-improvement project is a difficult step, and a robust technique should be used, so Lean Six Sigma, which is both speedy and accurate, was used during implementation.

In addition to the methods used for BPM, change-management techniques should be used to ensure successful implementation. A change-management solution should consider a combination of techniques based on the organization's culture and climate to facilitate process-improvement initiatives, as well as methods to monitor whether a project is going well according to organizational and financial goals (e.g., BSC).

5.2 Strategy

The organization's strategy had a significant effect on the BPM initiative. Many steps during the BPM implementation require decisions, and the prerequisites of decision-making are clear organizational strategies and management support. Without clear strategies, the BPM initiative cannot achieve the expected outcomes, as such a large BPM initiative drives organizational changes (e.g., structure, human resource tasks, responsibilities, infrastructures) that should be aligned to the overarching organizational strategies. BPM initiatives must be considered in light of the organization's strategic map and must be part of employees' performance evaluations. During the BPM initiative, process owners and members of the process-improvement project teams were still doing their regular work, and employees' performance evaluations had been designed based on this regular work, rather than their work on BPM projects.

5.3 Culture and People

In Iran, people are more individualist than collectivist (House, Hanges, Javidan, Dorfman, & Gupta, 2004). This cultural fact helps to explain why working in a team is more difficult in Iran than it is in more collectivist countries. Most employees in Iran prefer to work individually rather than as part of a team. However, Iranian people also have a culture of intergroup collectivism, so the project showed that the performance of the teams that featured friendly relationships between team members was better than that of teams that featured just formal relationships (House et al., 2004). Iran has also a high power distant culture (House et al., 2004). The System Group's organizational culture is less power distant than the national culture, but it still affected decision-making during the project. As a result, empowerment and delegation of authority were not complete during the project. Instead, decisions about some important issues were referred to senior-level management and even the company's board, which made the decision-making procedure long and difficult, as where empowerment is low, decision-making takes longer (Alibabaei, Bandara, & Aghdasi, 2009).

5.4 IT

The initial BPM office team had an IT background, and their IT knowledge and experience played an important role in the use of IT capabilities during the project implementation, the project's progress, and efficiency. However, BPM and IT were managed in separate departments, each of which had its own priorities. Therefore, the development of the IT requirements the BPM office specified were delayed. In addition, the IT department was developing solutions for the organization that had significant effects on organizational processes, but the BPM office was not aware of them, and changes in those processes were not at the top of the BPM office's priority list. The lack of clear functional strategies made the alignment between these two departments even more difficult. Based on The System Group's experience, BPM and IT should be under one manager's authority, and if they must remain in separate departments, the strategic and operational planning parts of these two departments should be aligned.

5.5 Governance

The idea of establishing a BPM office was necessary to build governance structures for the larger BPM initiatives, but the results showed that establishing a BPM office alone cannot ensure good governance of the smaller BPM initiatives. The difficulties during the project's progress, particularly the IT implementation and keeping employees motivated, were not expected because of the presence of the BPM office. Based on the experience in this case, successful governance requires an agreed strategy and an aligned structure before starting any BPM initiatives (Alibabaei, Aghdasi, Zarei, & Stewart, 2010).

Acknowledgments I am extremely grateful to The System Group (www.systemgroup.net/en/) for sharing information about the case, and I thank everyone who contributed to this project.

References

Alibabaei, A., Aghdasi, M., Zarei, B., & Stewart, G. (2010). The role of culture in business process management. *Australian Journal of Basic and Applied Sciences, 4*(7), 2143–2154.

Alibabaei, A., Bandara, W., & Aghdasi, M. (2009). Means of achieving business process management success factors. In: *Proceedings of the 4th Mediterranean Conference on Information Systems*, pp. 1348–1363.

AlKharashi, B., Jesus L., Macieira A., & Tregear R. (2010). *Establishing the Office of Business Process Management*. Leonardo Consulting Publication.

Dumas, M., La Rosa, M., Mendling, J., & Reijers, H. (2013). *Fundamentals of Business Process Management*. Berlin: Springer.

Hammer, M. (2007). *The process audit*. Harvard Business Review.
House, R. J., Hanges, P. J., Javidan, M., Dorfman, W., & Gupta, V. (2004). *Culture, leadership, and organizations: The GLOBE study of 62 societies*. Thousand Oaks, CA: Sage.
Rosemann, M., & vom Brocke, J. (2015). The six core elements of business process management. In J. vom Brocke & M. Rosemann (Eds.), *Handbook on business process management. Introduction, methods and information systems* (pp. 105–122). Berlin: Springer.
vom Brocke, J., Mendling, J., & Rosemann, M. (2021). Planning and scoping business process management projects and programs with the BPM billboard. In J. vom Brocke, J. Mendling, & M. Rosemann (Eds.), *BPM cases. Digital innovation and business transformation in practice* (Vol. 2). Springer.

Making Processes Patient-Centric: Process Standardization and Automation in the Healthcare Sector at Hirslanden AG

Thomas Kuhn, Jenny Bruhin, and Tecwyn Hill

1 Introduction

Healthcare professionals face many challenges that can be matters of life and death. The lack of effective healthcare processes and collaboration among local health and care services has resulted in people being unable to access the community-based care and support services that would avoid unnecessary admissions to hospitals, leading to increased demand for acute care (Care Quality Commission, 2018). If the objective of healthcare trusts and care service providers worldwide is to reduce costs without decreasing the quality of patient care, healthcare leaders must use modern process technologies and strategic planning to balance price and quality against efficiency.

While process management cannot cure personal healthcare problems, the BPM approach can modernize core processes and systems to support new clinical practices, regulatory standards, cost-reimbursement methods, and corporate governance regulations (Reichert, 2011). That way, the case serves as a great example to develop a BPM program that makes important strategic contributions (vom Brocke, Mendling, & Rosemann, 2021). The BPM lifecycle (Dumas, La Rosa, Mendling, & Reitjers, 2018) offers all this while optimizing processes and responding rapidly to changes introduced by healthcare and life sciences requirements.

Hirslanden AG, a private hospital group, has been implementing the three pillars of the "Transformation 2020" strategy program since 2014, with adoption across clinics since 2018. The process improvements, business–IT alignment, and business

T. Kuhn (✉) · J. Bruhin
Hirslanden AG, Zurich, Switzerland
e-mail: thomas.kuhn@hirslanden.ch; jenny.bruhin@hirslanden.ch

T. Hill
Signavio GmbH, Berlin, Germany
e-mail: tecwyn.hill@signavio.com

J. vom Brocke et al. (eds.), *Business Process Management Cases Vol. 2*,
https://doi.org/10.1007/978-3-662-63047-1_17

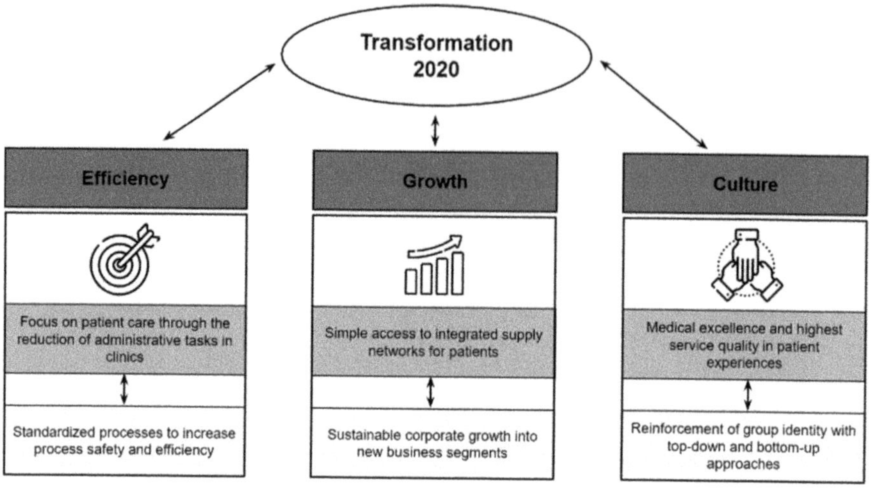

Fig. 1 The three pillars of the "Transformation 2020" program

transformations focus on the three pillars of efficiency, growth, and improved patient journeys, that is, "Patient Centricity." The efficiency pillar's goal is to standardize inpatient treatment while optimizing new and existing services. The objective of the second pillar, growth, is on faster access to specialists and treatments while aligning business performance with governmental regulations. The third pillar, culture, aims to strengthen the company's culture and identity by placing people at the center of change, where they can support and facilitate transformation (Fig. 1).

By fine-tuning the business–IT alignment strategy and micro-process design, the healthcare group can improve its scanning of best practices and standardize its efforts to ensure actionable feedback loops. Thus, the clinics are gradually relieved of administrative back-office tasks and can concentrate on their core work: patient care and well-being. When processes are unified, the patient journey naturally develops in tandem with modernized core processes and systems to support new clinical practices, regulatory standards, cost reimbursement methods, and organizational governance.

Hirslanden AG used an outside-in, patient-centric perspective that helped its healthcare professionals understand what patients experience during the entire patient journey while highlighting touchpoints for strategic outreach that improve engagement and satisfaction. This initiative simplifies and creates uniform processes and patient journeys by reducing variants in processes while mitigating complexity in the IT system to ensure streamlined organizational structures. Seeing through the eyes of the patient and removing operational chokepoints enhances "moments of truth" and staff efficiency and effectiveness.

As an effective institution, Hirslanden AG predicts that the use of BPM technology in its healthcare setting will result in a significant return on investment (ROI) and improve patient care and patient journeys. Outcomes of the use of BPM technology include: the provision of a single source of "truth" for physicians and nurses by storing and managing processes and documents across all clinics; benefits in optimization and quality improvement that staff notices and reports; and a reduction in the amount of time and resources devoted to administrative purposes through automation of workflows.

Hirslanden AG also noted that BPM empowers (1) the sharing of knowledge and information across business units with a holistic approach to problem-solving by reducing silos; (2) access and integration of clinical repository data for process improvement; (3) collaboration and ad hoc problem-solving in, for example, patient care activities; (4) the definition of to-be processes to target strategic initiatives and to then embed them across all clinics; and (5) a structural approach to overcoming the transition between as-is and to-be processes.

2 Situation Faced

The Swiss healthcare system takes a leading position among the member states of the Organization for Economic Cooperation and Development (OECD), and its high performance is reflected in its having the second-highest life expectancy of all OECD nations: 83.7 years (OECD, 2020). The number of primary care doctors and hospital beds per resident is also among the highest of all industrialized countries. However, Switzerland also faces significant healthcare expenditures. In 2017, the cost of healthcare in terms of the final consumption of healthcare goods and services was second only to that of the United States, at around 12% of GDP (OECD, 2019). Challenges for hospitals include cost containment and increased competition with the introduction of the DRG-based payment system. This change has had the effect of some interventions being newly treated as ambulatory, not stationary, thus generating less revenue for hospitals based on tariff systems. Clearly, Swiss hospitals are, more than ever, in need of ways to operate effectively. Hirslanden AG, one of Europe's leading private hospital groups, which consists of 17 hospitals and employs approximately 13,000 doctors and other personnel, is no different, as it is continuously challenged by three interest groups: the industry, competitors, and customers.

Switzerland's healthcare sector is a heavily regulated environment in which process documentation, and following regulatory requirements (ISO standards, SwissMedic), and quality management, is critically important. Competitors also pose challenges since competition between hospitals is rising, and the main differentiator is quality. Patients offer challenges as well, as they expect high-quality service on demand, whether they experience an accident or require elective treatment, and online services like arranging patient appointments and telecare services.

Against this backdrop, hospitals need to take a more patient-centric approach and to standardize their process models and ERP systems to reduce inefficiencies and eliminate rework, thus keeping the cost of healthcare from spiraling, and synergizing hospital sites by aligning processes and infrastructure. For Hirslanden AG, investing in information systems paved the way to optimize processes while coordinating the exchange of information required to deliver quality patient care.

Before Hirslanden AG could start "Transformation 2020," it considered the potential challenges to process automation. As the healthcare industry has historically been a manually intensive business with hands-on patient admissions, charts, billing, and care, automation of processes represented a challenge. Healthcare—diagnosis and treatment—in general, is complex because it is heavily regulated, making it challenging to implement standardization in patient treatment as it relates to process documentation fulfillment, following regulatory requirements, and quality management. Hirslanden AG also had to balance the tricky nuances of change management and acceptance, with staff from a wide variety of backgrounds facing process standardization for the first time. Change management requires the support of all involved parties company-wide and an understanding of a modern process culture (Rosemann & vom Brocke, 2015).

Despite the external and internal challenges, Hirslanden AG decided to embrace a new "process orientation" and the organic implementation of healthcare Enterprise Resource Planning (ERP) systems, which require a deep understanding of as-is processes within as-is organizational structures. A solid grasp of legacy systems and automation opportunities are needed to ensure the company is ready for new technologies and can design an effective process landscape. In this regard, Switzerland offers significant opportunities as one of the world's leading deployers of surgery robots (Bradley, 2015). Process mining initiatives can provide critical insights throughout automation and any robotic process automation (RPA) initiative, from defining the strategy to continuous improvement and innovation.

Hirslanden AG required a holistic ERP platform based on single data points and a process model that crossed finance, the supply chain, and human resources to support the emerging operating model. The same platform also had to be flexible enough to allow new entities to be assimilated and to support embedded cross-operational best practices, while also allowing variants in the infrequent case where standardization was impossible.

3 Action Taken

The scope of adopting process orientation is not limited to technology (e.g., workflow software tools), organization (e.g., clinical pathway specifications), or people (e.g., collaborating across functional silos) but must integrate all these capability areas (Reijers & Mansar, 2005). Capabilities must be developed in harmony to allow sustained adaptation of work practices that might be fundamental to governance. However, while process management is often a practical approach to improving business effectiveness by reducing costs and resources, healthcare shifts toward value-based care have resulted in simplified, improved patient journeys. In addition, targeting ROI has put pressure on hospitals to comprehend the actual cost of delivering care, regardless of whether it is per individual episode of care, per disease state, or per diagnosis. The need for clear insight into the cost of care, coupled with the obsolescence of many hospitals' ERP systems, has triggered interest in cloud-based ERP transformation systems.

Further demonstrating the transformation of standardized ERP systems in healthcare, a 2016 US report found that fewer than 30% of hospitals had an ERP system (PRNewswire, 2016). According to the survey, investments in electronic health records, cybersecurity, population health management, and analytics all have higher priority than ERP. While 30% seems low for the number of hospitals with ERP systems, it is not far from average. Software Advice found that only a third of enterprises across verticals use an ERP system, with another 44% using disparate systems (Burnson, 2015). However, for healthcare groups to succeed in the upcoming decades, their strategies must involve more than constant big-dollar upgrading or restructuring. Adaptive ERP technology can help hospitals to keep up not only with industry developments but also with the expansion of technology-enabled patient experiences and improved patient journeys.

In this medical instance, ERP refers to the integrated, real-time management of core business processes to support the assimilation of new entities with embedded cross-operational best practices. However, infrastructure and operations leaders must deal with the to-be scenario when they initiate such an IT monitoring strategy for evolved business intelligence based on new processes.

3.1 Managing Change Through the Transformation Program

To support Hirslanden AG's ERP transformation, the organization introduced a business transformation model called "Transformation 2020." The model consists of five steps: strategy development, strategy analysis, architecture planning, macro-design, and micro-design, and IS/IT implementation (Fig. 2). "Transformation 2020" is establishing a unique, group-wide business model for standardized and simplified processes across the group's IT systems and organizational structures. The business transformation model has helped to increase the efficiency of technology investments, the company's understanding of the challenges of aligning business with IT, and significantly reduced the financial and operational risks associated with healthcare and technical change (Herndon, Hwang, & Bozic, 2007). As part of the standardization journey, the organizational structure of process management is critical, requiring representatives from clinics, process owners, and managers from certain business units to collaborate closely.

With process standardization, employees can operate across locations to provide their patients with the care they need (Fig. 3). These operations include administrative processes like admissions and invoicing, as well as core processes like the coordination of doctors and attending physicians. Although these processes are fundamentally similar, they were carried out differently at Hirslanden AG's sites. Across all clinics, the long-term goal of process standardization is to drive the flagship value of "Patient Centricity" and to offer superior services for improved well-being. Thus, process standardization at Hirslanden AG helps to improve patient care and patient security and drives value by relieving the individual clinics of the

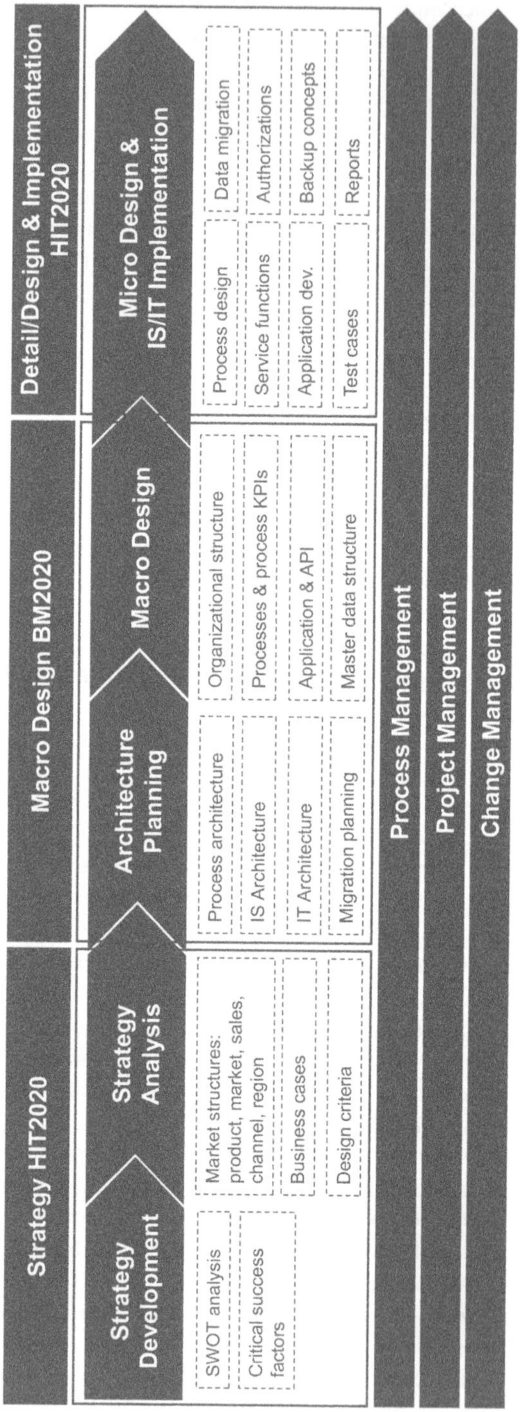

Fig. 2 The five steps of the "Transformation 2020" program

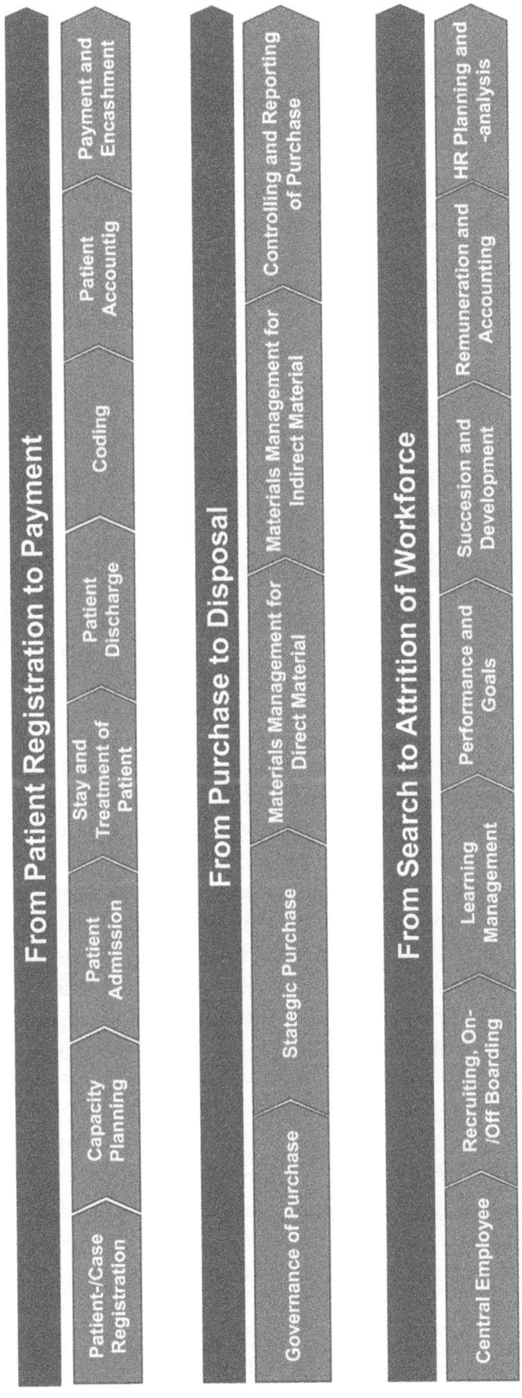

Fig. 3 End-to-end process standardization of the "Transformation 2020" program

administrative burden in favor of increased patient focus, developing universal standards for patient care, increasing efficiency, simplifying processes, and harmonizing the application landscape of the entire hospital group.

Standardizing medical processes also contributes to strengthening data security and process improvement initiatives, especially in relation to the General Data Protection Regulation (GDPR). Patients will experience smooth and secure processes, and employees will benefit from a systematic approach to the daily hospital routine. Staff can access a universally viewable overview of the map of processes and subprocesses. The collaborative capabilities of the BPM solution provide users with the ability to share these processes, develop them further, and automate transparently within a workflow tool. At the same time, regulatory requirements are reliably implemented, with a collaboration hub deployed as a central knowledge base for internal processes.

Reaching across people, processes, customers, technology, data management, and risk management, the ERP transformation is nothing less than a company-wide disruption. New processes, new ways of working, new paths through the system, and questions about the value and need for customization have all been critical aspects of the initiative. Avoiding the pain of historical time and revenue issues and ensuring more manageable cost strategies were critical.

3.2 Process Mining

To increase the value of process management in healthcare, the implementation of business intelligence must include KPIs, risk management, and mapping of corresponding processes. Process mining technology can help to detect bottlenecks and foster cost savings support with process standardization and optimization. BPM software supports process standardization throughout the hospital group, which offers (1) full project support across the corporation using process-driven requirements engineering and documentation of core administrative processes, and other medical and nursing processes; (2) an automation catalyst for numerous functionalities, such as information routing, escalation management, and task distribution; and (3) improved collaboration in process documentation and active process development using a collaborative commenting function so all employees can be involved.

The use of BPM crosses different IT architectures and any ERP system, including SAP®, which has the benefit of making networks scalable. Cloud-based IT infrastructure has also enabled rapid computing for various types of data and systems, from the physical network to the healthcare supply chain. As the process management system can be integrated with cloud ERP, it offers even simpler business–IT alignment. In this context, ROI originates from the reduction in the total cost of ownership, the development and improvement of business processes, and the increase in the productivity of business and process intelligence. For example, hosted workspaces can modernize the IT infrastructure without adding significant capital expenditure. Healthcare companies can then work to customize and implement a secure and effective cloud-based enterprise quality management strategy.

4 Results Achieved

Less than a year after the introduction of BPM software at Hirslanden AG, the first successes of the organization-wide process initiative are evident. The process optimization carried out in approximately 20 clinics for almost 13,000 employees created more than 2600 BPMN processes, produced 425 process maps, and filed 8245 documents, so process management is significantly facilitating efficiency in day-to-day tasks. These outcomes will continue to increase in scale and benefits as more clinics are onboarded. As digital needs grow, cross-departmental processes, in particular, will require renovating the operational environment.

According to global research and advisory firm, Gartner, "business alignment will need to be redefined to deliver successful digital experiences" (Prentice, 2017), so further business–IT alignment in healthcare requires next-generation standardization. BPM technology and Hirslanden AG's initiatives unfold in a common endpoint where business and technology activities link up, and leadership teams operate almost interchangeably.

Through the "Transformation 2020" approach, Hirslanden AG ensured that a web-based software solution is available around the clock, 365 days-a-year, making it suitable for the complex operations of medical needs. The web-based software makes it possible to model processes intuitively, thus increasing transparency, efficiency, and security through standardization.

However, Hirslanden AG is differentiating itself not only through technological progress but also, and most important, through its understanding of patients' needs, human behavior, and organizational structure, and through its drive for effective organizational change and governance. By improving the alignment of business and IT, BPM has improved the efficiency of health services and the quality of care and patient journeys. Radical process standardization supports the delivery and enhancement of capabilities through self-service and improved case management while keeping pace with policy changes and patient needs.

As unification becomes more widespread, business–IT alignment in healthcare will increasingly be impacted by the consumerization of IT such that corporate and personal technology, such as mobile technology, will dramatically change the provision and consumption of healthcare (Dadgar, Samhan, & Joshi, 2013). In this regard, the expectation that patients should have access to the same technologies at home as the doctor's surgery is growing. However, a more fundamental implication of business–IT alignment in medical care is the changing nature of corporate IT. In short, roles that have traditionally been embedded in IT departments are now formally integrated into business models. This change has significant implications for the IT infrastructure at Hirslanden AG because in a continuous, crowdsources business model, staff can be deployed reliably, safely, and cost-effectively across the enterprise and its applications to address any pain points that arise (Fig. 4).

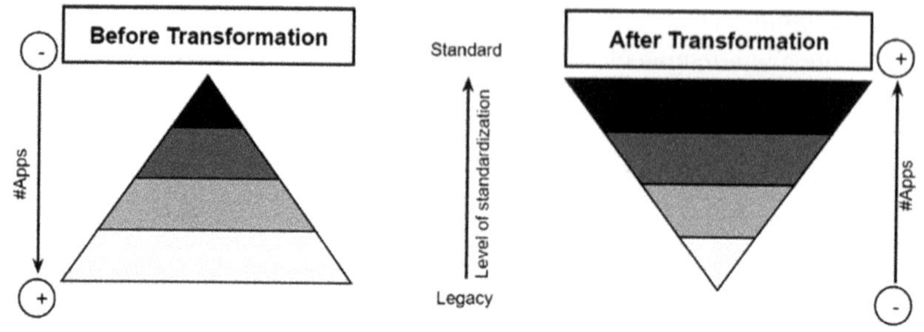

Fig. 4 Levels of standardization across applications, covering all four areas from standardized to legacy applications

Healthcare stakeholders who are struggling to manage clinical, operational, and financial challenges envision a future in which new business and care delivery models, aided by digital technologies, help to solve health-related problems. This vision goes hand-in-hand with building a sustainable foundation for affordable, accessible, high-quality healthcare.

5 Lessons Learned

Through reassessed and standardized business processes, Hirslanden AG is continually evolving and learning to improve its alignment with the changing economic environment (Naik et al., 2017). This move was triggered by several imperatives, including patients' and other stakeholders' demands for more innovative healthcare processes at more competitive prices, while the cost of doing business was rising, jeopardizing revenue growth.

Based on a process management approach, clearly linking process work to strategy (vom Brocke et al., 2021), Hirslanden AG modernized its core processes and systems to support new clinical practices, personalized outreach, regulatory standards, and cost-reimbursement methods and to meet government regulations. The BPM life cycle was a valuable tool in this effort, helping to modernize core processes while optimizing processes for rapid response to changes introduced by healthcare and life sciences (Dumas et al., 2018). Looking back, the analysis of "Transformation 2020" resulted in five significant lessons learned.

Common Understanding of the Hospital Ecosystem Since ineffective behavior often results from a lack of knowledge about one's actions, the analysis helped to clarify how current practice was leading to problems and complexity in the organization and the IT/healthcare ecosystem. This analysis was central to avoiding chasing silver bullets and aligning all stakeholders around a shared understanding of the issues they needed to address.

Shared Vision to Challenge the Existing Business Model A key driver behind the ERP and business transformation program was the entire company being united around one shared vision, which enabled the new business model to be tested under any number of conditions. It was essential to examine the internal part of the business model and its relationship to patients. Taking systematic steps enabled a transparent and flexible change agenda, where the shared vision functioned as a long-term guide.

Agility as a Change Management Approach Given that business transformation involves change across organizational boundaries, it requires interdisciplinary teams to ensure success. The use of certain agile principles helped this part of the ERP transformation because multidisciplinary teams were deployed in iterations and could continuously learn and adjust.

Workflow Automation as a Quality Enabler Implementing process management across clinics includes identifying segments of a business process that can be automated. These segments were often employee choke points where information was collected and handled manually. In such cases, the system can provide email notifications and reminders using web-based forms to prompt workers to perform tasks and keep things moving (Yeo & Ng, 2018). Emergency healthcare delivery across sites also involves a variety of interrelated activities, from a patient's admission to a clinic until his or her exit. Because these activities are inter-departmental processes, an appropriate technological infrastructure for automating and managing these processes was needed. The health sector is highly regulated, so after processes have been identified, process documentation can help the hospital group with compliance issues. BPM technology also provides significantly improved levels of management, collaboration, and timeliness for clinical research studies (Rentes et al., 2019). The company categorizes the benefits of process management as the "3 As," as they give medical professionals the power to: (1) adapt by reducing the time to implement change, (2) align by providing visibility and governance across the decision-management life cycle, and (3) act by sensing and responding to actionable situations based on precise information about events.

Process Mining for Continuous Improvement In the future, process mining initiatives will enable healthcare providers to manage process challenges with evaluation across the proof of concept for any proposed improvements, and by extracting relevant information from different data sets. By harnessing this raw data and continuously monitoring end-to-end processes, Hirslanden AG can control risk and keep track of improvement opportunities. The combination of process discovery, healthcare robotics, and conformance checking supports a future-state collaborative approach to process improvement (Cresswell, Cunningham-Burley, & Sheikh, 2018). This combination of factors drives improvement in as-is processes and removes exceptional and unwanted process steps by increasing visibility and transparency across IT processes. Data-based process mining will also be used to analyze working habits across teams and individuals, decreasing incident-resolution times, and improving patient impact through the discovery and validation of automation opportunities.

Another example of where process mining and strategic alignment will help experts is IT incident management. Here, an "incident" is an unplanned interruption to an IT service, whether complete unavailability or merely reduced quality. The goal of the incident management process is to restore regular service as quickly as possible and to minimize the impact on business operations.

References

Bradley, S., 2015. *Are robot-surgeons set to take over in Geneva?* Last accessed March 24, 2020, from https://www.softwareadvice.com/resources/erp-buyer-report-2015/

Burnson, F. (2015). *Enterprise resource planning software buyer report – 2015*. Last accessed from June 27, 2019, https://www.softwareadvice.com/resources/erp-buyer-report-2015/

Care Quality Commission. (2018). *CQC warns of growing 'care injustice', with access to good care increasingly dependent on how well local systems work together*. Last accessed June 26, 2019, from https://www.cqc.org.uk/news/releases/cqc-warns-growing-care-injustice

Cresswell, K., Cunningham-Burley, S., & Sheikh, A. (2018). Health care robotics: Qualitative exploration of key challenges and future directions. *Journal of Medical Internet Research, 20* (7), e10410.

Dadgar, M., Samhan, B., & Joshi, K. D. (2013). Mobile health information technology and patient care: A literature review and analysis. In: *Proceedings of the 19th Americas Conference on Information Systems (AMCIS)*, Chicago, IL.

Dumas, M., La Rosa, M., Mendling, J., & Reitjers, H. A. (2018). *Fundamentals of business process management*. Heidelberg: Springer.

Herndon, J. H., Hwang, R., & Bozic, K. J. (2007). Healthcare technology and technology assessment. *European Spine Journal, 16*(8), 1293–1302.

Naik, Y., Baker, P., Walker, I., Tillmann, T., Bash, K., Quantz, D., Hillier-Brown, F., & Bambra, C. (2017). The macro-economic determinants of health and health ine-qualities–umbrella review protocol. *Systematic Reviews, 6*(1), 222–214.

OECD. (2019). *Health spending (indicator) Homepage*. Last accessed June 27, 2019, from https://data.oecd.org/healthres/health-spending.htm

OECD. (2020). *Life expectancy at birth (indicator) Homepage*. Last accessed March 24, 2020, from https://data.oecd.org/healthstat/life-expectancy-at-birth.htm#indicator-chart

Prentice, B. (2017). *Business alignment will need to be redefined to deliver successful digital experiences*. Last accessed June 27, 2019, from https://www.gartner.com/en/documents/3667617/business-alignment-will-need-to-be-redefined-to-deliver

PRNewswire. (2016). *Hospitals remain underinvested in costing technologies, black book ERP survey results*. Last accessed June 27, 2019, from https://www.prnewswire.com/news-releases/hospitals-remain-underinvested-in-costing-technologies-black-book-erp-survey-results-300377359.html

Reichert, M. (2011). What BPM technology can do for healthcare process support. In M. Peleg, N. Lavrač, & C. Combi (Eds.), *Artificial intelligence in medicine* (pp. 2–13). Berlin: Springer.

Reijers, H. A., & Mansar, S. L. (2005). Best practices in business process redesign: An overview and qualitative evaluation of successful redesign heuristics. *Omega, 33*(4), 283–306.

Rentes, V. C., de Pádua, S. I. D., Coelho, E. B., Cintra, M. A. D. C. T., Ilana, G. G. F., & Rozenfeld, H. (2019). Implementation of a strategic planning process oriented towards promoting business process management (BPM) at a clinical research centre (CRC). *Business Process Management Journal, 25*(4), 707–737.

Rosemann, M., & vom Brocke, J. (2015). The six core elements of business process management. In *Handbook on business process management* (Vol. 1, pp. 105–122). Berlin: Springer.

vom Brocke, J., Mendling, J., & Rosemann, M. (2021). Planning and scoping business process management projects and programs with the BPM billboard. In J. vom Brocke, J. Mendling, & M. Rosemann (Eds.), *BPM Cases. Digital innovation and business transformation in practice* (Vol. 2). Springer.

Yeo, C. P., & Ng, W. Y. (2018). Automation and productivity in the clinical laboratory: Experience of a tertiary healthcare facility. *Singapore Medical Journal, 59*(11), 597–601.

BPM Adoption at the Industrial Services Provider Bilfinger

Seyed Amir Bolboli, Ludger Hasenauer, and Cristina Cabanillas

1 Introduction

Large corporations that adopt Business Process Management (BPM) invest heavily in BPM initiatives that focus primarily on identifying and standardizing best practices in the various phases of the BPM lifecycle (Dumas, La Rosa, Mendling, & Reijers, 2018). The goal is often to generate order in business processes and enable low- or mid-skilled employees to execute basic business functions following well-established procedures and using reliable systems (e.g., building information systems that can routinely process transactions), rather than responding to unique customer requirements, and to ensure that the end users of the business processes understand why they should think in terms of end-to-end processes. In successful implementations, such systems are usually simple and seen by most people as the standard way of execution. In addition, process modeling tools tend to be presented as a solution to all of the business problems in complex environments, disregarding their often low level of quality.

In fields like plant engineering, *flexibility* is required, so it is wrong always to want to simplify and impose standardization with existing BPM frameworks and tools (Hasan, 2012). In such flexible systems, the process members play an important role in delivering quality and innovative ideas, so they need a blueprint that can be adapted easily to various customer requirements. Such systems typically include change-management elements like communications oriented to the target group or the early involvement of affected members. However, the effects of such

S. A. Bolboli · L. Hasenauer
Bilfinger SE, Mannheim, Germany
e-mail: amir.bolboli@bilfinger.com; ludger.hasenauer@bilfinger.com

C. Cabanillas (✉)
University of Seville, Sevilla, Spain
e-mail: cristinacabanillas@us.es

J. vom Brocke et al. (eds.), *Business Process Management Cases Vol. 2*,
https://doi.org/10.1007/978-3-662-63047-1_18

change-management measures are often limited in reality. Therefore, the majority of process members do not understand the potential of process orientation and do not know why they can benefit from end-to-end processes or the difference between process orientation and traditional function orientation.

This case introduces a success story: a pragmatic approach to adopting BPM in complex environments with a clear focus on flexibility of processes related to customer requirements and a paradigm shift in people's mindsets. It therewith illustrates very nicely how the various elements of a comprehensive BPM approach link to one another and how they need to be aligned in order to deliver strategic value (vom Brocke, Mendling, & Rosemann, 2021). From a process map created previously, a blueprint process architecture and its process models were defined and adapted to more specific cases based on what customers required from the projects executed in various organizational units. The approach is inspired by the classifications and concepts introduced in the Cynefin framework (Kurtz & Snowden, 2003). We followed common practices for agile software development and used gamification (Deterding, Dixon, Khaled, & Nacke, 2011), among other techniques, to ensure the new paradigm's applicability and acceptance. The process members' initial reluctance before the initiative was put in place turned into satisfaction and positive feedback once they understood its results and advantages.

2 Situation Faced

Bilfinger[1] is a leading international industrial services provider that offers industrial plant maintenance services, modifications, and plant units (the last often on a turnkey basis) in two service lines: technologies, and engineering and maintenance. Bilfinger consists of numerous mid-sized companies that cover continental Europe, northwest Europe, North America, and the Middle East. These companies jointly execute projects, making use of synergy effects. With its 36,000 employees, Bilfinger upholds the highest standards of safety and quality and generated a revenue of 4.153 billion euros in financial year 2018.

For historical reasons, most of Bilfinger's companies are highly specialized and maintain discipline-oriented procedures as internal standards for their operative processes. A Bilfinger project consists of scope modules that can be executed by the Bilfinger's various units. (For example, engineering electrical is performed by Company A, the engineering process by Company B, and construction by Company C.) These scope modules are often modified by client-specific requirements. Bilfinger prepares for projects during the tender phase from a baseline that consists mainly of the project's execution plan, the schedule, and the budget. Changes to this baseline are allowed only for good reasons, usually because the client changes the scope, or external circumstances require changing the execution sequence. Therefore, the process model for the project must be frozen at the start of the project. The

[1] https://www.bilfinger.com/en/

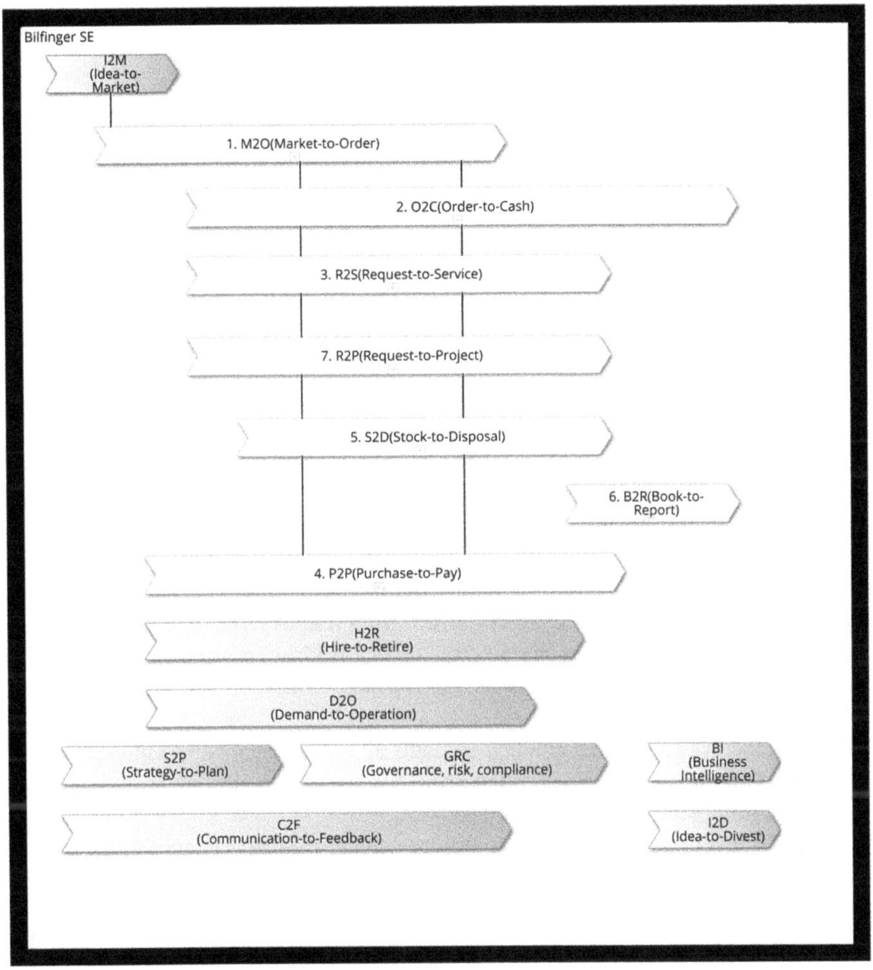

Fig. 1 Map of Bilfinger's commercial processes

baseline is a copy of the universal enterprise process model, stripped down to the relevant processes and altered in accordance with the project's specific needs. Improvements to the universal enterprise business processes are not automatically transferred but are manually introduced if necessary. A change in the project baseline requires a review of the respective project's process model. During execution, quality assurance (QA) is enforced using the project's process model as a basis.

As a first effort toward BPM adoption, the Bilfinger Process and System Harmonization (PSH) program was launched in 2017. The focus was first on the commercial processes. The process map (Dumas et al., 2018) depicted in Fig. 1 was defined for providing an overview of such processes. The definition of the process map was prior to the specific design, modeling, and implementation of every single process based on business process models, which took place in 2017 with satisfactory results. The standard Business Process Model and Notation (BPMN) (OMG, 2011) was used for process modeling purposes.

In that first BPM adoption effort, harmonization using the Enterprise Resource Planning (ERP) system was possible, but it was not possible in the remaining domains, especially in engineering processes. Therefore, the idea of pure harmonization, as previously conducted, was not an option in other domains.

The second phase of the program targeted the operations processes, which comprise the most value-adding functionalities for the business. These processes must be adapted for specific projects. Projects have specific requirements that must be considered by modifying standard company processes because, without such adaptations, there would be no possibility to check whether the processes fulfill the project requirements, and quality control and assurance could not be managed effectively.

Because of the impossibility of ERP-based harmonization and the significant need for justification and adaptation, the extension to the operations processes in engineering, manufacturing, and construction was much more challenging than handling the commercial processes. Although the advantages of process orientation (based on process models) over the traditional function orientation (with discipline-oriented procedures) had been recognized from the results of the commercial processes, reservations about application in engineering projects prevailed. The engineers identified two key requirements for a support of their operation processes:

R1. The general execution model that contains all processes must be tailored to each project by stripping it down to the project scope and modifying or adding steps to accommodate customers' requirements.

R2. It must be possible to change the process model if major changes occur during project execution.

In short, *flexibility* was necessary to satisfy customers' needs. Furthermore, the results of BPM adoption were acknowledged through the acceptance of the new work paradigm, especially by the internal stakeholders (employees and the management department).

3 Action Taken

The Corporate Project Management Office and one of the largest engineering units at Bilfinger jointly tackled the challenge of setting up a BPM system with all its advantages but also ample flexibility to accommodate engineering needs. The extension of the Bilfinger PSH program was carried out in 2018 and took place in two dimensions.

On one hand, horizontal development of a full process map was performed (Dumas et al., 2018) (called *process house* at Bilfinger) that contained all the processes at Bilfinger other than the commercial processes. As illustrated in Fig. 2,

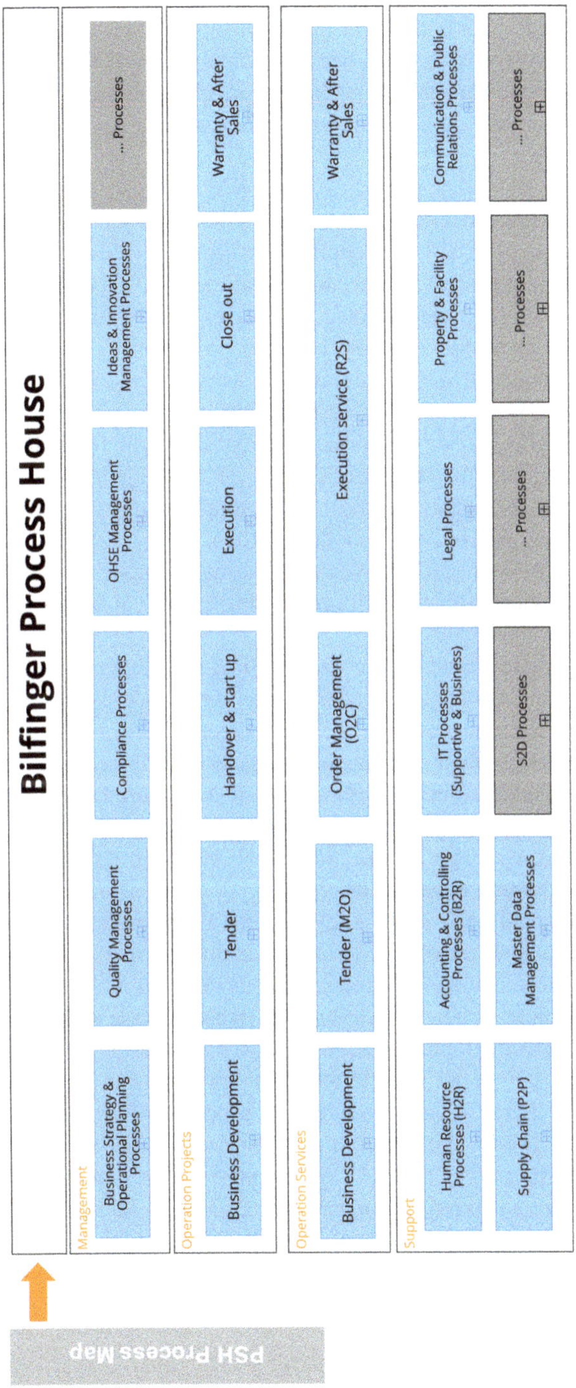

Fig. 2 Horizontal development toward a full process map

the processes were separated into four groups that can be classified into three categories in line with standard process classification frameworks (APQC, 1992): (1) operations (operative or core) processes, which involve projects and service operations (e.g., project management); (2) support processes, most of which encompass commercial processes (e.g., accounting and controlling); and (3) management processes (e.g., quality or legal). Special effort was put into simplifying the language for the end user.

On the other hand, vertical (top-down) development of a process architecture was conducted (Dumas et al., 2018). As depicted in Fig. 3, a drill-down option allows one to browse from the process map to the operative workflow level, which reflects detailed knowledge (e.g., project-related businesses like electrical engineering) in the form of executable business process models.

Defining the detailed BPMN process models as part of the vertical development was the most cumbersome task. We had been unsuccessful in standardizing at one time the whole business in complex project environments with huge BPM initiatives. To prevent similar problems, Bilfinger's plant engineering business provided an adaptable backbone for achieving the highest-quality results and increasing the operations processes' reliability by modeling them step by step. Such processes can be grouped into simple processes and best-practice processes. The hypothesis was that individual views (quick-starter maps) for individual businesses or entities would increase users' acceptance.

Therefore, we avoided establishing a huge BPM initiative at the corporate level and selected two pilot units in our project business sector. We also prioritized end-to-end processes into three waves with different types of processes. The first wave targeted Project Management and Engineering, while the second wave targeted Procurement, Sales, and Business Development, and the third targeted Construction and Commissioning. Because of the significant need for justification required by project management, we experimented with a novel BPM approach based on the Cynefin framework (Kurtz & Snowden, 2003).

Cynefin is a so-called *sense-making* framework, which means that its value is not so much in logical arguments or empirical verifications as in its effect on the sense-making and decision-making capabilities of those who use it. Cynefin gives decision-makers powerful new constructs that they can use to make sense of a wide range of unspecified problems, which is particularly useful in collective sense-making because it is designed to allow shared understanding to emerge. Key in Cynefin is the notion of un-order—which in process-oriented vocabulary, could be interpreted as *flexibility*—not a lack of order but a different kind of order, where the whole is never the sum of the parts, every intervention is also a diagnostic and every diagnostic is also an intervention, and any act changes the nature of the system. Thus, the Cynefin framework has five domains, as depicted in Fig. 4: two domains of order, two domains of un-order, and a fifth the domain of disorder. None of the domains is more desirable than any other, and there are no implied value axes. In short:

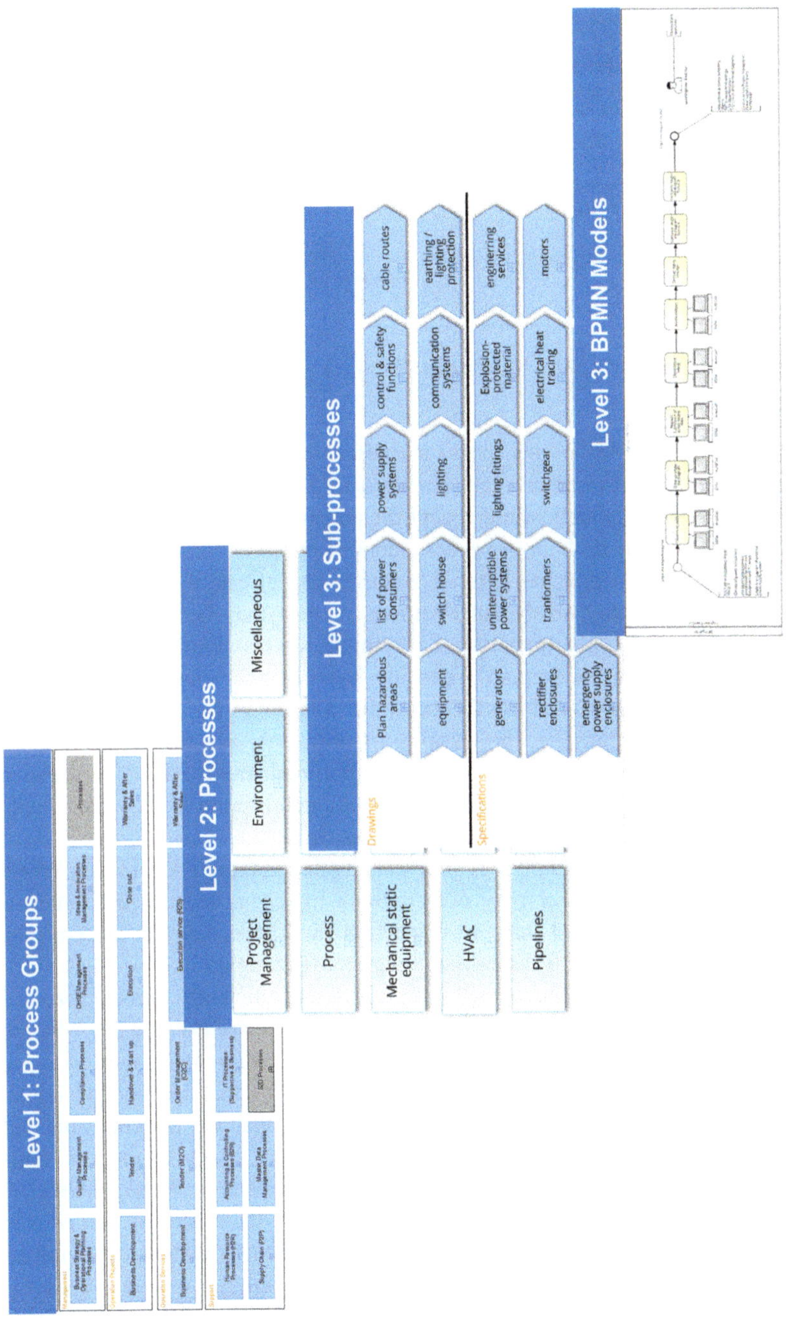

Fig. 3 Vertical development toward a process architecture

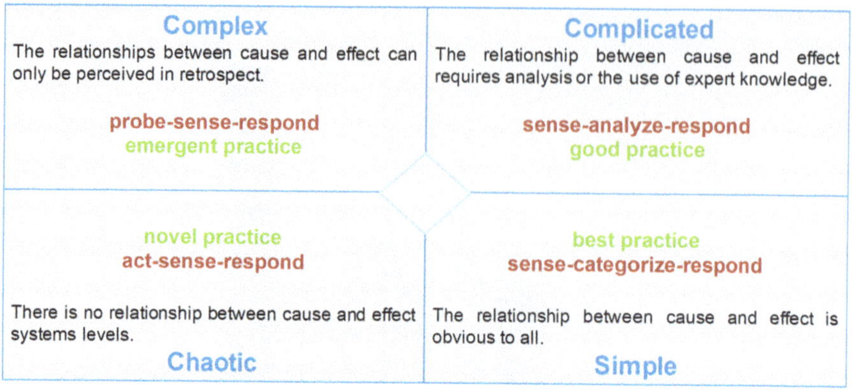

Fig. 4 Cynefin framework (inspired by Kurtz and Snowden (2003))

- The *Simple domain* has *known* causes and effects whose relationships are generally linear, empirical in nature, and not open to dispute. The objectivity is such that any reasonable person would accept the constraints of the best practice. The simple domain is the domain of process reengineering.
- The *Complicated domain* has *knowable* causes and effects whose relationships may be stable but may not be fully known, or they may be known only by a limited group of people (experts). Everything in this domain is capable of movement to the *known* domain. The only issue is whether we can afford the time and resources to move from the knowable to the known. This domain is the domain of systems thinking, the learning organization, and the adaptive enterprise, all of which are too often confused with complexity theory. The decision model here is to sense incoming data, analyze it, and respond in accordance with expert advice or interpretation of that analysis.
- The *Complex domain* has *complex* cause–effect relationships. Patterns may repeat for a time but they may or may not continue to repeat because the patterns' underlying sources are not open to inspection (and observing the system may itself disrupt the patterns). Therefore, relying on expert opinions based on historically stable patterns of meaning will not prepare us sufficiently to recognize and act on unexpected patterns. The decision model in this space is to create *probes* to make the patterns or potential patterns more visible beforehand, then to *sense* those patterns and *respond* by stabilizing the patterns that we find desirable. Sensing is performed by destabilizing the patterns that we do not want and seeding the space so the patterns we want are more likely to emerge. This approach requires gaining multiple perspectives on the nature of the system.
- The *Chaotic domain* has *chaos*, which means that there are no perceivable relationships between cause and effect, and the system is turbulent, giving us inadequate response time to investigate change. Applying a best practice is probably what precipitated chaos in the first place: There is nothing to analyze, and waiting for patterns to emerge is a waste of time. The decision model in this

space is to act quickly and decisively to reduce the turbulence and then to sense immediately the reaction to that intervention so we can respond accordingly.

When one uses the Cynefin framework, the way one thinks about moving between domains is as important as how one thinks about the domain because a move across boundaries requires a shift to a different model of understanding and interpretation, as well as a different leadership style. We faced a situation in which the information about the processes could be knowable and complex because the project-adapted processes were tailored to customer's needs. Consequently, we used the Cynefin framework to design business processes (and define the respective BPMN models) that lay in the *Simple*, *Complicated*, and *Complex* domains and to build an adaptable blueprint as a frame for the execution of the adapted processes.

First, we created a blueprint with the most developed organizational unit of Bilfinger, focusing on the first-wave processes in the form of a process map and the respective process model definitions. This blueprint was offered to other units as a reference model. For every project, a copy of the model(s) was adapted according to the customer's needs (cf. Fig. 5). The units encompassed processes that belonged to the three aforementioned domains, so they had to be treated differently.

The processes classified in Cynefin's *Simple domain* were considered well-known because of the large amount of data and knowledge that is available about them. In designing these processes, we evaluated the risks that typically bring projects from the *Simple* to the *Chaotic* category (e.g., a situation in which a project manager has an accident and is unable to fulfill his or her role for an unlimited period of time). Thus, process-based risk management was forced and mitigation measures were defined.

To handle the *Complicated* and *Complex domains*, we had to recognize *flexible* as a valid state in plant engineering, so we created one frame that covered both flexible socio-technical systems (for *complicated* scenarios) and flexible ecosystems (for more *complex* ones). In the *Complicated domain*, variants of good practices were offered to the end users with a company-specific approach to the adaption of processes based on the business case (cf. Fig. 6). The *Complex domain* included intricate components and complex interconnections that had to be adapted to rapid change. A *probe–sense–respond* approach with a fast reality check and evaluation of the probes was needed, and the lessons learned were captured for future needs. In general, Bilfinger's most challenging processes (with the highest potential for innovation regarding customers' needs) are often in the *Complex domain.*

During the execution of these actions, we had to make a number of decisions to address the challenges that emerged. These decisions and the methods used could be of help for other organizations that have to address similar problems and could be seen as guidelines for BPM adoption in complex settings. We classified them according to two goals:

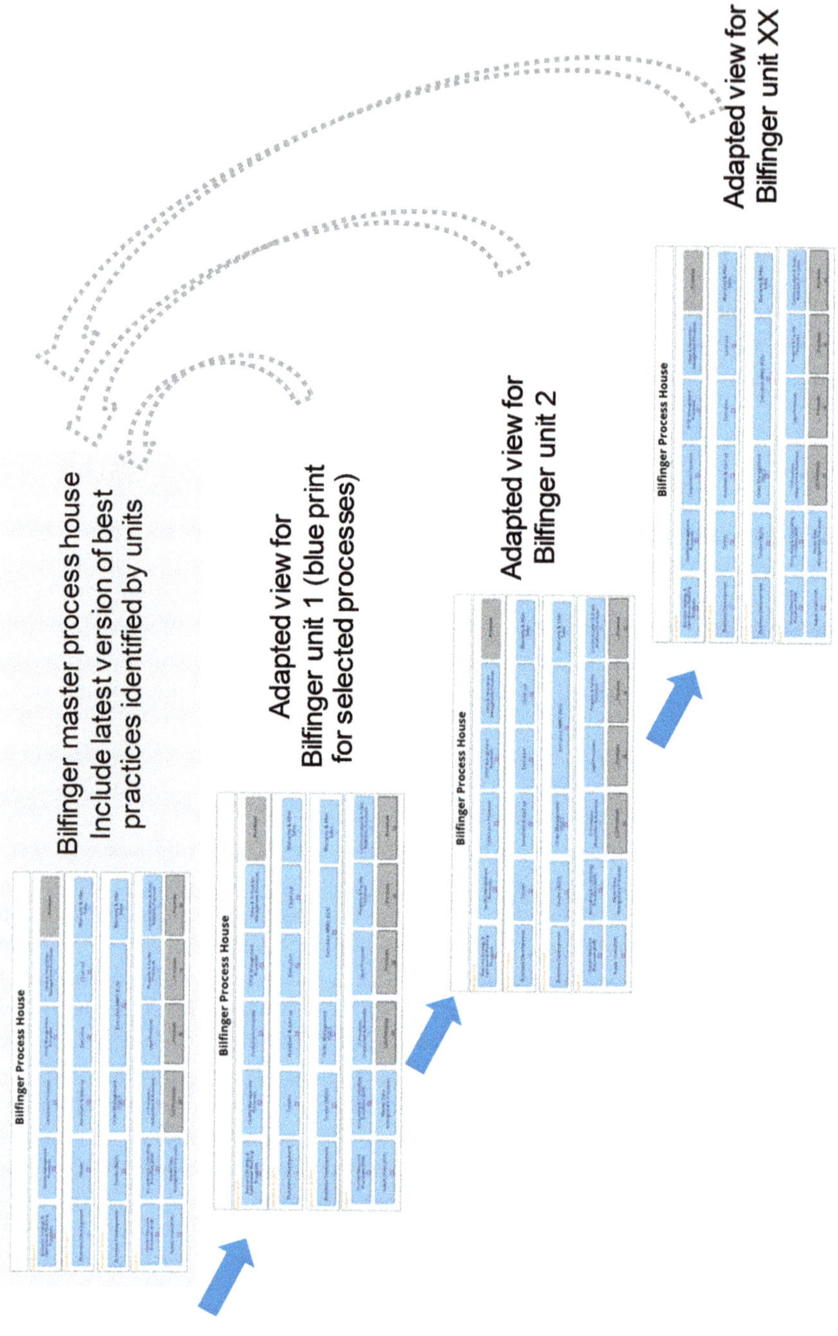

Fig. 5 Roll-out approach

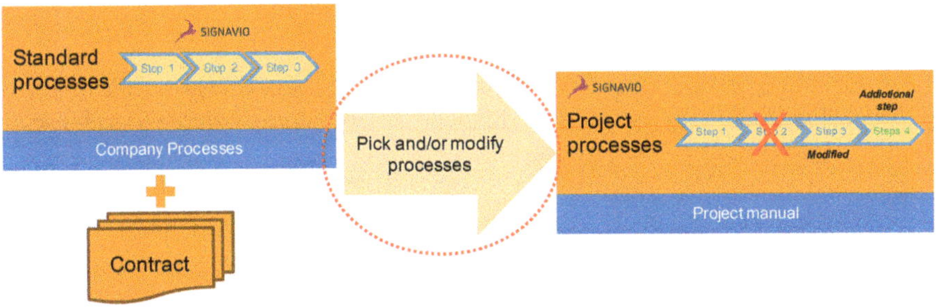

Fig. 6 Pick-and-modify approach

1. One of our main concerns was to ensure the BPM approach's applicability. Several actions were taken in this regard, specifically:
   (a) Rather than one big corporate project, we executed small BPM projects with a clear focus on a specific set of prioritized processes. We sought to harmonize and standardize operative processes only in the areas where doing so was reasonable. The goal of harmonizing the processes differed from that of establishing process orientation with a particular scope in each unit.
   (b) We established a blueprint for BPM governance and adapted it to the specific requirements of the selected pilot units.
   (c) We used Signavio[2] as the Business Process Analysis (BPA) system to enable fast process development and easy application for our end users. Specifically, Signavio Process Manager facilitated easy and detailed process modeling, and Signavio Collaboration Hub provided valuable functionality for accessing, sharing, and analyzing the processes.
   (d) We designed everything around the end users (end-to-end processes) and aligned all our execution activities with the particular (internal and external) customers' needs. We prioritized our customers and employees in all BPM decisions, rather than using standardized principles [e.g., BPMN language, ISO 9001 norm (ISO, 2015)].
   (e) We used agile tools like SCRUM[3] for challenges in the *Complex domain*. Following the SCRUM recommendations, we installed a strong moderator for the project development for such processes.
2. Typical process models and BPM initiatives have a limited long-term impact on execution quality in complex environments like our plant engineering project business. Making significant execution improvements required considerable work on our basic paradigm. We invested heavily in answering the questions, "Why do we need process orientation and why do we need the shift from thinking in functions to thinking in processes?" rather than focusing only on how we build process models and what to focus on for design and execution. Our goal was to

[2]https://www.signavio.com

[3]https://www.scrum.org

increase the acceptance of BPM activities, so we took several actions in this regard:

(a) We enabled the ability to find and work on mono-disciplinary content with a tailor-made view to allow individual disciplines to speed up end users' understanding of the processes.
(b) *Gamification* approaches (De Smedt, De Weerdt, Serral, & Vanthienen, 2016; Deterding et al., 2011) were developed to enable a paradigm shift in the mindsets of the affected stakeholders at various levels. We developed and applied a version of the famous coin-flipping game Slotter, among others, which we adapted to BPM. The goal was to experience differing levels of business processes' efficiency and stability and compare them to our daily business so we could clarify the added value of a process-oriented execution approach.
(c) We created a Bilfinger-specific SIPOC (Supplier, Input, Process, Output, and Customer) template (GoLeanSixSigma, 1988) to structure the content required to build a process model. We also analyzed typical best practices of successful project teams (the Formula 1 pit-stop teams, among others) and discussed lessons learned to improve the way of work.
(d) Finally, we created short videos to communicate the benefits of BPM that were being gained.

4 Results Achieved

At the beginning of this initiative, most of our stakeholders were reluctant and skeptical about the paradigm shift. However, after developing our novel approach to the step-by-step definition of process architectures for organizational units, we received positive feedback from our internal (e.g., employees) and external (e.g., customers) stakeholders. The positive feedback was also evidenced by improvement in several aspects of the organization:

(a) Every team member knew exactly what to do, how to do it, and which tool to use to reduce losses and increase the project's quality.
(b) Thanks to the standardized processes, flexibility in the application of processes to different projects' requirements increased.
(c) Because of intrinsic motivation by the management department, overall acceptance for the implementation of BPM increased.
(d) The focus on interfaces improved cross-departmental collaboration.
(e) Thanks to the live commenting feature of the selected BPA tool (Signavio), interactions increased and improved.

The paradigm shift with the adoption of BPM was a positive experience, which was clear in the pilot groups:

(a) The operative management team spread the idea of process orientation in their respective groups and platforms.
(b) There was no discussion about why we decided to invest time and effort into continuous improvement of the processes.
(c) The project managers started to expect team members to work based on the designed processes without feeling forced by the BPM rules.

In addition, flexibility in how business processes can be applied was achieved. Using the guiding principles described above, we looked at BPM from a completely different angle, which was an important step toward increasing BPM's impact and overcoming our business's complex environment.

The advantages the engineering community acknowledged were reduction of interface risks, more reliable process execution, much faster integration of temporary staff, and (hence) the opportunity to level resources between the companies.

5 Lessons Learned

We conclude that establishing BPM at large corporations is a complex task that must be done step by step and giving the implementation of the BPM practices and to the effort required to change the end users' mindset about process orientation the same importance. The approach must be flexible to accommodate different customers' needs and should be evaluated by applying it in several distinct scenarios. In successful cases, the positive feedback creates intrinsic motivation for other organizational units in the corporation so implementation can be rolled out more easily.

One of our key success factors was to design a blueprint as a universal enterprise process architecture and create a copy of it (and its process models) at the start of every project. The initial model was then stripped down to its relevant processes and amended in accordance with the project's specific needs. We will follow a similar approach when we have to face a similar problem in the future.

Another key success factor was the application of gamification to ease the paradigm shift and help end users understand the end-to-end processes. We could spend weeks, months, or even years laboring with process models trying to change our results and not even begin to approach the phenomenon of change that occurred spontaneously when our employees saw things differently and understood why. Using games and videos, we helped them understand and believe in the advantages of adopting BPM.

We also noticed that simply deploying process models in a process modeling tool does not necessarily lead to their employees' comprehending and using them. All employees must be taught that process models are a means of communication and that they are never finalized, as improvement is an iterative and continuous task.

Given the good results achieved, we are planning to continue to use our approach and practices in other Bilfinger units to address the requirements of other types of processes. Applying the approach to other projects will help us improve the blueprint and give visibility to our approach beyond our company's boundaries so other organizations apply what we learned in their own settings. Becoming informed about the benefits achieved in previous cases would help organizations to move from a top-down approach in which the top management pushes the adoption of BPM to the units by means of a harmonized approach, an approach organizational units tend to resist, to a bottom-up approach in which the units themselves are interested in adopting BPM, easing the creation of a blueprint.

References

APQC. (1992). *APQC's process classification framework.* Accessed March 19, 2020. www.apqc.org/process-performance-management/process-frameworks.

De Smedt, J., De Weerdt, J., Serral, E., & Vanthienen, J. (2016). *Gamification of declarative process models for learning and model verification*. BPM Workshops, pp. 432–443.

Deterding, S., Dixon, D, Khaled, R., & Nacke, L. (2011). From game design elements to gamefulness: Defining "gamification". *International Academic MindTrek Conference: Envisioning Future Media Environments*, pp. 9–15.

Dumas, M., La Rosa, M., Mendling, J., & Reijers, H. A. (2018). *Fundamentals of business process management* (2nd ed.). Springer.

GoLeanSixSigma. (1988). *SIPOC template description.* Accessed March 19, 2020 from goleansixsigma.com/sipoc/

Hasan, H. (2012). Unordered business processes, sustainability and green IS. In J. vom Brocke, S. Seidel, & J. Recker (Eds.), *Green business process management: towards the sustainable enterprise* (pp. 39–58). Springer.

ISO. (2015). ISO 9001:2015 on quality management systems. Accessed March 19, 2020, from www.iso.org/obp/ui/#iso:std:iso:9001:ed-5:v1:en

Kurtz, C. F., & Snowden, D. J. (2003). The new dynamics of strategy: Sense-making in a complex and complicated world. *IBM Systems Journal, 42*, 462–483.

OMG, Object Management Group. (2011). *"BPMN 2.0." Recommendation.*

vom Brocke, J., Mendling, J., & Rosemann, M. (2021). Planning and scoping business process management projects and programs with the BPM billboard. In J. vom Brocke, J. Mendling, & M. Rosemann (Eds.), *BPM cases. Digital innovation and business transformation in practice* (Vol. 2). Springer.

Adoption of Globally Unified Process Standards: The Case of the Production Company Marabu

Klaus Cee, Iris Bruns, Andreas Schachermeier, and Lena Franziska Kaiser

1 Introduction

For more than 150 years, Marabu GmbH & Co. KG has been an innovator and a reliable partner for businesses and users of screen printing inks, pad printing inks, digital printing inks, and creative colors. More than 500 qualified employees in the Marabu Group provide customers all over the world with a wide range of inks, with annual sales of more than 100 million euros. Founded in Stuttgart, Germany, in 1859, the family business has a worldwide presence with 16 subsidiaries and distribution partners in more than 100 countries. Marabu sets a gold standard in terms of high-quality special inks with the "Made in Germany" seal, the market launch of circa five new color series per year, and limited-edition inks to meet customer requirements. Top-class technical services, practical customer training courses, and a focus on environmental awareness are central components of Marabu's company philosophy. Marabu has established sustainable business practices as an important part of its operations and has proven itself in this regard with numerous actions and solid results. Marabu has received multiple awards, as the

K. Cee
Marabu GmbH & Co. KG, Tamm, Germany
e-mail: cee@marabu.com

I. Bruns
ConSense GmbH, Aachen, Germany
e-mail: i.bruns@consense-gmbh.de

A. Schachermeier
ConSense Management Systems GmbH, Aachen, Germany
e-mail: a.schachermeier@consense-gmbh.at

L. F. Kaiser (✉)
University of Liechtenstein, Vaduz, Liechtenstein
e-mail: lena.kaiser@uni.li

J. vom Brocke et al. (eds.), *Business Process Management Cases Vol. 2*,
https://doi.org/10.1007/978-3-662-63047-1_19

company develops products that are designed to reduce the impact on users and the environment.

However, Marabu has faced some challenges. As a result of corporate restructuring, its subsidiaries are more closely aligned with the parent company in Germany. This alignment requires the standardization of processes that are in line with the parent company's quality requirements. In addition, Marabu's customers have called for certified processes in the subsidiaries, which Marabu determined would be addressed by introducing a unified, certified quality management (QM) system (ISO 9001) and an environmental management system (ISO 14001). The International Organization for Standardization (ISO; http://www.iso.org) provides common standards between nations to facilitate world trade. In this regard, Marabu serves as a very rich case to show how a BPM program can be designed to support standardization in a global and distributed corporate setting in manufacturing (vom Brocke, Mendling, & Rosemann, 2021).

To master the challenge of implementing a new quality and environmental management system, Marabu took a holistic view of business processes and tackled complexity by breaking down processes into smaller parts (Rosemann & vom Brocke, 2015). The core pillars (i.e., strategic alignment, governance, methods, information technology, people, and culture) of business process management (BPM) provide guidance in the form of the critical success factors that should be achieved when seeking successful implementation (Rosemann & vom Brocke, 2015; Schmiedel & vom Brocke, 2015): Align BPM with the company's overall strategy (*strategic alignment*), clearly define roles and responsibilities (*governance*), use techniques or approaches that have a process focus (*methods*), use information technology solutions (*information technology*), involve the people (*people*), and create a BPM-supportive culture (*culture*) (Rosemann & vom Brocke, 2015).

The case of Marabu contributes to the broader discussion on adopting unified process standards, especially in terms of quality management and environmental management systems, QM itself, and process improvement. QM encompasses all activities and objectives that are intended to foster continuous improvement and organizational change (Kaynak & Hartley, 2005). Scholars have found that QM can lead to improved performance in terms of business results, innovation, operations, and quality (Kaynak & Hartley, 2005; Ravichandran & Rai, 2000). This chapter describes the case of Marabu's implementation of a quality and environmental management system, the actions that were taken, the results achieved, and the lessons learned.

2 Situation Faced

Good business performance is required for businesses to succeed, and sustainable quality plays an important role. In general, customers, business partners, and even company employees at Marabu were demanding a QM standard based on ISO 9001 (Najmi & Kehoe, 2001; Zhang, 2000). Many arguments favor introducing globally unified processes with the help of a QM system, as introducing such a system can improve, for example, customer satisfaction, documentation availability, internal communication, compliance, risk management, efficient working practices, performance measurement, and control of business processes (Noe, Hollenbeck, Gerhart, & Wright, 2017). Overall, the correct implementation and use of a QM system can lead to significant advantages for a company in terms of such factors as quality assurance and satisfying the requirements of the external environment (Najmi & Kehoe, 2001; Rusjan & Alič, 2010).

There were several reasons behind Marabu's decision to implement a management system. First, the new organizational structure required the company to standardize its processes globally. As a result of a strategic reorientation, the subsidiary companies had become more closely linked to the parent company over the previous few years. The parent company sets the standards for quality and environmental management and occupational health and safety, which are applicable to all subsidiary companies. The original plants have been certified according to ISO 9001 since 1995, and since 2003 according to ISO 14001. With the OHSAS 18001 certification in 2012 and its associated "Systematic Safety" seal of approval, the subsidiary companies have now embedded occupational health and safety within the company standards. These standards also had to be guaranteed in the other sites.

Second, key international customers expected that Marabu would implement a global quality and environmental management system to ensure that the product quality met and even exceeded their expectations.

Third, Marabu's own quality demands and the desire to receive TÜV SÜD multisite certification for the Marabu Group required the introduction of such a system. This certification is available for companies with multiple sites and is available only if the branches operate using a common quality and environmental management system. In addition, the management systems must be planned and controlled centrally, and the sites are then subject to a common annual audit program.

Finally, the subsidiaries wanted to improve as business locations and to have more responsibility. Unified and certified processes were key to achieving this goal.

Prior to the implementation of the tool, the overarching challenge was that the German sites were already using a computer-supported system that could not operate over multiple sites and did not include a tool for process modeling. This way of working not only made global cooperation more difficult but was also inefficient. For example, if any revisions were required, process flowcharts had to be prepared separately in another program and then transferred to the current management system via a "copy-and-paste" procedure, a complex process.

Marabu's intent was to satisfy the requirements mentioned above and to prepare the company for the future. To achieve this goal, Marabu decided in December 2012 that a new integrated quality and environmental management system would be rolled out, initially among the foreign plants and later among the whole Marabu Group. The schedule for the project was tight because the first certifications were scheduled for 2013.

3 Action Taken

Several actions were taken to achieve the overall goal of unified process standards and continuous improvement. The core pillars of BPM helped to break the complex project into smaller parts and served as guidance against disregarding any critical success factor (Rosemann & vom Brocke, 2015). First, the top management and the workforce had to be convinced of the plan's merit (i.e., critical success factors culture and people), and the decision had to be aligned to the company's overall strategy (i.e., strategic alignment, governance). Then suitable software had to be found that met the previously defined requirements (i.e., information technology), and software settings had to be worked out and preparations made for the software implementation. Next, the implementation took place, followed by continually revisiting the processes to allow for improvements in the system (i.e., method).

3.1 Commitment from the Top Management and the Workforce

The adoption of a QM system should be a strategic decision made by the company's top management (Deming, 1986; Hoang, Igel, & Laosirihongthong, 2010; Juran, 1986) and should be in line with the company's overall strategy (Rosemann & vom Brocke, 2015). Such decisions by the top management demonstrate its commitment to the development, implementation, and maintenance of the new system. This level of commitment is a vital factor in QM, as it helps to ensure that the vision is communicated, quality policies are developed, and the company culture is changed. Top management's commitment is associated with the successful implementation of ISO 9001 (Demirbag & Sahadev, 2008), but the relationship between the management and the employees is central to the ability to manage quality, which refers to culture as a critical success factor (Rosemann & vom Brocke, 2015). Therefore, the management team must know how to motivate and involve the workforce to enable smooth implementation (Zelnik, Maletič, Maletič, & Gomišček, 2012).

At Marabu, the entire top management team was convinced of the benefits of a QM system. Responsibilities were allocated in a way that ensured that employees were involved in the project. The correct distribution of responsibilities and ownership helps individuals to identify with the project (Rosemann & vom Brocke, 2015) and helps ensure that top management is always informed about the current state of affairs.

The Corporate Management Representative (CMR) and the Quality, Environment and Safety (QES) ISO team led the project, monitoring the management documentation and the modifications to the core processes in the joint management system, and controlling and carrying out the implementation of ISO 9001 and 14001 in various subsidiaries. The CMR, the key person involved in the transition, had an overview of the whole project. The CMR was responsible for the guidance and supervision of local QM representatives and environmental management representatives, managed the annual internal audit program of the Marabu Group, and was involved in steering activities regarding the continuous improvement process.

Top management support and a team or person who feels responsible for the project can help to ensure successful implementation, but successful implementation also requires employees, "the human capital of an organization" (Rosemann & vom Brocke, 2015, p. 113), to implement the project. Three types of training were offered to the employees: comprehensive training for all employees who would be working with the system, comprehension training for employees who would be working with the system but not making any changes to it, and process-owner training for employees who would be responsible for processes (Dumas, La Rosa, Mendling, & Reijers, 2018). The QM representatives and environmental management representatives also received intensive training at the company's headquarters since they would have to report directly to headquarters.

3.2 Software Selection

Software or information systems that enable or improve process activities refer to the critical success factor of information technology (Rosemann & vom Brocke, 2015). People from the QM and IT departments compared software providers based on predefined selection criteria that included the software's ease of use, an integrated tool for process modeling, process orientation via process maps, and versatile linking possibilities from main processes and subprocesses to other applicable documents in the software and other systems. Software providers that met the selection criteria were chosen based on market research and personal interviews at trade fairs. Only one software provider met Marabu's most important requirements: multilingualism and a multisite capability. ConSense GmbH from Aachen, a specialist in user-friendly and intuitive software for processes and QM, has been developing innovative solutions for the complete electronic support of ISO 9001 since 2003. The special features of ConSense software include a practical multilingual concept and site-specific deviations, both of which support the cautious harmonization of company-wide standards.

Since the selection of the right software provider should be done with care, a hands-on workshop was held to test ConSense's software products under live conditions. During the workshop, potential users received detailed information about the software's functions and modules and used the software on a sample project. The setting also facilitated the exchange with other prospective customers about their experiences with the various QM systems available on the market. The involvement of the employees in the selection process and the exchange with other users of the system was valuable since new technologies do not create value right away; people and processes must integrate the new technology into the company before value can be created (Schmiedel & vom Brocke, 2015).

3.3 Definition of System Properties

The selection criteria for the software were elaborated into extensive system properties, which contributed to employees' quick acceptance and adoption of the new system.

Multilingualism One important selection criterion was software multilingualism. The ConSense software not only covers a series of interface languages but also enables the use of two language concepts for documents and processes: identical content translated to other languages and varying content used in other languages. The varying-content concept is required if, as with Marabu, a simple translation of processes is not sufficient because local, regional, or national characteristics require variations. In this case, the software ensures an all-encompassing modification if a change is made to a central specification. This function is especially useful for the annual audits, which are executed in two languages.

System Operation The system should be easy to operate. Employees can find processes by using a search function since processes are named after the same structure worldwide. Moreover, the system has an appealing and intuitively designed interface (Fig. 1). One key aspect of the system is its process visualization feature, which allows the process managers to create and manage processes themselves. However, the headquarters still retains central control to ensure quality. Overall, employees enjoy working with the new system, reducing the risk of employees rejecting it.

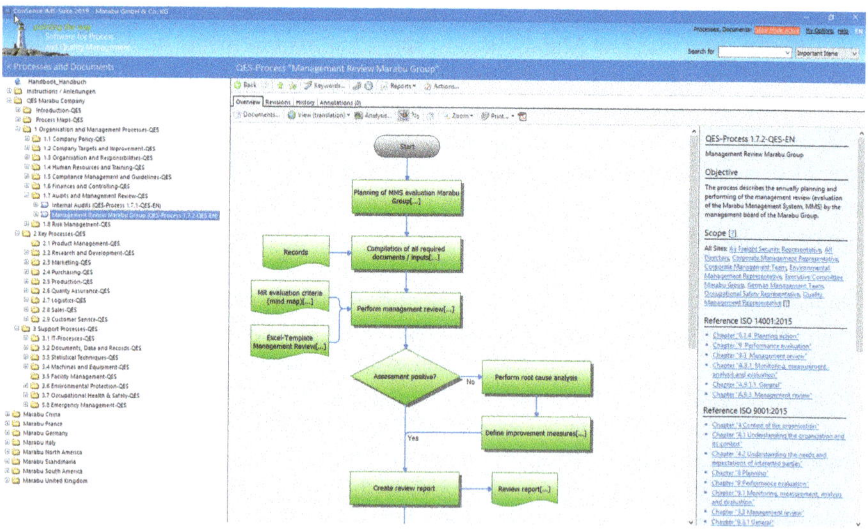

Fig. 1 Screenshot of ConSense IMS that depicts the management review process at the group level (as one example of a modeled process) while enabling variations in processes for special requirements at certain sites (source: Marabu)

Visualization The benefits of the unified visualization of processes include fostering global collaboration, reducing loss of knowledge if employees leave the company, and building a solid foundation for audits. The new system also includes internal specifications for visualizing processes through flowcharts that are globally applicable (e.g., concerning symbols, sizes, distances). These style guides prevent uncontrolled growth of process illustrations, as occurred with the previous system.

3.4 Rapid Adoption of Globally Unified Process Standards

Marabu adopted the new unified process standards within 2 years. The project started with developing the QES guidelines, preparing the most important documents, and selecting the appropriate ConSense IMS software. After the preparation phase, the process documentation was created and adapted, including local process variations and work instructions for each site. Where necessary, the process documentation was translated into other languages. In June 2013, Marabu France and its four sites (at that time) were certified. Four months later, in October 2013, the new management system supported the successful certification of the Chinese site to ISO 9001 and 14001. A team of employees from the central QES section assisted their French and Chinese colleagues with the implementation for approximately 6 months. The process landscape was developed in workshops and configured with ConSense. The integrated flow chart manager was particularly useful because of its quick and simple capacity for modeling processes. A month after China, the US plant was certified in November 2013. In July 2014, the sites in Tamm (Marabu HQ) and Bietigheim-Bissingen were audited based on ISO 9001 and 14001, followed by Brazil and Sweden in October 2014, Italy in 2015 and, finally, Marabu UK. All certifications were completed successfully within the planned period and with the desired quality.

3.5 Continuous Improvement

After the new system was implemented, the project was still far from over because the system formed the basis for continuous improvement. With the new system in place, adherence to processes could be checked, the continuous improvement of workflows could be ensured, and so the goal of operational excellence could be achieved (Schmiedel & vom Brocke, 2015). Deming's plan–do–check–act (PDCA) cycle was chosen as a method (Rosemann & vom Brocke, 2015) by which to support the continuous improvement process of the process lifecycle (Dumas et al., 2018). PDCA is a widespread, iterative, four-stage method that companies can use as they work toward continuous improvement (Kiran, 2016). Marabu uses Deming's PDCA cycle to ensure that all quality and environmental standards are met and are continuously improved.

Plan In the "plan" stage, quality and environmental aspects that need to be improved or changed to conform with legal and other requirements are worked out and objectives, targets, and the procedure are defined.

Do In this stage, processes are executed, the goal and the benefits of the changes are communicated, awareness is created, and employees are trained as needed. Changes are documented so they can be monitored later.

Check In the "check" stage, processes are measured and subsequent results are analyzed and contrasted with expected process performance. When results and expectations vary, potential causes are assessed to identify options to improve the processes.

Act In this stage, the improvement options are implemented. If the implemented improvement is found in the next "do" phase not to have solved the issue, the improvement options were not effective and the root-cause analysis is conducted again.

4 Results Achieved

The implementation of a unified quality and environmental management system was strategically important for Marabu to ensure compliance with local legal regulations, increase in legal security, and receive ratings as an A-supplier. Marabu implemented the system successfully as a result of the interplay between the socio side (e.g., skills, attitudes, values) and the technical side (e.g., process, task, technology) (Bostrom & Heinen, 1977; Lyytinen & Newman, 2008).

The new system ensures that there are no accidental local deviations in processes and provides more transparency since all employees have access to all relevant processes. This transparency fosters collaboration and support between the subsidiaries and their employees. When employees define a new process, they do not have to start from scratch but can see whether the process has already been implemented at another subsidiary. Since all processes are modeled in predefined standards, processes can be adopted and supplemented if necessary. The transparency of the new management system also simplifies the work of the QES team since the team can now access all sites anywhere in the world and can intervene at an early stage if required. Orientation is simple because the same interface is used everywhere.

The amount of support needed from headquarters to subsidiaries was reduced by 30–60%, depending on the subsidiary, since process owners maintain the system themselves instead of its being done centrally, as was once the case. Processes are modeled according to standards that were defined by local quality and environmental representatives at the sites after they participated in the appropriate training and workshops. Only the final test and its approval remained centralized.

Moreover, processes do not always have to be invented, as employees can learn from established processes even when they are at other sites, saving time and resources. Another valuable feature of the system is the translation function for processes and documents, which enables documents that are written in one language to be translated to another quickly (e.g., during audits). Audits are usually carried out bilingually, which facilitates quick recognition of deviations from the specified standards and, thus, immediate action.

Marabu contends that a worldwide standardized management system is not only useful for standard-compliant documentation but also helpful in the pursuit of a much more future-oriented goal: the continuous improvement process.

5 Lessons Learned

Marabu learned valuable lessons through the rapid introduction of its QM system.

Selection of the Right QM System Provider The selection of the QM system provider should not be made in a rush, as the company will use the system for many years. A suitable system that meets all requirements and enjoys reliable cooperation from the software provider is all-important, as the company's know-how is stored in the QM system. Having a strong partner while recording processes, migrating data from one system to another, and training employees on how to use the new software facilitates the whole project.

Involving the Entire Workforce In addition to top management, the whole workforce should be on board when adopting a new management system. If a management system is not accepted and "lived" in the company, it cannot be optimally used for continuous improvement and organizational control. Since continuous improvement is the goal, the system cannot be static, as it is subject to constant testing and change processes. The corresponding changes must be communicated to the employees and presented transparently so the necessary measures are implemented. More responsibility for Marabu's employees increased acceptance of the management system and led to a lived management system that drives the continuous improvement process.

Constantly Raising Awareness of the QM System in the Minds of the Work-Force The system should be in the minds of employees not only shortly before and during audits but always, as part of their daily routines. Training and regular refresher sessions can remind employees of the benefits of using the system. However, after initially strong skepticism, especially at sites that did not yet have a management system in place, a few training runs established a routine, and the employees quickly noticed the benefits, including higher customer satisfaction and more orders.

Not Underestimating Culture Cultural conditions differ in a globally operating company, and these cultural differences must be anticipated and prepared for. Intercultural communication workshops can be helpful, as can integrating time buffers into the project plan as, for instance, time management in Brazil and employee turnover in China differ from those in Germany. The key functions of the system—multilingualism and its multisite capability—had a significant impact on the appreciation of employees' cultures, as they could work in their own languages, but there was still transparency. Employees tend to feel more comfortable when they can move within their own cultural environments, an aspect that should not be underestimated.

It Is All About the Attitude From the outset, Marabu communicated to its employees that the company wanted to support them during the change and that it would not be monitoring them. In retrospect, this approach made a big difference, as employees reacted positively to the implementation of the new system, even though it was a big change for some employees.

Change that Has Paid Off The unified system ensures that there are no local variations in the quality and environmental management system while simplifying re-certifications. Marabu not only satisfied its customers and its own quality requirements but also created the basis for a learning and continuously improving organization. The newly established QM system provides a framework for measuring and improving Marabu's performance for many years to come.

References

Bostrom, R. P., & Heinen, J. S. (1977). MIS problems and failures: A socio-technical perspective. Part I: The causes. *MIS Quarterly, 1*(3), 17–32.

Deming, W. E. (1986). *Out of crisis, centre for advanced engineering study*. Cambridge, MA: Massachusetts Institute of Technology.

Demirbag, M., & Sahadev, S. (2008). Exploring the antecedents of quality commitment among employees: An empirical study. *International Journal of Quality and Reliability Management, 25*(5), 494–507.

Dumas, M., La Rosa, M., Mendling, J., & Reijers, H. A. (2018). *Fundamentals of business process management* (2nd ed.). Berlin: Springer.

Hoang, D. T., Igel, B., & Laosirihongthong, T. (2010). Total quality management (TQM) strategy and organisational characteristics: Evidence from a recent WTO member. *Total Quality Management, 21*(9), 931–951.

Juran, J. M. (1986). *Quality control handbook*. New York, NY: McGraw Hill.

Kaynak, H., & Hartley, J. L. (2005). Exploring quality management practices and high tech firm performance. *The Journal of High Technology Management Research, 16*(2), 255–272.

Kiran, D. R. (2016). *Total quality management: Key concepts and case studies*. Oxford: Butterworth-Heinemann.

Lyytinen, K., & Newman, M. (2008). Explaining information systems change: a punctuated socio-technical change model. *European Journal of Information Systems, 17*(6), 589–613.

Najmi, M., & Kehoe, D. F. (2001). The role of performance measurement systems in promoting quality development beyond ISO 9000. *International Journal of Operations & Production Management, 21*(1, 2), 159–172.

Noe, R. A., Hollenbeck, J. R., Gerhart, B., & Wright, P. M. (2017). *Human resource management: Gaining a competitive advantage*. New York, NY: McGraw-Hill Education.

Ravichandran, T., & Rai, A. (2000). Quality management in systems development: An organizational system perspective. *MIS Quarterly, 24*(3), 381–415.

Rosemann, M., & vom Brocke, J. (2015). The six core elements of business process management. In *Handbook on business process management 1* (pp. 105–122). Berlin: Springer.

Rusjan, B., & Alič, M. (2010). Capitalising on ISO 9001 benefits for strategic results. *International Journal of Quality and Reliability Management, 27*(7), 756–778.

Schmiedel, T., & vom Brocke, J. (2015). Business process management: Potentials and challeng-es of driving innovation. In *BPM-driving innovation in a digital world* (pp. 3–15). Cham: Springer.

vom Brocke, J., Mendling, J., & Rosemann, M. (2021). Planning and scoping business process management projects and programs with the BPM billboard. In J. vom Brocke, J. Mendling, & M. Rosemann (Eds.), *BPM cases. Digital innovation and business transformation in practice* (Vol. 2). Springer.

Zelnik, M., Maletič, M., Maletič, D., & Gomišček, B. (2012). Quality management systems as a link between management and employees. *Total Quality Management and Business Excellence, 23*(1), 45–62.

Zhang, Z. (2000). Developing a model of quality management methods and evaluating their effects on business performance. *Total Quality Management, 11*(1), 129–137.

A Processes Reference Framework for the Creative and Cultural Industries. The Case of the Puglia Creativa Cluster

Angelo Corallo, Mariangela Lazoi, Manuela Marra, Lorenzo Quarta, Aurora Rimini, and Cesare Liaci

1 Introduction

Cultural and creative industries' (CCIs) main purpose is the production or reproduction, promotion, distribution or commercialization of goods, services, and activities of a cultural, artistic, or heritage-related nature (EY, Italia Creativa, 2016). These organizations are facing considerable disruption. In the performing arts sector, the sales of physical products, which for years has been the main source of income, has dramatically decreased because of new ways for customers to consume the product (e.g., digitally). Even though digital sales are growing, their sales do not compensate for the loss incurred by the decline in in-person sales.

In this scenario, events can be significant sources of income and a way to advertise a cultural and creative product. From this observation emerges the necessity to organize more events in an attractive and efficient way to generate income from paying spectators and media exposure.

Cultural and creative products like festivals, concerts, events, tours, exhibitions, and theater performances have a life cycle that could be managed in a more efficient way by building on technologies and approaches that are well known in business process management (BPM). BPM initiatives can help companies to model and

A. Corallo · M. Lazoi · M. Marra · A. Rimini (✉)
Department of Innovation Engineering, University of Salento, Lecce, Italy
e-mail: angelo.corallo@unisalento.it; mariangela.lazoi@unisalento.it;
manuela.marra@unisalento.it; aurora.rimini@unisalento.it

L. Quarta
Bit.Arts SRL, Lecce, Italy
e-mail: lorenzo.quarta@bitarts.it

C. Liaci
Società Cooperativa Coolclub, Lecce, Italy
e-mail: cesare@coolclub.it

J. vom Brocke et al. (eds.), *Business Process Management Cases Vol. 2*,
https://doi.org/10.1007/978-3-662-63047-1_20

improve their processes quickly and cost-effectively to meet their business needs, but few projects and studies in the CCI field apply BPM techniques.

This work supports the introduction of BPM in arts and creative organizations. The case, therewith, serves as an example for the role of context in BPM (vom Brocke, Mendling, & Rosemann, 2021), and it specifically shows how the activities in the BPM program have been tailor-made to meet the requirements of a creative sector. The sector is represented by Distretto Puglia Creativa, a cluster association recognized by the Apulian Region that is largely representative of the industry's regional dimensions. Distretto Puglia Creativa is a productive cluster of companies that operate in the CCI and is distributed into the fields of performing arts (theater, dance, music, festivals), cultural industries (cinema, media, audiovisual, gaming, software, publishing), creative industries (design, "made in Italy," architecture, communication agencies), heritage (visual arts, cultural hub, cultural heritage, entertainment places, exhibitions), creative-driven services (social innovation, services, training), universities, and public and private institutions active in the field. The research focuses on the innovation needs for the market for performing arts.

We analyzed four companies that belong to the Puglia Creativa cluster and operate in the performing arts sector by means of interviews and focus groups. These companies are well known and appreciated in the Apulian Region, but despite many years of experience, they do not have an overall view of organizational processes and their relationships. They have never worked on identifying their processes (vom Brocke, Zelt, & Schmiedel, 2015), so it was necessary first to identify the organizations' business processes. The four organizations were chosen as representative of the four performing arts: theatrical performances (theater and dance), live music, festival production, and exhibition. The objective of this initial analysis was to learn how an arts and cultural organization works so we could maximize its value through a BPM initiative.

The interviews and focus groups identified the likely core processes, support processes, and management processes in an arts and creative organization and the relationships among them so as to define a process architecture. The method we followed can help organizations introduce BPM initiatives for defining an enterprise process architecture for strategic alignment (Rosemann & vom Brocke, 2010). Strategic alignment is fundamental to arts and creative organizations, which must now maximize their economic potential through improved resource allocation and reduced effort expended in producing a live event. One point that emerged from the study was that the organizations follow well-established activities during their work but without doing so in any formalized way. In addition, the organizations were in no way aware of how these activities are inputs for standardizing processes.

Suppose you are an art director: One of the biggest challenges you face is collecting information to be used in making predictions or assessments because each person on the team uses his or her own tools to collect and share information. Another problem that you may face is checking on the status of activities. If the team is not in the habit of receiving updates on the progress of planned activities, it may be difficult to resolve an unexpected issue. Of course, one of your biggest problems is your lack of awareness about the time and resources necessary to produce your event based on real measurements because your internal processes do not have a structure.

Based on this imagined context, the goal of this industrial case study is to propose a reference framework for the CCI performing arts companies that systemizes daily activities into complete and rigorous information flows involving input–output assets and a network of actors who work together to add value to each live event. The result of the study is a new process-classification framework. The framework is inspired by the APQC's process-classification framework (PCF) (APQC's Process Classification Framework (PCF)®, 2019), but no enterprise process framework—not even APQC's PCF focuses on the specific features of the performing arts sector.

2 Situation Faced

2.1 CCIs' Far from Process-Oriented Culture

Organizations in the arts and cultural industry have to manage their business processes, as these processes are subject to constant changes and are influenced by factors both internal and external to their environment. External changes can be cultural (e.g., participation in cultural activities and expenditures on culture and recreation), social (e.g., students enrolled in arts and humanities studies), demographic (highly educated people), economic (e.g., employment in cultural industries), political (e.g. government expenditures on culture), legal (e.g., safety standards for the performing arts), or technological (e.g., government expenditures on research and development) (Martinaityte & Kregzdaite, 2015). Internal changes can be related to the public, member organizations, boards of directors, staff, facilities, and growth and financial operations.

In recent years, CCIs have been characterized by large incomes (US$2.250 billion in global revenue in 2013) (EY, Italia Creativa, 2016) and have been the target of many public and private (regional and European) initiatives to drive economic growth and create jobs. Even so, definitions of which industries are part of the CCI domain are rare. UNESCO's definition includes 11 sectors: advertising, architecture, books, gaming, music, movies, newspapers and magazines, performing arts, radio, television, and visual arts (EY, Italia Creativa, 2016).

Despite these industries' potential, the dynamism and complexity of business processes in the CCI domain is proportional to the lack of process design, organization, and awareness. When the study began, the members of the organizations explained how they learned the best practices for producing an event only after several years of experience and that everyone in the organizations learned to play more than one role. This approach is the result of working methods that are not based on business processes. These organizations have never conducted a process analysis to help them reflect on the allocation of resources and distribution of responsibilities. In addition, the socioeconomic process and most of the governmental initiatives in the last few decades have underestimated the category's economic potential and reduced have this category to one merely of leisure activities. As a result, these enterprises have not been able to secure the necessary funding and cultural incentives to improve and seek organizational innovation, unlike other sectors (e.g., aerospace and manufacturing), where the explicit management of processes is much more sophisticated and established.

In a hypercompetitive business environment, the most successful companies are those that can propose a new idea, unique product, or application. To achieve this objective and secure a competitive advantage, companies can use the concepts of process innovation (Schilling & Izzo, 2012), but CCIs do not have the necessary financial resources or competences to do this by themselves. Therefore, BPM practices have to be developed inside these organizations with the objective of increasing process efficiency and effectiveness through established tools and management approaches like BPM (vom Brocke et al., 2015). Our work fills this need by systematically developing methods and organizational activities for CCI companies and by encouraging a culture of process orientation that highlights processes and process owners and encourages these companies to design their activities better and to sustain organizational improvements.

2.2 The Industry Case

Our industry case is the Distretto Puglia Creativa, an association recognized in 2012 by the Apulia Region in the south of Italy, according to the Regional law 23\2007. It represents more than 100 Apulian cultural and creative companies, bringing together heterogeneous, mainly Apulian, organizations that operate in various areas of the cultural sector at both the regional and national levels. Our study was carried out with the involvement of four companies in the Distretto Puglia Creativa, all of which operate in the performing arts and whose businesses are successful: *Cantieri Teatrali Koreja*, *Coolclub*, *Bass Culture*, and *Officine Cantelmo*.

We investigate each of the four firms as cases of representative internal business processes. These processes are parts of some of the companies' flagship events and relate to the activities that are carried out to produce a live event. During the interviews, a functional structure was documented for all four organizations that structures the processes into four phases: (1) "event design," which focuses on the artistic direction of the event and relationships with artists, (2) "production," (3) "administration," which focuses on the administrative relationships with stakeholders inside and outside the organization, such as public administration and suppliers, and (4) "promotion and communication."

Cantieri Teatrali Koreja ("Koreja" hereafter) is an innovation theater center with 30 years of history. We chose its staging of the theatrical performance "*Teatro in Tasca*" as a case study. Koreja has an autonomous location, which influences the entire life cycle of its live events. Benefits that emerged during documentation of the case were related to safety and regulations issues, while complications emerged in coordination tasks between the event's design activities and the many other activities carried out in the same structure.

Coolclub Cooperative Society has been involved for more than 10 years in the conception, planning, organization, and promotion of cultural events, press office, and events communications. We chose the live music event the "SEI Festival" as a case study. It is unique in terms of its cyclical nature and continual growth. The annual planning phase includes negotiation between the organization and the artists' managers and the planning of cultural activities that are complementary to the festival's various events.

Bass Culture is an entertainment agency with long experience in the organization, communication, and promotion of events and artistic productions. To investigate the internal process of this organization, we chose a concert by a popular singer as a case study.

Finally, Officine Cantelmo is a multipurpose space for the organization of public and business-oriented live events. Unlike the other three use cases, this case study refers to markets that are periodically organized within the structure. The process starts with the ideation phase, when the exhibition's theme is chosen, which usually depends on the time of year in which it is programmed.

All four organizations have well-established businesses and considerable potential for improvement, but all suffer from a lack of structure in their internal processes. All have redundant activities and activities that could be automated, and all four cases lack communication between the various actors in the process for each information flow. Each business unit is a black box to the others, which multiplies effort and generates qualitatively worse results than might be possible otherwise.

This research offers a complete overview of the performing arts sector, as it analyzes four companies, each of which represents a different subsector of the performing arts sector. The performing arts sector is largely fragmented and would benefit from bringing together the processes and best practices of cultural operators under one methodology. Factors like good management of physical and intangible resources could increase the quality of these companies' events.

3 Action Taken

The industry case study was followed by the action research method. This facilitated collaboration between the researchers and the industry representatives. In this method, several interactions and strong collaboration are required to develop the results from the data gathered (Bryman & Bell, 2015), so it is particularly suitable when undertaking a pragmatic exploration in a practical context and is well aligned with the objectives of this industry case.

The case study exploration started with an analysis of the available process frameworks, especially the APQC PCF Cross-Industry (APQC's Process Classification Framework (PCF)®, 2019), which provides insights into the analysis of processes in various contexts. Based on the framework's structure, the case study proposed a framework for the CCI that is similarly structured and supports the analysis of internal processes. The APQC PCF Cross-Industry framework was

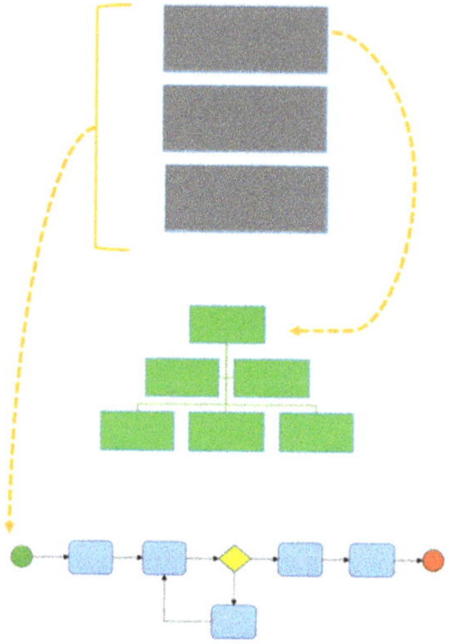

Fig. 1 The interview process analysis approach

used as a reference to guide the research team to define the levels of detail and the main reference categories.

The research started by designing semi-structured interviews and focus groups to collect information. As a first step, semi-structured group interviews were carried out to gather information on the organization, its roles, and its management. Certain key roles in each company were selected so people whose activities were distributed over the event lifecycle were interviewed: the artistic director, the technical manager, the communications manager, and the administrative manager.

Starting from a brief description of the event, information was collected about the types of actors (internal and external to the organization) involved in the event, phases and activities for the realization of the event, coordination of these activities, and the software technologies used.

The group interviews with each company confirmed that all of the activities are related to four process areas—event design, production, administration, and promotion and communication—and that all of these process areas are found in all four companies. Based on this classification, individual interviews and focus groups were designed and managed in each company with the people in charge of the activities for each process area. During the interviews, the weakness, wastes of time, and communication dynamics that slow down or block processes emerged. In addition, all the processes that are activated when the organizations have interactions with external stakeholders were highlighted.

Figure 1 summarizes the detailed information that was collected for the four case studies. The main phases found in the design and realization of the four events analyzed were formalized in a quick model that identifies a specific process area of the organization. Then the process hierarchies were represented using a tree structure that divides the process area into functions. Then we broke the functions down until

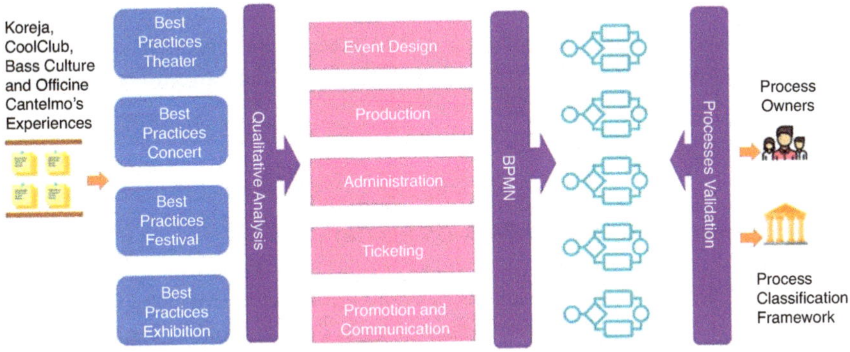

Fig. 2 Action taken

they could not be broken down farther. This approach yielded a description of the process areas, processes, subprocesses, process steps, and activities. At the final stage of analysis, the data on the processes that was collected in the interviews was modeled using BPMN 2.0 diagrams, and the mapped processes were validated with the respondents.

The second phase of the analysis used focus groups (Kitzinger, 1995). One of the advantages of the focus group is that it captures information, including critical issues, from groups of stakeholders in a short time and with a minimum effort. Unlike the semi-structured interview, the focus group is not a unidirectional tool, as interview techniques often have a rigid structure with well-defined roles. The focus group is multidirectional and tends to activate group dynamics, healthy confrontation, and discussion.

Figure 2 shows the actions taken and the results achieved.

Four focus groups were attended by 20 representatives of the four organizations involved in the study. During this event, which took place at the Koreja headquarters, participants discussed commonalities and differences in their organizations and in their ways of working. Long guided discussion sessions made it possible to formalize a shared technical language, which was fundamental to formalizing the framework. The focus group discussions also made it possible to confirm the available content, generalize the results in terms of decomposing processes and activities, and define process owners.

To increase the validity of the analysis, the focus group was open to all members of the Distretto Puglia Creativa association who work in the performing arts sector. The information collected during the interviews and the focus group was classified into either support or operative processes so as to structure the reference framework for the CCIs. These actions made it possible to define the process architecture in each organization (Dumas, La Rosa, Mendling, & Reijers, 2013). The primary challenge was to convince the companies' actors to be careful about the potentiality of the processes, especially about the unacknowledged need to improve how they execute their work. They were invited to think about their way of working and about ways to organize their daily activities. During the interviews, the technological issue emerged several times, and a challenge was to explain the roles certain ICT tools can play in making a difference in process management and the overall organization.

4 Results Achieved

4.1 Creating a Business Process Model for CCIs

We compared the processes of managing a cultural product (a live event in our case) with the help of similar information obtained from the four companies. In general, the interviewees did not have a unified view of their businesses; each function had its own understanding of its activities. The employees were unaware that, even though they produce different kinds of cultural products, they use the same processes. Ticket sales are ticket sales.

The evidence collected in the group and individual interviews and during the focus groups shows that the four companies and even other companies of the Distretto Puglia Creativa do not have significant differences in terms of processes. For example, the development of a business strategy is a process that is carried out informally, and business processes like event coordination and planning, ticketing, budgeting, analytics, asset management, promotion and communication, and safety management are typical for small performing arts organizations in the cultural and creative industries sector.

Using the results of this analysis and the APQC PCF structure, customized for the peculiarities of the performing arts, we developed a first version of a reference model for the business processes of performing arts companies. The framework provides an overview of the classification of processes so it can help companies to define best practices. Figure 3 shows the high-level structure of the reference model for improving performing arts organizations' business processes, which is a starting point for an analysis of how these organizations' processes can be classified.

The CCI framework is decomposed into 12 categories that distinguish among operating processes, management processes, and support processes. The framework classifies these three kinds of processes into four levels of detail (3 kinds of processes $\times$ 4 levels of detail $=$ 12 categories). The first level is classification into four defined "process areas" (from A to D). The second level is the "category" of processes, referred to by integers from 1 to 12. The third level is that of "process groups," indicated by 1.1 to 12.3. The fourth level captures "processes" as expressed by 1.1.1 to 12.3.11. The proposed "CCI Business Processes Reference Model" differs from the APQC PCF Cross-Industry in the classification and definition of categories, groups, and processes, as the proposed reference model groups the categories based on the four process areas defined during the analysis.

The number of categories also differs, as the APQC PCF Cross-Industry framework has 13 categories, while our framework has 12—11 if you consider that our last 2 categories are grouped together because they are not well defined for CCIs. The categories 1.0, 7.0, 9.0, and 10.0 have the same names as the APQC categories, but

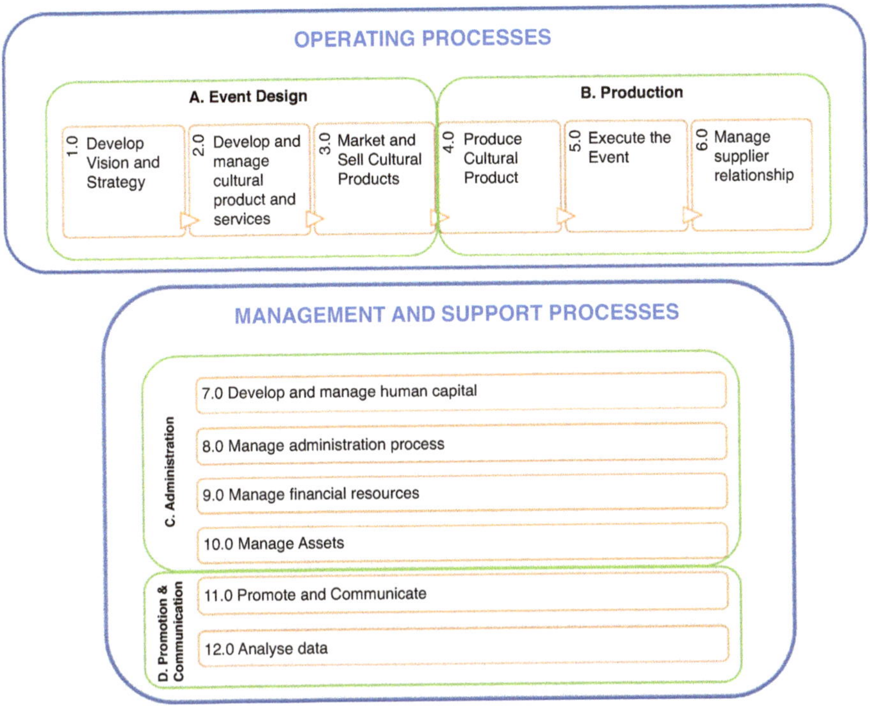

Fig. 3 High-level business processes reference model for cultural and creative industries operating in the performing arts sector (inspired by APQC PCF)

the names of the related process groups and processes are different, as are the names of all the other categories. Furthermore, in the CCI Reference Model, the level of detail arrives at the process level, without the specification of activities and tasks. This reference model, a taxonomy of processes for the performing arts, helps to increase awareness, order, and innovative elements in an unstructured context. The complete framework is available in Tables 1, 2, 3, 4, and 5.

Tables 1, 2, 3, and 4 shows the subsectors of the performing arts sector, from which the "Processes" emerged as best-practices.

In addition to the study's processes reference framework for CCIs shown in Tables 1, 2, 3, 4, and 5 suggests the processes owners for each "Process Group," which emerged from the interviews and focus groups. Thus, the processes framework is enriched by an organizational view that can be used in reengineering the internal processes and optimizing the allocation of human resources. The detailed distribution of "Process Groups" and related process owners is shown in Table 5.

The framework can be used in several ways. The "Processes" can be applied, with the appropriate consideration for each case, by companies that produce differing types of cultural products. In fact, one can use the proposed reference framework to develop a vision of multiple organizations' processes and to lead operational and technological innovation in the performing arts sector. The framework provides a

Table 1 Processes reference framework for performing arts companies: Event design

PA Sector T	F	M	C	ID	A. Event Design - Processes
				1	**Develop Vision and Strategy**
				1.1	**Evaluate external enviroment**
				1.1.1	Analyze artists' trend
				1.1.2	Evaluate artists' proposal
				1.1.3	Choice an artist/company
				1.1.4	Select the format
				1.1.5	Define the theme of the event
				1.1.6	Define event date
				1.1.7	Define the event name
				1.2	**Evaluate internal enviroment**
				1.2.1	Create programme timetable
				1.2.2	Check human resources available
				1.2.3	Check available time
				1.2.4	Design of internal activities related to the event
				1.3	**Bargain for an artist**
				1.3.1	Find artist personal data
				1.3.2	Define payment terms
				1.3.3	Negotiate terms of production
				1.3.4	Define promotion timetable
				1.3.5	Define promotion channels
				1.3.6	Formalize the agreement
				1.3.7	Pay the performance
				1.3.8	Retrieve technical material for event production
				2	**Develop and manage cultural product and services**
				2.1	**Team Design**
				2.1.1	Train the Team
				2.1.2	Sort data among functions
				2.2.	**Organize the Programme**
				2.2.1	Define the programme (i.e. festival/single event)
				2.2.2	Plan collateral activities
				2.2.3	Contact suppliers
				2.2.4	Request preventives
				2.2.5	Evaluate preventives
				2.3.	**Manage the Venue**
				2.3.1	Search the location
				2.3.2	Contact location managers
				2.3.3	Negotiate with the location supplier
				2.3.4	Select and contact engineer for inspection
				2.3.5	Retrieve security document (DUVRI and PSC)
				2.3.6	Measure usable space for exhibition stands
				2.3.7	Define price of each exhibition stand
				2.4	**Manage the Exhibitors**
				2.4.1	Contact loyalized exhibitors
				2.4.2	Contact new exhibitors
				2.4.3	Propose to purchase an stand for the event
				2.4.4	Manage stand reservation requests
				2.4.5	Assign a stand to each booking
				2.4.6	Communicate to exhibitors time, place and stand's number
				3	**Market and Sell Cultural Products**
				3.1	**Manage Ticketing**
				3.1.1	Retrieve main information (date, place, time, artist name)
				3.1.2	Choice ticketing platform
				3.1.3	Access ticketing platform
				3.1.4	Create the event on the platform
				3.1.5	Publicate the event on the platform
				3.1.6	Define sales opening date
				3.1.7	Obtain the link for the ticket's sale
				3.1.8	Forward links to the promotion and communication function
				3.1.9	Contact sale points
				3.1.10	Monitor sales on the platform
				3.1.11	Monitor sales on sales point
				3.1.12	Extract a report
				3.1.13	Control of sales trends up to the execution of the event
				3.1.14	Sales closing
				3.1.15	Extract the final report
				3.2	**Manage the Ticket Office**
				3.2.1	Manage the ticket office

Table 2 Processes reference framework for performing arts companies: Production

PA Sector				ID	B. Production - Processes
T	F	M	C		
				4	**Produce a Cultural Product**
				4.1	**Produce a Live Event**
				4.1.1	Verify technical data sheet
				4.1.2	Define technical data sheet
				4.1.3	Check the artist's backline
				4.1.4	Verify warehouse
				4.1.5	Contact affiliated structures
				4.1.6	Define an agreement with suppliers
				4.1.7	Coordinate affiliated structures
				5	**Execute the Event**
				5.1	**Control the Safety**
				5.1.1	Check safety regulations documentation
				5.1.2	Realize documentation in conformity with the regulations
				5.1.3	Obtain authorizations
				5.1.4	Measure usable space
				5.1.5	Define stand number
				5.2	**Set-up the Event**
				5.2.1	Define the production plan
				5.2.2	Share the production plan with internal staff
				5.2.3	Share the production plan with external suppliers
				5.2.4	Coordinate the production team
				5.2.5	Execute production plan
				5.2.6	Build-up the stage
				5.2.7	Set-up the scenography
				5.2.8	Set-up the exhibition space
				5.2.9	Execute the event
				5.3	**Deploy the assets**
				5.3.1	Disassembly the scenography
				5.3.2	Disassembly the stage
				5.3.3	Dismantle executive space
				5.3.4	Update warehouse
				5.3.5	Classify retrieved equipments
				5.4	**Update the Production Plan**
				5.4.1	Update the rider for next events
				6	**Manage supplier relatioship**
				6.1	**Retrieve the Assets**
				6.1.1	Contact suppliers of assets
				6.1.2	Contact service providers
				6.1.3	Send technical data sheet
				6.1.4	Request a preliminary quote
				6.1.5	Finding the equipment
				6.1.6	Return the equipment

Table 3 Processes reference framework for performing arts companies: Administration

PA Sector				ID	C. Adminsitration - Processes
T	F	M	C		
				7	**Develop and Manage Human Capital**
				7.1	**Manage artist's contracts**
				7.1.1	Define contract details
				7.1.2	Define payment method
				7.1.3	Define the contract subject
				7.1.4	Compose the contract
				7.1.5	Pay the performance agreed
				7.1.6	Compaire the payments
				7.2.	**Manage employee contracts**
				7.2.1	Take on new employee
				7.2.2	Make a contract
				7.2.3	Manage the employee
				7.2.4	Define the operational team
				7.2.5	Coordinate the staff
				7.2.6	Pay the salary
				7.2.7	Manage the internal relationships
				8	**Manage administration processes**
				8.1	**Manage organization's area**
				8.1.1	Manage the structure area
				8.1.2	Manage relations with public administrations
				8.1.3	Request for authorizations
				8.1.4	Request for licensing
				8.1.5	Produce documents for public authorities
				9	**Manage financial resources**
				9.1	**Perform palnning and management accounting**
				9.1.1	Forecast the activities
				9.1.2	Forecast the costs
				9.1.3	Forecast the ticket price
				9.1.4	Forecast the stand price
				9.1.5	Budgeting
				9.2	**Inspect previous results**
				9.2.1	Compare with precedent years
				9.3	**Systematization of performance**
				9.3.1	Make a report of the event
				9.3.2	Represent the Economic and Financial Performance
				9.3.3	Evaluate the event
				10	**Manage Assets**
				10.1	**Manage phisical resources**
				10.1.1	Define needed assets
				10.1.2	Check available assets
				10.1.3	Determine the missing assets
				10.1.4	Check on needed equipment
				10.1.5	Check on available equipment
				10.1.6	Determine the missing equipment
				10.1.7	Define the production team

Table 4 Processes reference framework for performing arts companies: Promotion and communication

PA Sector				ID	D. Promotion and Communication - Processes
T	F	M	C		
				11	**Promotion and Communication**
				11.1	**Text content production**
				11.1.1	Achieve artist information from the management
				11.1.2	Retrieve programmed event information
				11.1.3	Produce communication contents
				11.1.4	Define promotional contents
				11.1.5	Create press release
				11.1.6	Adapte the contents for the various promotion channels
				11.1.7	Launch digital tickets selling
				11.2	**Graphic content production**
				11.2.1	Finde official artwork
				11.2.2	Create visual concepts / Produce artwork
				11.2.3	Contact artwork suppliers
				11.2.4	Define distribution plan
				11.2.5	Book billboard spaces
				11.3	**Promotion plan definition**
				11.3.1	Define time line chart
				11.3.2	Find publication spaces
				11.3.3	Plan the Social Network sponsorships
				11.3.4	Plan billposting
				11.3.5	Plan dwell time
				11.3.6	Share time line chart
				11.3.7	Plan press conference
				11.3.8	Select Social Network channels
				11.3.9	Select other on-line channel
				11.3.10	Select newspapers
				11.3.11	Select sponsor
				11.3.12	Select radio channels
				11.4	**Strategy execution**
				11.4.1	Send content to newspapers
				11.4.2	Send content to social media channels (third parts)
				11.4.3	Publish content on social media
				11.4.4	Publish contents on newspapers
				11.4.5	Affix artwork
				11.4.6	Distribute artwork
				11.4.7	Launch event communication
				11.5	**Audience promotion**
				11.5.1	Contact loyal audience
				11.5.2	Contact potentially interested audience
				11.5.3	Contact new audience
				11.5.4	Contact institutional figures
				11.5.5	Contact journalists
				12	**Analytics**
				12.1	**Pre-event evaluation**
				12.1.1	Collect data
				12.1.2	Analyse data
				12.1.3	Evaluate event magnitude
				12.1.4	Analyse available resources (Budget for communication)
				12.1.5	Collect information from ticket sales
				12.2	**Ongoing evaluation**
				12.2.1	Monitor budget resources
				12.2.2	Monitor Social Network channels reactivity
				12.2.3	Monitor sales ticketing platforms
				12.2.4	Monitor tickets store sales
				12.3	**Final evaluation**
				12.3.1	Collect data from Social Network
				12.3.2	Collect data from ticketing platforms
				12.3.3	Collect data from box office
				12.3.4	Compare with previous results
				12.3.5	Check results
				12.3.6	Analyse customer satisfaction
				12.3.7	Evaluate overall performance
				12.3.8	Communicate event results
				12.3.9	Communicate festival results
				12.3.10	Communicate exhibition results

Table 5 Process Groups and Process Owners

ID	Process Group	Process Owner
1	*Develop Vision and Strategy*	
1.1	Evaluate external environment	Art Director
1.2	Evaluate internal environment	Art Director
1.3	Negotiate for an artist	Art Director
2	*Develop and Manage Cultural Products and Services*	
2.1	Design the team	Production Manager
2.2	Organize the agenda	Art Director
2.3	Manage the venue	Administrative Manager and/or Art Manager
2.4	Manage the exhibitors	Production Manager
3	*Market and Sell the Cultural Product*	
3.1	Manage ticketing	Administrative Manager
3.2	Manage the ticket office	Administrative Manager
4	*Produce the Cultural Product*	
4.1	Produce a live event	Production Manager
5	*Execute the Event*	
5.1	1. Control for safety	Administrative Manager
5.2	Set up the event	Production Manager
5.3	Deploy the assets	Technical Manager
5.4	Update the production plan	Technical Manager
6	*Manage Supplier Relationships*	
6.1	Retrieve the assets	Technical Manager
7	*Develop and Manage Human Capital*	
7.1	Manage artists' contracts	Administrative Manager
7.2	Manage employee contracts	Administrative Manager
8	*Manage the Administration Process*	
8.1	Manage the organization's physical spaces	Administrative Manager
9	*Manage Financial Resources*	
9.1	Perform planning and management accounting	Administrative Manager
9.2	Inspect previous results	Administrative Manager
9.3	Systematization of performance	Administrative Manager
10	*Manage Assets*	
10.1	Manage physical resources	Technical Manager
11	*Promote and Communicate*	
11.1	Produce textual content	Communication Manager
11.2	Produce graphic content	Communication Manager
11.3	Define the promotion plan	Communication Manager
11.4	Perform activities	Communication Manager
11.5	Develop an audience	Communication Manager
12	*Analyze Data*	
12.1	Evaluate the pre-event phase	Communication Manager
12.2	Evaluate the ongoing event phase	Communication Manager
12.3	Evaluate the final event phase	Communication Manager

guideline for performing arts companies in executing their activities and increasing their awareness of their processes. For consulting and IT companies, the framework offers a complete picture of the sector and can help them define and develop new techno-organizational solutions based on the execution of processes or on integrated systems for managing and tracking data and information about processes and activities. The framework also provides an overview of the organizational aspects that can be re-engineered to optimize the allocation of physical and human resources.

The BPM implementation initiative with CCIs achieved substantial benefits. The process reference framework helped the four organizations increase the efficiency of their processes. The value contribution was analyzed for core, management, and support processes for each organization, as every process was characterized by repetitiveness, a high level of interdependence, and a medium level of variability. The scope was the intra-organizational processes. The results for two of the six core elements of BPM, strategic alignment and governance, were all but immediate, as a better definition of a strategic vision emerged, which was aligned with the organizations' core activities. Each organizational structure was also formalized. As for the governance component, process roles and responsibilities were formally defined (Rosemann & vom Brocke, 2010).

5 Lessons Learned

The Distretto Puglia Creativa companies' new awareness of their processes and related process owners confirmed that, even if they produce different kinds of cultural products, they use the same processes, reuse the same information, and incur similar problems. The managers' new ability to think about their processes with a view to improvement and in an all-encompassing way led them to decide that everyone should specialize in solving problems in their own areas instead of overburdening themselves with work for which they have no specific skills. From a methodological point of view, the use of both interviews and a focus group made it possible for similarities among the four companies to emerge and, therefore, to define best practices for the performing arts sector. We define four key lessons learned from this work:

- The application of BPM methodologies and technologies allows the life cycle of cultural and creative products to be managed in a more efficient way, much like complex products are managed.
- Event production has four process areas—design, production, promotion, and communication and administration. Every process area has a process owner, regardless of the format of the event produced, and every event has the same critical issues.
- Based on the Capability Maturity Model's (CCM) levels (Paulk, Curtis, Chrissis, & Weber, 1993), the companies involved in the case studies are largely at level 1. These immature organizations are companies that are based on heroes; the artistic director, the technical manager, and even the administrative manager carry

out activities based on their own experiences and a way of working that is in their heads as highly experienced people. They apply their approaches as routine, but they have difficulty describing the routine or transferring it to new resources.
- The proposed framework can be used to determine how many processes are used in an organization and to explore the details of the processes to determine when and why problems arise and verify whether the employee's positions have been designated to the right activities.

This methodology and the framework development were carried out based on the experience of small and medium-sized organizations. One of the researcher's objectives in the future is to replicate the research on large entertainment organizations to validate and enrich the process framework.

Acknowledgments The authors thank all of the MYA project partners for their valuable contributions to the study and for sharing their experiences, skills, and processes, particularly Cesare Liaci and Osvaldo Piliego of Coolclub Cooperative Society; Anna Petrachi, Salvatore Tramacere, and Marco Chiffi of Cantieri Teatrali Koreja; Vincenzo Bellini and Silvia Rossini of Bass Culture; and Marco Cataldo, Eleonora Leucci, and Andrea Sanità of Officine Cantelmo Cooperative.

References

APQC's Process Classification Framework (PCF)®. (2019). Available at https://www.apqc.org/pcf

Bryman, A., & Bell, E. (2015). *Business research methods*. Oxford Press.

Dumas, M., La Rosa, M., Mendling, J., & Reijers, H. A. (2013). *Fundamentals of business process management* (Vol. 1, p. 2). Heidelberg: Springer.

EY, Italia Creativa. (2016).

Kitzinger, J. (1995). Qualitative research: Introducing focus groups. *BMJ, 311*(7000), 299–302.

Martinaityte, E., & Kregzdaite, R. (2015). The factors of creative industries development in nowadays stage. *Economics and Sociology, 8*(1), 55.

Paulk, M. C., Curtis, B., Chrissis, M. B., & Weber, C. V. (1993). Capability maturity model, version 1.1. *IEEE Software, 10*(4), 18–27.

Rosemann, M. & vom Brocke, J. (2010). *The six core elements of business process management*. doi: https://doi.org/10.1007/978-3-642-00416-2_5.

Schilling, M., & Izzo, F. (2012). *Gestione dell'innovazione*. The McGraw-Hill Companies.

vom Brocke, J., Mendling, J., & Rosemann, M. (2021). Planning and scoping business process management projects and programs with the BPM billboard. In J. vom Brocke, J. Mendling, & M. Rosemann (Eds.), *BPM cases. Digital innovation and business transformation in practice* (Vol. 2). Springer.

vom Brocke, J., Zelt, S. & Schmiedel, T. (2015). *Considering context in business process management: The BPM context framework*. bptrends.com.

Exploring BPM Adoption and Assessing the Strategic Alignment of Processes at Raiffeisen Bank Kosovo

Elheme Azemi and Saimir Bala

1 Introduction

Raiffeisen Bank Kosovo (RBKO) began in 2003 as a subsidiary of Raiffeisen Bank International AG. Since then, it has provided a wide range of banking products and services to all categories of customers in the individual and business segments through an extensive branch network throughout the country and through leading-edge electronic banking facilities like cash machines and telephone and internet banking. In the first 6 months of 2018, the bank's profit was 11 million euros, the highest in Kosovo's banking market. RBKO's excellent results and commitment to improving its customer service through both its branch networks and alternative channels has also been recognized by two international financial magazines, *Euromoney* and *EMEA Finance*, which awarded RBKO the title of "Best Bank in Kosovo" in 2018.

Business process management (BPM) is well known at RBKO and is applied there. The organization is divided generally into CEO, IT and Operations, Retail Banking, and Corporate Banking. The department of organization and process management (OPMD), which falls into the IT and Operation Division, is divided into three units: the Process Management Unit (BPM, Lean and Agile methodology), the Project Office Unit, and the Procedures and Organizations Unit. Kettinger and Teng (1998) showed that successful BPM implementation requires an alignment between BPM and organizational strategy and that organization's structure is central to effective and efficient processes. To what extent was this the case for RBKO?

E. Azemi (✉)
Raiffeisen Bank J.S.C., Prishtina, Kosovo
e-mail: elheme.azemi@raiffeisen-kosovo.com

S. Bala
Vienna University of Economics and Business (WU), Wien, Austria
e-mail: saimir.bala@wu.ac.at

J. vom Brocke et al. (eds.), *Business Process Management Cases Vol. 2*,
https://doi.org/10.1007/978-3-662-63047-1_21

This chapter explores RBKO's adoption of BPM and its importance to the company's strategic alignment. In this regard, the chapter provides an insightful case of how to assess a BPM program for further development (vom Brocke, Mendling, & Rosemann, 2021). In particular, it explores: (1) to what extent BPM is implemented and understood at the bank and (2) how the BPM methodology is linked to the bank's strategic goals. The study takes two approaches in answering these questions: First, a literature review helps to scope the area of BPM and its key aspects. Then semi-structured interviews are used to collect evidence about BPM's status at RBKO and to reveal BPM's relationship to the bank's strategic objectives.

The rest of the chapter is organized as follows. Section 2 describes the situation the bank faced when this study began. Section 3 presents the approach used to explore the bank's BPM-related status. Section 4 shows the results of our interviews and explains the role of BPM at RBKO. Finally, Sect. 5 reflects on the lessons learned from the case study.

2 Situation Faced

RBKO, one of the largest banks in Kosovo, provides services like loans, credit cards, and bank accounts to its customers. Customer satisfaction is a priority at RBKO, not only to retain existing customers but to pursue the objective of increasing the number of clients. To improve customer satisfaction, the bank concluded that its internal processes should be as simple as possible, that customers should be treated fairly, and that the steps in their applications should be transparent.

As growing the number of customers would require more resources, RBKO had put in place several practices to make its processes easier to manage, including methodologies like Six-Sigma, BPM, and Lean, and Agile. BPM in particular was used to make the internal steps of their application processes visible and manageable. Process and business owners were assigned to processes and a BPMS was also in place.

However, the bank's BPM adoption was still suboptimal. For instance, dedicated teams were not set up according to RBKO's objectives, which would have been possible had teams been more empowered. More specifically, BPM was working well in improving existing processes, but the goals and outcomes of these processes were not always directly mapped to specific strategic goals. As a result, monitoring the bank's efficiency in achieving its predefined objectives was problematic.

Therefore, the bank needed a direct connection between BPM and its strategic objectives, since BPM can be a framework that helps business make continuous improvements. Hence, the goal of this research was to determine how BPM, as a methodology, was implemented at RBKO, and its impact on the bank's vision and strategy related to its business processes.

3 Action Taken

This study applies a twofold approach to explore the extent to which RBKO adopted BPM and BPM's role in the bank's strategic alignment. First, a literature review is conducted to define the BPM concept and understand its multiple facets. The purpose of this first step is to identify which of BPM's aspects are applicable in the bank's context. Then field interviews in the field are conducted to collect data from the real world and compare them to the concepts learned from literature. This chapter uses a qualitative approach that includes interpretation, discovery, and explanation.

3.1 Literature Review

Scoping the BPM Methodology Next, we present the main works in the literature that helped to explain how to link BPM to strategy. The literature review focused on the BPM methodology, its concept and governance, and the key elements in linking BPM with the organization's strategy. BPM is among the most powerful concepts in managing business processes, as it contributes to process vision and strategy execution by continuously addressing process optimization.

Dumas, La Rosa, Mendling, and Reijers (2018) explained that BPM refers to managing and controlling business processes end to end, which involves the full cycle of Identification, Discovery, Analysis and Improvement, Redesign, Implementation, and Monitoring and Controlling. An essential component of control is the ability to measure correctly, as something that cannot be measured cannot be controlled and managed. According to the BPM lifecycle, control and management happens in an infinite loop, so BPM facilitates continuous improvement, even beyond the targets of a single project. With the help of the BPM life cycle, implementing a business process can be an ongoing process in response to changes that occur in the business environment.

In addition, Jeston and Nelis (2015) elaborated on the idea that cultural empowerment must be present to pull people toward accepting changes and that the identification and publication of the process owners will help with the adoption of changes, as the real commitment and coordination necessary to make BPM work begins with process ownership (Motwani, Prasad, & Tata, 2005). Kohlbacher and Gruenwald (2011) considered process owners to be among the key pillars of process-based organizations.

Considering BPM as an organizational capability includes taking into account more aspects than merely the execution of the tasks along a process life cycle (identify, model, analyze, improve, implement, execute, monitor, and change). This standpoint requires an organization to have a wider perspective than just process goals. In fact, literature on BPM maturity models suggests that successful BPM requires the identification of core capability areas. Moreover, the organizations' strategy division should be involved in planning the transition to BPM. Rosemann and vom Brocke (2015) also stress that BPM should be viewed as a whole, not just as fulfilling a specific organization's activities along the process life cycle (design, configuration, execution, control, and diagnosis).

This study also takes into account the perspective of the six core elements that Rosemann and vom Brocke (2015) identified, as these elements are central to an organization's strategy. Each of the six core elements—strategic alignment, governance, methods, information technology, people, and culture—is a critical success factor for BPM. These six elements can guide the definition of KPIs that would then reflect the performance and efficiency of BPM.

An alignment model has also been developed that addresses the alignment of BPM with the organization's strategy, processes, structure, management, information technology, performance measurement, people, and culture. If the organization's strategies are well defined and aligned with BPM, the organization can benefit from such advantages as a shorter time to market, lower costs, a high-quality product, and improved customer satisfaction. Kramp (2003) confirmed that performance measurement is fundamental to continuing quality improvement.

Research Questions Two research questions were derived from the literature review, the first author's experience, and RBKO's market position.

RQ1: How does RBKO adopt and implement BPM?

RQ2: What is BPM's impact on RBKO's strategy, vision, management, and decision-making as they relate to business processes?

3.2 Case Study

Selection Criteria The researchers chose RBKO for a case study because the bank has an experience in BPM methodology development. Since 2006 RBKO has used Six Sigma methodology, after which they also used BPM, Lean methodology, and most recently Agile methodology. The research was exploratory so as to offer clarification regarding the activities undertaken for BPM as a methodology of management and decision-making for business processes.

We consulted the literature for similar research on business process methods related to improving quality and relied on case study analysis (Yusof, 2001). Thereafter, we investigated guidelines on the selection of a research strategy (Yin, 2014), a choice that depends on the type of research question, the control an investigator has over behavioral events, and the research's focus on contemporary (as opposed to historical) phenomena. Yin (2014) explained that, if the research seeks to answer "how and why" questions, it should be performed as case study research. The first author's BPM experience also affected the choice. A significant amount of data for the study was readily available, and the first author was familiar with almost all of the interviewees, eliminating the need for searching and formal introductions.

Participant Selection Criteria The nine semi-structured interviews conducted averaged around 45 min in length. The interviewees, who all played key managerial roles in a variety of departments were the Chief Operations Officer (COO), Head of Finance, Head of Organizations and OPMD, CEO of Leasing at RBKO, Head of Corporate Banking, Head of the Private Individual Segment, Head of Audit, Head of the Risk Management, and Head of Operations. The participants were selected using the purposeful sampling method and based on their positions and decision-making roles in the organization. The interviews provided information that helped meet the study's targets and objectives.

Given the research purpose and the purposive sampling technique applied, non-probability sampling was used. Research participants had to meet three qualification criteria:

- Top or middle manager (B = member of the management Board; B-1 = department head; B-2 manager) at RBKO.
- At least 5 years' experience in vision of business processes.
- Familiarity with the research themes, particularly knowledge about the company's business processes.

Data Collection Interviewing is a kind of data collection technique that not only gets comments and answers interviewees but also seeks clarifications (Kvale & Brinkmann, 2009). Interviewing also facilitates data collection done at a distance.

In addition to the semi-structured interviews, data were collected via document analysis and observation. The qualitative data gathered through the nine interviews were fully transcribed and coded, then analyzed and compared with the documents analysis, observation notes, and business process reports data (quantitative secondary data). Then the main findings were summarized and the interviews were transcribed and analyzed using qualitative data analysis methods. The interview sessions and other secondary data helped the researchers to acquire information that was credible and reliable, directly from the sources. Additionally, irrelevant aspects have been filtered out and only content that is significant to the research objectives was taken into account (Dresch, Pacheco Lacerda, & Cauchick Miguel, 2015).

During the data collection, the researchers had to integrate real-world observations collected during the different interviews into the needs of this data collection plan (Yin, 2014). Interviews are considered the most suitable approach to gathering data for this research, as Saunders, Lewis, and Thornhill (2009) demonstrated.

4 Results Achieved

This section outlines the results achieved by this case study. Findings are presented with respect to each key factor of the framework (Rosemann & Vom Brocke, 2015).

4.1 The Role of BPM at RBKO

Documentation is an essential part of day-to-day business, and BPM helps to ensure that documentation is correct and current. RBKO always documents and visualizes its core business processes, with the COO Division primarily responsible for BPM and process quality control. Strategic performance measurement and analysis is also part of BPM. In addition to the BPM methodology, RBKO uses Six Sigma, Lean methodology, and Agile methodology because of the need for optimization, visualization, and continuous management of business processes. The COO mentioned that BPM gives the firm a clear view of processes' performance, as well as processes related to people, governance, and IT.

Adoption of BPM at RBKO The interview data revealed that the process of implementing BPM is largely clear. The interviewees confirmed that visualizations of processes, development of systems, responsibilities that come with process ownership, and the governance setup allows the organization to continue with process improvement and process management:

> Requests for implementations of BPM sometimes come from the local office and sometimes from the head office. After identifications of all stamps, systems, full-time equivalents involved in the particular process, and identification of process owners and responsibilities, we build the automatic process/timestamps, set up the governance, and proceed with continuous improvement. (Participant 1)

> BPM is implemented to measure, step by step, visualizations of activities, timestamps, and stakeholders end to end. BPM is implemented in two contexts: technical and concept of BPM: 1. In the technical part, end-to-end processes are put into systems/tools in the core system's automatic process and timestamps 2. In terms of concept, a framework with responsibilities and process owners and governance is used to decide about any optimizations within processes. (Participant 3)

Role of Executives and Senior Managers in Supporting BPM The interviewees stressed that input from the executives and senior management is necessary for a successful BPM implementation, as inspiration and motivation can be drawn from top management to other levels. The participants also agreed that there is a need for supportive leadership, and dedication and involvement by senior managers to complete the implementation successfully and maintain the process.

> The role of top management is to provide recourse and help implementations move toward success. Top managements are process sponsors and owners. (Participant 6)

> Support is very high: We have regular meetings, and we are interested in BPM methodology. Our role is main support, sponsorship, and ownership (Participant 4)

Business Processes' Customer Focus The interviews made clear that customer satisfaction is a primary concern. Although some internal procedures must be used even when the customer has another focus, but everything is dependent on customer satisfaction and on how customers experience the company's products and services. Since the BPM methodology also has the Critical to Quality (CTQ) measurements tool, the tool from the Six Sigma methodology, which is the voice of the customer, and as one of the referred points for continuous improvement, the participants were asked whether the bank has a customer focus.

> In our bank we consider a customer-focus approach as key to business success. This means that BPM is designed in such a way that customer satisfaction is the backbone of all current and new processes. (Participant 7)

> We have regulatory processes (risk process and internal procedures) that do not let us definitively be only client-focused, but in principle we take into consideration the voice of the customer (VOC) in making improvements by considering their requests. (Participant 7)

> Yes, we absolutely focus on the customer because of continuous improvement. (Participant 1)

4.2 Alignment Between BPM and Organization Strategy

The participants believe in the need for alignment between business processes and strategic objectives to improve profits and customer satisfaction, product quality, response time, and delivery time. However, not all interviewees agreed on the benefits of alignment, as some suggested that BPM cannot align with all strategic objectives unless they are financial objectives.

> Yes, I have already thought about linking BPM with the bank's objectives and strategy. (Participant 1)

> We have some factors that we take into account when we decide on a strategy. Usually, we have to figure out how to get there. (Participant 5)

The interviews also revealed that the effect of aligning business strategy with BPM is significant in that doing so helped the bank improve customer satisfaction, reduce operational costs, and consider employees as an important part of the organization. Moreover, most of the participants said that the bank does not consider it difficult to find a proper fit between the business processes and business strategy when good documentation and key indicators are available, but a few of the participants were skeptical about realizing all of the bank's strategic objectives through BPM.

Key Factors in Aligning the Bank's Strategy and BPM This section is divided into two questions, the first of which concerns, in the context of the organization, the importance of key factors within RBKO and the second of which concerns, in the context of BPM, how successful the bank sees those key factors as being. The key factors are drawn from major concepts that emerged during the interviews, most of which correspond to factors identified in the literature review (Jeston & Nelis, 2015; Rosemann & Vom Brocke, 2015). Each element proposed has sub-elements. In our case, we have adapted the identified factors. These factors have guided the interviews in such a way to provide material for answering the research question. Interviews highlighted *people* and *leadership and management* as central factors that build alignment.

4.2.1 How Successful Is RBKO in Addressing the Key Factors?

People The interview data underscored that people are important in organizational processes because they help to make the processes work using the skills, knowledge, behavior, and culture that are so important for a successful organizational strategy.

> The bank is aware that people are key to the company's success and that they are the bank's most valuable asset in terms of BPM. Staff members who have the necessary levels of expertise and skill are assigned to set new business process. In this way, the bank empowers the staff members, as they are key to the bank's overall success. (Participant 7)

> RBKO has invested in staff, especially in BPM training. (Participant 1)

Governance The aspects of BPM governance identified were BPM integration in organizational management, performance assessment, assigning process-based responsibilities, and disseminating a process-management culture. According to the interviews, governance is related to the decision-making that relates to expectations, giving power to the employees, and authenticating the execution. Governance is also the factor that ensures organization's responsibility and decisions harmonize with BPM.

> We have defined and structured ways to initiate a process changes, optimizations, and reengineering at the bank. We have set up a process committee that addresses the governance and decision-making processes related to BPM. (Participant 6).

> The model that RBKO created is so successful. Decisions are made through governance. (Participant 2)

Information Technology The participants confirmed that the biggest challenge they have in implementing BPM is with IT issues, as the effort from IT required too much time. They affirmed that they used several technology platforms, so the collection and reporting of accurate data have been difficult.

> We are working in a dynamic environment that requires aligning IT with business strategies. Organizations need to provide strong IT support for the process activities and model designing. At the moment, we can say that we have a gap in IT that is due to turnover of IT staff. (Participant 3)

> Usually, all BPM requires IT involvement, but the main issue is IT resources. (Participant 5)

Performance Measurement Performance measurement can be applied at different levels of organizations. The interview data confirmed that measurement of performance is fundamental for continuing quality improvement at RBKO. The participants affirmed that, where KPIs are implemented, the bank is successful, but there is a need for more measurements in the organization.

> The measurements are important because we have to have an assessment of where staff performance and process performance are if we are to continue to improve. (Participant 7)

> Where we have KPIs we are successful, but we need more measurements to have control of processes, products, and people. (Participant 9)

Management and Leadership Support for successful BPM should come from top management. Almost all participants stated that, even if the project team creates the best processes and BPM systems, if people refuse to use them or use them poorly, the project will not be successful. Therefore, support for successful BPM should come from top management.

> Yes, we have good support, without which we could not implement BPM methodology. When planning a process, managers are concerned with defining and achieving the objectives and goals. We also have to decide on the steps to achieving these goals while allocating and identifying the resources that they require. (Participant 8)

> Our bank has a very good structure with the committee where the support for and decisions about changes and implementation of BPM are made. (Participant 1)

Culture Culture is a soft skill and is difficult for people to change. The interviews described culture as a soft factor but as having a strong impact on the success of the BPM.

> Culture plays a vital role in successful BPM. (Participant 1)

> A BPM culture embraces various values and beliefs that can help the organization become more process-oriented. (Participant 2)

Communication Communication includes the evaluation patterns between process stakeholders and how related knowledge is discovered and explored. Interviewees advocated the need for strong communication across departments as a requirement for running successful BPM.

> To achieve the desired process results individuals and groups should work together in process collaboration, as communication between them plays a vital role. (Participant 4)

> Communication is key to the success of every business process. In the case of BPM, the bank is ensuring transparent results for all business processes and fostering communication between all stakeholders at all hierarchical levels to make sure that everyone is informed about the results and data. Sharing the data means fostering the communication between all business lines and between all layers of same business lines. (Participant 1)

4.3 Answers to the Research Questions

Implementation of BPM at RBKO (RQ1) The first objective of this study is to determine how RBKO implements BPM. From feedback and the opinions of the participants, awareness of BPM within departments is evident where RBKO has implemented it. They know that BPM is a methodology for the effective use of people, processes, assets, and technology in business measurement and achieving business goals. It enables real-time access to data and continuous process and data flow for proactive business management. Process visualization, a core element of BPM projects, is often achieved with a series of as-is and to-be process modeling tasks.

The research reveals that RBKO has an effective process for BPM implementation with sufficient investments in the people involved in implementation and identification of responsibilities. However, more awareness is needed, particularly in departments and units where BPM has not been implemented and in lower levels of management. Moreover, there is a need for process ownership definition and responsibilities in all departments that are involved in end-to-end processes.

The research also revealed that the accomplishments of the BPM implementation process can be challenging. For some of RBKO's activities, the major problems that affected BPM implementation were IT issues, lack of IT resources, and commitment to further BPM development, which had significant effects on the implementation of BPM. Another challenge identified is related to BPM training and the lack of budget to support the staff involved in BPM. Based on the interviewees' feedback, there is a need to provide training tailored to BPM's needs so those involved can understand the methodology, the perspective of BPM, and process modeling as a decision-making tool, as described in the literature review.

Impact of BPM on Strategy (RQ2) The research reveals a significant impact if BPM and the bank's strategic objectives are aligned, as the bank is a service- and process-orientated organization. Processes should be improved continuously per market requirements.

The systematic process monitoring that is included in BPM allowed the major objectives of the bank's strategy to be met. First, BPM helped in characterizing the use of BPM in the organization by quantifying the absolute frequency of the core elements (strategic alignment, governance, methods, information technology, people, and culture) that Rosemann and Vom Brocke (2015) proposed. Second, it helped in identifying many of the dimensions related to organizational performance and the main measures, variables, and indicators that correlate BPM with bank performance. Third, it allowed a model that proposed linking BPM's key elements with organizational objectives.

5 Lessons Learned

This case study is a first step toward the conviction that banks' strategy objectives can be linked with BPM's elements. The recommendation from this research is that BPM should be strategy-driven. This process will lead RBKO to think about its internal and external processes and to expand how it thinks about how its products and services are delivered to the customers. Our proposed approach will help organizations to create direct alignment between BPM and strategy. Several factors are involved in such an alignment, including people, management, leadership, governance, culture, information technology, performance measurement, and communication, all of which can create a link between organizational strategy and BPM. BPM can encompass other methodologies, such as Lean, Agile, and Six Sigma, which can also help in improvement in innovative ways.

The researchers recommend additional study that combines the effects of these alignment factors on the overall alignment process and to investigate the differences between the factors presented in multiple banks.

References

Dresch, A., Pacheco Lacerda, D., & Cauchick Miguel, P. (2015). *A distinctive analysis of case study, action research and design science research. Review of business management.*

Dumas, M., La Rosa, M., Mendling, J., & Reijers, H. (2018). *Fundamentals of business process management* (2nd ed.).

Jeston, J., & Nelis, J. (2015). *Business process management practical guidelines to successful implementations.*

Kettinger, W., & Teng, J. (1998). *Aligning BPR to strategy: A framework for analysis. Long range planning.*

Kohlbacher, M., & Gruenwald, S. (2011). Process orientation: Conceptualization and measurement. *Business Process Management Journal, 17*(2), 267–283.

Kramp, M. (2003). *Exploring life and experience through narrative inquiry. Foundations for research: Methods of inquiry in education and the social sciences*, pp. 103–121.

Kvale, S., & Brinkmann, S. (2009). Learning the craft of qualitative research interviewing. In S. Kvale & S. Brinkmann (Eds.), *InterViews: Learning the craft of qualitative research interviewing* (pp. 81–96). Sage.

Motwani, J., Prasad, S., & Tata, J. (2005). The evolution of TQM: An empirical analysis using the business process change framework. *TQM Magazine, 17*(1), 54–66.

Rosemann, M., & Vom Brocke, J. (2015). The six core elements of business process management. In M. Rosemann & J. V. Brocke (Eds.), *Handbook on business process management 1: Introduction, methods, and information systems* (pp. 105–122). Berlin: Springer.

Saunders, M., Lewis, P., & Thornhill, A. (2009). *Research methods for business students* (5th ed.). New York: Pearson.

vom Brocke, J., Mendling, J., & Rosemann, M. (2021). Planning and scoping business process management projects and programs with the BPM billboard. In J. vom Brocke, J. Mendling, & M. Rosemann (Eds.), *BPM cases. Digital innovation and business transformation in practice* (Vol. 2). Springer.

Yin, R. (2014). *Case study research: Design and methods* (5th ed.). Thousand Oaks, CA: Sage.

Yusof, S. (2001). Case studies on the implementation of TQM in the UK automotive SMEs Lean implementation in SMEs. Smart Manufacturing System for process industries. *International Journal of Quality and Reliability Management.*

Developing Business Process Architecture at Poland's Ministry of Finance. An Uneasy Journey Toward BPM

Renata Gabryelczyk, Artur Grygorowicz, and Agnieszka Bitkowska

1 Introduction

The Ministry of Finance (MF) in Poland is a central government administration body that is responsible for public finance. As a nonprofit institution in the public sector, the MF operates under specific conditions of institutionalization and bureaucracy and performs activities required under the influence of the political environment (Boyne, 2002). Even though increasing numbers of public sector organizations take up the challenge of adopting Business Process Management (BPM), the topic of successful BPM applications in this sector is still under-researched (Syed, Bandara, French, & Stewart, 2018), and each new use-case has a chance to contribute to the development of BPM practice and theories. Accordingly, the MF case describes how business process architecture has been developed in a large government institution. This case refers to the initial stages of the BPM life cycle (Dumas, La Rosa, Mendling, & Reijers, 2013) and documents the first difficult task of the organizational unit that was set up at the MF to be responsible for business process architecture.

The fundamental activities of the MF include designing, executing, and controlling the state budget, managing tax issues and public debt, dealing with the financing system for local governments, and supervising the operation of financial

R. Gabryelczyk (✉)
University of Warsaw, Warszawa, Poland
e-mail: r.gabryelczyk@wne.uw.edu.pl

A. Grygorowicz
Ministry of Finance in Poland, Warszawa, Poland
e-mail: artur.grygorowicz@mf.gov.pl

A. Bitkowska
Warsaw University of Technology, Warszawa, Poland
e-mail: Agnieszka.Bitkowska@pw.edu.pl

J. vom Brocke et al. (eds.), *Business Process Management Cases Vol. 2*,
https://doi.org/10.1007/978-3-662-63047-1_22

markets and institutions (Ministry of Finance, 1999). The MF is also responsible for cooperating with foreign countries and implementing provisions regarding customs. An extensive and important area of responsibility of the Minister of Finance in Poland is supervising the National Revenue Administration (NRA), creating the policy related to performing its tasks, and initiating tax and customs law. The NRA started in March 2017 as the result of a reform process that merged the tax administration, fiscal control, and Customs Service. The consolidated NRA focuses on establishing standards for serving key taxpayers, maintaining the professional service of the large taxpayers' service, providing uniform interpretations of tax law and tax and customs information, and preventing economic crime. The purpose of the reform was to make better use of its human, financial, and organizational resources (NRA, 2016). However, the reforms also forced organizational changes in structures, processes, workflows, and managerial decisions.

Currently, the MF consists of a number of organizational units, including:

- Thirty-three departments that implement the substantive tasks of the MF.
- Seven main offices that perform tasks related to serving the MF.
- Secretariats that provide service to the Minister and committees, councils, and teams.
- Faculties and teams as organizational units within departments and offices.

The Minister sets out, by way of an ordinance, the organizational regulations of the MF, which define the scope of tasks and the mode of work of the MF's organizational units.

The NRA, which is organizationally associated with the MF, has an even more complex organizational structure, consisting of:

- Sixteen tax administrative chambers.
- Four hundred revenue offices.
- Customs and tax offices (45 delegations and 144 customs branches).

Such an extensive organization translates into a large number of employees, with almost 2500 working in the MF headquarters and more than 64,000 in the NRA. Such a complex organization reflects the complexity of the management processes for which it is responsible.

In view of citizens' growing expectations and the need for efficient and effective state management, the MF since 2011 has undertaken initiatives related to adopting process management methods. An additional reason for the interest in the BPM concept has been the requirement to spend public funds in a reasonable and cost-effective manner, in accordance with the Polish Public Finance Act (2009). Following the Act's principle of "*maximized effects and optimized selection of methods and means to be used to achieve the intended objectives*," the MF recognized BPM as a management concept that could enable a focus on activities that create value for the citizen while reducing the costs of public administration activities. This case presents five approaches that have brought the MF closer to adopting BPM. In each approach, the MF started the journey toward BPM by identifying and defining process architectures. The case sets a great example of the importance of comprehensive BPM approaches, that go beyond modeling activities in order to deliver strategic value (vom Brocke, Mendling, & Rosemann, 2021).

The case is structured as follows: The opening section presents the situation the MF confronted in the face of the functioning conditions of the government administration organizations. Then brief descriptions of a succession of projects and initiatives related to adopting BPM at the MF are provided to approximate the complexity of the MF and the multifaceted problems it faced in adopting BPM. Finally, we highlight lessons learned from the long and costly path that public sector organizations travel in moving toward process-oriented management.

2 Situation Faced

As with any other organizational change in public sector organizations, implementing a process-oriented approach has been an ongoing challenge. Two groups of conditions and circumstances are particularly important for the functioning of these organizations in Poland: (1) As a result of reforms, political changes, and other changes in legal regulations and organizational structures, managerial positions are taken and responsibilities are subject to dynamic and continuous change; (2) the public sector suffers from issues related to its inefficient and bureaucratic business processes, outdated IT systems, lack of market mechanisms, nonexistent or limited performance measurement systems, excessive involvement in regulations, and extensive systems of hierarchical dependencies (Ferlie, Lynn Jr, Lynn, Pollitt, & Lynn, 2005; Saxena, 1996; Syed et al., 2018).

Unfortunately, these conditions are reinforced by management salaries in the public sector in Poland being significantly lower than those in the private sector, resulting in difficulty attracting appropriately qualified employees. In turn, senior decision-makers often take political positions but do not have the power to make decisions that contribute to the development of an organization, which is "*often due to political control, as politicians do not necessarily restrict themselves to policy-making; they often wish to involve themselves in the execution of policy*" (Saxena, 1996, p. 704).

The MF in Poland performs its statutory activities in such an environment. Beginning in 2011, decision-makers in the MF began to notice the benefits of process-based management and planned steady organizational-change projects aimed at implementing BPM, especially when these projects could be funded by the EU. However, the conditions under which the MF operates result in the cancelation of BPM initiatives and projects before they reached their full effect or were implemented using trial and error.

The "Actions Taken" section below presents the projects and initiatives related to developing business process architecture in the MF and the ultimate adoption of BPM. The section outlines the goals, results obtained, and the main difficulties and obstacles in adopting elements of BPM. All of them contributed to the development of the process-oriented approach at the MF and taught lessons regarding the adoption of BPM in public sector institutions. Moreover, they all shaped the current (2020) situation and actions taken by the Business Process Architecture Division (BPAD), which was established in the MF's Department of Strategic Management.

Figure 1 provides an overview of the succession of BPM initiatives/projects on a timeline as a preview of "Actions taken" in BPM adoption. We highlight the years in which these initiatives were implemented, their nature, and the areas in which actions were taken to develop process architecture.

Analysis of the documentation justifying the succession of projects shows that, in each approach to BPM adoption, the MF attempted to follow a set of basic principles of process management, including the pervasiveness of process management principles throughout the organization, process ownership, process documentation, process measurement, and process inspection (Lee & Dale, 1998). To implement the process-oriented approach, the MF began each project by defining the process architecture and establishing appropriate and transparent accountability in terms of roles and responsibilities for processes. The MF's BPM initiatives focused primarily on how to adopt BPM and, in the execution phase, on designing process architecture and identifying processes. Each subsequent project brought the MF closer to constructing a process-oriented organization, an uneasy journey.

3 Action Taken

3.1 First Approach to Adopting BPM: 2011–2013

The first attempts to build the process architecture and implement BPM at the MF were implemented as a part of the e-Customs Program. The program was implemented as part of the National Strategic Reference Framework under the EU Community budget for improving the functioning standard of public institutions and the development of partnership mechanisms. As a result of the full implementation of the e-Customs Program, a modern electronic environment was to be built for services provided by the Customs Service to improve cooperation between the Polish Customs Service and cooperating institutions abroad. In addition, expenditures on IT were to be rationalized by introducing the logically uniform information system of the Customs Service, which is based on process management. Covering the entire country and worth approximately EUR 40 M, the project was carried out by the MF and the organizational units of the Customs Service. Part of this project, termed "SZPADA," concerned the adoption of BPM.

The first steps toward adopting BPM were to create the Business Process Architecture for the Customs Service (CS) and to define the management and supporting process roles, the scope of tasks, and responsibility for processes. This governance provides principles, methods, mechanisms, and tools for use in the management of the CS through a process approach. The content of the documentation for planning BPM implementation was developed with participation by representatives of the management and key employees of the CS. The project was conducted by experts from external consulting companies who were selected in a public tender.

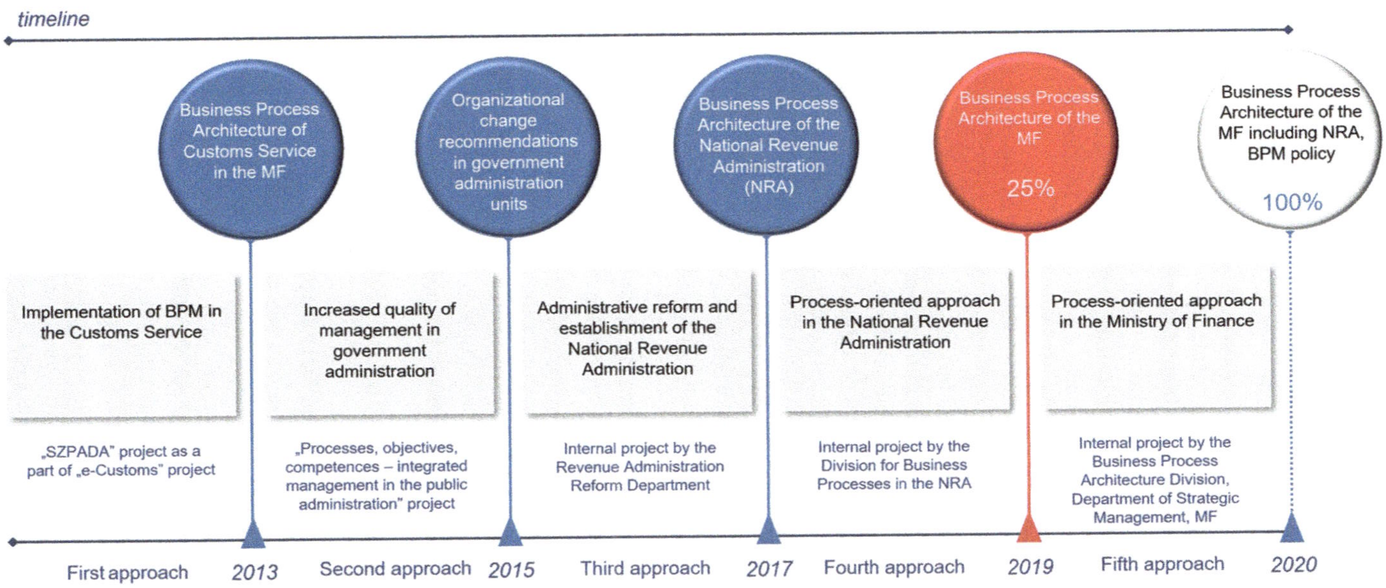

Fig. 1 The timeline of business process architecture development at the Ministry of Finance

3.1.1 Results Achieved in the First Approach

- An organizational unit (the Process Management Division) dedicated to the implementation of the process-approach was established in the CS.
- Documents that outlined definitions, tasks, and process roles related to the planned implementation of BPM were developed.
- The first business process architecture (*to-be*) was built for the CS area at the MF (Fig. 2). Five levels of process hierarchy—strategic, tactical, operational, process stages, and activities—were identified in this architecture. Processes' scopes, goals, measures, products, and responsibilities for achieving goals were divided into three traditional types of processes: key, management, and support. (Figure 2 presents only two levels of process architecture.) The owner of the CS Processes Architecture was the head of the CS.
- The Process Architecture Repository was created as one of the key products of the SZPADA project.
- Documentation of ten selected business processes was developed in preparation for detailed modeling and monitoring of process indicators.
- A detailed scope of responsibilities for possible changes in the architecture and processes at various levels and of various types was established.
- Workshops on the proposed organizational change were held for project stakeholders (managers in the CS, experts in identified processes, employees).
- Using a public tender, the ARIS Designer system was selected and purchased (corporate license) for the entire MF.
- Employees started to use the term "process language" when discussing their work and began using concepts like "gaining input and delivering output" in their communications (Reijers, 2006). In addition, an awareness of processes and a basic knowledge of BPM emerged in the organization.

Despite the significant financial resources and effort invested in the project, the BPM was not implemented, as the head of the CS decided to stop the project in 2014. Although the SZPADA project was implemented with the support of top management in the MF, readying the business process architecture and detailed implementation plans were abandoned.

3.1.2 Main Obstacles in the First Approach

The main obstacle to the adoption of a process-oriented approach in the CS was a firmly established hierarchical organizational structure, with its associated dependencies. Both the internal project team and external consultants underestimated the strength of these structures, which were built over the years. The newly proposed flat organizational structure based on processes and radically changed responsibilities of managers were too revolutionary for the organization and contributed to the final decision to stop adopting BPM.

Despite the large amount of work involved in developing the concept of process ownership associated with the new architecture, the consultants could not disconnect the ownership of the new processes from the deep-rooted organizational structures

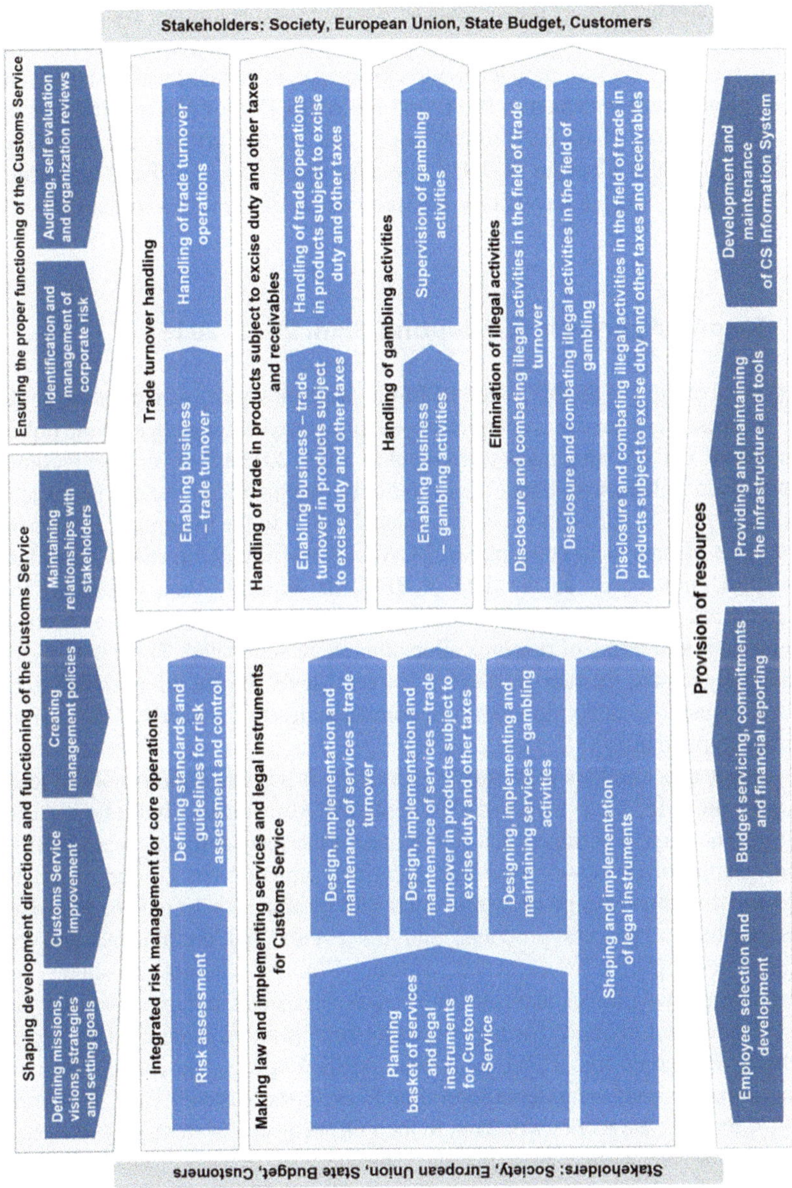

Fig. 2 Business Process Architecture of the Customs Service, 2013

and habits. This problem was not solved in the first approach to BPM and contributed to the abandoning of the implementation.

Extending the work over 3 years was another significant problem. Only after this period, when the concept was fully developed, did project leaders begin trying to convince top management of the benefits of the proposed solutions. By then it was too late.

Finally, the lack of a system that supports process management was an issue. The SZPADA project was launched in 2011, and the ARIS IT tool was delivered at the end of 2013. Before that, the primary tool used in the project was an Excel spreadsheet. With the adoption of ARIS, the data saved in spreadsheets was transferred to the newly created Repository of Architecture of Processes in the CS.

3.2 Second Approach to Adopting BPM: 2013–2015

The next involvement of the MF in the BPM initiative took place as part of the larger project, "Processes, Objectives, Competences—integrated management in the public administration" (POC), which was carried out in 2013–2015 for government administration units in Poland with financing from the European Social Fund. The project, worth about 7 million euros, included activities directed to the integrated implementation of three management concepts: BPM, Management by Objectives, and Management by Competences. In the field of BPM, the identification, modeling, and improvement of processes for government administration institutions, as well as their examination in terms of resource allocation, were scheduled. The creation of a coherent management system by objectives and development of a competency model that focused on adapting employee competencies to the needs of the institution were also planned.

The project was implemented for 63 government administration units, one of which was the MF, and involved 130 external consultants and about 3000 employees. The project assumed that in the part of the project that addressed BPM adoption, groups of processes would be identified and that ten groups would be modeled and five business processes in each unit would be selected for improvement. Stakeholders, process products, and the events that initiate and end the processes were identified by means of workshops run by external consultants for members of internal project teams. However, the project's requirements did not specify the rules and methods for implementing such process changes. The project was carried out using free BPM tools like ARIS Express and Bizagi and the modeling notations that the external consultants preferred (usually EPC, less often BPMN). At the MF, the work carried out in the POC project was in no way related to the results achieved in the first approach, especially as the POC project did not include areas of activity that were covered in the first BPM initiative. The project ended with the completion of funding that coincided with a change in the political staff and decision-makers at the MF.

3.2.1 Results Achieved in the Second Approach

Most of the objectives of the second approach were not achieved. The tangible benefits included documentation of several unrelated processes and increased awareness of BPM among the small group of employees involved. The expected benefits of the project included reduced costs through rational planning of budgets and resources based on actual costs incurred, defined responsibilities, improved horizontal and vertical cooperation and communication, and improved quality of services provided by improving the efficiency of operations, organizing activities in terms of creating added value for the customer, and eliminating unnecessary activities. Other results presented in the report that summarized the project concerned the identification of processes, the possibility for measuring their effectiveness, and risk management in processes. It was assumed that, as part of the activities, the organization's goals (strategy) would be integrated with individual levels of business process architecture and BPM would be included in internal documents, which would affect the efficiency, timeliness, and quality of implemented processes. The assumed benefits also concerned a strong focus on the needs and expectations of external and internal customers.

3.2.2 Main Obstacles in the Second Approach

Significant barriers to BPM adoption that were observed in the second approach resulted from the siloed organizational structure, which was based on a functional approach, as well as an organizational culture that was typical of public administration.

- It proved impossible to identify the full process architecture or even the relationships between processes. Some of the processes were closed within departments or units.
- An important barrier was insufficient top management support for changes and the lack of adequate employee involvement in the process of change.
- In summary, the second approach resulted in increased awareness of process orientation among a small group of employees. Although the main goal of the project was to prepare the MF for effective BPM, this initiative was not implemented, and the business process architecture was not built.

3.3 Third Approach to Adopting BPM: 2016–2017

The third approach to adopting BPM at the MF was associated with the reform that led to the CS's being combined with the tax administration to form the NRA. Preparatory work for the reform aimed at building a new business process architecture for the MF to create a foundation for all MF activity. Thus, this next planned architecture was to cover a larger scope of MF activities than was covered in the first BPM approach. As a result of this reform, the MF became even more complex than it was prior to the reform not only because of the combination of two organizational cultures but also because of diverse solutions in the information technologies used.

The CS already had some experience and results from the first BPM adoption initiative, so its process awareness was at a much higher level than it was in tax administration, where the concepts of process and process management were unknown to most employees, as only a small group of employees in the tax administration area had been involved in BPM initiatives (under the second BPM approach) and they were only fundamentally familiar with process language and process thinking. The lack of clear, uniform solutions in the two units that were to create a coherent new NRA resulted in low interest in the process approach among executives and decision-makers, who were not convinced of the benefits of implementing a process-oriented approach in the MF.

Work on the new architecture was carried out by the newly established Business Process Division under the NRA Reform Department. A characteristic feature of the BPM initiative under the third approach was the perception of procedures and regulatory tasks as processes. Hence, the preparation for the workshops during which processes were identified and described consisted primarily of taking inventories of the external and internal regulations, procedures, instructions, and guidelines that were collected for the purpose of defining processes later. This dispersed paper documentation was principally used to develop the second business process architecture for the NRA, the newly constituted unit that performs the vast majority of the MF's statutory tasks. At the beginning of the work on architecture, the topic of BPM, particularly MF's business processes after the reform, seemed to be the last topic executives and decision-makers were interested in.

3.3.1 Results Achieved in the Third Approach

The main result of the third BPM approach by the MF was the development of a process architecture for the NRA (Fig. 3). At the beginning of the work on the architecture, the topic of BPM, particularly the MF's business processes after the reform, seemed to hold little interest for those who made decisions about the shape of NRA reform.

However, at the end of work on the process architecture for the NRA, its printed poster became an integral component of the reform, its main pictorial language. The image of the process architecture was a prototype of how the NRA should look and act after the reform. This business process architecture combined a multitude of documents that described structures and scopes of activity. Despite numerous shortcomings and an incorrect approach to many aspects of process definition, the NRA process architecture became the starting point from which the newly created organization would try to convince decision-makers in the MF that they should support additional BPM initiatives and adopt BPM in the future.

Apart from the indisputable media value of the developed architecture, the most important result for the organization was the establishment at the end of the third approach of the Business Process Management Division within the NRA structure, the primary task of which was to introduce a process-oriented approach to the new NRA organization.

As in the first version of the architecture (Fig. 1), the architecture presented in Fig. 2 includes only two levels of processes. However, these processes differ from

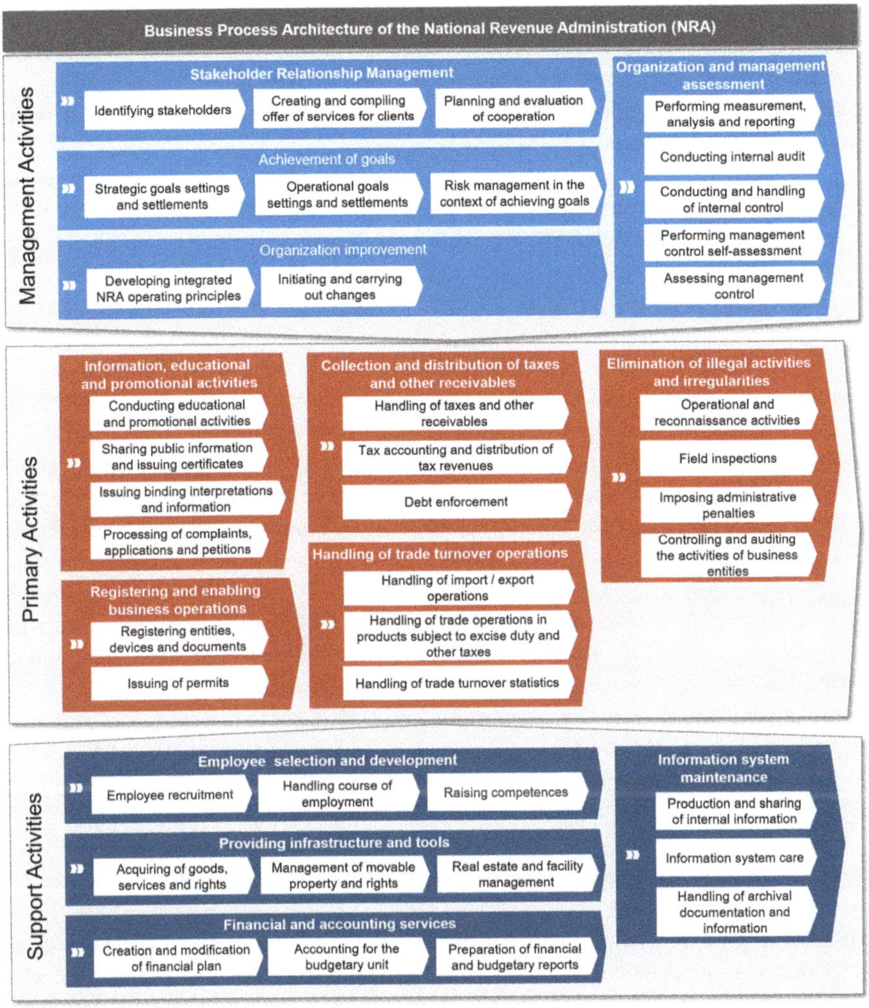

Fig. 3 Business Process Architecture of the National Revenue Administration, 2017

those of the first process architecture, so work related to the identification and discovery of processes in the second approach to BPM adoption was performed without taking into account the experience in the first approach to BPM adoption.

3.3.2 Main Obstacles in the Third Approach

The biggest obstacle to achieving lasting effects from the third BPM initiative in the MF was the low level of awareness of processes in the newly created organization (the NRA).

The previous experience in building process architecture for CS (the first approach) was only partially used in preparing the general assumptions for the process architecture. Instead of adapting the first architecture, it was built again, without using any methodology and in too little time. In this context, the main obstacles to the adoption of BPM included:

- Lack of support from experienced BPM consultants. Neither employees with experience from the first BPM approach nor external consultants were involved in this initiative.
- Lack of methodology for process identification. The development of architecture was ad-hoc.
- The identification of processes was based on the inventory of procedures and instructions carried out in parallel for each of the two units that were to constitute the new organization, the NRA. This approach was considered to be required for the merger of the two entities' organizational structures and areas of responsibility, but the negative effect of these actions was the application of the principle that *if there is a procedure for something, then there should be a process to which this procedure applies*.

In summary, as a result of the third approach, the concept of architecture was developed by presenting in detail the areas of the newly created NRA's activities. Despite calling it a business process architecture, it tended to present a chain of activities divided into primary, supporting, and management activities, rather than a business process architecture.

3.4 Fourth Approach to Adopting BPM: 2017–2019

The fourth approach began with the formal start of the activity of the huge new organizational unit, the NRA. As a result, the next changes to take place at the MF were in the organizational structures, subordination of departments, and names of organizational units. The Business Process Division (BPD) was moved directly under the umbrella of the MF, while within the structures of NRAs, work on business process architecture was largely done by the new Process Optimization Competence Center (POCC) in the city of Katowice. These two units, both of which were dedicated to the development of process-oriented management in the MF, began work on updating the architecture developed for the NRA in the third approach and developing it for the entire MF. The updating of architecture was necessary because the last edition of the business process architecture for the NRA had taken place a few months before it started to operate, so the first task in this fourth approach was to determine to what extent the previously developed (*to-be*) architecture was reflected in reality. Work on the detailed identification of processes at the MF was supervised by the BPD, while identification of specific processes within the NRA architecture was overseen by POCC.

Table 1 Process identification cycle used in the fourth approach

1st step	The team for process identification methodology plans to identify processes in an organizational unit, selects employees from that unit to participate in the workshops, and prepares them for further activities in the initial training.
2nd step	Together with previously trained employees (process identification team inside the units), the managers of the organizational units develop sheets of identified processes and/or process stages. This activity is carried out in accordance with the method presented at the training and its attached instructions, examples, and patterns.
3rd step	The team for the process identification methodology analyzes the process sheets, uses the process identification team inside the unit to clarify any concerns, and develops preliminary process models using ARIS Designer, modeling notations, value-added chain diagrams, EPCs, and function allocation models.
4th step	The methodology team conducts three full-day workshops for each organizational unit. Members of the process identification teams and other employees of organizational units take part in the workshops using the brainstorming method. During the workshops, process models are verified and tasks are assigned.
5th step	The managers of organizational units submit the process sheets and process models, published in the ARIS Portal system, for approval to their supervising directors. All organizational units involved in the execution of the process are consulted regarding the final description of the identified processes.

The identification of processes took place in the so-called process identification cycle, as shown in Table 1. The green light for BPM development, lit by the decision-makers in the third approach, allowed for a much broader scope of BPM initiatives throughout the MF. For example, teams for process identification methodologies were set up within departments, supervised by the BPD and POCC, and tasked with identifying and modeling the processes in detail, starting from the lowest level.

The method used to identify the processes involved describing detailed processes from the "bottom-up" and then matching them to the overall outline of the architecture previously developed for NRA.

Most organizational units that perform tasks in public sector organizations are characterized by routine execution of processes that are formalized to a significant degree (Saxena, 1996; Syed et al., 2018). Thus, the approach used to identify processes highlighted the divergent goals of the workshop participants and the generally negative perception of the activities carried out. Particularly noteworthy was how the workshop leaders tried to reduce the number of processes by combining tasks, while the participants tried to increase it. Such conflicts significantly extended the process identification process and had a negative impact on the quality of data that emerged from the workshop participants. The workshop participants preferred to share their detailed knowledge of the tasks performed in their positions, rather than to think holistically and define process goals, process products, and process relationships. Moreover, employees involved in the identification of processes did not see the business benefits for their units and were also busy performing appropriate daily tasks, so they were reluctant to devote time to the workshops. The fourth approach to adopting BPM and building a business process architecture for the MF was brought to an end by the sound judgment of the project team. The division responsible for processes realized that using the adopted method of identifying and modeling processes for the MF, which employed 66,500 people, would take 8 years, so only 25% of the next business process architecture for the entire MF was built before the use of the approach was discontinued.

3.4.1 Results Achieved in the Fourth Approach

The main achievements of the fourth approach were the lessons learned from individuals' own mistakes, as the results obtained made clear that improved results would be obtained only by using a *top-down* approach and decomposing processes to lower levels of the hierarchy (Dijkman, Vanderfeesten, & Reijers, 2016). At this stage, the need to use the knowledge and experience that was already available in the BPM management literature and practice was recognized. In particular, the BPM initiatives were implemented without the participation of external consultants, who usually bring with them valuable knowledge and experience from other projects. The new organizational units dedicated to BPM adoption also did not include all of the employees who had gained experience in the previous three BPM initiatives. Paradoxically, seeing and understanding the problems and obstacles to BPM development proved to be the biggest achievement of the fourth approach.

3.4.2 Main Obstacles in the Fourth Approach

- Process identification was closely linked to the organizational structure, leading to incorrect results. Identifications were carried out in subsequent departments and their organizational units (i.e., in accordance with the silo organizational structure), which created undesirable competition between departments to achieve the largest number of processes identified.
- Strategic processes were not identified, processes were not prioritized, and processes were not linked to the organization's goals, probably because the bottom-up method was used to identify processes.
- Another important problem in the third BPM initiative was appointing process owners and defining their responsibilities and tasks. In the MF, the owner of the process, by default, is a manager in the organization, usually the director of the organizational unit. Such an approach only strengthens the silo thinking and constitutes the existing functional system.
- The resistance from middle management was strong, often because processes run through multiple departments. As a result, the managers of these departments are obliged to share part of their power with the process owner.
- Employees involved in the workshop reported problems in understanding the process language and modeling notation, especially if BPMN was used. The choice of notation was usually determined by the habits and experience of narrow expert groups. BPMN began to be used for the requirements specification of the implemented IT system, but most processes were first described in Excel sheets using the function-allocation model, and even then only some of them were in EPC notation.

- Difficulties arose in trying to go into the process-measurement phase when setting measures or building indicators for individual processes because of the improperly constructed catalog of processes that was based heavily on tasks taken directly from organizational regulations. The catalog of identified processes too often resembled a list of statutory tasks, supplemented by a list of applicable regulations (or names of areas covered by legal regulations).

3.5 Fifth Approach to Adopting BPM: 2019–2020

The current approach to BPM, the fifth approach, commenced because of changes in personnel in the BPAD and resulted in a higher awareness of BPM. New individuals responsible for process architecture quickly understood that poor architecture, improper development methodology, and the general lack of a BPM development strategy can quickly lead to the failure of BPM adoption. Their actions taken in response mainly concerned three issues:

- Embedding BPM adoption on three main levels of improving the performance of the organization in accordance with Rummler and Brache (1995).
- Defining the policy and standards of planned BPM adoption.
- Changes in the approach to the development of process architecture from *bottom-up* to *top-down* and basing it on the established reference model proposed by Dijkman et al. (2016).

According to Rummler and Brache's (1995) concept of "three levels of performance," the strategy is established at the organizational level, workflows are improved at the process level, and the work is done at the performer/job level. The factors that affect the organization's performance at the organizational level include the organization's mission and vision, strategy, overall objectives (and methods for measuring the objectives), and structure. In the government sector, the role of BPM is to support the implementation of the goals set by the organization's statutory tasks (Tregear & Jenkins, 2007), so it can be said that BPM policy is created for the needs of the organizational level, constituting the principles and framework for creating BPM standards, which are the main carriers of principles for the process level. A characteristic feature of the process level is management at the interface between functional departments, which, in practice, comes down to the management of the "*white space*" between departments or stages in the process. The reference for this level is not only the policy that provides the most important principles for BPM (Vom Brocke et al., 2014), but also the set of standards that dictate how to deal with the processes. Figure 4 illustrates how the BPAD is involved in the BPM application at three levels of performance.

The performer/job level is mainly influenced by BPM standards and its process description notations. In addition to BPM standards, variables that affect performance at the workplace level include applied labor standards, recruitment methods,

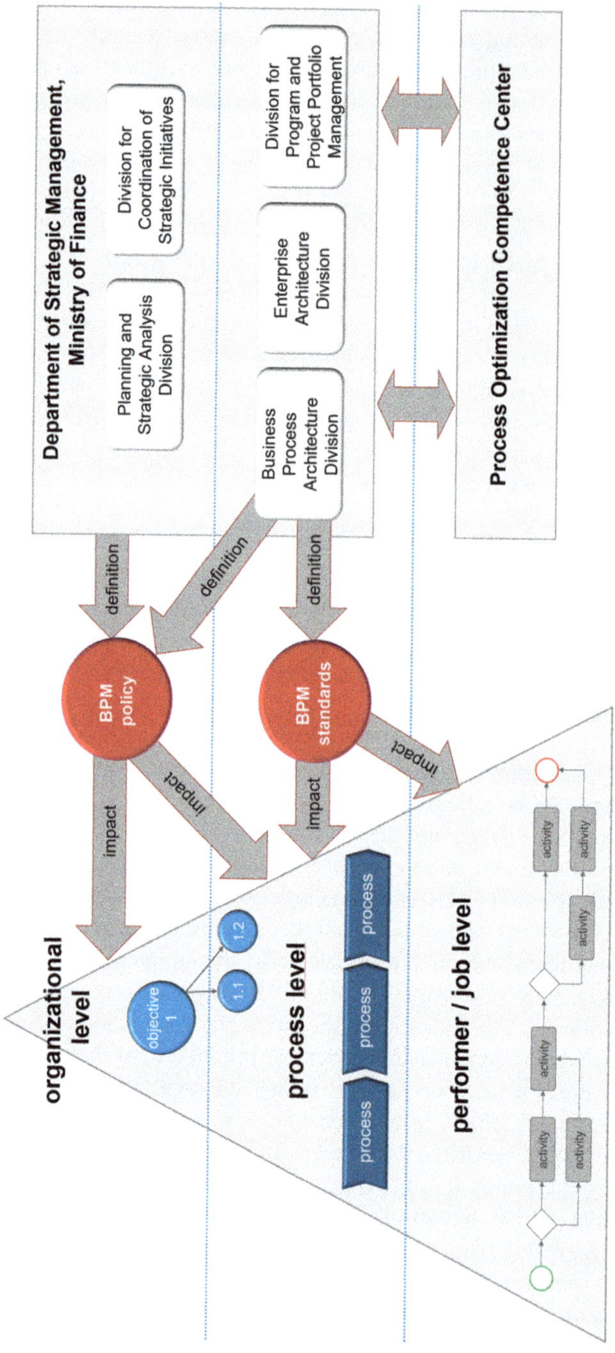

Fig. 4 Three levels of performance improvement in the context of the BPM adoption strategy by the Ministry of Finance, 2019

training, and scopes of tasks, duties, and powers. This area remains primarily in the POCC's sphere of activity.

Bearing in mind the experience of the fourth approach, for which the biggest problem was the slow progress of work, the most important result of the fifth approach was the acceleration of work on the process architecture while maintaining established BPM policy and standards. The process identification method changed from bottom-up to top-down, for which the BPAD used proven best practices in the form of reference models (Dijkman et al., 2016) and the Process Classification Framework (PCF) from the American Productivity and Quality Center (APQC, 2019), especially the City Government Process Qualification Framework version 7.2.1 (2019). The APQC framework provides the foundations for architecture development by offering:

- Process hierarchy with decomposition.
- Process classification, including operating processes and management and support services.
- Methodologies, standards, and definitions that provide a common approach and guidelines.

The choice to use the APQC framework in the MF was due to the need for a uniform approach to process identification and to ensure comparability in the information transmitted between the NRA and the MF and the need to build an architecture of processes whose structure would be stable over a long period of time, that is, independent of political factors and radical organizational changes.

While the development of process architecture was generally compliant with the reference model, there were significant discrepancies in decomposing processes into subprocesses and activities. However, the advantage of the top-down approach was the logic and simplicity of conducting it, while the disadvantages were the risk of not taking some activities into account, particularly those related to the specificity of the MF's activities. In the fourth approach, the bottom-up approach, the identified top-level processes were composed into subprocesses, taking the relationships between them into account. In this case, it was necessary to formalize this type of procedure, which required establishing appropriate categories of relationships and criteria for their assessment, as in only this way could connections between processes be established. Changing the process identification method to top-down quickly bore fruit, as all of the architecture was estimated within 6 months, as opposed to the estimated 8 years with a bottom-up approach.

Other actions taken for the development of a business process architecture at the MF were:

- A general architecture outline built based on the categories proposed under the APQC's PCF (level 1—category).
- Transfer of the processes identified so far to the structure, prepared in the appropriate way, and adjusted to the level of process groups (level 2—process groups).

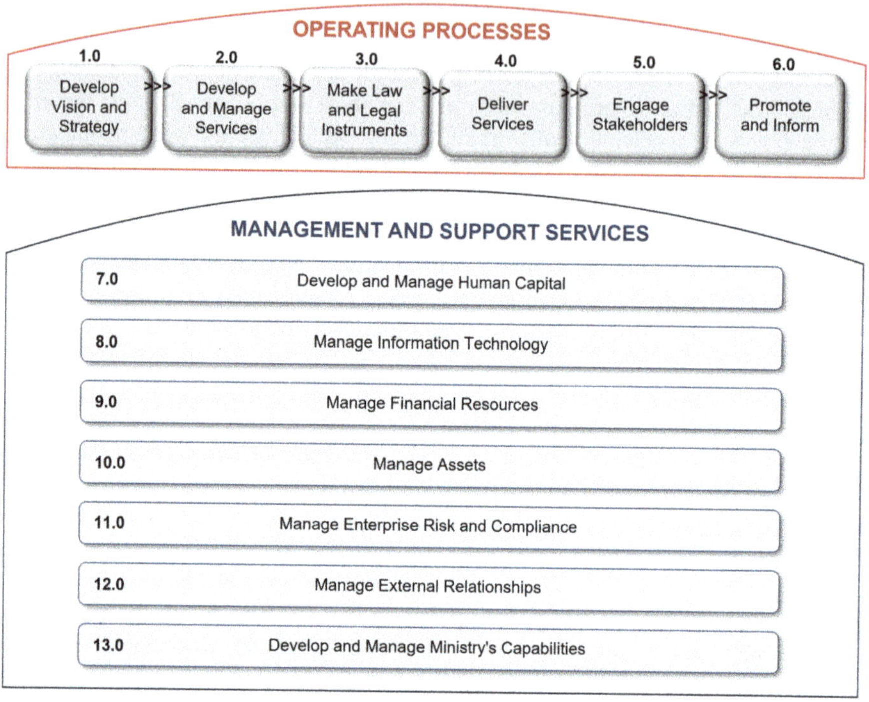

Fig. 5 High-level business process architecture at the Ministry of Finance, 2019

- Supplementation of each of the process groups with a list of processes identified thus far (level 3—process), a level that deviates sharply from the solution proposed in the APQC model (although the point of view used in PCF significantly contributed to how the available catalog of processes was ordered).

Figure 5 presents the highest level of the MF's process architecture after adapting it to the APQC model's assumptions. To comply with this model, the tactical level that caused problems in previous architectures was removed, particularly in the context of determining the ownership of processes and increasing levels of process decomposition.

Conducting process identification makes sense only when one intends to supervise the identified processes and measure and carry out improvement activities so they create value of strategic importance for the organization (Dumas et al., 2013, p. 35). In the case of public sector organizations, one often forgets about such basics as the purpose of identification, so the process identification itself becomes only a census or inventory of "*what we do.*"

To ensure the consistency between the built architecture and the organization's goals and strategy, the ARIS Strategy module, which uses the cascade of goals and strategic scenarios for modeling, was launched. The objects from these models will be used in process allocation models. Using ARIS's technical capabilities allows one to prepare reports quickly based on SQL queries, so decision-makers can receive the current process model with reference to the goals and activities that are implemented as part of the adopted strategy.

The introduction of BPM adoption mechanisms at the MF was possible because of the establishment and extension of the scope of the BPAD's tasks that were adapted to the concept of the BPM Center of Excellence (Jesus, Macieira, Karrer, & Rosemann, 2009). Compared to previous approaches that limited BPAD's or similar units' tasks to identifying and documenting processes, BPAD significantly expanded the possibilities of adopting BPM (Fig. 6).

The framework presented for operating a BPAD is also the answer to the question: What comes after documenting all processes? Establishing transparent BPM policy and standards allows the full BPM life cycle to be implemented, which is the long-term goal of the BPAD in the MF. Unlike the previous approaches that carried out no improvement activities but focused entirely on documenting, the fifth approach carried out pilot activities in optimizing the purchasing process.

3.5.1 Results Achieved in the Fifth Approach

- The most important result of the fifth approach was the BPAD's location in the MF's organizational structure as being responsible for BPM adoption. BPAD develops guidelines for BPM adoption and introduces these guidelines to other units that operate independently, such as the POCC.
- Another important result of the fifth approach was the establishment of the BPM policy, created from scratch and based on previous experience, that covers the entire MF, including the NRA. This approach ensures consistency in the solutions developed and the concepts and methods used, including modeling principles.
- Only after the introduction of a uniform policy and BPM standards did BPAD receive positive signals of employee involvement in changes and of employees' understanding of the need for a common and coherent approach to BPM adoption. Understanding the need to use good BPM implementation practices should be considered an important achievement.

3.5.2 Main Obstacles in the Fifth Approach

- The BPM adoption initiative still does not come from the top management level, and decisions are not made in the MF but at the middle management level that has expressed interest in BPM and understands it. As a result, each activity related to the development of the process architecture must be agreed upon and planned, which uses unnecessary resources. Without a directive from the highest level, not all activities that the BPAD undertakes are easily adopted by other departments, especially since the scope of activities undertaken by various departments (Fig. 6) partly overlaps. The lack of directives at the highest level also hinders cooperation, although the problem has been partly solved by using the APQC model, which forces a holistic view of the entire organization.
- The term "process" is still identified with internal regulations or the procedures indicated in the organizational regulations. This problem is typical of public

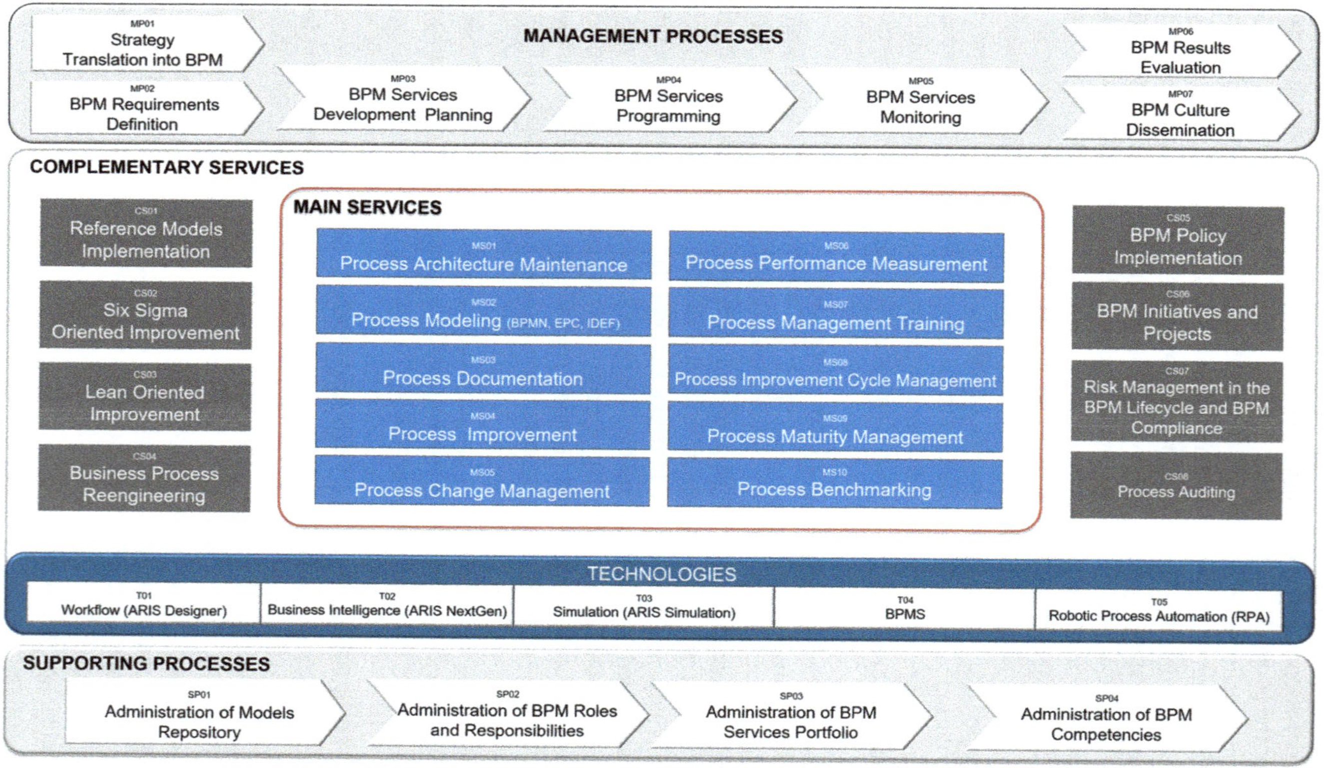

Fig. 6 Framework for the operation of a Business Process Architecture Division in the Ministry of Finance, 2019. Based on Jesus et al. (2009)

sector organizations, which are keen to ensure their compliance with the laws and regulations under which they perform their tasks (Ferlie et al., 2005; Saxena, 1996; Tregear & Jenkins, 2007). In practice, this approach always results in a huge number of identified processes—often several hundred—which the BPAD has termed "modeling madness." Such an approach involves the preparation of a huge amount of documentation containing process descriptions, although the question of who will consult this documentation—and when and why—remains open.

- An important obstacle to BPM adoption that the BPAD noticed in the fifth approach was the malfunctioning of the management control mechanism. As a mechanism imposed by law, management control has become a consistent element of organizational culture in the public sector and is treated as a panacea for preventing any type of dysfunction and inefficiency in operations. In accordance with the Polish Public Finance Act (2009), management control in the public finance sector units consists of "*all activities undertaken to ensure the achievement of objectives and tasks in a lawful, effective, economical and timely manner*," so public sector entities tend to consider the mechanism sufficient to ensure efficiency of operations, diminishing the significance of the process approach. Public sector organizations often fail to notice that the process-oriented approach also concerns efficiency and helps eliminate unnecessary work, delays, and re-works through better management of the *white space*. However, decision-makers in the public sector interpret management control as not only supporting the functional division of labor but also strengthening it by imposing an additional structure of duties and responsibilities on the existing structure.

4 Results Achieved

Results achieved were presented in the previous section after describing the actions taken in each of the five approaches.

5 Lessons learned

The case study of the MF provides lessons learned regarding three main issues:

- We learn how (not) to develop business process architecture in a large government institution (Dijkman et al., 2016) and diagnose the research gap regarding shaping business process architectures for public sector institutions.
- We verify the list of critical success factors for BPM adoption in the public sector using a practical example, thus filling part of the research gap indicated in the BPM literature (Syed et al., 2018).
- We draw conclusions concerning the barriers and restrictions related to BPM adoption in public sector institutions.

5.1 Lessons Learned with Regard to the Development of Architecture

The MF saw the business process architecture as defined in the BPM literature: "*a tool to design a structure for the processes that exist in an organization, before those processes are designed in detail*" (Dijkman et al., 2016, p. 3). The purpose of developing the architecture was "*to provide a representation of the processes that exist in an organization*" and "*to face the complexity of the whole organization*" (Dumas et al., 2013, p. 41). This complexity, as it occurs in a huge institution, turned out to be most problematic for designing an architecture. The MF needed several approaches and lessons learned from trial and error over almost 9 years to rely, albeit only partially, on a proven APQC Framework reference. A valuable lesson in the development of the architecture is the need to show how the characteristics of the public sector are conducive to falling into "modeling madness," which led to the documentation of thousands of procedures and internal regulations that were mistakenly understood as business processes. The reasons for this state of affairs can be seen in many factors, which certainly include a lack of sufficiently documented practices from similar initiatives in similar organizations to benchmark and a shortage of literature that focuses on the specificities of public sector institutions. Even the APQC framework used in the fifth approach does not have government reference models and required that the value chain and high-level processes be adapted.

Moreover, the architecture development in the first four approaches was followed by only a few—or even no—other BPM core elements (Rosemann & vom Brocke, 2010). Strategic alignment was identified only with the implementation of statutory tasks, and obtaining BPM governance was heavily burdened with long-term habits, strong hierarchical structures, and political decisions, fundamentally preventing any change. A significant challenge in the public sector relates to appointing process owners. With the exception of the first approach, none of the initiatives provided for any analysis or modification of organizational structures or the related consolidated dominance of vertical organizational relationships over horizontal ones. The proposed modification of structures probably contributed to the decision to stop the first approach. In addition, even after establishing new units in the Strategic Management Department, there remains the problem of integrating the enterprise architecture with the process architecture. In general, the first four approaches attached almost no importance to the organizational culture and people, which often resulted in unexpected negative impacts. Only in the fifth approach did the BPAD consistently attempt to popularize process-oriented management through thematic training and newsletters. In addition, with the exception of the first approach, no initiative provided for any analysis or modification of organizational structures or the related dominance of vertical organizational relationships over horizontal ones.

In summary, research on the design of process architectures for powerful public sector organizations is needed, as are practical solutions to the problem of integrating these architectures with other areas of the organization, such as IT. Developing process architecture cannot be self-focused; failure to consider other BPM core elements, such as BPM governance, IT, people, and culture, will make the practical implementation of an architecture impossible.

5.2 Lessons Learned with Regard to the BPM Critical Success Factors in the Public Sector

To verify BPM's critical success factors using the example of the MF case study, we reviewed the factors identified as critical in Syed et al. (2018), as shown in Table 2.

5.3 Lessons Learned with Regard to the Barriers and Restrictions Associated with BPM Adoption in Public Sector Institutions

The case study of the long and difficult journey in adopting BPM at the MF revealed a number of barriers to and restrictions on process-oriented management in the public sector. These include the inability to adopt the key perspective of the client (citizen, entrepreneur) in defining values that relate to, for example, the lack of competition in the provision of public services. Managers accounted only for tasks performed in accordance with the regulations established in the organization. External oversight and restrictions related to control and the political dynamics of change (and sometimes even political pressure) mean that managers in the public sector have less power and influence over the organization being managed than those in the private sector do, which makes it difficult to achieve the planned results. Therefore, managers who are willing to establish further hierarchical controls and give opinions on decisions made by lower-level managers are reluctant to delegate power (Ferlie et al., 2005).

An important obstacle to adopting BPM in the MF was also the insufficient knowledge about and experience of BPM inside the organization, although the fifth approach shows that it is possible to develop this knowledge if appropriate organizational units and individuals dedicated to BPM adoption are established. It also draws attention to the lack of sufficient knowledge and support from external consultants, who, in the first and second approach, should have provided the organization with the appropriate methodology, but they did not know how to develop process architecture. In addition, managers in the public sector are less well paid than those in the private sector are, which results in the inability to attract well-qualified staff. The lack of qualifications is also connected to focusing on the implementation of process management without fully understanding the principles of the BPM concept. Employees see internal organizational regulations as more important than the proposed process model, as employees regard process models as not being anchored in the organization's formal regulations, which are pillars of public sector institutions' identities. Breaking employee habits is one of the leading challenges in adopting BPM in public sector organizations.

Moreover, the cadence and frequency of personnel changes result from the lack of continuity in organizational changes, the rejection of the implemented changes, or the interruption of activities that support their implementation. An organizational culture that is characterized by bureaucracy, unwillingness to change, lack of quality orientation, and lack of results is unfavorable to adopting BPM in the public sector. Organizational cultures that exhibit these features arise mainly as a result of

Table 2 Verification of BPM's critical success factors using the example of the Ministry of Finance

Critical success factor (Syed et al., 2018)	How critical?	Comments
Top Management Support	Critical	This factor in the public sector is manifested by issuing regulations with legal force that will not be altered when the managers change. The first two BPM initiatives undertaken by the MF did not have top management support, resulting in the cessation of these initiatives as soon as the funding ran out.
Communication	Important but not critical	The MF did not set appropriate rules for effective cooperation and team collaboration, which prolonged the duration of initiatives and resulted in needing more resources. This type of mismanagement goes unnoticed because of a malfunctioning management control mechanism.
Preparedness for Organizational Change	Important but not critical	This factor is strongly associated with top management support. The external consultants at the MF did not bring with them knowledge about the methodology for developing the architecture and did not include a methodology in the design assumptions, such as those related to the changes in organizational culture. As a result, the implemented projects had no lasting effects.
Enlisting Customer Support	Not important	No attempt was made to seek stakeholder support or involvement, as this factor is irrelevant in the MF.
Choosing the BPM Team	Critical	This factor was important, particularly as it relates to specialized skills and experience and setting up an organizational unit dedicated to BPM. The lack of both external consultants' and internal teams' knowledge led to the development of a process architecture using a *trial-and-error* method, so the BPM initiatives had no lasting effects.
Alleviation of Downsizing Fears	Important but not critical	If the BPM initiative is not established by regulation, individuals resist the additional work under the initiative. If the initiative achieves some success, then the decision-makers claim credit.
Empowerment	Critical	This factor is especially important for internal teams that initiate BPM initiatives from the middle management level. These initiatives do not come from top management or result from the organization's needs, strategic goals, or other factors at the strategic level. Only empowerment made it possible to interest top management in BPM at the end of the fourth approach at the MF.
ICT Infrastructure	Important but not critical	This factor is important in terms of the IT tool for supporting modeling and process analysis, but it was not critical at the MF, which, despite having the ARIS system, used Excel sheets successfully to identify processes.

(continued)

Table 2 (continued)

Critical success factor (Syed et al., 2018)	How critical?	Comments
Project Management	Important but not critical	See comments under the factor "choosing the BPM team."
ICT Awareness	Important but not critical	See comments under the factor "ICT awareness."
Culture	Critical	Although an element of organizational culture that is conducive to BPM was not planned or included in any of the approaches in the MF, culture made a strong contribution to obtaining or not obtaining lasting effects from each of the initiatives.
IT-BPM Governance	Critical	The factor is difficult to implement in the public sector. It does not operate without top management support or ordinances introduced by law.
Strategic Clarity and Alignment	Important but not critical	BPM in the public sector must support the implementation of statutory tasks efficiently and effectively. Therefore, understanding the essence of BPM and its benefits is important, although in the MF it is mainly the units that are dedicated to BPM that understand it.
External Environmental Factors	Not important	These factors may be important for further process improvement and enhancement of BPM maturity at the MF after the organization adopts BPM.

formalization, leading to too many or too detailed behaviors included in organizational regulations.

The understanding, implementation, and application of management control could be a remedy for all these obstacles and limitations, but the example of the MF shows how the current application of management control is not conducive to BPM adoption and other organizational changes. In the MF's documentation, each of the described approaches to adopting BPM was successful, confirming that "*the government initiatives only require plans and performance measures. Specific guidance on how to link these planning objectives to business processes and eventually align organizational information systems is not included*" (Gulledge & Sommer, 2002, p. 374).

5.4 Concluding Remark

Figure 7 summarizes the case study of the MF in Poland. The lessons learned about architecture development are based on the MF experience, although it is likely that other large public sector institutions have met similar obstacles to adopting BPM. It is also likely that these institutions could learn from the MF's mistakes.

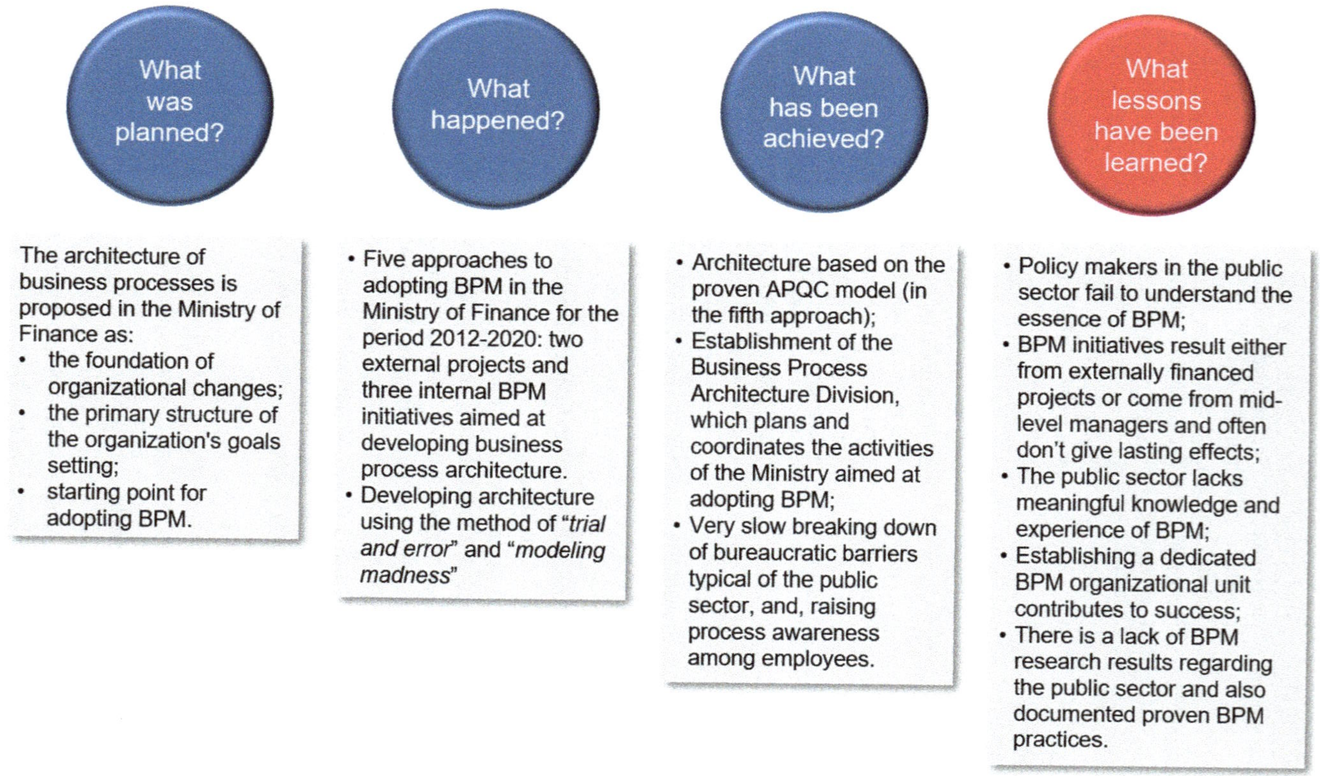

Fig. 7 An uneasy journey toward BPM at the Ministry of Finance at a glance

We hope that the experiences of the MF presented in this case study will contribute to the development of BPM theory and practice in public sector organizations.

Acknowledgments This work was supported by the Polish National Science Centre, Poland, Grant No. 2017/27/B/HS4/01734.

References

APQC. (2019). *Process classification framework by American Productivity and Quality Centre.* Version 7.2.1 (2019). https://www.apqc.org/process-performance-management/process-frameworks

Boyne, G. A. (2002). Public and private management: What's the difference? *Journal of Management Studies, 39*(1), 97–122.

Dijkman, R., Vanderfeesten, I., & Reijers, H. A. (2016). Business process architectures: overview, comparison and framework. *Enterprise Information Systems, 10*(2), 129–158.

Dumas, M., La Rosa, M., Mendling, J., & Reijers, H. A. (2013). *fundamentals of business process management* (Vol. 1). Springer.

Ferlie, E., Lynn, L. E., Jr., Lynn, L. E., Pollitt, C., & Lynn, L. E. (2005). *The Oxford handbook of public management.* New York, NY: Oxford University Press.

Gulledge, T. R., & Sommer, R. A. (2002). Business process management: public sector implications. *Business Process Management Journal, 8*(4), 364–376.

Jesus, L., Macieira, A., Karrer, D., & Rosemann, M. (2009). *A framework for a BPM center of excellence.* BPTrends.

Lee, R. G., & Dale, B. G. (1998). Business process management: A review and evaluation. *Business Process Management Journal, 4*(3), 214–225.

Ministry of Finance. (1999). Regulation of the Council of Ministers of November 3, 1999 regarding the establishment of the Ministry of Finance. *Journal of Laws No. 91*, item 1020.

National Revenue Administration. (2016). Act on the National Revenue Administration of 16 November 2016. *Journal of Laws*, item 1947.

Polish Public Finance Act. (2009). Act of 27 August 2009 on public finance. *Journal of Laws No. 157*, item 1240.

Reijers, H. A. (2006). Implementing BPM systems: The role of process orientation. *Business Process Management Journal, 12*(4), 389–409.

Rosemann, M., & vom Brocke, J. (2010). The six core elements of business process management. In *Handbook on business process management* (Vol. 1, pp. 107–122). Springer.

Rummler, G. A., & Brache, A. P. (1995). *Improving performance: How to manage the white space on the organization chart.* Jossey-Bass.

Saxena, K. B. C. (1996). Re-engineering public administration in developing countries. *Long Range Planning, 29*(5), 703–711.

Syed, R., Bandara, W., French, E., & Stewart, G. (2018). Getting it right! Critical success factors of BPM in the public sector: A systematic literature review. *Australasian Journal of Information Systems, 22*, 1–39.

Tregear, R., & Jenkins, T. (2007). *Government Process Management: A review of key differences between the public and private sectors and their influence on the achievement of public sector process management.* BPTrends

vom Brocke, J., Mendling, J., & Rosemann, M. (2021). Planning and scoping business process management projects and programs with the BPM billboard. In J. vom Brocke, J. Mendling, & M. Rosemann (Eds.), *BPM cases. Digital innovation and business transformation in practice* (Vol. 2). Springer.

vom Brocke, J., Schmiedel, T., Recker, J., Trkman, P., Mertens, W., & Viaene, S. (2014). Ten principles of good business process management. *Business Process Management Journal, 20* (4), 530–548.

Integrating Hoshin Kanri into Business Process Management: A Holistic Approach at Siemens Electronic Works Amberg

Konrad Schießl, Andreas Weigert, and Gunter Beitinger

1 Introduction

The initiative for this change was not driven by the management team but originated from practice. The improvement process is a lived culture of EWA, as the three to five realized ideas per employee per year show.

The challenge was to transfer the requirements of the international standard for management systems into an adjusted x-matrix (as we know it from the Hoshin Kanri methodology) to be aligned with the business strategy planning, which was already based on the Hoshin Kanri process (Fig. 1).

Re-introducing a strong lean-management philosophy in 2015, Siemens Electronic Works Amberg, Germany (EWA), one of Siemans AG's leading digital factories, moved from the nearly 20-year-old three-level target agreement-setting process to the Hoshin Kanri method. The case, therewith, is an example of how methodological support can contribute greatly to BPM success (vom Brocke, Mendling, & Rosemann, 2021).

The initial driver for improving the management review process in combination with business process management (BPM) was to set the established principles of the Hoshin Kanri matrix as a basis for all business process views. Managing the interdependence of all business processes as a system increases their effectiveness and efficiency in achieving the expected targets while enhancing their overall performance.

Previously, to drive business performance, EWA focused on the methods based on Hoshin Kanri and on management review for certified management systems. Successful strategy execution requires no longer handling information based on spreadsheets, PowerPoint presentations, or even unrecorded email traffic. A

K. Schießl (✉) · A. Weigert · G. Beitinger
Siemens AG, Amberg, Germany
e-mail: konrad.schiessl@siemens.com

J. vom Brocke et al. (eds.), *Business Process Management Cases Vol. 2*,
https://doi.org/10.1007/978-3-662-63047-1_23

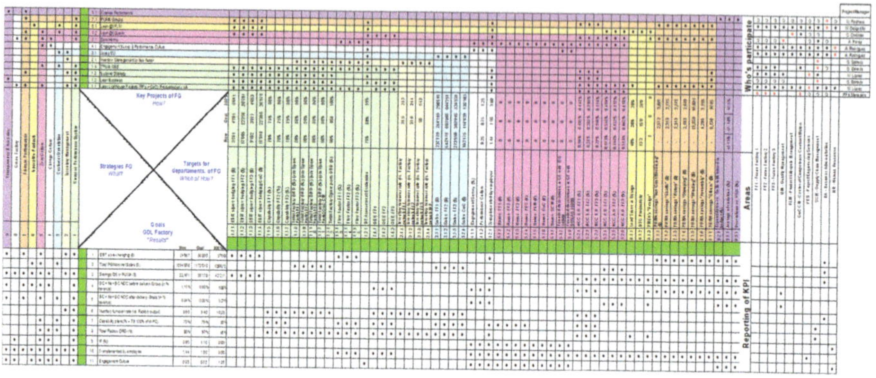

Fig. 1 Classic Hoshin Kanri X-Matrix

centralized dashboard system eliminates the risk of wrong, imprecise, and outdated data handling and ensures the ability to manage the intended strategy's execution and to turn strategy into reality. Continuous improvement and long-term strategy deployment by digitalizing existing processes will deliver the expected business results.

With an even greater emphasis on the process-oriented approach from the High-Level Structure-Based Management System Standards (HLS), the interdependence between BPM and management systems had become even more intense. Referring to the management system, BPM is set on the principles of the HLS: one requires the other.

Process control as a measure of BPM's ability means implementing the defined procedures and processes cost-effectively, quickly, error-free, and satisfactorily from the customers' perspective. The required responsibilities, competencies, and interfaces must be described as exactly as possible. Access to information should be given to all employees, with the information as understandable as possible. The aim of effective process control is to ensure the company's long-term competitiveness, especially given the increasing trend of digitalization of business processes [*The journey from a Factory to a Lean Digital Factory* (Beitinger, 2019)].

2 Situation Faced

The "Hoshin Kanri Strategic Planning" and the "Management Review" are independent management tools with overlapping coverage on some topics, such as strategy, goals, and processes, but are only connected via participation of management in meetings.

2.1 Hoshin Kanri

Coming from the Japanese language, Hoshin Kanri refers to something like a compass needle (Hoshin) and management (Kanri). Other frequently cited meanings are "management by policy" and "policy deployment." The method is a lean-management tool for holistic planning, target-setting, and strategy implementation. In general terms, Hoshin Kanri is a step-by-step strategic-planning process whose main purpose is to deploy strategies, goals, and actions in a way that they are aligned with the organization's general vision. The idea behind the method is to ensure that everyone in the organization knows the strategic direction and its associated goals and actions (Fig. 2).

As a planning and control system, Hoshin Kanri:

- Involves all managers (at all levels) and employees
- Requires a systematic and stringent derivation and coordination process among the participants ("cascading"), which runs simultaneously vertically (across hierarchical levels) and horizontally (across business units, departments, and team boundaries)
- Includes the development and definition of strategic and operational goals ("breakthroughs") from the company's vision
- Derives strategies and goals for all employees (including managers) from these breakthroughs so as to focus all company members' activities on the same vision and the same goals. Internal agreements, communication, and a common approach are essential. Hoshin Kanri is not a one-time action but a long-term and repetitive process. Against the background of the company's vision and the goals derived from it, a holistic strategy is developed and implemented.

The goals of the EWA-Hoshin Kanri are hierarchical and are represented in an X-matrix, as shown in Fig. 1. They consist of newly defined key projects from which all other key projects are derived, long- and medium-term goals, department goals,

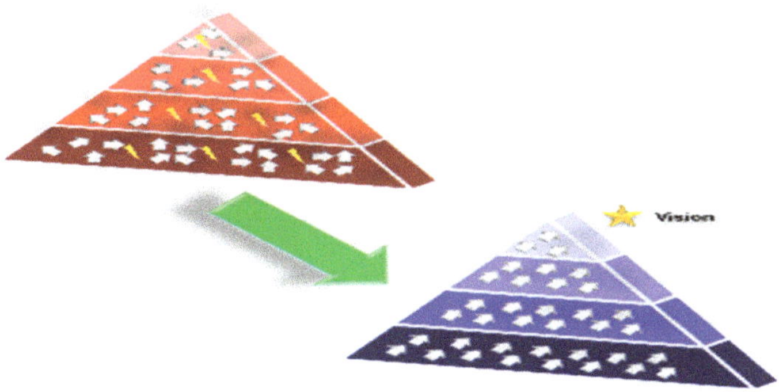

Fig. 2 Hoshin Kanri principle

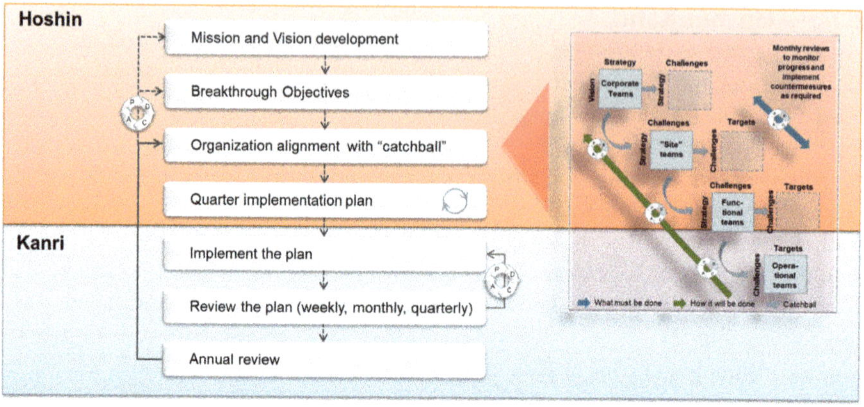

Fig. 3 The Plan-Do-Check-Act Cycle as part of the Hoshin Kanri process

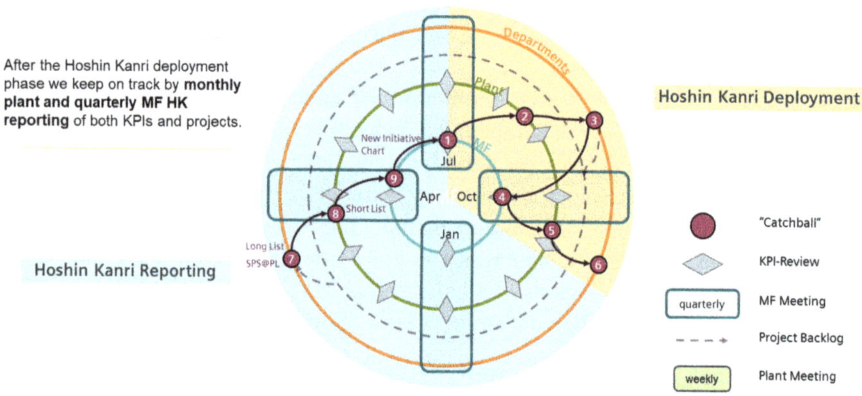

Fig. 4 Catch-ball process

and the six pillars of EWA's long-term strategy and key initiatives from the upper levels of the organization.

The Hoshin Kanri process also includes the prominent role of the Plan-Do-Check-Act improvement cycle (PDCA) (Fig. 3).

The dependencies between the activities in each of the four sections of the HK-matrix (Fig. 1) are visualized as strong relationships or minor correlations. Using the Hoshin Kanri approach, EWA defined a clear vision and list of breakthrough goals.

HKM is processed according to the catch-ball principle, with mandatory quarterly reviews of the key projects and key process indicators, as shown in Fig. 4.

2.2 Management Review

In addition to the ISO 9001:2015 Quality Management System, EWA also holds certificates for the ISO 14001:2015 Environmental Management System and ISO 45001:2018 Occupational Health and Safety Management Systems. All three systems follow the HLS for certifiable management systems. The procedure for management review is based on ISO 9001:2015. In general, a management review must be performed by the management in a systematic and regular way via many rules, regulations, and processes to ensure the effectiveness of the management system itself. Normally, it is not designed to solve current problems but to analyze long-term trends and results. Management reviews the management system at planned intervals to ensure its continuing suitability, adequacy, effectiveness, and alignment with the strategy. (ISO 14001:2015 Quality management - Quality of an organization - Guidance to achieve sustained success, n.d.; ISO 45001:2018 Quality management - Quality of an organization - Guidance to achieve sustained success, n. d.; ISO 9001:2015 Quality management systems. Requirements, n.d.).

ISO 9001:2015 Subchapter 9.3.2 *Entries for the management review* stipulates which information must be included:

- Measures from previous management reviews
- Changes in internal and external topics
- Information on the management system's effectiveness and performance
- Adequacy of resources
- Effectiveness of measures implemented on opportunities and risks
- Possibilities for improvement

Subchapter 9.3.3 Results of the management assessment stipulates the topics on which decisions and measures must be taken:

- Improvement
- Any need to change the quality management system
- Need for resources

Historically, EWA performed the management review according to Siemens' internal quality standard of the "Nine Mandatory Elements," which are intended to provide clear guidance in daily practice. Together with the quality strategy, they form the Quality Management System (Siemens Nine Mandatory Elements, n.d.).

The mandatory elements are divided into four categories:

1. Excellent Processes for Quality, with the subcategories Customer Integration, Quality Standards in Processes and Projects, and Consistent Supplier Management
2. Quality Control, with the subcategories Business-driven Quality Planning and Focused Quality Reporting

3. Quality Mindset and Outstanding Capabilities, with the subcategories Comprehensive Qualification for Quality and Continuous Improvement
4. Leadership for Quality, with the subcategories Spirit by Management Involvement and Control and Support Role of the Quality Manager

The Nine Mandatory Elements provide the framework for the quality management system, so they are also applied to other management systems.

Because the management system and the Hoshin Kanri process share aspects of strategy and objectives, combining both in a new holistic approach was obvious.

3 Action Taken

After several trial runs to determine the best configuration of the topics Management System/Business Process Management, Key Projects, Process Cluster, Vision, and Main Targets for the Management Review Cockpit (MRC), EWA decided to use the x-matrix structure as a tool for the new management review approach to achieve a multi-grade line-up of the respective financial years. (Schießl, 2019).

Structure of the MRC:

- North:
  Management Systems and BPM Structure
- South:
  Long- and mid-term goals
- West:
  Newly defined yearly key projects plus process clusters
- East:
  The six pillars of the EWA long-term strategy and key Initiatives (from upper levels of the organization)

The west, north, and south quadrants are added with each review (Fig. 5).

Unlike a classic HK x-matrix, the MRC uses the traffic-light system to mark correlations at the intersection of the horizontal and vertical aspects (e.g., "Process

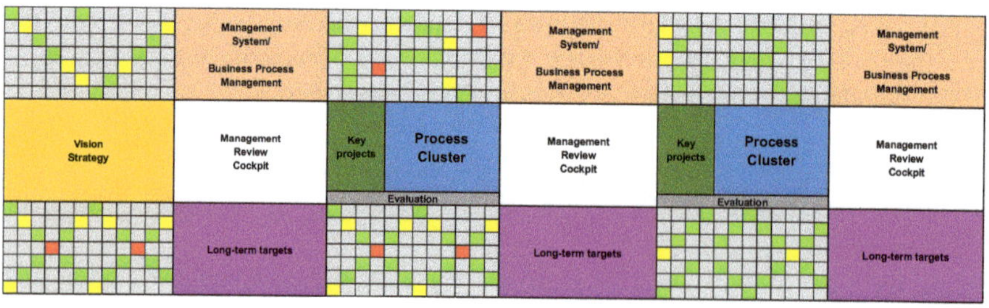

Fig. 5 Management Review Cockpit

cluster" versus "Long term targets") from adjacent quadrants, where green means that everything is on track, yellow means that significant deviations are expected, and red means that achieving the goal no longer seems to be possible. Other colors are used to visualize the status in terms of whether a goal has not yet been evaluated or has been stopped by the management during the year because of changes in priorities (Siemens SIPEX, Siemens Process for Excellence. Siemens internal documentation (Standard 001 - Policy of Siemens Business Process Management), n.d.).

The advantage of a color-oriented evaluation system is that it is easy to understand and provides a quick overview of the general situation. The disadvantage is that the choice of colors depends in some cases on the subjective feeling of the persons involved in the evaluation process.

Therefore, a performance evaluation of the key projects and of the process clusters was added, based on the three criteria from the HLS-based management systems:

- **Suitability** of the key project's objective or the purpose of the process cluster to improve or maintain compliance of the management system
- **Adequacy** of the cost use ratio
- **Effectiveness**, related to whether the key project has already been successful based on the defined measures and whether the control groups of the process clusters have worked correctly (Fig. 6)

3.1 Initial Setup

The matrix is filled in by performing five steps (Fig. 7):

1. North:
   The relevant elements of the BPM/Management System
2. South:
   The main KPIs
3. West:
   The process clusters
4. Area (4):
   The relationships between main KPIs and the process clusters
5. Area (5):
   The overview of the correlations between the elements

3.2 Annual Setup

After the initial setup, the matrix is supplemented by the results of the catch-ball process Therefore, a West, a North, and a South pillar are added to the matrix to represent a new fiscal year.

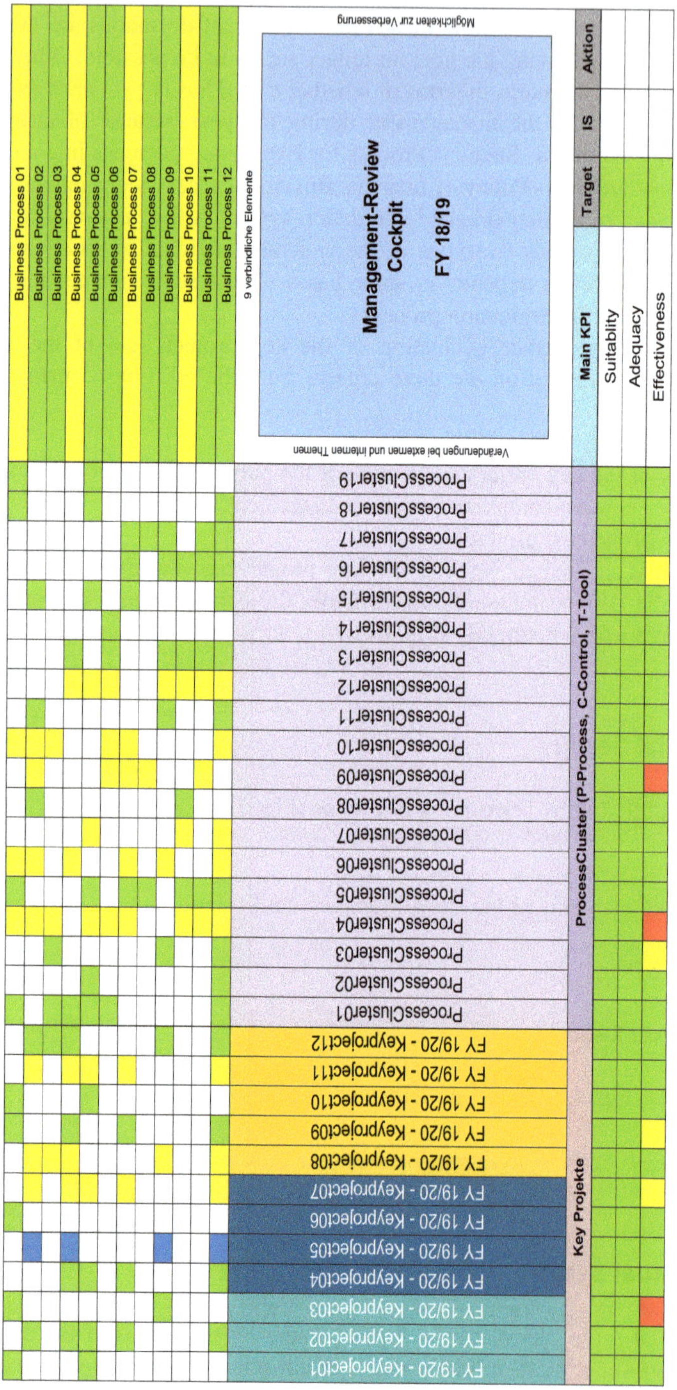

Fig. 6 Additional HLS based criteria's in the east of the HK x-matrix

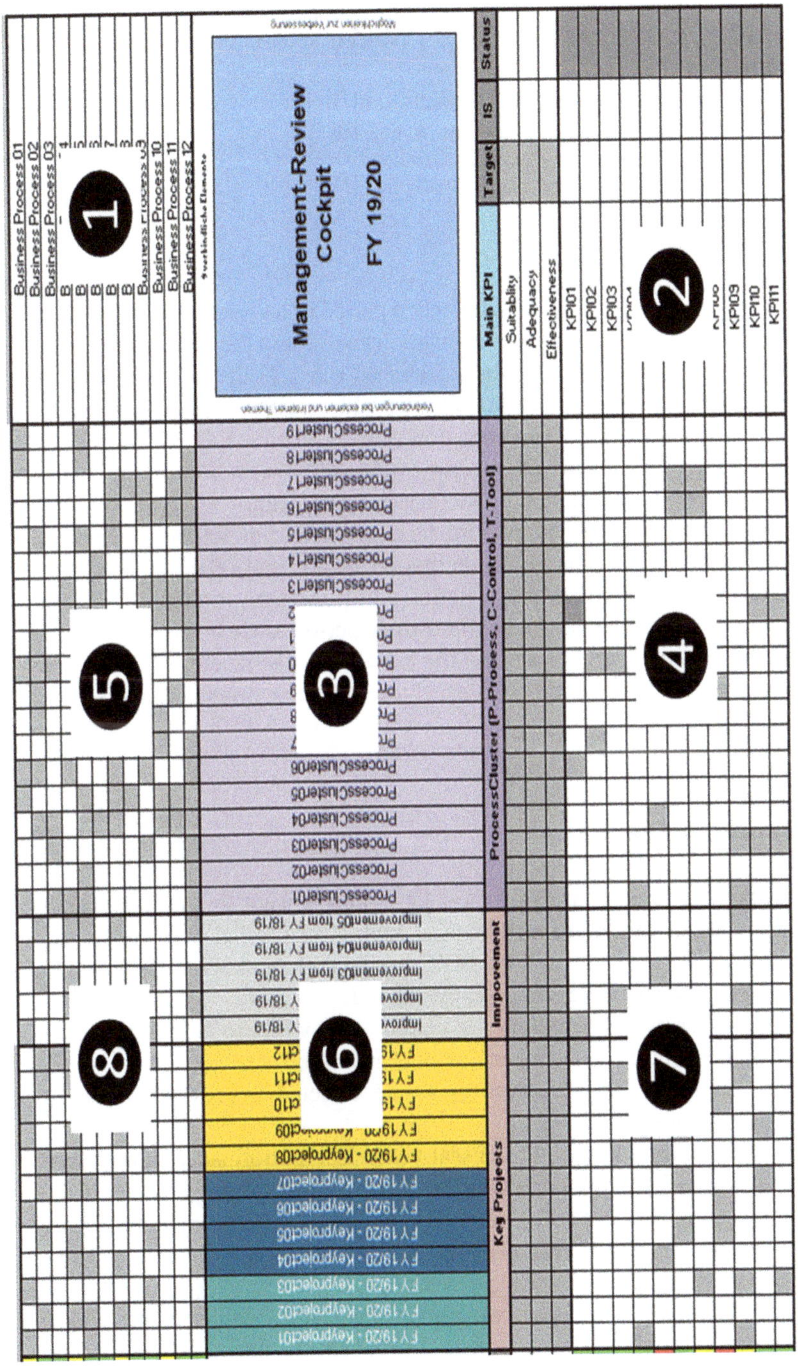
Management-Review
Cockpit
FY 19/20
Main KPI
Target
IS
Status
Suitability
Adequacy
Effectiveness
Key Projects
Imrpovement
ProcessCluster (P-Process, C-Control, T-Tool)

Fig. 7 Setup

1. The key projects for the new fiscal year and the defined improvement topics from the review of the previous fiscal year are set in the West (6).
2. Mapping of related main KPIs against key projects and the improvement actions are fixed in area (7).
3. The correlation between the key projects and improvement actions and the business processes from area (1) are set in area (8).

3.3 Evaluation Process

The evaluation of all relevant information over a period of a year follows steps in the MRC. Determining the main KPIs' performance levels allows the appropriate traffic-light status to be assigned based on the established rules. In the next step, the key projects and process clusters are assigned to the KPIs and the performance level is transferred to the intersection. The evaluation is done when a KPI is assigned to a key project or a process cluster. If several assignments have been made, a final summary score must be determined by the management team.

Assessment of the key projects' performance, improvement actions, and process clusters are based on three criteria: suitability, adequacy, and effectiveness. In the next step, the overall performance is determined by merging the three individual evaluations into one overall assessment. If the three performance levels differ, which is likely, the final assessment is based on the individual assessments of the persons involved in the review. There is no established mechanism to determine a final value from the various ratings.

4 Results Achieved

Throughout the transformation period, new key projects were set and consistently met. In the first year, the target method was applied in parallel to the other two management tools. In years 2 and 3, the MRC increasingly took over, BPM and the Business Strategy Process were strategically aligned.

Accordingly, year-by-year columns are placed side by side to help management draw conclusions about the current performance and objectives.

The setup shown in Fig. 8 serves to define targeted improvement projects strategically for the next fiscal year.

The example in Fig. 9 shows three fiscal years. The performance development can be understood easily in the context of the corresponding strategy elements. For example, if a business process was evaluated as "yellow" for 3 years, a key project must be defined in the fourth year to bring the level to green. Alternating colors indicate a lack of stability in the business process.

Since this systematic approach was implemented and established to achieve process excellence at EWA, the company's productivity increased significantly 3 years in a row. EWA was awarded as a Smart Factory in terms of its processes

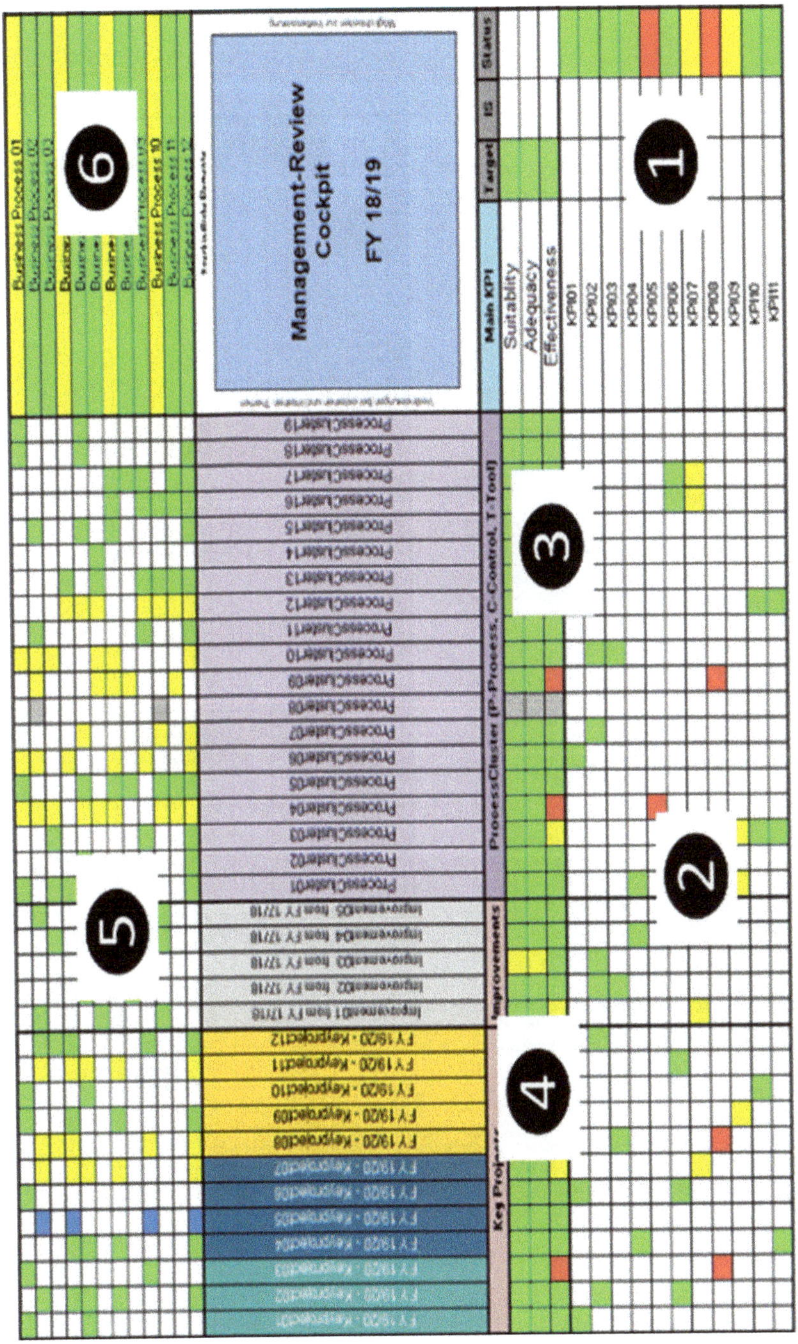

Fig. 8 Evaluation

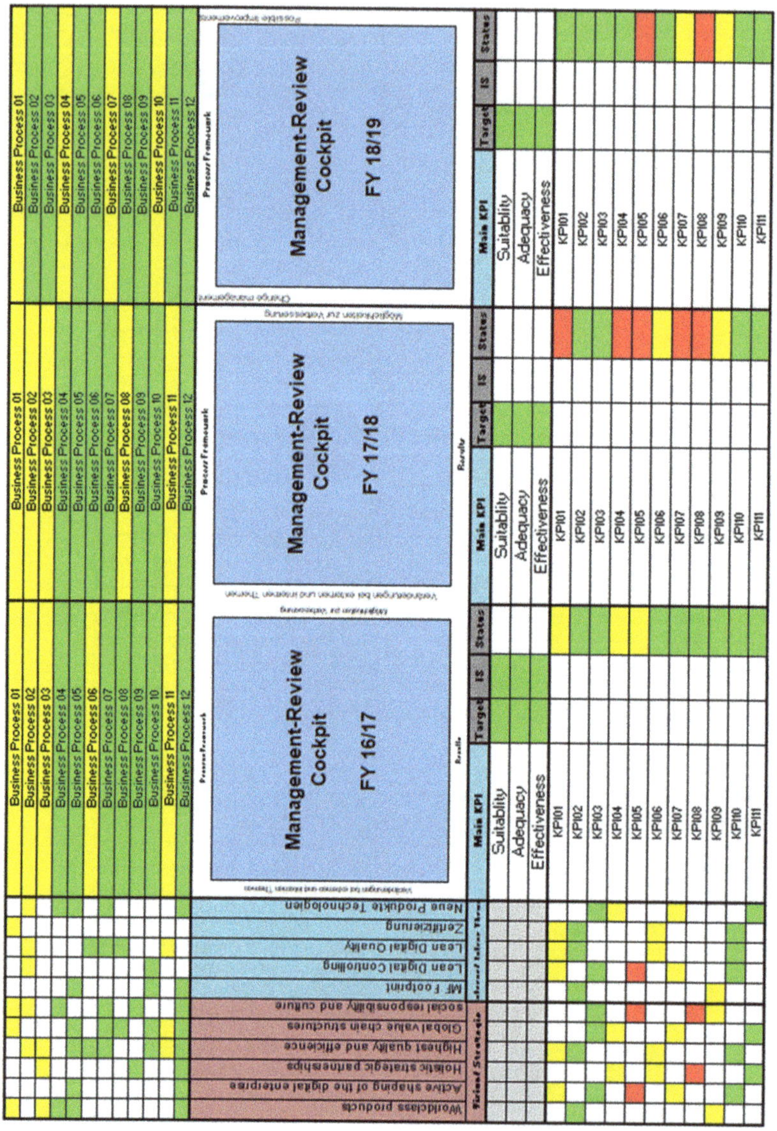

Fig. 9 Orientation for strategically deriving improvements

and its performance, the Diamond Star Award 2019, and the Industrie 4.0 Award in 2018.

5 Lessons Learned

The stakeholders of EWA's management systems and the Business Strategy Planning Process provided overall positive feedback. Everyone is confident based on the view that the implementation of additional improvements will lead to even better and faster application of the new method.

In addition to the cultural aspect, the traditional presentation of slides followed by a concluding discussion was transferred to a workshop-like event in which the participants digitally review the MRC. This cultural change, as Rosemann and vom Brocke (2015, p. 113) mention, is also seen as a main driver of change management and changes in how decisions are put into action.

Developing the MRC required a central organized MRC managing team with strong governance and an open communication culture in regard to process improvement, lean operational excellence, and BPM initiatives. This team, which consisted of members of Quality Management, EHS (Environmental, Health and Safety), and Lean Operation Excellence, is responsible for gathering all relevant data during the preparation phase and supports the review meeting itself. In the future, this team will focus on further development of the MRC to shift it to the next maturity level. The next step will be further evaluation of all existing relationships between various topics and the traffic light system (which is not a topic in the Hoshin Kanri approach).

In short, we find out that the MRC is a highly efficient management tool for obtaining a large quantity of information by focusing on the most relevant information at a glance.

References

Beitinger, G. (2019) Internet of things, *The journey from a Factory to a Lean Digital Factory published on Siemens Internal Ingenuity*.

Heckl, D., & Moormann, J. (2010). Process performance management. In J. vom Brocke & M. Rosemann (Eds.), *Handbook on business process management* (Vol. 2, pp. 115–135). Berlin: Springer.

I-nexus website. www.i-nexus.com

ISO 14001:2015 Quality management - Quality of an organization - Guidance to achieve sustained success.

ISO 45001:2018 Quality management - Quality of an organization - Guidance to achieve sustained success.

ISO 9001:2015 Quality management systems. Requirements.

ISO 9004:2018 Quality management - Quality of an organization - Guidance to achieve sustained success.

ISO/IEC 33000 Process Assessment Standard.

REFA website. www.refa.com

Rosemann, M., & vom Brocke, J. (2015). Six core elements of business process management. In J. vom Brocke & M. Rosemann (Eds.), *Handbook on business process management: Introduction, methods, and information systems (International handbooks on information systems)* (Vol. 1, 2nd ed., pp. 105–122). Berlin: Springer.

Schießl, K. (2019) *Management review based on Hoshin Kanri*. In Paper Presented at the 14. Konferenz für Organisation und Unternehmensstrategie Prozess Management, May 2019.

Schmelzer, H. J. *Wolfgang Sesselmann: Geschäftsprozessmanagement in der Praxis*. 7. Auflage. Hanser, München 2010, ISBN 978-3-446-42185-1.

Siemens Nine Mandatory Elements.

Siemens SIPEX, Siemens Process for Excellence. Siemens internal documentation (Standard 001 - Policy of Siemens Business Process Management).

The Policy of BPM@Siemens. Siemens internal documentation (Standard 001 - Policy of Siemens Business Process Management).

vom Brocke, J., Mendling, J., & Rosemann, M. (2021). Planning and scoping business process management projects and programs with the BPM Billboard. In J. vom Brocke, J. Mendling, & M. Rosemann (Eds.), *BPM cases. Digital innovation and business transformation in practice* (Vol. 2). Springer.

GPSR Compliance
The European Union's (EU) General Product Safety Regulation (GPSR) is a set of rules that requires consumer products to be safe and our obligations to ensure this.

If you have any concerns about our products, you can contact us on

ProductSafety@springernature.com

In case Publisher is established outside the EU, the EU authorized representative is:

Springer Nature Customer Service Center GmbH
Europaplatz 3
69115 Heidelberg, Germany

www.ingramcontent.com/pod-product-compliance
Ingram Content Group UK Ltd.
Pitfield, Milton Keynes, MK11 3LW, UK
UKHW020704041026
15590UKWH00001B/470
* 9 7 8 3 6 6 2 6 3 0 4 9 5 *